REMAINING KAREN

A STUDY OF CULTURAL REPRODUCTION AND THE
MAINTENANCE OF IDENTITY

REMAINING KAREN

A STUDY OF CULTURAL REPRODUCTION AND THE MAINTENANCE OF IDENTITY

ﹾ

ANANDA RAJAH

MONOGRAPHS IN ANTHROPOLOGY SERIES

THE AUSTRALIAN NATIONAL UNIVERSITY

E PRESS

E PRESS

Published by ANU E Press
The Australian National University
Canberra ACT 0200, Australia
Email: anuepress@anu.edu.au
This title is also available online at: http://epress.anu.edu.au/karen_citation.html

National Library of Australia
Cataloguing-in-Publication entry

Author:	Rajah, Ananda.
Title:	Remaining Karen : a study of cultural reproduction and the maintenance of identity / Ananda Rajah.
ISBN:	9781921536106 (pbk.) 9781921536113 (pdf)
Notes:	Bibliography.
Subjects:	Sgaw Karen (Southeast Asian people)--Ethnic identity.
	Ethnology--Thailand--Chiang Mai (Province)

Dewey Number: 305.895

Cover design by Teresa Prowse.
Cover image:
Printed by University Printing Services, ANU

Table of Contents

Foreword

This publication of *Remaining Karen* is intended as a tribute to Ananda Rajah and his consummate skills as an ethnographer. It is also a tribute to his long-term engagement in the study of the Karen. *Remaining Karen* was Ananda Rajah's first focused study of the Sgaw Karen of Palokhi in northern Thailand, which he submitted in 1986 for this PhD in the Department of Anthropology in the Research School of Pacific and Asian Studies at The Australian National University. It is a work of superlative ethnography set in an historical and regional context and as such retains its value to the present.

Throughout his academic career, Ananda would return again and again to the study of the Karen. Initially his focus was specific to the Sgaw Karen but increasingly he took up a concern with the issues of Karen refugees both in Thailand and Burma. At the time of his sudden, untimely death, Ananda was finishing a paper on the Karen naming system and preparing an edited volume on the refugee situation for which he had proposed the tentative title: *Karen refugees in the Thailand-Burma borderlands: Ethnic conflict, flight and cultural change*. Ananda's ethnographic investigations involved a continuing engagement with the Karen and his hesitation in publishing his thesis stemmed from a hope that he would, one day, be able to write an even more comprehensive account of Karen social life. His death has ended this possibility; hence, the need now to make publicly available the considerable work that he had already done on understanding the Karen.

Anthropological fieldwork invariably begins in some microcosm of a much larger community. In Ananda's case, as he makes clear, the Sgaw Karen settlement at Palokhi consisted of just twenty households. It was in the intimacy of this community that Ananda mastered his understanding of Karen ritual and social practice – the basis, as he argued, for a distinctive local Karen identity. His work centred on domestic organization and agricultural rituals from which he developed his notion of a 'procreative model' of social life and, in his final chapter, endeavoured to compare this conception with contrasting notions of origin and identity held by other Karen groups.

The acknowledgements in this work are themselves revealing. They chart Ananda's progress through the different stages of his doctoral research. He alludes to the contributions of his three supervisors. Clearly Gehan Wijeyewardene and Ted Chapman, both Thai specialists and scholars were crucial in their support of his research and formative in their advice to him. My task, as the supervisor with the least knowledge of Thailand, was one of continual interrogation, probing him to explain what needed to be made clear. No less important, however, was the community of fellow students with whom Ananda was in continual discussion while he was in Canberra and a similar community of close colleagues at the Institute of Southeast Asian Studies in Singapore where he eventually completed his thesis.

Ananda was the most affable of scholars who enjoyed the conviviality of good company and never tired of engaging conversation. He was able to derive a special personal and intellectual sustenance from this engagement. If there is one memory of Ananda that persists, it is of his love of the camaraderie of his friends and acquaintances. This virtue allowed him to seek out new acquaintances with whom to engage in a variety of different settings and made him an ideal fieldworker and a notable ethnographer.

James J. Fox

Abstract

There are an estimated 242,000 Karen in Thailand making them the largest ethnic minority in the country second only to the Chinese. In Burma, they number approximately 2.2 million. The Karen, of whom the Sgaw and Pwo represent the two largest groups based on dialectal differences, speak a number of related languages which are now recognised as belonging to the Sino-Tibetan group of languages. Since the early part of the last century, the Karen have been the subject of a number of studies by missionaries and British colonial administrators in Burma and, more recently, by anthropologists in Thailand.

Two major areas of interest in the long history of Karen studies have been the nature of Karen religious systems which appear to draw on various traditions, and the nature of Karen identity which appears remarkably resistant to change. While Karen religious traditions and customs were a dominant concern in earlier studies, the question of Karen ethnic identity (or identities) has been the focus of interest in contemporary studies, matched perhaps only by an interest in Karen subsistence or economic systems. Though the more recent anthropological studies of the Karen have retained an interest in Karen religious systems, related in most part to the study of Karen ethnicity, it is remarkable that there has not been a detailed contemporary account of the indigenous, non-Buddhist, non-Christian religion of the Karen.

This study is concerned with both issues — the nature of indigenous Karen religion and the maintenance of identity in a small Karen community which is firmly located, as much by necessity as by choice, in a predominantly Northern Thai socio-economic milieu in the highlands of Northern Thailand. It is also concerned with sociological explanation as well as anthropological description, in the case of the Karen, namely the part played by an indigenous religion (which draws little from Buddhism or Christianity, both of which have had considerable influence on Karen elsewhere) in the maintenance of identity. At one level, therefore, this study may be regarded as an attempt to fill a gap in the contemporary ethnography of the Karen, that is, to provide an account of an indigenous **Karen** religious system as a system in its own right but taken broadly to show how it encompasses different facets of life in one Karen community. At another level, this study addresses a larger sociological issue in the study of the Karen: how a **cultural** identity may be constituted (and reconstituted as an on-going process) and the implications that this may have for an understanding of Karen ethnicity the principles of which, though perhaps sufficiently established as a matter of conventional sociological wisdom, have not been adequately demonstrated in relation to hard ethnographic fact.

The major argument in this thesis, stated in its most general terms, is that religion and ritual sustain and reproduce what is best regarded as a cultural ideology which provides a cultural identity, and from which an ethnic identity may be constructed according to the particular circumstances and details of the contexts of intergroup relations. In the case of the Sgaw Karen of Palokhi, in Chiang Mai in Northern Thailand, who are the subject of this study, it is argued that this cultural ideology consists of the structured relations between what is best described as a "procreative model" of society and social processes, an integral part of which is a system of social classification based on the difference between male and female, cultural definitions of the relations between the two and the relationship between men and land, and a "model" of agricultural processes. The cultural ideology of the Palokhi Karen is "reproduced" in and through their religious system and ritual life, which is dominated by men who play a crucial role, and it is this which provides them with their distinctive cultural identity.

Acknowledgements

This thesis and the research on which it is based would not have been possible without the support of several institutions and individuals. The Institute of Southeast Asian Studies (ISEAS), Singapore, with which I am privileged to be associated, was instrumental in enabling me to embark and complete the research and course of study which this thesis represents. My first year of study at the Department of Anthropology, Research School of Pacific Studies, Australian National University (RSPacS, ANU) was financed by a grant from the Ford Foundation made possible only through ISEAS. Fieldwork in Chiang Mai, Thailand, conducted under the auspices of the National Research Council of Thailand and the sponsorship of Chiang Mai University (CMU) and the Tribal Research Centre, Chiang Mai, was funded by two grants. The first was a grant under a United Nations University (UNU) Fellowship, through its Natural Resources Programme, in connection with the UNU-CMU Joint Research Project on Agro-Forestry and Highland-Lowland Interactive Systems. The second grant was very generously provided by the Stiftung Volkswagenwerk, again made possible only through ISEAS. The ANU awarded me a one year scholarship for thesis writing at the university. This was later extended in the form of a grant from the Director's Discretionary Fund (as I believe it is called), RSPacS. Long though it has taken, this thesis would have taken even longer to complete had it not been for the further support and allowances in time unstintingly given by ISEAS. It is a manifestly inadequate acknowledgement, but I am extremely grateful to these institutions for their support and consideration.

However benign and philanthropic they may be in supporting research, even by the unimportunately impecunious, research institutions, funding agencies, and universities do not — at least in my own experience — act out of some anonymous impulse. I therefore feel compelled to acknowledge my debt of gratitude to Professor Kernial S. Sandhu, Director, ISEAS, for his unfailing but always unobtrusive support, patience and, if I may say so, a realisation that the "art of the possible" is possible; Peter Geithner of the Ford Foundation for initial encouragement; Wolfgang Wittwer of the Stiftung Volkswagenwerk for his interest and considerable patience; E.C. Chapman who, as consultant to the UNU-CMU Project (and another master of the "art of the possible") made the UNU Fellowship indeed possible; and James J. Fox (yet another master of what can be made possible) for administering extreme unction, as it seemed then, in the form of the grant from the Director's Discretionary Fund, RSPacS.

Theses are, of course, written under supervision of one sort or another and, just as it is usual to acknowledge one's intellectual debt to one's supervisors, it is also usual to absolve them of any shortcomings and deficiencies. I do not see why this should be so. Apart from a certain fallaciousness in the reasoning that underlies this reprehensible practice, it seems rather unfair that they should share in any credit, if there is any, and yet be excused from blame, should it come to that. I therefore feel obliged to say that I am profoundly indebted to my supervisors, Ted Chapman, James J. Fox, and Gehan Wijeyewardene, for all that I have been privileged to learn from them and that this thesis is in large part a testimony of the intellectual debt I owe them; but, if there are any shortcomings and deficiencies in it, we are all collectively responsible. This may not be a refraction of some Theravada Compact, but it certainly makes good Durkheimian sense.

Nevertheless, there is also a great deal else for which I am grateful to them which, as with all that I have learnt from them, made everything worthwhile. Not being a practitioner of the art of the possible, I consequently find it impossible to express it all, but some things seem to stand for everything else, rather like dominant symbols and the totality of the ideological structures which, as I claim, they uphold and help to reproduce. They are: with Ted, an introduction to the mysteries of field-book-and compass-traverses and elementary map-making at Kioloa, an initiation into the somewhat complex and confusing world of applied research in Northern Thailand, an awareness of the importance of commonsense, a fear of prolix, and the question of Karen identity; with Jim, an introduction to the ethnography of the societies of Eastern Indonesia, the critical roles of the Head of the Earth, **ina,** and **ama,** the issue of procreative models, and occasionally relentless "bemused" questioning; with Gehan, Meskin functions, a pathological fear of sociological fallacies, a painless introduction to Chiang Mai and **kham myang,** that things like **Ayutthaya maa tii Chiang Mai** are worth thinking about, Northern Thai cuisine, olive planting and an introduction to chain saws (fortunately well away from the forests of Northern Thailand), and epistemological problems. There is in all of this another debt I owe them, and Professor Sandhu as well, rather more difficult to express; it is of the kind that generally leaves prodigal sons thoroughly abashed. That, perhaps, comes closer to saying all of it.

In the course of work on this thesis, I benefitted from discussions of certain problems in the ethnography of the Karen with Peter Kunstadter, Ronald Renard, Roland Mischung, and Peter Hinton. Some analytical problems were also clarified by Geoffrey Benjamin, who first introduced me to anthropology, and whose work on Temiar kinship and naming systems read so long ago, is the original inspiration for an analysis contained in this study. I am, however, particularly grateful for his interest and encouragement throughout all these years.

At the Department of Anthropology, RSPacS, ANU, I was fortunate to enjoy the friendship and support of a great many people. However, I feel I must mention especially Jimmy Weiner, Wayne Warry, Douglas Lewis, Satoshi Nakagawa, Greg Acciaioli, Penny Graham, and Nerida Cook for sharing with me their views of anthropology, and their concern and interest expressed in so many ways in what I was doing which made a difference then.

At ISEAS, Singapore, the interest, encouragement, and companionship of many, no less than at the ANU, made all the difference this time. I must mention Sharon Siddique "about whom I have nothing but nice things to say", as we agreed I must say, and who introduced me to the administration of social science research at ISEAS which eventually helped me put my own work more appropriately in its larger context, namely, its proper (and much smaller) place, Subbiah Gunasekaran and Ng Chee Yuen for outrageously hilarious moments with "lizard forecasts", "long haired operations", and lunch time gourmet tours which, if I understand their intentions correctly, are meant to stand for life after a thesis if not death, Kenneth James for "computerising" me, Yao Souchou for explorations in ideological analyses, and Tim Huxley and Pauline Khng for, amongst many other things including explorations in the "ideologically unsound", **not** asking me (too often) when the "thing" would be done — all of which has made the completion of this thesis a rather less excruciating experience than I thought it would be.

Also at ISEAS, a great deal of the production of this thesis would not have been possible without the highly professional assistance, always cheerfully given, by Betty Kwan, Jane Ong, Rahim bin Mohd. Amin and Ramlee bin Othman, and I thank them too. All too often, so it appears to me at least, acknowledgements of this nature sincere though they may be are expressed in somewhat perfunctory fashion. That seems like yet another reprehensible practice. I would, therefore, like to say that I am very grateful indeed to Betty Kwan for making major and more difficult portions of earlier versions of this thesis much more presentable and, intended or otherwise, instruction in how to do it; Rahim bin Mohd. Amin for advice and help with diagrams and figures always given with lordly good humour (though I must confess to some feeling of umbrage at his gleeful reception of my wholly innocent mistakes), and Ramlee bin Othman for patient support, invariably given with enviable modesty, without which none of this would be readable. I am, however, especially grateful to Jane Ong for her care in rejuvenating a somewhat "ancient" document.

Fieldwork in Chiang Mai is, I believe, always regarded by the old Chiang Mai hands, or most of them anyway, as an extremely rewarding and pleasant experience. Though I may not have eaten as much rice as they have had salt, and presumptious though it may seem, that too has been my experience. Much of it was due to Cecilia Ng Siew Hua to whom I owe amongst a great many other things an interest in Karen clothes and cloths even if they may not appear to be splendid symbols, Donald Gibson for his friendship and hospitality, Thra Phy and Thra My Phi Ta Moo for showing me what being Karen meant to them, and Phongwattana Na Chiang Mai. It would be remiss of me if I did not also mention that much of my understanding of conditions in the Mae Muang Luang-Huai Thung Choa area where this study was conducted was gained through my association, in the UNU-CMU Project, with Pakorn Jringsoongnoen, Thannarong Viboonsunti, Sompote Nuntapong, Samer Lympchuvong, Tongchai Pratoonsuvan, Chusak Wittayapak, Chaiwoot Hongthong, Hans Hurni, and Wieland Kunzel. But most of all, if I have gained some understanding of working in Northern Thailand, and any feeling for it, I owe it to Gehan Wijeyewardene and Ted Chapman.

If these acknowledgements seem rather lengthy and excessive, I can only say that I feel they are necessary because that is what it took. My other more personal debts are better acknowledged elsewhere even if, like the ones here, they cannot be fully discharged.

To the Palokhi Karen who are the subject of this study, my debt is enormous and quite impossible to express. Though it is hardly adequate, this thesis stands as my acknowledgement of all that they gave in the twenty-two months when, as I would like to think, they admitted me into their collective conscience and allowed me glimpses of their cultural ideology. It may not be a "golden book", but they have never expected one anyway. All the same, this "book" is really in large part theirs. I only hope I have been able to do them some justice in it.

A.R.
ISEAS
November 1986

Note on Transcription

The system of transcription for Sgaw Karen, Northern Thai and Central Thai terms employed here is essentially based on that of Robert Jones in his **Karen Linguistic Studies** and Mary Haas in her **Thai-English Students' Dictionary**. The exceptions are:

VOWELS

Mid central unrounded vowel /∂/:	oe
Low front unrounded vowel /ɛ/:	ae
Mid back rounded vowel /ɔ/:	au

For Northern and Central Thai terms, long vowels are represented by a duplication of their respective symbols with the exception of the vowels indicated above for reasons of economy and neatness. In Karen, no distinction is made between long and short vowels.

CONSONANTS

Voiced palatalised nasal consonant /ñ/:	nj
Voiced velar nasal consonant /ŋ/:	ng
Unvoiced velar unaspirated consonant /χ/:	x
Voiced velar consonant /γ/:	gh
Unvoiced glottal unaspirated consonant /ʔ/:	'

The voiced palatalised nasal consonant is common to Karen and Northern Thai but does not occur in Central Thai. The the consonants /χ/ and /γ/ occur only in Karen.

Except for Karen place names, all other place names are romanised according to published Thai government practice.

Chapter I

Introduction

This study is concerned with how a small Karen community of 20 households, in the highlands of Northern Thailand, maintains its cultural identity in the context of a predominantly Northern Thai socio-economic environment and a slowly growing presence of the administrative apparatus of the larger polity of Thailand.

The nature of the economic relations between this Karen community, Palokhi, and its Northern Thai neighbours and its contacts with Thai government agencies raises an important issue. Palokhi is, quite evidently, integrated at various levels into this wider socio-economic and political system. Yet, the Palokhi Karen offer every indication of having what can only be described as a distinctive identity in their individual and community life which reflects little of this integration.

The identity of the Palokhi Karen in this sense is most evident in their language, religion, and ritual life which distinguish them from the Northern Thai. Although Palokhi Karen adults and many older children speak the Northern Thai dialect, **kham myang,** which they invariably use in their dealings with the Northern Thai, their ability falls short of that of the Northern Thai due to phonological interference.[1] In such interactive situations, they are immediately distinguished not only as non-Northern Thai but, indeed, as **Karen.** More importantly, within the community itself the dialect of Sgaw Karen which they speak is the medium by which social and cultural meanings are expressed beyond the mundane day-to-day communicative function of language and speech. While this holds true for perhaps every aspect of life in the community, it is decidedly marked in their religion and ritual for two reasons: first, the language or dialect is integral to the representation of symbolic meanings in their distinctive non-Christian, non-Buddhist religion and ritual practices; second, religion and ritual encompass virtually every aspect of social life in Palokhi but not beyond.

The religious system of the Palokhi Karen is central to the construction of a particular form of social reality which reflects little of the socio-economic and political realities outside the community. Furthermore, although there are some similarities between Palokhi Karen ritual practices and those of the Northern Thai, there is one major difference: the Palokhi Karen cannot be said to be Buddhist by any means. At the level of this general distinction, the difference not only means that to be non-Buddhist is also to be non-Northern Thai; it implies that the meanings contained in Palokhi Karen religion and ritual, as well as the social reality that they sustain, are indeed autonomous to the extent that they are not shared with the Northern Thai. In other words, this religion and ritual life, as well as the social reality they maintain, are particular to the Palokhi Karen.

From a sociological perspective, what is significant is that their integration in a larger socio-economic and political system has not resulted in social and cultural changes which would make them indistinguishable from the Northern Thai. In short, the Palokhi Karen possess a social and cultural identity which is quite unambiguously their own.

This poses a key issue which forms the focus of this study: given the larger circumstances of the community life of the Palokhi Karen, what is the nature of this identity and how is it maintained?

The Problem: Ethnic Identity, Cultural Distinctiveness and Religion

The question of the nature and maintenance of identity in non-Buddhist, non-Christian Karen communities is an important one for several reasons. Despite the long history of Karen studies, it is a phenomenon that is not well understood; it is only comparatively recently that the beginnings towards its understanding have been made with reassessments of studies on the Karen.[2]

The question raises several related issues, analytical and ethnographic, of some complexity. These issues involve the relation between ethnicity, or ethnic identity, and cultural distinctiveness or, as I would put it, the "identity of a culture". Quite simply, the relation concerns the correspondence between processes: the construction and maintenance of identity in the context of **intergroup** relations, and the constituted distinctiveness (or identity) and continuity of a culture within a group, to the extent that it assumes a separate identity **vis-a-vis** other groups. They also involve religion which, together with language, appear to be important variables in Karen community life and identity. For instance, although the Karen have various religious traditions, nevertheless, it appears that they are undeniably Karen in one way or another. The diversity, or eclecticism, of Karen religious beliefs is very much taken for granted; yet, it is remarkable that very little detailed information is available on the religious systems of Karen communities, especially those which are non-Buddhist and non-Christian.

In the contemporary literature on the Karen, these issues are most clearly to be seen in two key essays by Keyes and Lehman in the volume **Ethnic Adaptation and Identity,** edited by Keyes (1979), which is specifically concerned with "The Karen on the Thai Frontier with Burma".

In his introductory essay, Keyes examines the relationship between cultural distinctiveness, ethnic identity and structural oppositions between groups by which ethnic boundaries may come into being.

Keyes takes the view, the utility of which is well established in studies of ethnicity, that ethnicity is an emergent phenomenon (see, for example, Mitchell 1974) in the context of intergroup relations. However, Keyes argues, **contra** Barth (1969), that rather than culture which acts to define ethnic groups, it is ethnic identity which provides the defining cultural characteristic of ethnic groups (1979a:4). He also adds that the cultural expressions or symbolic formulations of ethnic identity may be found in, for example, myth, religious beliefs, ritual, folk history, folklore and art. By this, I take it that ethnicity provides the **context** within which these "expressions" or "formulations" assume a distinctiveness as diacritica of an ethnic identity. This is a view which is expressed more succinctly in another paper where he outlines a theoretical approach to ethnic change: "An ethnic identity thus becomes a personal identity after an individual appropriates it from a cultural source, that is, from the public display and traffic in symbols" (1981:10).

Keyes also goes on to point out that while "the cultural distinctiveness an ethnic identity provides is a necessary condition for the existence of an ethnic group, it is not a sufficient condition" (1979a:4). The other condition without which an ethnic group cannot be said to exist is the "structural opposition" between groups in terms of which there is a structural differentiation in the competition for scarce resources such that members of the same group share a "common interest situation" as well as a "common cultural identity". The resources in question may take a variety of forms, for example, productive resources, access to power or the reproductive capacities of women, and so forth. Accordingly, ethnic identification and adaptation (or change) also involves the element of relative advantage in the membership of groups. Keyes concludes with the observation that any examination of ethnic group relations should therefore treat both the cultural definition of groups and the structural oppositions between groups as problematical (1979a:8).

While there undoubtedly have been movements between Karen and other non-Karen ethnic groups (see, for example, Wijeyewardene, **in press**), the fact that there are Karen who remain quite unambiguously Karen would, thus, indicate that it is advantageous for them to do so. This in itself is entirely possible as part of the dynamics of ethnicity. Or, as Wijeyewardene also points out — in discussing Karen political strategies in the context of the Theravada Buddhist states of Thailand and Burma — "distinctiveness is sometimes more important than assimilation". Lehman has provided an answer as to why distinctiveness might be preferable to assimilation where the Karen are concerned. He says:

Karen might just as well have become, and in fact many are, Buddhists, but it is clear that their interests do not lie that way. For that way their choice is to try to acculturate to the Burmans, which would mean, given their relatively backward and remote habitat, being predictably poor Burmans and thus relative failures at the very levels of aspiration they would be adopting. In fact it can be argued that one of the very reasons for an historical and continued Karen identity is that peoples in relatively poor areas are often better off in their own eyes if they maintain cultural styles and aspirations distinct from those of their richer neighbours. (1979:248).

This, I suggest is precisely the case with, for example, the Palokhi Karen. In the context of their particular circumstances, it is advantageous for them to "make use" of the economic opportunities in a larger Northern Thai milieu while at the same time remaining separate. Indeed, I would further suggest that this very separation provides, "in their own eyes", the assurance of a certain degree of independence from the very socio-economic system that they are linked with. At this cognitive level it is the belief in their own distinctiveness which is important in the positive value placed on a Karen identity. The point to note, however, is that at this level they are predisposed towards a certain view because they are "Karen". There is, in other words, a certain tautology in Lehman's observations. I shall return to this later.

This brings us to further considerations in the relationship between the cultural distinctiveness and ethnic identity of the Karen, namely, change, the role of religion, and the status of an indigenous Karen religious tradition. In his discussion of this aspect of Karen ethnic identity, Keyes considers various examples most of which are drawn from the work of others. They are presented to illustrate the principle that in intergroup situations, it is the cultural belief held by the Karen themselves about what makes them distinctive that is relevant to the definition of Karen identity (1979a:10-3). His observations about religion, however, reveal what is the most outstanding gap in the ethnography of the Karen.

At the beginning of his introduction, Keyes quotes a short passage by Father Vincentius Sangermano written at the end of the eighteenth century dealing with Karen living amongst the Burmese and Mon. In this passage, Sangermano observes that the Karen still retain their language, dress and so on and "what is more remarkable, they have a different religion" (Sangermano, quoted in Keyes 1979a:1). Commenting on the relationship between religion and Karen ethnic identity, Keyes says:

> ... unlike Father Sangermano in the eighteenth century, those who have studied the Karen in Thailand have not found that the Karen associate their identity with a distinctive religion. Rather, Karen follow a number of different religions while still remaining Karen: traditional forms of spirit and ancestor worship, a tattooing cult (**cekosi**), several varieties of millenialism (cf. Stern 1968), Christianity, and different types of Buddhism. That there is no single Karen religion does not make religion irrelevant to our considerations; quite the contrary .... However, for the

moment, it is worth noting that few, if any, local groups of Karen in Thailand hold that particular religious forms distinguish Karen from non-Karen. (1979a:12).

Whether or not the Karen claim that a certain religion distinguishes Karen from non-Karen is not quite the issue, though it is interesting that it has not emerged in the ethnography of the Karen. It may be language or some other feature; it is only the **belief,** or claim, that some cultural feature or other **is so** that is relevant to actor-definitions of ethnic identity.

The main difficulty here is the lack of documentation, in contemporary studies, on a distinctive Karen religion (which Sangermano found so remarkable in his time) as well as the status of the "different religions" which Keyes refers to. This has led Hinton to state, quite categorically, that "There is no distinctive Karen religion" on the grounds that, in the region, "religions are very fluid" and that the Karen are "eclectic in religious matters" (1983:161-2). Although Hinton's general observations about religion in Northern Thailand are correct, his conclusion is precipitate. Where the Karen are concerned, to take religion as a world religion, a syncretic mix of a world religion with spirit beliefs, or a hodge-podge of various spirit beliefs is to miss the point in many respects. The point is whether or not there is, among the Karen communities which do not espouse Christianity or Buddhism in one form or another, a religious **system.**[3] The issue is, admittedly, problematic in the border areas of Thailand and Burma where a great many Karen communities have been exposed to Buddhism and Christianity. Nevertheless, the likely existence of what might be regarded as an indigenous Karen religious tradition should not be overlooked.

On the basis of a 1977 survey by the Tribal Research Centre (Chiang Mai), Kunstadter (1983:25) indicates that 42.9 per cent of the Sgaw Karen surveyed were "animists", 38.4 per cent were Buddhists, 18.3 per cent were Christian while 0.2 per cent were Muslims and another 0.2 per cent belonged to other, unclassified religions. In the case of Pwo Karen, 37.2 per cent were "animists", 61.1 per cent were Buddhists and 1.7 per cent were Christian. Too great a reliance should not be placed on these statistics, but I refer to them to point out that, even as rough approximations, they indicate the existence of a substantial number of Karen who do not see themselves as being Christian or Buddhist. This, of course, raises the obvious question of what is the nature of their "animistic" religion?

Christianity and Buddhism (whatever their forms including syncretic Karen millenial cults) are quite obviously religious traditions which the Karen have **adopted** and have the status of religions amongst the Karen, but they immediately beg the question of what sort of religion existed prior to Karen conversion. "Spirit and ancestor worship" and the "tattooing cult", on the other hand, are problematic issues in the Karen ethnography. Though "spirit and ancestor worship" are undoubtedly part of Karen religious traditions, they are aspects of the religious life of the Karen which suffer from several misconceptions. As I have shown elsewhere (1984), the so-called "ancestor worship" is a variable phenomenon and its significance differs, in all likelihood, from community to community. It cannot be construed to be a religion in itself, though in some cases it may be regarded as a cult. As for the "tattooing cult", little enough is known about it, and to regard it as a religion would be a hasty and premature conclusion indeed.[4]

The central problem as I see it here, however, is the question of religious conversion and whether anything may be said about the sociological relationship between, if not an identifiable then, at least, a posited "Karen religion" and Karen identity.

This is an issue which is implied in Lehman's discussion of Karen conversion to Christianity and why it may be advantageous for the Karen to do so rather than to convert to Christianity. He is, in fact, concerned with the relationship between cultural change and change in ethnic identity in general. Taking religious conversion to Christianity as a case in point, his conclusion is that cultural change expressed as religious conversion is nothing short of a change in ethnic identity:

> The answer in recent times seems to have been both to maintain their separateness and to identify with a modern social and religious system, that is, to identify with Christianity, even while not necessarily adopting Christianity wholesale.

> … I have to make it as clear as I can that, as this last observation about religion shows, cultural change itself, especially insofar as it is determined by intergroup relations, amounts precisely to a change in ethnicity, an alternation in identity. This is too frequently not understood. I will even go so far as to assert that the tendency for Karen, Sgaw, and Pwo in particular to develop millenial and messianic cults that seem to change their religion almost totally is exactly this, an alternation in ethnic identity in response to changing intergroup relations. (Lehman 1979:248).

There are two points in these observations which warrant serious consideration.

First, these examples of religious, cultural, and ethnic change, when placed in their historical context, have the following implications: providing that intergroup relations do not change, Karen cultural distinctiveness or identity is directly related to an indigenous, non-Christian, non-Buddhist religion; furthermore, assuming again that intergroup relations do not change, the maintenance of Karen cultural identity is directly related to continuity of such a Karen religion. Although Lehman does not discuss the nature of indigenous Karen religion, it is quite clear that he implicitly acknowledges it must exist.

More generally, it is also apparent that he sees religion as a critical aspect in cultural distinctiveness or identity. This is a point which I take up again later.

Second, religion is **implicated** in cultural change as part of the modification of ethnic identity in the context of changing intergroup relations. The central issue is the relationship between religious, cultural and ethnic change.

The point, I suggest, may be expressed more generally, if somewhat simplistically, in another way. Karen ethnic identity however it may be defined or arrived at as a consequence of processes in intergroup relations has to do with cultural distinctiveness or identity as it is constituted within the community. Or, to paraphrase Keyes' observations noted earlier: ethnic identities are appropriated from cultural sources (which, I would add, are themselves part of the lived experience of the community) to become personal and hence group identities. Furthermore, change in one means a change in the other. This is the critical issue in the relationship between ethnic identity and cultural identity and, I suggest, it constitutes the thrust of Lehman's remarks. But, Lehman also emphasises the role of religion.

The importance that Lehman gives to religion is worth noting. Although cultural distinctiveness or identity may be associated with any feature or sets of features, religious systems are important for many reasons in various societies. However their general social and cultural significance, to take one anthropological definition of religion as a **cultural system,** is that they are "a system of symbols which acts to establish powerful, pervasive, and long-lasting moods and motivations in men by formulating conceptions of a general order of existence and clothing these conceptions with such an aura of factuality that the moods and motivations seem uniquely realistic" (Geertz 1966: 4). Whatever else religion may entail, it clearly involves cognitive processes where, as Geertz and Geertz have said (in another context), "a way of seeing is also a way of not seeing" (1964). It is for this reason that if the Karen place a positive value on their identity in relation to others, it is tautological, as I noted before. However, given the importance of religion in predisposing individuals in a society towards particular ways of looking at things, including themselves and others, it does mean that a great deal of their culture and their behaviour may be understood by investigating their religion in its own right. Religious systems, however, are also important for another reason. They possess considerable symbolic content; they are part of the "traffic in symbols" which are the means by which ethnic identities may be appropriated from cultural sources.

In reviewing the discussions of Karen identity by Keyes and Lehman, what I wish to stress is that, first, it is essential to make a distinction between ethnic identity and cultural identity and, second, it is necessary to establish the relationship between ethnic identity, cultural identity, and religion which is clearly an important factor in the maintenance or change of these identities.

Where ethnic identity, cultural identity and religion are concerned, cultural distinctiveness is necessary to ethnic identity but ethnicity itself is an emergent phenomenon in the context of integroup relations. Furthermore, cultural identity is closely associated with religion in cognitive and experiential terms, and religious change amounts to cultural change which may be taken as a response to changing intergroup relations. There is, in other words, a dialectical relationship between ethnic identity and cultural identity in which religion is an operative factor.

The general observations, and these points in particular, made by Keyes and Lehman are instructive. But, they raise two major problems.

First, current understandings of what might be regarded as the non-Buddhist, non-Christian religious tradition of the Karen are limited indeed because little is known about it. Accordingly, although the dynamics of ethnic **adaptation** are clear enough, the relationship between a Karen religion, a Karen cultural identity and their continuity are still a problematic issue in the case of non-Christian, non-Buddhist Karen who possess an unambiguous Karen ethnic identity. The fact of the matter, quite simply, is that we really do not know enough about it.

This thesis is an attempt to explore precisely this issue on the basis of the ethnography of the Palokhi Karen.

I propose to deal with this in terms of the following question: how do the Palokhi Karen maintain their cultural identity, given that they have a religion which is distinctively their own, in the context of fundamental economic relations which extend beyond their own domain of life and control, and an awareness of their incorporation within a larger polity?

Following Keyes and Lehman, I accept that ethnicity in general is constructed as part of the process of intergroup relations. I also take the view that religion is essential to a cultural identity and, hence, an ethnic identity. In the case of the Palokhi Karen, I begin with the assumption that they possess a distinctive religion of their own and take the relationship between this religion and cultural identity as the central concern of this study. I have not attempted to substantiate my claims about what constitutes the religion of the Karen in general and the Palokhi Karen in particular; the rest of this thesis will be evidence and justification enough for my assertion.

The second problem, a more general one, which arises from Keyes' and Lehman's observations is this: if Karen ethnic identity is an emergent or situational phenomenon, and if at the level of the actors themselves ethnic groups are defined by some set of "cultural traits" (Lehman 1979: 235, 247) or "commonsense constructs" (Mitchell 1974:22-4), what then is it that is "Karen" about these instances of ethnic adaptation? To take one example if, as Lehman argues, religious and cultural change amount to a change in ethnicity, in what way or ways are Christian, Buddhist and "animist" Karen "Karen"? The problem is, ultimately, an analytical one, namely, that if we take ethnicity too far as an analytical concept, what we are left with is a much too relativistic notion of ethnic identity in which the only irreducible element is the cultural distinctiveness of this identity. The answer to this question, I suggest, can only be arrived at through an answer to the first question and I, therefore, take up this issue at the end of this study.

In the rest of this chapter, I set out the general geographical and economic context of Palokhi and show briefly why the Palokhi Karen may be regarded as having, quite unambiguously, a Karen ethnic identity. I also set out an interpretative framework and argument which underlies my analysis of religion and the maintenance of cultural identity in Palokhi which forms the principal concern of the rest of this study.

FIGURE 1 The Location of Palokhi in the Mae Muang Luang-Huai Thung Choa Area, Amphoe Mae Taeng, Changwat Chiang Mai

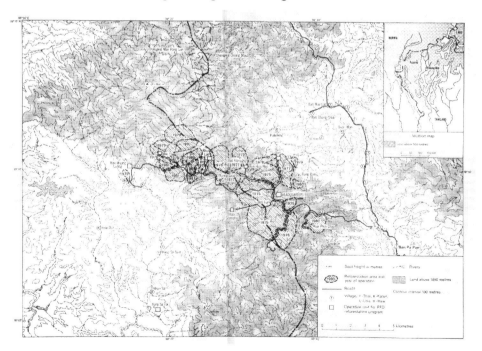

Note: This map is based on one published for the United Nations University-Chiang Mai University Joint Research Project on Highland-Lowland Interactive Systems (Chapman 1983: 319).

Palokhi: The Geographical and Economic Context

Palokhi is situated some 90 kilometers north-west of the provincial capital of Chiang Mai in Northern Thailand (Figure 1.1). The village lies in a generally hilly area which, in this thesis, I call the Pa Pae hills after the largest Northern Thai settlement in the area.[5] The Pa Pae hills, which are generally above 700 metres in elevation, are part of a larger area of hill country which forms the eastern edges of the Doi Inthanon mountain range stretching from North to South. Through this area, there is a road which begins at Mae Malai in Amphur Mae Taeng and leads up to Pai in the province of Mae Hong Sorn. Palokhi is situated several kilometres off this road within an inter-montane valley system which forms the drainage of the Mae Muang Luang, a river, and several streams. The largest stream is the Huai Thung Choa by which Palokhi is located.[6]

The Mae Muang Luang-Huai Thung Choa drainage system is essentially an area of dissected hill country with a central ridge over 1,000 m which rises to approximately 2,000 m. Above 1,000 m, the landscape is marked by the extensive presence of **Imperata cylindrica.** Since 1975, reforestation programmes of the Royal Forestry Department have resulted in the overplanting of much of this grassland with **Pinus kesiya,** an indigenous species of pine. Below 1,000 m, however, land cover consists of multi-storeyed evergreen forest and woodland.

The Mae Muang Luang-Huai Thung Choa basin has a total area of 220 km^2. In 1979–80, it had a total population of 1,438 of which 976 were Karen, 247 Northern Thai, 169 Lisu and 46 Yunnanese Chinese living in 23 settlements distributed throughout the area. Of these 23 settlements, 14 were Karen, 6 Northern Thai, 2 Lisu and 1 Yunnanese Chinese (Thannarong **et al.,** n.d.).[7] Population density in the area was, therefore, 6.5 per km^2. Compared to other highland areas in Northern Thailand, the Mae Muang Luang-Huai Thung Choa area is relatively unpopulated and there is a high proportion of forest and woodland even in the vicinity of Karen villages (Chapman 1983:322). As Chapman also notes, overall there is little pressure on the Karen swidden system and Northern Thai farming activities in the area. This general observation is true for the Palokhi Karen and Northern Thai within the Huai Thung Choa valley. The Palokhi Karen occupy the middle section of the valley while the Northern Thai (at Ban Mae Lao and Ban Thung Choa) inhabit the lower end near the Mae Malai-Pai road at the confluence of Huai Thung Choa and Mae Lao. Given the distribution of population in the Huai Thung Choa valley and a general separation of areas of exploitation for subsistence purposes between the Karen and Northern Thai, there is little competition for natural resources in the valley.

There is also a Royal Forestry Department Watershed Development Unit headquarters which is located next to the Lisu village of Ban Lum. Scattered throughout the Mae Muang Luang-Huai Thung Choa area are several sub-units of the Watershed Development Unit at Ban Lum which are engaged in various activities and projects such as reforestation, as well as a Flower Plantation which is engaged in ornamental flower horticulture for a crop replacement programme. These activities have had a direct impact on some of the settlements in the Mae

Muang Luang-Huai Thung Choa basin but Palokhi has only been indirectly exposed to them thus far.[8] Where the Palokhi Karen are concerned, these sub-units offer opportunities for wage work which they take advantage of from time to time.

Palokhi, at the time of my fieldwork (1980–1982), varied between 18 and 20 households with a corresponding population of 109 and 116. Its closest neighbours, approximately 2 kilometres away downslope the Huai Thung Choa, are two Northern Thai settlements — Ban Thung Choa and Ban Mae Lao. The contact between the Palokhi Karen and Ban Mae Lao is, by far, the more important although it is further away than Ban Thung Choa. The reason is that Ban Mae Lao, which lies next to the Mae Malai-Pai road, functions as an important node in the network of economic linkages in this particular part of the Pa Pae hills. The reasons for these contacts are, therefore, primarily economic.

The principal features of the economic linkages between Palokhi and Ban Mae Lao, as well as some other Northern Thai settlements (including Ban Thung Choa) may be summed up quite simply as follows. In broad general terms, the subsistence economy of Palokhi consists of a dual system of cultivation based on swiddening and wet-rice agriculture. The Palokhi Karen, however, are not self-sufficient in rice production and they therefore purchase rice in Ban Mae Lao and, to some extent, in Ban Pa Pae.

In 1980–81, for example, there was an overall deficit in agricultural production which amounted to 16 per cent of total consumption requirements. This could only be met by recourse to external sources of rice by various means.[9] If this deficit is translated into expenditures on husked glutinous rice (which is what the Palokhi Karen purchase in Ban Mae Lao and Ban Pa Pae) at the 1981 price of Bht 4.5 per litre in the Pa Pae hills, it amounts to the very considerable sum of Bht 49,135.5. These aggregate figures serve to indicate the extent to which 10 out of the 18 households in Palokhi are dependent on external sources for their rice requirements.

In order to purchase the rice they need, the Palokhi Karen require cash. This they earn primarily through the sale of tea leaves (**Camellia sinensis**) for the dry leaf and **miang** (fermented tea) industries, wage labour in related activities and, secondarily, from the sale of forest products, and services. The rice which the Palokhi Karen purchase is not, in fact, surplus rice grown by the Northern Thai in the Pa Pae hills; it comes from the markets of Chiang Mai and is sold by shop-keepers in Northern Thai settlements such as Ban Mae Lao and Ban Pa Pae.[10]

The tea and **miang** industries, based in Mae Taeng, are therefore of considerable importance to the Palokhi Karen. What is noteworthy about Palokhi Karen involvement in these industries (especially the **miang** industry), as I show later in this study, is that there is a marked absence of institutionalised credit arrangements and on-going indebtedness on the part of the Palokhi Karen. This also holds true of the relationship between them and the shop-keepers in Ban Mae Lao and Ban Pa Pae from whom they buy rice and other commodities. In other words, although the Palokhi Karen are dependent on these external sources for rice, they are not locked into institutionalised or rigidly defined external socio-economic relationships.

This too is a feature of the wage work undertaken by the Palokhi Karen in Northern Thai settlements in connection with the tea and **miang** economy. The work consists essentially of clearing tea gardens, chopping firewood for steaming **miang,** and portage. It is obtained on an **ad hoc** basis and employer-worker relationships, correspondingly, last only for the duration of the work with wages generally being paid at its conclusion.

For all practical purposes, the Palokhi Karen are therefore dependent to a significant extent on an external, regional economy in order to meet their consumption requirements in rice. It is a relationship which rests essentially on an important function characteristic of Northern Thai settlements situated along the Mae Malai-Pai road in the Pa Pae hills, that is, their role as conduits for exchanges and transactions in a regional economic network which links the Pa Pae hills with the lowlands of Chiang Mai.

The point I wish to stress here is that although the Palokhi Karen are integrated into a network of local and regional economic linkages through the necessity of obtaining rice and the need for cash to purchase it, they are not bound in structured socio-economic relationships.

Apart from being integrated within the larger economic system of the region, Palokhi has relatively recently experienced greater and more regular contact with agencies of the Thai government in the form of the Provincial Government's District Office at Mae Taeng and, of course, the Royal Forestry Department.

In 1975, for example, the Pa Pae area was given **tambon** (sub-district) status whereas it had previously been part of **tambon** Sopoeng. A registration exercise, for the purposes of issuing official documents such as identity cards (**bat pracam tua**) and household registration certificates (**baj thabian baan),** was also conducted in the same year. All households in Palokhi were registered and most adult males now possess identity cards. One result of this extension of the District Office's administration into the area has been that the Palokhi Karen are required to register births, deaths and children when they reach 18 years of age for identity cards. Another consequence has been that they have to pay a tax for the upkeep of the locality (**phasii bamrung thaung thii 6).** The tax is collected annually by the **kamnan** (the head of a cluster of villages by government appointment), a Northern Thai, living at Ban Mae Lao. The Palokhi Karen have difficulty in comprehending the rationale of these administrative measures, but they are conscientious in observing them and to this extent they have already accepted the reality of an external authority which impinges on their lives. They also do not fully understand the nature of the tax. There is a general misapprehension that it is related to the ownership of wet-rice fields and that it implies a certain official recognition of their rights to these fields which is one reason why they are concerned to pay their dues.

The significance of this establishment of District Office administration in the area is that the Palokhi Karen acknowledge the authority of government agencies. They are also fully conscious of being part of a larger polity though they do not quite grasp the implications of this fact in terms of their rights and obligations.

The presence of the Royal Forestry Department in the Huai Thung Choa area has also impressed upon the Palokhi Karen that they are not an isolated, independent community. This is particularly evident where their farming activities are concerned. For example, officials of the Royal Forestry Department have visited them occasionally bearing the message that swiddening should be limited or curtailed because of its deleterious effects on forest cover. They tend to ignore such exhortations but they are, at the same time, apprehensive that in so doing they may incur penalties although they are quite unable to specify the nature of these penalties. It may be noted that the Royal Forestry Department's officials do not, in fact, attempt to coerce the Palokhi Karen into abandoning swiddening through specific or even vague threats of punishment. Their belief that they will be penalised should be understood in terms of reactions to institutional authorities with functions which are not fully comprehended but which are regarded as having considerable power to affect their lives.

The presence of the Royal Forestry Department is also important from another point of view. It has provided various opportunities for work which the Karen have taken advantage of on a short term basis. This has taken the form of very short term wage work such as clearing **Imperata** grasslands for reforestation to earn some cash as well as longer term employment in order to save money to buy wet-rice fields prior to settling in Palokhi.

It is indeed true that the Palokhi Karen (and for that matter other Karen in the area) and the Northern Thai see each other as being culturally different. In the wider context of the Pa Pae hills area, it is also true that there is competition between Karen and Northern Thai for land due to upland migration of Northern Thai. This is part of a more general trend in Northern Thailand which Chapman (1967) has described. In the specific context of the Huai Thung Choa valley, this competition for productive resources is reflected only to a limited extent. It is confined to access to wild tea bushes growing in the forest between Palokhi and the two Northern Thai settlements, rather than farming areas because the Northern Thai prefer to cultivate wet-rice fields (and sometimes swiddens) near their villages. The competition is also limited because of low population densities and a general separation of their respective areas of exploitation for subsistence purposes. However, it exists to the extent that where the Northern Thai utilise the forest between Palokhi and Ban Thung Choa and Ban Mae Lao the Palokhi Karen are therefore pre-empted from picking the tea bushes in the area. Most Palokhi Karen tea gardens are, thus, to be found around the village and on the western slopes of the Huai Thung Choa valley near the village. Nevertheless, neither the Palokhi Karen nor the Northern Thai regard this as a source of potential conflict.

The most important feature of the relations between the Palokhi Karen and Northern Thai, however, is the **dependence** of the Palokhi Karen on an external economy that is at their point of contact dominated by the Northern Thai who act as middle-men or as employers in wage work. This may well be regarded as a very specific kind of "structural differentiation", though not necessarily in Keyes' sense. By this I mean a distinct separation of economic arrangements between the Northern Thai and the Palokhi Karen which is mediated only through direct cash transactions in, for example, seller-buyer and employer-worker relationships.

In terms of the principles underlying ethnic adaptation discussed by Keyes, it could be argued that it would, perhaps, be to the advantage of the Palokhi Karen who are significantly dependent on this economy to "become Northern Thai" and, therefore, compete on a more equal basis for the resources that they are dependent on by necessity. The agricultural systems of the Palokhi Karen and Northern Thai are not radically different and, indeed, the Northern Thai themselves often do not produce enough rice for their needs. However, they have access to a wider economy which offers greater opportunities by which their rice deficits may be made up. One of these opportunities consists of acting as middle-men between the Palokhi Karen and other Northern Thai and Chinese merchants who are further links in the chain of economic networks stretching up to Pai and down to Mae Taeng. It is thus conceivable that it would be advantageous for the Palokhi Karen to integrate themselves more fully into such a system, by "becoming Northern Thai" and availing themselves of the opportunities which are open to the Northern Thai.

The same might also be said of the relations between the Palokhi Karen and the Thai bureaucracy. The Palokhi Karen actually do recognise quite clearly that when it comes to dealing with officials of the Mae Taeng District Office, for example, they are less able to do so compared to the Northern Thai. And they are aware that the difference lies in the fact that the Northern Thai are more informed about the workings of the Thai bureaucracy. Nevertheless, this does not prevent them from also viewing the matter in terms of ethnic affiliation and its attendant advantages or disadvantages. In addition to this, the Palokhi Karen occasionally complain that while some Northern Thai cultivate swiddens, officials of the Royal Forestry Department appear to be less concerned about it whereas they themselves are told to limit their cultivation of swiddens. The insinuation in these complaints is that the Northern Thai are privileged in some sort of way because they are Northern Thai.

Yet, the fact of the matter is that notwithstanding their dependence on the Northern Thai dominated local economy for rice to make up their deficits and other commodities, and whatever advantages they may attribute to being Northern Thai in dealing with the Thai bureaucracy, the Palokhi Karen present every semblance of having a life and identity of their own. Indeed, it is probable that **even if** they could "become Northern Thai", they would not wish to do so. Although they are quite able to see that they are dependent on external sources for rice to make up their deficits up to a certain extent, this does not go beyond a pragmatic assessment of economic realities. It is an economic fact which has little impact on their consciousness or sense of being a community to themselves.

In their view one of the more discernible features of life in Northern Thai communities (such as Ban Mae Lao and Ban Pa Pae) is the proximity to figures of authority and exposure to official demands. For example, although the Palokhi Karen are conscientious about paying their taxes, they do not seek out the **kamnan** at Ban Mae Lao to hand over the money. Instead they wait for him to come around before they part with their money. This is reflective of a more general feeling that if they establish regular contacts with the **kamnan,** they would become more open to other official intrusions through the person of the **kamnan.**

Another example of how they view the Northern Thai and life in Northern Thai settlements is an attitude that there is total exposure to Northern Thai (in general) who cannot be trusted at best, and who are dangerous at worst. This is reflected most clearly in the constant fear that the Northern Thai will steal their cattle or buffaloes. It may also be seen in the way they explained, without hesitation, the six Northern Thai homicides in the Pa Pae area in 1980–81, in the following terms: "because the Northern Thai are like that".

In terms of their own perceptions, the Palokhi Karen thus have good reasons for remaining unambiguously Karen in the context of their relations with the Northern Thai. At this cognitive level it is the belief in their own distinctiveness which is important in the positive value placed on a Karen identity. The Palokhi Karen, in short, possess a very definite "Karen" **ethnic** identity. But what, then, of their cultural identity?

The Argument: Religion, Ideology, and the Maintenance of Cultural Identity

The major argument in this study is that the maintenance of the cultural identity of the Palokhi Karen depends on the perpetuation of a "cultural ideology" which is reproduced in and by their religious system and their system of subsistence agriculture. By this, I mean that the subsistence agricultural system in Palokhi, which only partially sustains the community, is nevertheless sufficient and necessary for the maintenance of a cultural order which provides it with its essential identity. More specifically, it is the rites associated with swidden cultivation, integral to the ritual life of the community, together with other aspects of the religion of the Palokhi Karen, which form the key elements in the construction of a social and cultural order that is unequivocally Karen.

On the other hand, this social and cultural order is at the same time expressed, asserted and re-affirmed through the performance of rituals and other social institutions such as marriage and domestic organisation. This social and cultural order which constitutes the social reality of the Palokhi Karen, thus, exists in a dialectical relationship with their religion and ritual practices. But, their religion and ritual practices are grounded on their system of subsistence agriculture. To put it another way, the religious life of the Palokhi Karen only has meaning, or "makes sense", in relation to their system of swiddening and to some extent wet-rice agriculture. Without their agricultural system, their religion would hold little meaning.

Religion and Ritual

My view of religion is essentially similar to that of Geertz's, referred to earlier. While religion may be a matter of belief and a system which provides a moral order for the Palokhi Karen themselves, it is for all that a system of symbolic representations. It is thus made up of cultural categories, concepts and ideas. Accordingly, whatever else religion may involve, it also consists of conceptual associations which represent some underlying schemata of cognition or, in other words, models. While I would not claim that there is, necessarily, a **single** cognitive model in Palokhi Karen religion, an important aspect of my argument consists in demonstrating that there is, at least, a **dominant** (or primary) model. This, I call a "procreative model of society" in the religion of the Palokhi Karen. As I attempt to show, the procreative model of society in Palokhi is based on a very fundamental difference, namely, the difference between male and female. This is a model which is identifiable in symbolic representations in the domain of kinship and marriage. It is also to be found in agrarian rites: two key swidden rituals are also based on this fundamental difference between male and female and their **conjunction.**

Furthermore, I suggest that there are other identifiable models and their significance can only be understood in terms of the dominant model. For example, I attempt to show that the linguistic system of sex and gender differentiation in Palokhi contains an essential distinction between non-fecundable and fecundable human females. This is related to the system of kin terms and a naming system, both of which mark out the conjugal bond and the continuity of generations.

The cultural significance of these systems (or the models in these systems) lies in their relation to the dominant model.

Religion, however, has its behavioural aspects. One of these is, of course, ritual. I therefore take ritual to be the expressive, practical activity characteristic of religion. However, I do not necessarily accept that ritual is behaviour or activity which only takes place in a context which would be conventionally recognised as "religious". This is a view that is by no means new in anthropology. Leach (1964:12-3), for instance, has suggested that actions may be placed on a continuum with the purely technical at one extreme and the highly sacred at the other, and that most actions would fall in between with their significance being drawn partly upon both. It is a view of behaviour which has considerable utility because it enlarges the analytical base on which meaningful interpretations may be made.

To give one example, which is an important one in the ethnography of the Palokhi Karen, consider eating. The consumption of food is, at one level, a technical act in the sense that it serves the function of nutrition. On the other hand, it is at other levels, a highly symbolic act involving commensalism in ritual situations. Indeed, it would appear that this very basic human activity is employed (as it is with many other societies) to express symbolically the nature of social relations in domestic social organisation, community organisation, as well as various ritual relationships. Depending on context, one important feature of eating as a ritual act is that it may be "transformative" in Kapferer's sense (1979:3–19), as well as being "constitutive" as I call it.

Between the strictly functional and the highly symbolic, eating is also part of day-to-day domestic activity in the sense of a non-reflective routine. Nevertheless, it occurs in situations which are very much social and domestic. It is part of my argument that at this level of routine activity, eating and commensalism is also symbolic; it is a **practical** ritual in which the principal aspect is the "constitutive".

There is one further aspect to ritual which I wish to touch on briefly. In Palokhi, ritual activity involves both verbal and non-verbal performances often in conjunction. Thus, by ritual I also mean those aspects of behaviour (in "religious" contexts) in which the use of language is a "performative" in Austin's sense (1962) and as Tambiah (1968, 1979) has elucidated it.

Ideology

I also argue that in terms of the more general relationship between economy, social organisation and the social and cultural order of the Palokhi Karen, their dependence on external sources for rice represents a paradox. This dependence does not significantly alter the social cultural order which provides the Palokhi Karen with their particular sense of identity. On the contrary, it helps to sustain this order; it enables the community to meet its subsistence requirements, but because they have an on-going system of subsistence agriculture which is intimately linked to their religion, the reality of the social and cultural order in Palokhi remains undisturbed. The reason for this lies in what we might call the "unassailable" character of their cultural ideology — at least as it has remained up to the present time.

At the heart of the maintenance of their social and cultural order is this cultural ideology, built up of symbolic representations, which links agricultural production to social processes. As a working definition, which forms part of the interpretative framework on which my argument is based, I take cultural ideology to be the structured relations between symbolic representations, social organisation and agricultural production in Palokhi.

The concept of "cultural ideology", as I use it, ultimately comes from Althusser's treatment of ideology. Ideology, according to Althusser,

> is a matter of the **lived** relation between men and their world. This relation ... is not a simple relation but a relation between relations, a second degree relation. In ideology men do indeed express, not the relation between them and their conditions of existence, but the way they live the relation between them and their conditions of existence: this presupposes both a real relation and an **"imaginary"**, **"lived"** relation. (1969:233).

The important aspect of Althusser's definition, as I see it, is the attention it gives to ideology as a "relation between relations" and the distinction between the relations in the objective ("real") conditions of existence and these relations as they are **thought** ("imaginary") and experienced ("lived").[11] It is not a simple distinction between objectivity and subjectivity. Rather, ideology is the "second degree" relation between the relations which are established in thought, and as they are lived, about objective conditions.

Thus, in the case of Palokhi Karen religion the cognitive models which I depict are, as I would call it, first degree relations established in thought. It is the relations between models, however, that constitute a cultural ideology. To take one example, there is in Palokhi a dominant "procreative model of society", as I call it, which exists in the domain of social organisation and the domain of agriculture. It is the relation between them (or the extension of the model from society to cultivation) which constitutes part of the cultural ideology in Palokhi.

Following Yao (1983:22), I do not make a distinction between "ideology" (conventionally understood in its "political" sense) and "cultural ideology". The reason is that "ideology" is, as Yao observes, by its very nature "cultural" because it is **constituted by culture**.[12] Nevertheless, I find it convenient on occasion to use the term "ideology" as it is conventionally understood. I use the term in this sense to describe, for example, the way in which the headman and elders in Palokhi are impelled to "enforce" certain marriage rules (see below). The different senses in which I use the term will be apparent from their contexts.

Here, I wish to deal very briefly with what I termed the "unassailable" character of the cultural ideology in Palokhi up to the present time. By this, I do not mean to imply that the ideology is incapable of change but, rather, that given the particular configuration of "objective conditions" in the history of the Palokhi Karen, the cultural ideology has not only remained the same but has been extended to include certain changes in these conditions. One important example, which I shall not be able to discuss in any detail later because of limitations of space, is the cycle of wet-rice agricultural rituals in Palokhi. The Palokhi Karen have not only adopted wet-rice agriculture from the Northern Thai, but they have also adopted some Northern Thai agricultural rituals as well. Nevertheless, both have been subsumed within an existing form of social organisation and agricultural production, namely swidden cultivation, and a cycle of swidden rites. In other words, the pre-existing system of agriculture has exerted a "priority" which has enabled the Palokhi Karen to include wet-rice agriculture and accompanying Northern Thai agricultural rituals within their ideological system without any substantial change in the system.

The Maintenance of Cultural Identity

An important part of my argument also rests on showing that the perpetuation of the cultural ideology in Palokhi depends on the performance of various rituals at domestic and communal levels, and a concern with the continuity of ritual relationships. Central to this is the role of the headman of the community and other males in senior generations who are the religious functionaries in all important communal rituals, including marriage ceremonies. Their role may otherwise be described as the ritual management of reproduction in younger generations and agricultural production in Palokhi. In this respect, Palokhi resembles a great many other societies in which age and sex act as **natural** principles of social differentiation (La Fontaine 1978). In Palokhi, however, the role of the headman and males in senior generations is best understood in the following terms: as religious functionaries whose positions are defined according to these principles, these men are the managers of the "symbolic capital" of the community.

The nature of headmanship and the position of males in senior generations cannot be usefully considered in terms of "political leadership" or "political organisation". It is best considered in terms of the exercise of moral and jural authority. If, however, "political" is taken in the sense of "acting to influence the actions of others" then, to take the example of the enforcement of marriage rules, it may be regarded as such. It is important to realise that, in this particular sense, the "political" aspect of authority in Palokhi is that the headman and older men act to influence others on the basis of the "moods and motivations" generated by the symbolic system rather than the cultural ideology itself. To this extent their actions would be "ideological" as conventionally understood. It is, however, in these kinds of actions, including their officiation of important rituals — in short, the management of the "symbolic capital" of the community — that the system of symbolic representations is regenerated and the cultural ideology perpetuated.

It is, therefore, through these relationships between agriculture, religion, social organisation, the authority of males in older generations and their central role in the religious life of the community, that the cultural ideology of the Palokhi Karen is perpetuated in highly symbolic, as well as "practical", ritual activity. It is the reproduction of this ideological system, in these ways, that enables the Palokhi Karen to maintain their distinctive identity. For, it pre-empts the emergence of significantly different ways of seeing things which could conceivably lead the Palokhi Karen to view themselves as being anything other than what they regard themselves to be.

The argument is presented in the following chapters through a close examination and analysis of a series of data from Palokhi.

I begin, in Chapter II, with a description of Palokhi's history as a settlement and an examination of the institution of headmanship. This entails an examination of Palokhi Karen ideas about what it means to be a community, the importance of continuity in the ritual relationship between the headman and the tutelary spirit of the domain (the "Lord of the Water, Lord of the Land"). I also introduce the concepts of "heat" and "cooling" which are important in Palokhi Karen ideas about harmony in the on-going existence of the village as a community.

In Chapter III, I discuss kinship and domestic social organisation in order to draw out the ideology of kinship and marriage as a central aspect of the cultural ideology of the Palokhi Karen. The chapter is essentially concerned with an explication of a "procreative model of society" in Palokhi. This requires an extensive examination of kinship terminology, the system for naming individuals, the system of sex and gender differentiation, and dress and colour symbolism. It also entails a further analysis of the concepts of "heat" and "cooling" and the role of the headman and village elders in the maintenance of the symbolic and ideological significance of marriage. Following from this, I discuss the sociology of household formation and fission, relating the ideology of kinship to social organisation in Palokhi.

Chapter IV is concerned with rather more general issues in Palokhi social organisation, namely, the role of kinship in relation to patterns of household production and consumption. Here, I also explore the symbolic aspects of the consumption of food which are related to the ideology of kinship and the household as the basic unit of production and consumption in Palokhi. The symbolism of eating is integral to the representation of social relations in the routine consumption of food as well as in ritual contexts which include domestic rites and agricultural rituals.

Chapter V is mainly given to a consideration of the subsistence economy of the Palokhi Karen. In this chapter, I discuss in some detail swidden and wet-rice cultivation in order to show the extent to which agricultural cultivation fails to meet the consumption requirements of the Palokhi Karen. This is followed by a description of the ways in which rice deficits are made up in the cash sector. Overall, the chapter attempts to show how the Palokhi Karen are integrated into a larger socio-economic environment and how they utilise it according to their own needs. The chapter, however, also contains a discussion of an important aspect of the sociology of agricultural cultivation: the crucial role of men in the ownership and inheritance of wet-rice fields which, I argue, is an important aspect of the relationship between social organisation and agriculture. As such, it forms an integral part of the cultural ideology of the Palokhi Karen.

I further explore the cultural ideology of the Palokhi Karen in relation to agriculture in Chapter VI through an examination of the cycle of swidden rites in Palokhi which are integral to the religious life of the Palokhi Karen. In this chapter, I describe and analyse several key rituals. Among the many symbolic representations contained in these rituals, perhaps the most significant for an understanding of the cultural ideology of the Palokhi Karen are the ritual practices associated with "heat" and "cooling" and certain symbolic expressions related to marriage and commensalism. This chapter, thus, sets out the "procreative model of society", discussed earlier in Chapter III, in the context of swidden cultivation.

In the final chapter, I draw together the main threads of the argument contained in my examination of the ethnographic data from Palokhi and return to a consideration of cultural identity and its maintenance in Palokhi. I discuss this in relation to the ethnic identity of the Palokhi Karen and examine the general implications for an understanding of Karen ethnic identity with reference to other Christian and Buddhist Karen groups.

ENDNOTES

[1] The general familiarity of the Karen (especially men) with the Northern Thai dialect is itself a good indication of the contacts between Karen and Northern Thai. Some interesting observations on Karen competence in Northern Thai may be found in Grandstaff (1976:287–94).

[2] The Karen are by no means new to ethnological and anthropological study. Studies of the Karen began well over a hundred years ago and the development of trends in Karen studies, since then, may well be described in terms of a shift of interest from ethnology to ecology, economy and ethnicity. The earliest accounts on the Karen come mainly from missionary sources, for example, Cross (1853–54), Mason (1865, 1866, 1868) and Gilmore (1911) amongst others. A list of these earlier publications may be found in the bibliography to the study by Marshall (1922), also a missionary, whose work is perhaps the most informative. Early works on the Karen were also published by British colonial administrators in Burma such as Smeaton (1887) and Scott (1922). I might also add that because of some of these and

other sources, the Karen have featured (though not in any particularly significant way) in some of the classic works in ethnology and anthropology. References to the Karen may be found in, for example, Morgan (1871:441–7), Frazer (1919:138) and Levi-Strauss (1969:41). Contemporary academic interest in the Karen was foreshadowed by two dissertations written in the early part of this century (Heald 1900; Lewis 1924), including Marshall's monograph. These were followed by yet another dissertation (Truxton 1958). All of these studies, however, were by missionaries which followed the tradition set by the earlier missionaries working in Burma. Since then, the Karen have been the subject of several contemporary anthropological studies. These studies reflect broader trends in anthropology since the 1960s up to the present time. The parallel trends were, first, social and ethnic change following Leach's work on the Kachin beginning with Kunstadter's series of papers (1967, 1969 amongst others) and culminating in a collection of papers on Karen ethnic adaptation edited by Keyes (1979). The other trend was problem-oriented approaches in anthropology arising from the interest in development problems, anthropology as an applied discipline, and socio-economic change. Where the Karen are concerned, these approaches were manifest in studies dealing with cultivation systems, population growth and problems of natural resource management (for example, Kunstadter 1969, Hinton 1975, Grandstaff 1976, Madha 1980). There have also been other studies which deal with other aspects of Karen history, society and culture, for example, Keyes (1979b) and Renard (1980) on the history of the Karen, Somphob (1975) on Karen medicine, Mischung (1980) on religion, and Hamilton's rather more general study which also emphasises change (1976). If Karennic speaking groups, other than the Sgaw and Pwo, are also taken into account, it would be necessary to include Lehman's work on the Kayah (1967) and Hackett's dissertation on the Pa-O or Thaungsu (1953). This review of work on the Karen is not, by any means, exhaustive.

[3] The question, in other words, is whether or not religion in Karen communities possesses an internal coherence in relation to social organisation, political institutions and other aspects of social life, and whether or not a logical structure may be discerned in it.

[4] See Keyes (1979a:21). There are also other problems in understanding the nature of Karen religious traditions. Keyes has pointed out elsewhere (1977b:52) that the interpretation of Karen myths has been coloured by the fact that they were first recorded by American Baptist missionaries. Keyes presents an alternative interpretation of some of these myths which is by far the most consistent with what we know of other aspects of life of the Karen. It is worth noting that missionary interpretations of Karen myths, and some of the early ethnological speculations about the origins of the Karen, have found their way into contemporary Karen theories of racial origins and ethnicity. I discuss this in an unpublished paper (1985, but see Chapter VII, pp. 451–5) in relation to the Karen separatist movement in Burma. I should also point out here that the Palokhi Karen have very few myths; the little they have bear hardly any resemblance to the myths documented by the American Baptist missionaries. They are rather like just-so stories which appear to have little relevance to their religious system.

[5] Throughout this thesis, I use the place name Pa Pae to refer to the Northern Thai settlement Ban Pa Pae, the **tambon** which has the same name and of which it is a part, as well as the general area which I call the Pa Pae hills. Kunstadter has written on **The People of Pa Pae** (in Mae Sariang) which, in 1979, was due to be published as Monograph No. 2 of the Thomas Burke Memorial Washington State Museum (Keyes 1979:261). Unfortunately, I have not been able to refer to this work and all references to Pa Pae in this study therefore pertain to the area of my fieldwork. Pa Pae is, in fact, a fairly common place name in Northern Thailand. It is very often used to designate places or settlements which lie at the fringes of uninhabited areas or forests well away from major human habitations (Wijeyewardene, pers. comm.).

[6] A brief but informative description of the geography of the Mae Muang Luang-Huai Thung Choa basin may be found in Chapman (1983). In the existing literature on the area (most of which are reports and papers from the United Nations University-Chiang Mai University Joint Research Project on Highland-Lowland Interactive System with the participation of the Royal Forestry Department of Thailand), the area is known as the "Huai Thung Choa Project Area". This designation does not reflect the full extent of the area, hence my use of the term "Mae Muang Luang-Huai Thung Choa area". The official designation comes from the fact that when the Watershed Development Unit of the Royal Forestry Department first began their operations in the area, it was initially intended that it would be based in the Huai Thung Choa valley on the basis of a first reconnaissance. Subsequent reconnaissance established that a site deeper within the area (at Ban Lum near a Lisu village) was more suitable where the unit headquarters was in fact built. The name "Huai Thung Choa", however, remained and was applied to the area under its purview and has been used for all subsequent projects carried out. The area has also been designated a "King's Royal Hilltribe Development Project Area".

[7] The survey by Thannarong, Benchaphun and Prasert was conducted to establish base-line socio-economic data on the communities inhabiting the area as part of the United Nations University-Chiang Mai University Joint Research Project. It will be noticed that the number of settlements, especially Karen, shown in Figure 1.1 does not tally with the number given by Thannarong **et al.** The reason for this discrepancy is that whereas the map in Figure 1.1 (source: Chapman 1983:319) shows only villages which have been independently established by the Karen, Lisu, etc. themselves, the survey by Thannarong **et al.** includes not only these villages but clusters of mainly Karen households (classified as villages) doing full-time wage work, attached to operational units of the Royal Forestry Department's Watershed Development Unit in the area.

[8] Several published papers now exist on the conditions in the Mae Muang Luang-Huai Thung Choa valley system and the impact of the presence of the Royal Forestry Department in the area. See, for example, Chapman (1983), Hurni (1979,1982), Hurni and Sompote (1983), and Kunzel (1983, n.d.) amongst others. Kunzel (1983) deals specifically with the impact of the Royal Forestry Department's presence on wage work patterns among the Karen, Lisu and Northern Thai inhabitants in the area.

[9] I discuss the subsistence system of the Palokhi Karen in more detail in Chapter V. In Palokhi, ordinary rice is preferred to glutinous rice for daily consumption. Glutinous rice is usually grown in small amounts for making rice liquor and certain kinds of cakes which are eaten on ceremonial occasions such as the rites of the New Year. When the Palokhi Karen purchase rice from shops in Northern Thai settlements to meet their consumption requirements, they buy the glutinous variety because it is cheaper. It is also the main form of rice available because the Northern Thai themselves grow it in preference to ordinary or non-glutinous rice.

[10] It is worth noting also that the province of Chiang Mai is a net importer of rice because rice production even in the high-productivity rice-farming areas of the province is insufficient to meet the needs of a rapidly increasing population (Wijeyewardene, pers. comm.).

[11] To discuss this further would require far more space than is possible here and it would be a digression into issues which are far removed from my present concerns. Most of these issues, including reviews of earlier marxist anthropological works, may be found in Kahn and Llobera (1981) who suggest that marxist approaches in anthropology are far from consolidated and may very well be heading towards an "unavoidable fragmentation". However, I should perhaps add that one reason why the data from Palokhi will not sustain a marxist analysis is simply that the conceptual tools of such an analysis are in considerable disarray. One such tool which has been used in diverse ways in marxist anthropological analyses is the concept of "mode of production" which is perhaps far more important, analytically, than "ideology". The subsistence system of Palokhi would require yet another idiosyncratic (or highly specific) definition of "mode of production" which would only bear out what now appears to be all too true: that there are as many marxist anthropologies as there are marxist anthropologists! The same, of course, might be said of other theoretical orientations in anthropology. I should, however, make it quite plain that I am not interested here in theories. My concern is with an interpretative framework which will permit a sociologically reasonable, or even commonsense, understanding of what happens in Palokhi. Thus, I have no hesitation in attempting a working definition of "cultural ideology", derived from Althusser's formulation, because the formulation is indeed a useful one in a general sense. This is necessary because along with marxist uses and understandings of the term "ideology", the term is also used a great deal in anthropology with notorious imprecision. Despite Althusser's theoretical intentions, his definition is general enough to be used, or applied, without necessarily implying the analysis he advocates.

[12] Cultural ideology, then, as Yao points out would be "political" in Barthes' (1972) sense of the "political uses" of culture. For another earlier view of ideology and culture which emphasises the importance of symbolic representations, see Geertz on "Ideology as a Cultural System" (1973).

Chapter II

Settlement History, Headmanship, and the Lord of the Water, Lord of the Land

Of the eight Karen villages in the Mae Muang Luang-Huai Thung Choa area, Palokhi (first settled in 1953) is the most recently established Karen community in the area while the oldest, at Huai Dua and Mae Muang Luang (see Figure 1.1), have been in existence for about one hundred years. Although the history of Palokhi as a settlement is a comparatively short one as far as Karen communities in the immediate area are concerned, it has nevertheless been an eventful one. The village has undergone four changes of location and two successions of headmen. It has also grown considerably as a consequence of steady in-migration and natural increase.

The history of Palokhi forms an important background for the rest of this study. It reveals how a pioneer Karen settlement has been able to establish its viability and consolidate its existence as a result of a variety of factors which include favourable ecological conditions and the advantages of being linked with an economic network which covers the Pa Pae hills and spreads to the plains of Chiang Mai. The changes in location and headmen also highlight some significant aspects of what is entailed by settlement, not only as a process, but a state of **being a community** according to Karen ideas and experience. This concerns the relationships between the people in the community, the headman, and the tutelary spirit of the domain known to the Karen as the "Lord of the Water, Lord of the Land".

In this chapter, I examine both these sets of issues in the history of Palokhi and set out the basic elements of the ethnography of the community which appears in the chapters that follow.

Toponym, Village, and Domain

The general term for village, in the dialect of Sgaw Karen spoken in the Mae Muang Luang-Huai Thung Choa basin is **zi**. The term refers essentially to a group of dwellings while a single house, on the other hand, is known as **doe'**.[1] In this sense of a human habitation, **zi** therefore also describes what we might call a village "community". In the Mae Muang Luang-Huai Thung Choa area, all eight **zi** are known by toponyms whose invariant feature is the suffix **khi** which means "headwaters" or the upper reaches of streams. Indeed, this is an almost universal feature in the naming of Karen villages in general.[2] The principal topographical referent in village names is, thus, the upper section of streams.

However, the toponyms of villages imply rather more than the fact that villages are, generally, situated near the headwaters of streams which often, though not always, give their names to villages as well. They also imply, more broadly, the geographical area within which these streams are found, that is, stream valleys which are roughly bounded by their surrounding mountains, hills or ridges which act as natural lines of demarcation between communities inhabiting contiguous stream valleys.[3] This pattern in the distribution of Karen settlements in the Mae Muang Luang-Huai Thung Choa river system is immediately apparent from any topographical map of the area. Such an area, conceived of as being roughly circumscribed by prominent natural features, is known as a **kau**. The term, however, is not simply geographical or topographical in its meaning. It also connotes the idea of an area of land which a community lives off, as well as in. Equally important is the fact that each **kau** is also believed to have its own principal tutelary spirit, the **Thi Koe'ca, Kau Koe'ca** or Lord of the Water, Lord of the Land. **Kau,** therefore, are distinct territories or domains with a religious aspect and they are closely bound up with the identities of villages and their modes of subsistence.

The name "Palokhi", thus, refers to a particular Karen village situated near the headwaters of a stream which lies within a domain with its own territorial spirit. The toponym, however, is not a true Karen term. Its etymon is **pang luang** ("almost great"), the name of a Northern Thai village (Ban Pang Luang) which is one of three which make up the larger settlement of Ban Mae Lao, as it has come to be known, further downstream. Because Sgaw Karen lacks final consonants, other than the glottal stop, and diphthongs (as well as a distinction between long and short vowels), there is a tendency for Northern Thai final consonants to be elided and diphthongs to be approximated by either Sgaw Karen vowels or a modification of their phonological shapes, by Karen speakers of Northern Thai. Thus, **pang luang** has become **pa lau** and hence the name of the village: **Palaukhi.**

The Northern Thai name of the stream is, in fact, Huai Thung Choa which is one of the two major tributaries of the Mae Lao, the other being Huai Non. The reason why the Huai Thung Choa is generally known to the Karen as "Pang Luang" is because they have taken the name of the village, which is one of the oldest Northern Thai villages in this particular area, to be the name of the stream in the way that they themselves often name their villages. Indeed, it is not unusual by any means for Northern Thai villages to be named after streams and rivers, but in this instance it happened not to be the case. The names of other Karen villages in the Mae Muang Luang-Huai Thung Choa area are derived, similarly, from Northern Thai names or terms. Thus, for example, we find villages called "Maulaukhi" (Mae Muang Luang) and "Hedoekhi" (Huai Dua) from the Northern Thai names of a river and a stream, "Khusakhi" (Khun Sa) from the

Northern Thai name for a peak, and so on. The only exception to this is "Toeloekhi" (Pong Thong) which is, possibly, a Karen eponym.[4]

It is worth noting here that the derivation of Karen toponyms from Northern Thai is a conspicuous feature in the naming of a great many Karen villages throughout Northern Thailand and its significance is clear.[5] Where these toponyms are found to contain Northern Thai names or terms, we may be certain that the Karen have migrated to areas already inhabited by Northern Thai or which were, at the very least, known and named by the Northern Thai before the Karen arrived. This, undoubtedly, has been the case in the Mae Muang Luang-Huai Thung Choa valley system and, probably, most if not all of the Pa Pae area.

As I have noted before, the two oldest Karen villages at Mae Muang Luang and Huai Dua were established approximately one hundred years ago and this is worth a brief comparison with the ages of some Karen villages to the west, in Mae Hong Son, in order to place Karen migration into the Mae Muang Luang-Huai Thung Choa area within its wider context. Kunstadter, for example, reports that Karen from Burma first settled in the Mae Sariang area some one hundred and twenty years ago (1979: 127–29) while Hinton places the migration of Pwo Karen into the Omkoi area at around one hundred and fifty years ago (1975:25). Elsewhere in Chiang Mai, Mischung estimates that the Karen around Chom Thong first arrived about eighty-five years ago (1980:16).

It is clear, therefore, that the eastward migration of the Karen from Burma has had a long, if variable, history. Nevertheless, the general trends are there and the approximate ages of the villages at Mae Muang Luang and Huai Dua are consistent with these trends. The more easterly position of the Mae Muang Luang-Huai Thung Choa drainage system which straddles the provincial borders of Chiang Mai and Mae Hong Son, suggests however that the fore-runners of the Karen communities in the area probably left Burma much earlier than those of the communities now found in Mae Hong Son. Most, if not all, Karen in the Mae Muang Luang-Huai Thung Choa area in fact claim that they have always lived there, while those who do not have moved in from a southerly direction. It is also significant that the men and women of 50 or 60 years from these two villages, with whom I have spoken, have no recollection of any connection with Burma in their own generation or that of their parents.[6] It is impossible, therefore, to reconstruct anything of the circumstances surrounding the founding of these older Karen villages in the Mae Muang Luang-Huai Thung Choa area. It may be noted, however, that at the latitude of the area, the Karen approach the marchlands of their eastward migration (Kunstadter, pers. comm.); but, as the map **Distribution of Major Highland Ethnic Group Village Settlements** prepared by the Tribal Research Centre, Chiang Mai, in 1978 (and also to be found as a supplement to MacKinnon and Wanat [1983]) shows, elsewhere the frontiers of Karen expansion lie well to the east in Chiang Rai and, indeed, Karen communities may also be found in the provinces of Lampang and even Phrae.

The more recent history of Palokhi, however, assures a reasonable degree of accuracy in oral histories which provides for a better understanding of the circumstances, motivations, events and related processes which have led to the establishment and consolidation of the village as a community in its own right, along with the older communities in the watershed.

Settlement History

Karen settlement in the Huai Thung Choa valley first began in 1953 and it is a process that has continued at different times and in varying numbers right up to the present, that is, 1981. In all cases, the settlers who now make up the community of Palokhi cite two principal reasons for moving into the valley: first, the favourable ecological conditions in the valley which offered ample opportunities for more productive swiddening for these migrant families who also report coming from villages where there was a shortage of land for swidden cultivation; second, the considerable attraction of reclaiming abandoned Hmong wet-rice fields requiring lower labour inputs to bring them under cultivation than would have been the case if new terraces were opened up along the banks of the Huai Thung Choa. In short, the reasons for Karen occupation of the Huai Thung Choa valley have been a combination of ecological and demographic factors. From a general perspective, this is consistent with prevailing conditions in the highlands of Northern Thailand now well-recognised in various studies. However, perhaps for reasons of historical accident, the Huai Thung Choa valley represents rather different conditions in microcosm which the Karen have recognised and have proceeded to take advantage of.

Unlikely though it may seem on the basis of popular stereotypes about Hmong cultivation systems, the existence of these abandoned Hmong wet-rice fields must be accepted as fact rather than the product of some fanciful speculation on the part of the Palokhi Karen. Some of the Northern Thai from Ban Mae Lao (now living in Ban Thung Choa) confirm that these fields were opened up by the Hmong who subsequently left the valley some years before the last war.[7] Both the Karen and Northern Thai also agree that the Hmong migrated to Khun Sa in the vicinity of the Karen village of the same name mentioned earlier.[8] I might also add that in the time that elapsed between the departure of the Hmong and the arrival of the first Karen settlers, two Northern Thai from nearby villages and a Burmese from Pai, to the northwest near the Thai-Burmese border, in fact came to the Huai Thung Choa valley primarily to cultivate these abandoned Hmong terraces. However, as I discuss the relations between the Karen and their immediate predecessors in some detail within the specific context of the acquisition of these fields and Karen entry into wet-rice cultivation in Chapter

V, I shall not therefore deal with the presence of the Northern Thai and Burmese any further. They, in any case, eventually left the Huai Thung Choa valley as the Palokhi Karen established themselves there.

In Table 2.1, I have summarised the history of Karen settlement in Palokhi according to the years in which families first arrived and some salient demographic indicators, namely, household size, number of dependents, the ages of spouses, and the residential and migration histories of these households prior to settling in the Huai Thung Choa valley. The small population of Palokhi does not allow for any meaningful statistical tests of significance for trends and characteristics on the basis of the values of the variables represented by these indicators. Nevertheless, they are useful for drawing a rough socio-demographic profile of these families which migrated to the Huai Thung Choa valley as they describe the particular characteristics of individual households which nonetheless share some important features in common, as I discuss below. There is one other consideration which has been an important factor in the migration of families to the Huai Thung Choa valley, and this is the genealogical relationships between families — relationships which have been cited by some Palokhi households as a reason, though by no means the most important, for migrating to the Huai Thung Choa valley.[9]

From Table 2.1, it can be seen that Karen settlement in the Huai Thung Choa valley has been distributed somewhat irregularly over time with the arrivals of the first families concentrated in 1953 and two families following in 1954, after which there is a more even spread of families migrating in subsequent years broken by three time gaps, the first of which was relatively long (1955–60) while the other two were comparatively short (1969–71 and 1975–78). The characteristics of the five families in 1953 and the two families in 1954 are worth noting for not only do they reveal something of the conditions which have led to their migration and those under which they have had to establish themselves, but they also foreshadow the conditions and circumstances of the families which came later in several important respects.

Table 2.1. Karen Settlement in the Huai Thung Choa Valley

Year	Household*	Household Size	Number of Dependents**	Age of Husband	Age of Wife	Mean Age of Spouses	Residential and Migration History***
1953	H16+	3	–	NA	NA	NA	Pong Thong (20)
	H9+	6	4	47	49	48	Khun Sa (38); Pong Thong(4)
	H14+	5	3	33	28	30.5	Khun Sa(1); Pong Thong(4)
	H5+	3	1	31	18	29	Huai Khon Kha(4); Mae Maeng(1); Pang Ung(2); Pong Ma Kwaeng(1)
1954	HA	3	1	NA	NA	NA	Huai Dua(?)
	H1+	3	1	33	27	30	Huai Dua(1)
	H5++	3	1	58	51	54.5	Khun Mae Poeng(7); Huai Pong Faw(1); Huai Sai Luang(11); Huai Khon Kha(4); Mae Maeng(1); Pang Ung(2); Pong Ma Kwaeng(1)
1961	H2	4	2	45	31	36.5	Huai Sai Luang(2); Pang Ung(3)
1962	H11b	2	–	25	18	21.5	Mae Mong(1)
	H12	8	5	NA	33	NA	Maukhakhi(?); Pong Ma Kham(?); Mae Mong(?)
1963	H11a	3	–	NA	44	NA	Mae Lao(?); Huai Khon Kha(2); Pang Ung(4);
1968	H13+	7	5	41	36	38.5	Mae Poeng(2); Huai Sai Luang(2); Huai Khon Kha(2); Mae Poeng(3); Pang Ung(4)
1971	H3	8	5	34	NA	NA	Mae Thol(2)
1974	H4	5	3	52	40	46	Pang Ung(3); Mae Lak(9)
	H8	7	4	30	35	32.5	Mae Lak(9)
1979	H6	6	3	30	29	30.5	Huai Hia(4); Mae Lak(4); Huai Mao(2); Plaeng Dauk(3)
	H7	4	2	30	24	27	Mae Lak(3); Huai Mao(2); Plaeng Dauk(3)

* The composition of households has, of course, changed since they first arrived in the Huai Thung Choa valley as a result of natural increase, death, reconstitution through in-marriage and fission through out-marriage. However, to facilitate cross-references in this thesis, I have retained the system of coding households which I have employed on the basis of genealogical proximity and shared economic functions in 1980–1. To indicate that these households are not necessarily constituted by the same personnel in 1981, I have marked them with the "+" symbol. Thus, H1 has become H1a and H1b, H5 and H5 have become H5, and so on. The household HA no longer exists in Palokhi in any form. Little is known of its past history. This table indicates only initial (or first-time) migration to Palokhi; it does not include the remigration of some households back to Palokhi after temporary residence elsewhere.

** Dependents include children below the age of fourteen and adults above the age of sixty.

*** Residential and migration history, here, refers to previous residence and migration from the time when spouses were first married leading up to residence in Palokhi. This does not include the migration of husbands as a consequence of the custom of uxorilocal residence at marriage (see text and Chapter III). The figures contained in brackets indicate the length of time, in years, that couples have been resident in a particular village or locality. All place names are Northern Thai with the exception of Maukhakhi, a Karen toponym and village name, the Northern Thai derivative of which I have been unable to ascertain. The periods of residence in this column, as with the ages of spouses at the time of settling in the Huai Thung Choa valley, are essentially estimates which I have arrived at from the oral histories of the individuals concerned who were still living in Palokhi at the time of my field work. The time estimates of informants themselves, especially older men and women, are generally unreliable. However, such inaccuracies can usually be reduced to a large extent and, indeed, eliminated in some cases, where there is sufficient independent corroborative evidence which may allow dates or time frames to be established with a reasonable degree of accuracy. Furthermore, while the recollections of individuals may not be reliable in establishing durations in individual life histories, the reproductive histories of women, on the other hand, may be reconstructed in most cases with remarkable clarity. The reason for this is that even though women may not necessarily be able to state what the ages of their children may be, nevertheless, they are almost always able to recall intervals between the births of children and this, coupled with their recollections of where their children were born, considerably assists the reconstruction of residential and migration histories. The histories of younger couples are, of course, far more accurate than those of older men and women.

One important feature of these founding families and those which migrated to the Huai Thung Choa valley later is that they are relatively young (though there are a number of older families), but not immediately post-marital (except for H1[+], H2 and H11b), as indicated by the clustering of the mean ages of spouses around 30 years. This, very generally, agrees with the number of dependent children that they have although the correspondence is not altogether regular. In some cases (H5[+], H5[++], H4, H8 and H6) the dependents were, or included, an aged parent of one or the other of the spouses in the household. Under normal circumstances, we would expect the mean ages of spouses to show a regular correspondence with the length of time that they have been married (that is, within a given cohort) and the number of children that they have, in any given population. In Table 2.1, the duration of marriages of spouses may be determined by the total number of years they have been resident elsewhere prior to migrating to Palokhi, and simple inspection will show that when they are matched against the number of children, by households, there is a considerable degree of variation amongst these three indicators or variables. There are two main reasons for this. First, the irregularities, especially those between durations of marriages and the mean ages of spouses (which exhibit a wide range in general as a result of large discrepancies in the ages of some spouses), take on a larger significance than would otherwise be the case if the population were larger. Second, the high infant mortality rates of some households have resulted in their having less children than they would have had under normal circumstances. Nevertheless, the clustering of the mean ages of spouses around the 30-year mark is significant, at least sociologically, because it means that they had not exhausted their reproductive potential at the time they settled in Palokhi. Thus, in the course of their residence in Palokhi, most households have continued to increase in size, and this has contributed to the expansion of the settlement as I show in Table 2.2. This clustering is also significant from another point of view: it indicates that while couples were relatively young when they migrated to Palokhi, nonetheless, they were not newly married (except for H1[+], and H2) with an even greater reproductive potential. Consequently, although the size of households and the community has increased with further births (accentuated by in-migration and off-set to some extent by out-migration), this has not occurred at an excessively high rate — with the result that there has been a net increase in the dependency ratio of the community from 42 per cent in 1953–54 to close to 55 per cent in 1980–81.[10] In Table 2.3 may be found some relevant demographic data on the population of Palokhi in 1981.

Table 2.2. Demographic Changes in Palokhi 1953–1981[*]

	1953–1960	1961–1970	1971–1980	1981
Base population	–	31	66	109
In-migration	28	31	46	8
Out-migration	–	4	31	3
Births	6	23	41	4
Deaths: Children	2	8	5	–
Adults	1	7	8	2
Total	3	15	13	2
Total population	31	66	109	116

[*] The Northern Thai and Burmese who preceded the first Karen settlers in the Huai Thung Choa valley are not included in this table, hence the zero base population for 1953. The present population of Palokhi is now, however, composed entirely of Karen. There is a Khamu' man (originally born in Laos) who came to Palokhi in 1972 and became a dependent of H2, and a Yunnanese Chinese deserter from a Kuomintang garrison in Chiang Rai who came to Palokhi in 1975 and eventually married 'Ae' of H11a. Both men were unequivocally regarded as members of the community although they were not Karen and for this reason I have included them here. I have, however, excluded two Northern Thai brothers and a Karen who own wet-rice fields and **miang** gardens in the Huai Thung Choa valley because they were permanently resident in Ban Mae Lao and Ban Pa Pae respectively. They, in fact, had houses near Palokhi in which they stayed during the planting and harvesting seasons, for wet-rice, but they were not regarded by the Palokhi Karen as being a part of Palokhi.

Although the increase in dependency ratios has not been excessively high, it is high nevertheless as are the dependency ratios themselves. These ratios represent important constraints on subsistence production as I discuss in some detail in Chapter V. However, suffice it to say that the reclamation of the abandoned Hmong wet-rice fields (which were an important reason for migrating to the Huai Thung Choa) could only be carried out gradually because of limited domestic supplies of labour. These families, on first settling in Palokhi, thus, practised swiddening in the initial years of their residence in the Huai Thung Choa valley and slowly embarked upon wet-rice agriculture as the Hmong terraces were slowly recovered for cultivation. Wet-rice cultivation, however, did not replace swiddening for most of these families have all continued with a dual system of swiddening and wet-rice cultivation up to the present time, with new terraces being opened up as the Hmong terraces have all been fully reclaimed. The exceptions to this general pattern were H6, H7 and H16 which migrated to Palokhi after working as wage labourers in the Flower Plantation (Plaeng Dauk) of the Royal Forestry Department's Watershed Development Unit and took up wet-rice cultivation without swiddening when they first arrived.[11]

Table 2.3. The Population of Palokhi by Age and Sex in 1981

Age Group	Males	Females
0 – 10	21	20
11 – 20	10	16
21 – 30	8	6
31 – 40	7	4
41 – 50	4	3
51 – 60	4	4
61 – 70	2	3
71 – 80	1	1
81 and above	1	1
Total	58	58

For some families, kinship has been an important consideration in migrating to Palokhi. These households are related by primary kin relations, that is, parent-child and sibling ties or step-sibling ties which, for all practical purposes, are equivalent to true sibling ties. However, these ties also include affinal relations, specifically, parent-in-law and son-in-law or brother-in-law relationships. These ties, from the perspective of the rationale adduced by some Palokhi Karen for migrating to the Huai Thung Choa valley, that is, to be with kin for mutual aid in agricultural production, are probably as important if not more so than the primary kin relations existing between these families. The reason for this is that given the general rule on uxorilocal residence at marriage which the Palokhi Karen observe (see Chapter III), male affinal relationships tend to take on a considerable degree of importance in the management of labour by related households in the heavier tasks associated with agricultural production (see also Chapter IV). Thus, for example, H5$^+$ and H1$^+$ are related by the fact that the head of H5$^+$, Thi Pghe, was the younger brother of Tamu', the head of H1$^+$. H5^{++}, on the other hand, is related to H5$^+$ by virtue of the fact that Rae', the head of H5^{++}, is the father-in-law of Thi Pghe. It is worth noting here that the dependent of H5$^+$ was the father of Thi Pghe and Tamu'.

It is clear from this example that despite the rule on uxorilocal residence at marriage which the Palokhi Karen share with other Karen, the exigencies of household members' life circumstances can result in modifications to the rule, usually after an initial period of such residence. Under the rule, Thi Pghe and his wife should, in fact, have been residing with Rae' (H5^{++}).

But as he had an aged father, Thi Pghe set up house independently after a nominal period of uxorilocal residence in order to look after his father because his brother, Tamu', had gone to live with his wife's family in Huai Dua, leaving no one to support their father.[12] In any event, both brothers decided to settle in the Huai Thung Choa valley and as they did so, one consequence was that H5++ also migrated as well. H5++ had, as a dependent, Rae''s aged mother-in-law, but what is significant in Rae''s decision was his relatively advanced age and that of his wife. In their case, they decided to settle in the Huai Thung Choa valley to be with their daughter, Do' Kwi, and her husband Thi Pghe, in order that the burden of agricultural cultivation could be shared with H5+.

A similar reason underlies the migration of H11a and H11b, where H11a was the original parental household. The step-sibling relationships between H4 and H8, likewise, were a factor in their migration to the Huai Thung Choa valley in 1974. In the same manner, the joint migrations of H6 and H7 from the time when they were co-resident in Mae Lak until they settled in Palokhi were influenced by the fact that the two households are related by parent-child, sibling and male affinal ties where La Zi, the head of H6, is the brother-in-law of Thi', the head of H7 and brother of La Zi's wife, with Thi''s old mother being resident in H6.

It is clear that these kinship relations have been an important consideration in the migration of various related families to Palokhi because of the perception, at least at the actual time of migration, that mutual assistance could be rendered by kin within these limited ranges in agricultural tasks. There can be no doubt, of course, that sentimental attachments and affective considerations have also played a part. However, as I noted before, the composition of households in Palokhi has changed with time and this has been accompanied, in several cases, by a realignment of these relationships between households in the management of labour in subsistence production and, indeed, even the degree of importance placed on sentimental attachments.

These changes, clearly, are the concomitants of the developmental cycle of domestic groups in which uxorilocal residence at marriage plays a part, insofar as the Karen are concerned. A contributory factor to these changes has been the very growth of Palokhi where the range of people, kin and non-kin, with whom the members of a particular household may choose to work has increased considerably. Thus, as I discuss in the next two chapters, while kinship is important in several respects, we find that at the present time (that is, 1981) a great deal of the arrangements in co-operative labour exchanges for example are not, in fact, necessarily dependent on kinship relationships in Palokhi.

Another noteworthy feature about Karen migration to the Huai Thung Choa valley is a distinct pattern in the migration histories of families. This pattern is related to the distribution of Karen and non-Karen populations (specifically, Northern Thai) within and outside the Mae Muang Luang-Huai Thung Choa river system. From Table 2.1 and Figure 1.1, it will be noticed that, generally, those families with a low incidence of migration and change in post-marital residence all came from villages within the Mae Muang Luang-Huai Thung Choa area, namely, the villages of Khun Sa, Huai Dua and Pong Thong. There were, of course, some exceptions to this where after a short period of post-marital residence in these villages, married couples moved on to Palokhi. Nevertheless, the households with long or short periods of residence in these villages within the area migrated to Palokhi in the space of a few years of one another. The generally stable residential histories of some of these families suggest that ecological and demographic conditions in Khun Sa, Huai Dua and Pong Thong were, by and large, stable until approximately thirty years ago at which time the only viable means of gaining access to resources for subsistence cultivation was migration to the Huai Thung Choa valley.

"Stable", however, is a relative term. Of these three villages, Khun Sa and Huai Dua are, on the basis of present-day observations, more hard-pressed in terms of population relative to land available for swiddening purposes but Huai Dua has the advantage of lying in an alluvial plain eminently suitable for wet-rice cultivation. Pong Thong, on the other hand, lies within a very small stream valley which has just sufficient resources for both systems of cultivation and its population. The families with unstable residential histories, however, were all resident in villages situated outside the Mae Muang Luang-Huai Thung Choa area, with several families having been resident in the same villages at different times, or with some overlap in durations of residence. Their relatively high frequencies of migration are indicative of comparatively unstable ecological and demographic conditions in the areas where they were previously resident. Indeed, in all cases, the changes in residence are consistent with their explanations for these changes, that is, the search for new swiddening areas.[13]

The difference in conditions obtaining within and without the Mae Muang Luang-Huai Thung Choa drainage system is intriguing and requires some explanation. Although there is insufficient documentation on the areas lying outside the drainage system, some general observations and an examination of topographical maps of these areas indicate that they are far more densely populated by Northern Thai settlements than is the case in the Mae Muang Luang-Huai Thung Choa valley system. In the areas outside the Mae Muang Luang-Huai Thung Choa valley system where the Karen households were previously resident (southeast and south of the river system on either side of the Mae Malai-Pai road), a great many Northern Thai settlements are distributed in a linear pattern a long the road, but they are also to be found along many stream valleys on the eastern side of the road at elevations which are lower than those of the hills, ridges and stream valleys of the Mae Muang Luang-Huai Thung Choa area. Interspersed among these Northern Thai settlements are to be found Karen settlements.

On the basis of the distribution of Northern Thai and non-Northern Thai (that is, principally Karen) settlements within and outside the Mae Muang Luang-Huai Thung Choa area, it is reasonable to assume that the difference in ecological conditions existing in these areas has been the outcome of differentials in demographic pressure on available resources. That is, outside the valley system this has been caused by a larger, more mixed population (predominantly Northern Thai) per unit area of land. The presence of the Northern Thai in these areas has very likely been due to a history of upland migration (going back at least sixty years ago judging by the oral histories of some Northern Thai now resident in Ban Mae Lao and Ban Thung Choa) whilst the pressure on natural resources in these areas is probably to be explained by the natural increase in both the Northern Thai and non-Northern Thai populations, of which the Karen are the majority.

The migration of Northern Thai from plains areas to the foothills of highland areas in Northern Thailand has undoubtedly occurred as Chapman (1967) has shown and it is almost certainly true that they are continuing to move further upslope according to local circumstances (Chapman, pers. comm.) Indeed, the general northward and upslope movement of Karen into the Mae Muang Luang-Huai Thung Choa valleys mentioned before may well be indicative of a much broader trend, not only of Karen but of Northern Thai communities as well, in response to population increase. The high rates of natural increase of Karen populations, on the other hand, are now well-documented by Kunstadter (1972, 1983).

Within the Mae Muang Luang-Huai Thung Choa valley system, in-migration by Karen has so far not been accompanied by a similar movement of Northern Thai on the same scale. The residential histories of the Karen families from Huai Dua, Khun Sa and Pong Thong, together with existing distributions of Northern Thai communities in the watershed, (for example, at Pong Sa Nua and Pong Sa Tai) suggest that Karen resettlement has been the consequence of natural increases in mainly Karen populations over a long period of time. To the extent that other communities have affected the movement of Karen locally, only the small Northern Thai and Lisu populations inhabiting the Mae Muang Luang valley have been involved.[14] Within the valley, especially around Khun Sa, Huai Dua and Mae Muang Luang, other factors were probably operative as well. Pressure on resources in the past (and the present) were in all likelihood compounded by the ecologically deleterious effects of opium cultivation practised by the Hmong around Khun Sa, and the Lisu around Huai Dua and Mae Muang Luang. Where Huai Dua is specifically concerned, the shortage of swidden land has also undoubtedly been due to the fact that tracts of land were, and still are, occupied by pine trees (**Pinus kesiya**) which the Karen quite rightly regard as being unsuitable for swiddening. Nevertheless, they protect these trees in order to use the resinous, inflammable wood as firestarters and torches.[15] Since 1975, the area under pine trees has increased significantly as a result of reforestation by the Royal Forestry Department.

The overall consequence of these various conditions and developments has been that those Karen who have been long-term residents within the Mae Muang Luang-Huai Thung Choa area, as well as those approaching it from outside, have sought to take advantage of the opportunities now only to be found in small forested pockets within the Pa Pae hills, such as the Huai Thung Choa valley.

Headmanship and The Lord of the Water, Lord of the Land

In its twenty-eight year history between 1953 and 1981, Palokhi experienced a change in headmen and four changes in the actual physical location of the settlement in the Huai Thung Choa valley. These changes are related in part, and they provide an important indication of the kinds of issues which are regarded as significant in the way in which a community is constituted according to Karen ideas.

The institution of headmanship in Karen communities has its roots in ideas and concepts in the non-Christian, non-Buddhist religious tradition of the Karen. Where it has been associated with some form of political or politico-religious organisation, this has been the result of the influence of ideas derived from Buddhist religious traditions and millenarian movements (or, for that matter, from Christian religious ideas) occasionally melded with, amongst others, the Karen notion of **pgho**, that is, religious power or "charisma" (Keyes [1977b:54–5]). In other words, political organisation and political leadership are not a primary part of indigenous Karen traditions and social organisation. On the other hand, headmen of Karen communities who are appointees of the Thai bureaucracy may in some cases be recognised as such within the community, and according to indigenous Karen ideas about headmanship.

In Palokhi, headmanship falls well within traditional definitions of the position, without political or politico-religious implications and without bureaucratic responsibilities. Headmanship, in Palokhi, is essentially a religious office which others (for example, Lewis and Lewis [1984:86]; Hinton [1975:41]) have described in terms of the role and functions of "village priest". It does not carry with it jural authority of any significance except in matters, such as the enforcement of customary rules on marriage (which I discuss in the next chapter), where the headman does attempt to apply his authority. Even in such matters, however, attempts to exercise what may be regarded as a form of jural authority — although moral or religious authority would be a better term — are ultimately based on the belief that these matters do, indeed, have religious and ritual significance. In these matters, the headman does not act alone but with four older men in the community who are known as "old hearts" (**sa' pgha**) or "elders". Hinton (1975: 42–3) has described this collection of men, including the headman or "village priest", by the term "council of elders". The term suggests an institutionalised, formal group which, at least in the context of Palokhi, is inappropriate. While it is true that these men do get together to discuss matters of communal interest, more often than not such discussions take place in piecemeal fashion with two or three of the four men taking part at a time. These discussions may occur at any place or time, though usually it is in the headman's house, after evening meals when the Palokhi Karen visit one another for pleasure, or for some business at hand such as recruiting labour for agricultural work on the next day. Such visits frequently involve both pleasure and business.

Through these back and forth discussions over a period of time (which depends on the urgency of the matter at hand), a "consensus" is arrived at. But, as Mischung has astutely observed (1980:34–5) such "consensus" is not necessarily the outcome of an unanimity or majority of opinion; frequently, it is the product of being able to "speak well" with a demonstrable knowledge of traditional Karen axioms and proverbs applied to the matter at hand which sways the opinions of others.[16] Mischung's observations are almost wholly applicable to Palokhi.

The important point to note, however, is that there is a certain degree of egalitarianism in which all of these men, including the headman, may express their opinions, and that these processes involve **men** who are generally, or relatively **old** (but cf. Mischung [1980:33]). That is to say, the "jural" process involves gender considerations and some form of age-grading or, in other words, principles based on natural differences which are employed to effect a form of social differentiation (see, for example, La Fontaine [1978:1ff.]).

Where Palokhi is specifically concerned, the pre-eminence of men in this regard is related to their dominance in agricultural and ritual matters, which are a major concern in the lives of the Palokhi Karen as I discuss below and in other chapters, whereas the generally old — or older — age of men who participate in such matters is related to a more universal phenomenon, namely, experience and knowledge which accrue with time. Even this, however, has a particular implication in Palokhi where, very generally, it is related to the notion of precedence which is an important consideration in religious and ritual concerns. While this explains the "jural" process in Palokhi (to the extent that such a process may be said to exist), nevertheless, these considerations do not account for the nature of headmanship, because the role and functions of the headman are primarily ritual and religious in substance.

Perhaps the most important consideration in Karen headmanship is precedence in residence which involves establishing a ritual relationship with the tutelary spirit of the domain, the **Thi Koe'ca, Kau Koe'ca** or Lord of the Water, Lord of the Land. This relationship consists of the annual propitiation of the Lord of the Water, Lord of the Land. It is regarded as a necessary condition not only in the opening up of a settlement but also in the on-going process of inhabiting a particular **kau.** Thus, the first headman (**zi kho,** literally, "village head") of Palokhi was Lauj (H9[+]) who was the first to settle in the Huai Thung Choa valley in 1953, and who was the first to propitiate the Lord of the Water, Lord of the Land of the stream valley.

The village was initially situated towards the upper section of the stream where Lauj had built his house and was joined by the various families which settled shortly afterwards (see Figure 5.2, p. 275). After approximately one and a half years there, Lauj decided to move the site of the village further downstream to a more favourable location because it was felt that the initial site of the village was too damp and cold due to its proximity to the stream. In 1958 or 1959 the village was moved yet again, this time because pigs from the village tended to forage in the swiddens which were being opened up on the northern slopes of the stream valley and, thus, lay close to the village itself. After three years (that is, in 1960) in this new location, the village was rebuilt in its immediately previous location. The reason for this move, according to the Palokhi Karen, was that several children had died in the new location and this was taken as an indication that the villagers had somehow incurred the displeasure of the Lord of the Water, Lord of the Land, although no specific reasons were given for this. The Palokhi Karen also claim that even after the change in village site, children continued to die, but it is not clear from their accounts as to the nature of the causes of these children's death. An examination of the life histories of households indicates, that a number of children had indeed died during this time although the number does not appear unusually large in comparison to child mortalities in previous years.

What emerges clearly, however, is that in shifting their village site within its first ten years, the Palokhi Karen obviously attached considerable significance to the children's deaths, leading in 1964 to a decision by three households (H5[+], H1[+] and HA) to hive off and settle in a new location. This happened to be the site of an old swidden that had been cultivated several years before by a Northern Thai from Ban Mae Lao. They were joined subsequently by H5[++] and other households, and the village remained in this location.

This last change in the site of the village was significant because it resulted in a change of headmen. It highlights an important aspect of village organisation in general as well as the crucial nature of the relationship between headman and the Lord of the Water, Lord of the Land, as a basis for the existence of the community in particular. It demonstrates that despite the interdependence of households as a community — which is conspicuous, for example, in the co-operative labour exchanges that take place in agricultural activities and which is ritually marked in the rites of the New Year, as I discuss in Chapter IV — they are, nonetheless, essentially autonomous units within the community. This is to be seen in the independent decisions taken by the three households to resettle themselves in 1964 and those of the households which followed subsequently.

The resettlement of the three families clearly shows the importance of the relationship between headmen and the Lord of the Water, Lord of the Land. Where it is felt that this relationship has not been sufficiently or successfully established (and, perhaps, even abrogated by the Lord of the Water, Lord of the Land), it can lead to the dissolution of the community, at least as it was previously constituted. When the three families moved to the present site of Palokhi, Thi Pghe (H5$^+$), Tamu' (H1$^+$) and Chwi' (HA) jointly assumed responsibility for propitiating the Lord of the Water, Lord of the Land, through an annually held rite called the Head Rite (**Talykho**) because they had simultaneously settled in the new location. In the time that Chwi' was still resident in Palokhi (that is, up to 1974) and Thi Pghe was still alive (until his death in 1978), none of these three men was regarded as headman over the other two, although some of the Palokhi Karen say that Tamu' was more or less so by virtue of the fact that he was the oldest of the three men, which is an indication of the importance placed on age as a criterion in determining precedence in Palokhi.

The overall ambiguity as to which of the three men was headman in the ten years after Palokhi was relocated in 1964 underlies the importance placed on precedence. The fact that the three men had established themselves in the new site of the village at the same time meant that none had clear-cut precedence. Instead, for ten years until 1974 (when Chwi' left Palokhi) the three men were the ritual leaders of the new settlement which they had established and to which the other households came. Although Thi Pghe, Tamu', and Chwi' decided to form their own settlement as a result of the deaths of the children, the ultimate reason for leaving the village of which Lauj was still headman was that they felt Lauj was no longer able to maintain the ritual relationship with the Lord of the Water, Lord of the Land.[17]

This very clearly demonstrates that, conceptually, the legitimation of headmanship in Palokhi rests on the successful maintenance of this relationship with the tutelary spirit of the domain. In effect, then, the legitimacy of Lauj's role as headman which rested on his ability to propitiate successfully the tutelary spirit of the domain was called into question. According to Nae' Kha, Tamu''s son, there were also misgivings in the early 1960's about Lauj's effectiveness as headman because of his growing addiction to opium. It is evident, however, that these three families were not the only ones to doubt Lauj's abilities, for they were soon followed by other households. When they did so, Lauj could no longer claim to be headman of the village since most of the village had, for all practical purposes, left him. He and his family, in fact, finally moved to join the others in the present location of Palokhi where he had no part to play in the Head Rite. As an elder, however, he was required to participate in some of the communal rites performed in Palokhi.

For Palokhi, as a Karen community, the overall significance of the headman is that he acts essentially as a mediator between the community and the Lord of the Water, Lord of the Land. Individual households do, in fact, perform rituals which are directed at the Lord of the Water, Lord of the Land as the tutelary spirit of the domain, but these rituals (although propitiatory in content) are primarily **agricultural** rituals unlike the Head Rite which is performed only by the headman (or co-founders of a settlement) and which is specifically conducted with the aim of propitiating the tutelary spirit of the domain in order to ensure favourable conditions and a harmonious state of affairs for the community.[18] In terms of the **logic** of the cycle of ritual activities in Palokhi, (which are predominantly agrarian rites), all else follows from the Head Rite which is consistent with the notion of precedence that underlies the role of headman. It is only because the headman performs the Head Rite that other households may then perform their own agricultural rituals. In other words, the Head Rite is a precondition for agricultural cultivation of land in the **kau,** or domain; subsequently, households may perform their own propitiations of the tutelary spirit of the domain as part of the cycle of agrarian rites in Palokhi.

The importance of the headman and the Head Rite, in this respect, is clearly to be seen in the way that both are described by the term **kho** or "head" which not only implies superordination but also connotes, in more general applications of the term, the idea of temporal priority as well, in the sense of "that which comes first". The first libations of rice liquor in the ritual propitiations of the Lord of the Water, Lord of the Land, for example, are called **khwae' si' 'a' kho** as opposed to the last libations which are called **khwae' si' 'a' da'** whilst in another context — the production of rice or maize liquor — prime liquor, which is the first distillate, is called **si' kho thi'** (literally, "liquor of the head water" or, as we might say it, of the "first water"). Similarly, rice that is first harvested and eaten (in a ritual which I discuss in Chapter VI) is called **by kho,** "head rice" (or "first rice"). All of these terms with **kho** imply precedence or priority of one kind or another and, in the context of headmanship and the Head Rite, it is the fact of precedence that gives headmanship its mediatory significance.

Precedence, however, is not the only important principle in the ritual or symbolic relationships between the headman, the Lord of the Water, Lord of the Land, and the community. The other equally important principle is **continuity** of these relationships which is, of course, the corollary of precedence. This was, undoubtedly, implicit in the reasons for the last resettlement (1964) of the Palokhi Karen although they themselves expressed these reasons merely in terms of Lauj's inability to propitiate successfully the tutelary spirit of the domain. Before the deaths of the children (and, perhaps, Lauj's increasing addiction to opium) the Palokhi Karen did in fact remain together as a community, with Lauj as the headman, on the assumption that he was able to maintain the relationship with the Lord of the Water, Lord of the Land. But then events caused his efficacy as headman to be questioned, at least as the Palokhi Karen viewed it.

The principle of continuity in the relationships between headman (or headmen), the Lord of the Water, Lord of the Land, and the community as a whole is probably best illustrated at Palokhi by the fact that the Head Rite must be performed **annually**. This renews the relationship between the headman (and his co-founders) with the tutelary spirit of the domain, and that between the community and the spirit of the domain through the intercessionary role of the headman. This renewal, or continuity, is re-affirmed by the genealogically-based succession to headmanship and the duty and obligation to perform the Head Rite on the part of the male descendants of Tamu' and his co-founders.

Headmanship and Succession

As I describe, in some detail, the Head Rite and its key features in the next section of this chapter, I shall therefore consider first the question of succession, and its implications for the continuity of the ritual relationships between headman, community, and the Lord of the Water, Lord of the Land in Palokhi.

In Palokhi, Tamu' is now regarded as the headman of Palokhi and, as one of the original founders of the village at its present site, he continues to perform the Head Rite which he first performed in 1964 with Thi Pghe and Chwi'. When Thi Pghe died in 1978, his eldest son Chi Choe (then sixteen years old) was required to participate in the rite in Thi Pghe's place. Chwi', on the other hand, who had migrated to Huai Dua in 1974, returned to Palokhi each year to perform the rite until his death in 1980. Tamu''s only son, Nae' Kha, was also included in the ritual when he returned to Palokhi after a few years of residence in Huai Dua where he went to marry. Nae' Kha's return was dictated by, amongst other considerations, the expectation that he would succeed Tamu' as headman in Palokhi. It is worth noting that Chwi' had a one year old son in Huai Dua (where he went to marry again) at the time of his death, but the son — quite apart from his age — was not considered to have any rights or responsibilities to the performance of the Head Rite because he was born in Huai Dua and not Palokhi.

Although there are two issues involved in the question of succession (succession to headmanship and succession to participation in the Head Rite), the rule is the same in both cases, namely, affiliation through the male line and primogeniture. This kind of succession to headmanship (or office of "village priest") in Karen communities is a well-established ethnographic fact noted by

Hinton (1975:41–2), Kunstadter (1979:130), Mischung (1980:33) and Madha (1980:61). Palokhi is, therefore, no exception in this regard. On the other hand, the importance of co-founders in association with headmen, thus far, has not been reported in existing accounts of the Karen. Nonetheless, the general principle of succession whether it be to headmanship or participation in the Head Rite is clear. However, insufficient attention has been given to the importance of the idea of **continuity of ritual relationships** entailed by this rule of succession.

Expressed more generally, there are two considerations involved here: succession on the basis of genealogical relationships, and the symbolic significance attached to these relationships and/or succession.

It is clear that the cognatic kinship systems of Sgaw and Pwo Karen societies do not preclude certain forms of social organisation (constituted for ritual purposes) whose principle of recruitment is based on maternal affiliation or, in some instances, what may be regarded as matrilineal descent properly known. On the other hand, succession to headmanship and participation in the Head Rite is based on affiliation through the male line. Except for the "matrilineal cults" of the Sgaw and Pwo Karen which I have briefly reviewed elsewhere (1984; see also Cohen and Wijeyewardene [1984a:252]), I hesitate to use the terms "matrilineal" and "patrilineal" in describing these principles of recruitment and succession (in the context of Palokhi) although Hinton and Madha have, in fact, used the term "patrilineal" with regard to succession to headmanship. The reason is that the construct "descent" is implicated in the use of these terms which, in my view, is not justified by the data from Palokhi. As Cohen and Wijeyewardene point out in their general introduction to the volume **Spirit Cults and the Position of Women in Northern Thailand** (1984), the application of the term "matrilineal" necessarily implies, according to traditional anthropological usage which restricts "descent" to a minimal three-generation span, at least recognition of a line of predecessors traceable to a common apical ancestress, and some ideology of matriliny. The same conditions would, of course, apply to the term "patrilineal" as well. In the absence of such recognition and ideology, only successive affiliation may be said to exist.

In Palokhi neither of these conditions apply to the domestic ritual called **'au' ma xae** (see Appendix A) which, though similar in several respects to the matrilineal spirit cults found in some Sgaw and Pwo communities, differs from these cults on these very grounds. Nor do these conditions apply to succession to headmanship and participation in the Head Rite. Hence, my use of the term "affiliation". I might add, in this connection, that individual genealogies in Palokhi are very frequently shallow with a **maximum** range of three ascending generations (see next chapter). This and the fact that descent is never traced to an apical ancestor or ancestress, as well as the absence of any discernible unilineal ideology, make the use of the neutral term "affiliation" (qualified appropriately) necessary if a better understanding of social arrangements in Palokhi is to be gained. As I discuss kinship and the domestic ritual **'au' ma xae**, more fully in the following chapter and Appendix A, I shall therefore now consider the question of succession to headmanship and participation in the Head Rite according to these two principles of affiliation and the notion of continuity in ritual relationships as they are to be found in Palokhi.

Succession to any office or role is a matter of considerable importance in most societies and where this is effected by genealogical principles, as distinct from other means, there are only two fundamentally logical alternatives for doing so, namely, through patrilineal or matrilineal principles — or, in Palokhi, by affiliation through males or females as I prefer to call it. There may also exist variations of these principles where there is some other contingent factor such as residence which acts to modify them which is not uncommon in the case of cognatic systems. The view that I take of these principles or, more generally, of cognatic kinship, in approaching the various aspects of social organisation in Palokhi is that they do not necessarily operate **independently** in determining the particular configurations that characterise various forms of social organisation in Palokhi. More specifically, the view that I take is that these configurations are the result of the **application** of genealogical reckonings guided by **non-genealogical** considerations, that is, by ideological considerations (as defined before) and the attribution of particular meanings to kinship relationships. In Palokhi, one such range of meanings is that which is attached to one of the more important aspects, if not the most important aspect, of kinship: sexual difference.

Thus, in the case of Palokhi, succession to headmanship and participation in the performance of the Head Rite, pose two different, but related, questions: why succession and why **male** succession? The answer to the more general question of succession, in Palokhi, has to do with the idea of continuity of ritual relationships, as I have already suggested, which informs most matters of ritual significance or religious importance of which the association between the headman, the community and the tutelary spirit of the domain is but one. The evidence for this lies, therefore, in the general characteristics of ritual performances and religious beliefs in Palokhi rather than the succession to headmanship and participation in the Head Rite (as well as its annual performance) alone.

The concern for continuity is evident more widely in the "connecting up of generations" in a variety of ritual contexts. For example, in the domestic ritual of **'au' ma xae**, the Palokhi Karen are concerned with the maintenance of generational lines in the pigs and chickens that are consumed in this ritual. Furthermore, they say that all **'au' ma xae** rituals must be conducted in the

same way in their details as when it was **first** conducted by a married couple. Continuity is also to be found in the cultivation of a special crop of rice, called the "Old Mother Rice" (**By Mo Pgha**) which is grown successively in each agricultural season for ritual purposes from its own seed (see Chapter VI).

Taken together, the undoubted concern with establishing continuity of ritual relationships in one form or another in these various ritual practices, including the succession to headmanship and participation in the Head Rite, indicate that continuity is an important aspect of the religious conceptions of the Palokhi Karen. It is significant, however, that it is expressed primarily in generational terms. The implication of this is that succession or continuity is conceived of as a process of affiliation, or association, through successive steps of biological reproduction rather than strict genealogical lineality. However, when the matter is brought to their attention, the Palokhi Karen are of course quite able to see that this can be represented as a "line". The important point to note, nevertheless, is that they do not have cultural categories for "lineage", "descent" (or "descent group") or, for that matter, "line" applied specifically in a genealogical context. This is strong evidence for the absence of any concept of genealogical lineality as such.

Male succession, on the other hand, has to do with a more general characteristic of ritual activities in Palokhi: the domination of men in the ritual life of the community. It is also related to the fact that despite the minimal sexual division of labour in agricultural activities, men are the decision-makers. Indeed, as I show in Chapter V, they are essential as managers of land, which is by no means irrelevant to ritual matters; an important part of the "management" of land in fact entails the performance of a series of agricultural rituals throughout the year which constitutes the annual ritual cycle in Palokhi. The dominance of men in the ritual life of the community is, thus, intimately linked with agricultural cultivation or, more generally, with the use of land within the **kau**. Male succession to headmanship and participation in the Head Rite, therefore, are part of a complex of conceptual associations or ideas which link men, land, agriculture and ritual activities together.

The Head Rite

The Head Rite, (**Talykho**), was, after 1980, performed by Tamu', his son Nae' Kha, and Thi Pghe's son, Chi Choe. It is held in May (or La De' Nja', the "frog, fish month" as it is known in Palokhi) which is the month when it was originally performed in 1964 by Tamu' and his co-founders, Thi Pghe and Chwi'. The agricultural season in Palokhi, in fact, commences in January-February when swiddens are first cleared in Palokhi and when the rites of the New Year (**kau lau wae** or **thau ni sau**) which symbolically mark the transition from the old season to the new are held. Thus, the performance of the Head Rite does not actually precede the commencement of the agricultural season in each year. The reason why the rite is held in May, rather than before the beginning of the agricultural season in Palokhi, is that it was first conducted by Tamu', Thi Pghe and Chwi' in this month after they had completed building their houses when they first established their settlement.

The performance of the rite itself is exclusive: when it was first, and subsequently, performed, it was conducted by Tamu' and his co-founders whilst at the present time only Tamu', Nae' Kha and Chi Choe participate in the rite. No other villager was, or is, permitted to attend the rite or even to witness it.[19] This restriction applied to all "outsiders" as well and the description of the Head Rite that follows is based on an account provided by Chi Choe immediately after the rite was held.

As with a great many rituals in Palokhi, the Head Rite is simple, comprising three characteristic features: offerings of food and rice liquor, commensalism, and prayers distinguished by semantic parallelism.[20] Another feature which the rite shares in common with agricultural rituals in Palokhi, as against rites of curing or healing individuals, is that it is proleptic in orientation and aoristic in form: it is directed towards the future as a renewal of the past. It seeks to obtain, through the propitiation of the Lord of the Water, Lord of the Land, auspicious and harmonious conditions for the well-being of the community as a whole and the successful cultivation of rice and other crops on which the community depends. In more general terms, the rite may well be regarded as a renewal of the compact between the headman and his co-founders (or their descendants) with the Lord of the Water, Lord of the Land, through which these conditions are obtained.

In the Head Rite described by Chi Choe (performed in the evening of 28 May 1981), various offerings were first prepared by Tamu' (and his wife) in his house, which included two stews made from a cock and a hen, roasted popped rice, six wax candles (a pair for each of the participants) and a bottle of rice liquor distilled by Tamu''s wife and daughter.[21] The rite itself was performed at the base of a tall tree (**se mi**, a species of **Eugenia**) located approximately three hundred metres east of the boundaries of the village along the ridge where the village is situated. There is no particular significance attaching to the species of the tree, but the presence of the tree is undoubtedly of some importance in the performance of the ritual.[22] The tree is said to "belong to the Lord of the Water, Lord of the Land" (**Thi Koe'ca, Kau Koe'ca 'a' se**) but the real significance of the tree is that it is a medium of communication or mediatory ritual device, which may be inferred from the only other ritual in Palokhi which employs trees. Without going into the details of this other ritual, suffice it to say that this ritual is designed to recall the souls (**kau' koela**) of **old** people. It is said that "the trees can see faraway" and, thus, assist in calling back the souls of old people which are believed to wander (or be enticed to do so by spirits, **tamyxa**) further afield than those of younger people.[23] In the same manner, the tree in the Head Rite is a medium by which access is gained to the Lord of the Water, Lord of the Land. The offerings are laid out on a woven bamboo mat which is placed at the foot of the tree, and the three participants (with Tamu' as officiant) squat around the mat.

As recounted by Chi Choe, the ritual commences with Tamu' making offerings or libations of rice liquor (the **khwae' si' 'a' kho** or "first libations of liquor") to the Lord of the Water, Lord of the Land. The libations are made by dripping the liquor from a cup, using the fingers with the cup tilted at a slight angle, onto the base of the tree. As this is done, the following invocation and prayer is recited by Tamu':

Sa, Palokhi 'a' Koe'ca, Palauklo' 'a' Koe'ca	O, Lord of the headwaters of Pang Luang, Lord of Pang Luang stream
Mauliang 'a' Koe'ca, Tung Cau' 'a' Koe'ca	Lord of Mauliang, Lord of Tung Choa (stream)
Maungau' 'a' Koe'ca, Maulaukhi 'a' Koe'ca	Lord of Maungau', Lord of the headwaters of Mae Muang Luang
Hedoeklo' 'a' Koe'ca, Lekoepau 'a' Koe'ca	Lord of Huai Dua stream, Lord of the Shining Cliff
Ha' 'i, hae kwa pgha	Come here, watch over the people
Dau' phau'khwa, dau' phau'my	Together the women, together the men
Dau' bau', dau' pgha	Together the children (literally, "the plump"), together the old
Dau' tapho, dau' taxa	Together the children, together the animals
Ta 'a' 'oe' 'a' sau hae, toe' ghe	That which is inauspicious (literally, "dirty") that comes again (literally, "anew"), it is not good
Kwa di' 'a' ghe, kwa di' 'a' gwa	Watch over well (literally, "good" or "beautiful"), watch over purely (literally, "white")
He di' 'a' loe', 'a' cau	Giving everything, giving (?) completely
'I pgha, kwa pgha kau' gha	Here (are) the people, watch over each person
Khaenjakhau, poe' koe' ly 'a' na dau'	Next year, we will propitiate (literally, "rear" and feed") you together again
Kwa gha ghe ghe	Watch over the people well

The prayer is a simple one and its intentions are fully and clearly expressed. It is worth noting, however, that although the ritual is directed towards the Lord of the Water, Lord of the Land of Palokhi, nonetheless the tutelary spirits of other domains and prominent topographical features are included in this prayer.

They are all seen as being essentially similar and there is no implication that one is superordinate to the others, apart from the priority accorded to the Lord of the Water, Lord of the Land of Palokhi. This spirit is addressed before all others. While this is to be expected, given that the Palokhi Karen inhabit the stream valley or **kau** known to them as the Pang Luang, and the importance placed on precedence in ritual matters as I have already noted before, the inclusion of tutelary spirits of other domains and prominent topographical features is of some importance in the conceptions held by the Palokhi Karen about the relationships amongst these tutelary spirits and the domains that they are believed to preside over. Perhaps the most important consideration is that the Palokhi Karen (and the Karen elsewhere in the Mae Muang Luang-Huai Thung Choa area) attribute a symbolic significance to prominent natural features which include those that define **kau**. Thus, while Palokhi, Huai Dua and Mae Muang Luang (and, possibly, Mauliang and Maungau) are recognised as domains in their own right, Lekoepau is also given recognition because it is a prominent natural feature near the headwaters of the Mae Muang Luang with a tutelary spirit of its own. The same reason underlies the references to the tutelary spirits of Huai Dua and Mae Muang Luang. Mae Muang Luang originates from the highest hills in the watershed, while Huai Dua which is a tributary of Mae Muang Luang in its lower section, flows through a valley bottom dominated by the hills from which Mae Muang Luang has its source. The inclusion of the tutelary spirits of Mauliang and Maungau are, however, problematic. They are not identifiable in the topography of the Mae Muang Luang-Huai Thung Choa valley system, but it is entirely possible that they refer to places which were, in the distant past, important in similar prayers which have been passed on from generation to generation. That such prayers have an old provenance, is unquestionable. In the prayers that Lauy used to recite, for instance, the tutelary spirit of Chiang Dao (which none of the Palokhi Karen have been to) was invoked as was the "Lord of Great Silver, Lord of Long Silver" (**Ce' Do' 'a' Koe'ca, Ce' Thu 'a' Koe'ca**). The latter is based on a historical knowledge which has not been wholly lost in Palokhi; it contains an implicit reference to the silver bar coinages of Northern Thai principalities first minted some four hundred years ago but which remained in circulation for some time after (see, for example, Oliver [1978:96]).

In terms of the rituals performed at the present time, however, one important feature of the prayer is the formula "watch over well, watch over purely" (**kwa di' 'a' ghe, kwa di' 'a' gwa**) which recurs consistently in agricultural ritual texts. **Di'** is a particle indicating continuing action (equivalent to the present continuous tense), whilst **ghe** and **gwa** which mean "good" or "beautiful" and "white" (in their literal senses), respectively, are best translated as "auspicious and harmonious" through their parallel juxta-position. These terms represent the conditions which are, ultimately, being sought after in the Head Rite and the various agricultural rituals performed in Palokhi.

Another important theme which appears in the Head Rite and agricultural rituals is the creation or induction of a "cool" state which is believed to be essential for the successful cultivation of crops and, more generally, for the well-being of the community. It is a state implied by the conditions represented by the terms **ghe** and **gwa** but is ritually produced by sprinkling lustral water which may simply be ordinary water, or water with acacia pods (**pychi sa**) and it is a practice that the Palokhi Karen share with their Northern Thai neighbours (see also Davis [1984:106–7]).

For auspicious and harmonious conditions to prevail, the Palokhi Karen believe that the Lord of the Water, Lord of the Land, and the land itself must be "cool". In the same way, the successful growth of the rice crop depends on the production of a "cool" state in the crop while auspicious and harmonious conditions for and in marriages are thought to be brought about by "cooling" the bride and groom which is an important part of marriage ceremonies (see Chapter III). In all cases, the application of lustral water is required. Thus, in the Head Rite, after the first libations of liquor have been offered to the Lord of the Water, Lord of the Land, lustral water is sprinkled onto the "head" of the spirit although this is in fact done at the base of the tree. The head, generally, is the focus of these applications of water because it is believed to be the most important part of the body, containing the principal soul (called the **koela kho thi'**) of a person.[24] The following short prayer accompanies the lustrations to the Lord of the Water, Lord of the Land:

Pghi noe' kho	Sprinkling your head
Pghi khy	Sprinkling cool
Pghi ba' na	Sprinkling directly onto you[25]
Kwa pgha ghe ghe	Watch over the people well

After the completion of these lustrations, the food offerings are then made to the Lord of the Water, Lord of the Land. This consists of placing some rice onto a banana leaf followed by the beaks, claws, wing tips, intestines and livers of each fowl. These parts represent the whole fowls offered to the spirit which is then invited to partake of the offerings. The invitation simply consists of asking the spirit to "come and eat, come and drink" followed by a repetition of the prayer said at the first libations of liquor.

Divination is then carried out to establish whether or not the Lord of the Water, Lord of the Land has eaten the offerings. This consists of tearing up three leaves, taken from any nearby bush or tree, in random fashion and then counting the number of pairs which the torn pieces make up. If there is a full set of pairs, whether odd or even in number, it is deemed that the spirit has consumed the food offerings, after which the three participants in the rite then eat the main portions of rice and chicken. The divination is important because it determines if the Lord of the Water, Lord of the Land has **accepted** the offerings and thereby renewed the compact, as it were, with the headman and his co-participants in the rite.

The other important aspect of this part of the rite, also present in the first libations, is commensalism. In the first libations, after the liquor has been offered to the spirit, the headman takes a sip of the liquor remaining in the cup and then passes the cup to Nae' Kha and Chi Choe who do likewise. Thereafter, they may then drink freely of the liquor leaving, however, enough for the last libations which are performed after the eating of the food. The principle of commensalism in the drinking of liquor at the first and last libations and the eating of food is the same and it expresses ritual and social relationships at two levels. First, there is in one sense a commensalism with the spirit which is given precedence in drinking and eating and this is symbolic of its superior ritual position. Second, the commensalism of the participants expresses their own communality and, indeed, equality as supplicants of the Lord of the Water, Lord of the Land. It is worth noting, here, that this is perhaps the single most pervasive aspect of ritual performances in Palokhi — the expression of social and ritual relationships, specifically the solidarity and egalitarian nature of relationships amongst co-participants in communal rituals, through commensalism in the drinking of liquor or the eating of food. The Head Rite ends with the last libations which are made after the three participants have finished eating the meal of rice and chicken stew.

With the completion of the Head Rite at the base of the tree outside the village, a subsidiary rite is performed in Tamu"'s house which brings together all the members of the community in a ritual similar in principle to the Head Rite. The structure of the ritual is identical to that of the Head Rite, the only difference being that food is not offered to the spirit or eaten by the congregation of villagers assembled in the headman's house. The fact that it is performed after the Head Rite, however, points unequivocally to the intercessionary nature of the Head Rite and the role of the headman for it is only after the Lord of the Water, Lord of the Land has been propitiated by the headman that the rest of the community may then participate in this more generalised ritual which further propitiates the spirit.

Although the ritual is considered by the villagers to be a village-wide performance, open to all Palokhi Karen adults to participate, what happens in practice is that men usually assemble in Tamu"'s house for the ritual. The reason for this is partly pragmatic because not everyone in the village can be accommodated in the house, but the more important reason is that men enjoy precedence in ritual matters.

The ritual commences with the first libations of liquor to the Lord of the Water, Lord of the Land which, in these circumstances, is performed by Tamu' and other older men in the village, the "old hearts". The libations are made at the walls of the house where these men happen to be closest (usually near the hearth where they often sit together with Tamu'), that is, directed away from the other villagers. The prayers which accompany the first libations are essentially similar to those said by Tamu' in the Head Rite and I shall not, therefore, describe them here. When these prayers are completed, each of the officiants sips from the cup of liquor from which the libations were made. The cups are then passed back and forth amongst the officiants until all have sipped from the various cups. If there is any liquor left in these cups, they are then passed on to the rest of the congregation who do likewise. When these first cups have been consumed, they are refilled by Tamu' or his son and then redistributed amongst the members of the assembly. The drinking continues in this way until it is judged that there is just sufficient liquor for the last libations at which time the cups which have been passed around are returned to Tamu' or his son to refill. They are then given to the officiants again to perform the last libations. When the final libations are completed, the liquor remaining in the cups is once again shared by the officiants and the people present. This time, however, concerted efforts are made to ensure that **everyone** takes a sip from **all** the cups. The cups, therefore, are passed to and fro with each person raising the cups to his mouth such that the liquor merely touches his lips before they are passed around yet again. The reason why such care is taken in the sharing of liquor at this time is that the Palokhi Karen believe it is an auspicious sign if there is still some liquor remaining in the cups even after everyone has sipped from them. What this means, however, is that everyone in the entire congregation makes a **conscious** effort to produce this result. It is almost as if the entire ritual and its key symbolic aspects have become sharply focussed in its last stages where the Palokhi Karen **act out** their communality and solidarity through the, now, deliberate sharing of liquor.

It is, I think, clear that the sequel to the Head Rite is primarily concerned with the "community" of the Palokhi Karen although it is expressed within the context of a more general propitiation of the Lord of the Water, Lord of the Land. It does, however, follow logically from the earlier performance of the Head Rite, and the two rituals express in symbolic terms the ritual and social relationships which are believed to be the essential basis of being a community according to ideas in the religion of the Palokhi Karen. The annual performance of these two rituals, and the succession to headmanship and participation in the

Head Rite, on the other hand, indicate that an equally important aspect of being a community lies in continuity of these relationships.

In this chapter, I have attempted to set out the history of Palokhi as a settlement in the Huai Thung Choa valley with particular emphasis on family residential histories, the ecological context of the establishment of the village, and the ritual relationships between the headman, co-founders of the village, the community, and the tutelary spirit of the domain. An important consideration in the establishment of Palokhi has been, and still is, the continuity of these ritual relationships.

This description of settlement history and the relationship between the headman and the Lord of the Water, Lord of the Land thus serves to introduce contemporary issues in the ethnography of the Palokhi Karen which I present and discuss in the chapters that follow. I begin with aspects of the kinship system, domestic social organisation and ritual in Palokhi.

ENDNOTES

[1] One aspect of Karen villages and dwellings which has received some attention in previous studies of the Karen is the question of villages consisting of a long-house (Marshall [1922:56]; Iijima [1979:101–2]; Hamilton [1976:247, n. 3]). Hamilton is correct in saying that **zi** and **doe'** which now refer to "village" and "house" may have described, in the past, "long-house" and "apartment" but his suggestion that this confirms the existence of long-houses as a form which Karen villages traditionally took in the past is untenable. The suggestion is unsupportable because the terms only indicate that different house forms may be described in similar ways. The linguistic evidence alone offers no indication of which form was historically prior. Following Marshall, Iijima suggests that long-houses were built as a defensive measure against slave raids by the Kayah who often preyed on the Karen. The disappearance of Karen long-houses in present times, therefore, may well be the outcome of the fact that Kayah slave raids eventually ceased in the last century as a result of their pacification by the British in Burma, and various agreements between the British and Northern Thai princes and, subsequently, the Bangkok government which dealt with, amongst other issues, the question of slave raiding and the sale of slaves across the Thai-Burmese border (see Renard [1980:135ff.]). It may well be, therefore, that the traditional form of Karen villages was a clustering of separate houses until Kayah slave raids made the construction of long-houses a necessity. The Karen in the Mae Muang Luang-Huai Thung Choa valley system have no recollection of villages which took the form of long-houses although in Palokhi an attenuated long-house was in fact built primarily out of ritual considerations as I discuss in Chapter III.

[2] Karen villages may, however, also be named with streams (**klo'**) and plains (**tha**) as their topographical referents (see, for example, Marlowe [1969:53] and Mischung [1980:13]) but the referent "head-waters" is, by far, the most common in the naming of Karen villages.

[3] See also Mischung (1980:13) and Marlowe (1969:68) for a similar discussion of the definition of **kau** in topographical terms. While Marlowe has probably been the first to remark on this fact, Mischung's discussion is the more detailed of the two.

[4] The derivation of Karen village names from Northern Thai names for rivers and streams is an extremely common phenomenon particularly with villages situated further east of the border between Thailand and Burma. The villages listed by Marlowe (1969:68), for example, are almost without exception based on Northern Thai names. Eponymous Karen village names are highly uncommon, but this has been reported by Madha (1980:25).

[5] Apart from Marlowe's work (1969), this is also apparent from the names of Karen villages studied, or reported on, by Hinton (1975), Kunstadter (1979), Iijima (1979), Hamilton (1976), Madha (1980) and Mischung (1980).

[6] This is, to some extent, confirmed by Dr Ronald Renard (pers. comm.) who has worked on the history of Karen-T'ai (that is, Thai) relations and who, in the course of his researches, briefly explored the area south of the Pa Pae hills in Mae Taeng. Dr Renard's informants were of the view that their ancestors

may have left Burma perhaps more than 100 years ago, stopping somewhere in-between before arriving in Mae Taeng. In collecting genealogies in Palokhi, I was able to establish that only one person (within the range of recountable genealogical relations) had any connection with Burma and this existed merely by virtue of the fact that this person, Lae Bghe (now dead), had visited and stayed for some time in a Kayah village in Burma though the circumstances surrounding this were wholly obscure. The name, Lae Bghe, was in fact the consequence of this sojourn with the Kayah; it means, literally, "went to the Kayah" where **lae** means "to go" and **bghe** is the Sgaw Karen term for the Kayah. While this throws hardly any light on the Burma connections of the Karen in the Mae Muang Luang-Huai Thung Choa area, if indeed they exist at all, it is extremely important from the point of view of the system of naming individuals in Palokhi, and I shall deal with this in more detail in the next chapter.

[7] There is, however, evidence to suggest that the Huai Thung Choa was, in the distant past, in fact occupied by Lua' although this has little relevance to present conditions. In the course of opening up new wet-rice terraces (as opposed to the Hmong terraces which have been reclaimed) along the banks of the Huai Thung Choa, the Palokhi Karen have unearthed tobacco pipes and pots which are distinctively Lua' in design suggesting an earlier Lua' presence. That this must have been in the distant past is suggested, on the other hand, by the fact that these discoveries frequently occur together with ash layers (probably laid down by the burning of swiddens) several centimetres beneath the present surface of the earth in the areas where these terraces are being cut.

[8] The Khun Sa Hmong have, in fact, been investigated by Cooper (1984) but Cooper makes no mention of Hmong from the Huai Thung Choa valley. Cooper's research which was conducted in 1972–74 shows quite clearly that the Hmong now inhabiting the area came from elsewhere, south of Khun Sa, beginning in 1952 (1984:77–82); he also states that some of the Hmong now at Khun Sa migrated to the area because they were interested in opening up wet-rice fields. Cooper, however, does not indicate whether these fields existed prior to the migration of these Hmong or whether they were first opened up by them. The northward migration of these Hmong, however, is interesting because it suggests, along with the northward migrations of the Karen, I have mentioned earlier, that this is a general trend. The conclusion that must be drawn from this is that demographic pressure, perhaps with a concomitant deterioration in ecological conditions, was building up in the foothills in the area south of the Mae Muang Luang-Huai Thung Choa valley system, that is, in Tambon Sopoeng before the 1950's. Nevertheless, we are still left with the problem of explaining what happened to the Hmong from the Huai Thung Choa valley who are said to have gone to Khun Sa. The Palokhi Karen and Northern Thai in Ban Mae Lao and Ban Thung Choa claim as well that the Hmong who inhabited the Huai Thung Choa cultivated opium and this is, to a large extent, corroborated by the existence of broad swathes of **Imperata** or cogon grass on the slopes of Doi Mae Ya (that is, Mae Ya mountain). **Imperata,** as it is now commonly recognised, is the most characteristic form of succession in areas which have been under opium swiddening regimes because the intensive weeding necessary for the successful cultivation of opium permits only the establishment of more tenacious species such as **Imperata** once opium swiddens are left fallow. In view of this, the only plausible explanation must be that the Hmong left the Huai Thung Choa for two reasons: first, because their opium swiddens became unproductive; second, because alternative swidden sites on the Mae Ya were out of reach as a result of a sedentary existence imposed by the need to remain close to their wet-rice fields. Thus, once available resources for opium cultivation were exhausted under these circumstances, the Hmong probably migrated to Khun Sa where, as Cooper shows, conditions were suitable for a similar dual system of opium and wet-rice cultivation. These Hmong may then have departed from Khun Sa yet again for perhaps similar reasons.

[9] I discuss this in more detail in Chapter IV where I present several case studies of households or domestic groups to illustrate general features in the domestic organisation of production and consumption in Palokhi. Here it may be noted that while most Palokhi households are related to one another by primary or collateral kin links, the emphasis or weight placed on these links varies from one case to another especially in the context of the organisation of economic activities.

[10] Dependency ratios are given by the proportion of dependents to the total population (in this case that of households) expressed in percentage terms. Dependents are defined as those under the age of fourteen and over the age of sixty. Thus, the dependents of these various households include not only young children but old people as well.

[11] H16 was, of course, one of the first migrant families in the Huai Thung Choa. It consisted initially of a middle-aged couple and their only daughter. They were later joined by Chwi who married the daughter. When the parents of the daughter died, the couple decided to move to Plaeng Dauk (the Flower Plantation of the Royal Forestry Department's Watershed Development Unit) to become wage labourers. The reason why these families, upon migrating (or remigrating) to Palokhi, did not embark

on swidden cultivation was that they did not have sufficient supplies of domestic labour to manage both systems of rice cultivation.

[12] I discuss in more detail, in Chapter III, the kinship system in Palokhi and the place that uxorilocal residence at marriage has within this system. I wish to stress here, however, that the "rule" is not quite so thorough-going as the term "rule" suggests or implies. It is quite subject to modification as with other "rules" (such as those on marriage) according to the exigencies and pragmatics of the life circumstances of the Palokhi Karen. I might add, in this regard, that they are equally amenable to manipulation — within limits — according to the idiosyncracies of individuals as I also discuss in the context of violations of marriage rules in Chapter III.

[13] I might add here that much the same pattern is to be found in the migration and residential histories of these individuals who came from outside the watershed before they were married and still part of their parental households. In one case (H5[++]), which is interesting from an economic perspective, the household spent three to four years (1923–27) picking **miang** (tea which is fermented and eaten as a relish and stimulant) as its sole subsistence occupation. Although this was the only case which I recorded in Palokhi, it suggests that the tea industry south of the Pa Pae hills may have been economically important to the Karen (apart from the Northern Thai) many years ago. This is a subject which I take up from the point of view of present-day economics in Palokhi, in Chapters V.

[14] This has changed in recent years as a result of the presence of the Royal Forestry Department's Watershed Development Unit. The Unit, which has several sub-units including the Flower Plantation mentioned earlier, has had to recruit large numbers of Northern Thai from settlements outside the watershed to work in its various reforestation projects because labour from the Karen and Lisu settlements in the watershed is only seasonally available. See Kunzel (1983) for a detailed account of this aspect of the Unit's operations in the Mae Muang Luang-Huai Thung Choa area.

[15] The reason why land dominated by coniferous species is generally unsuitable for swiddening is that these species have a lower biomass than land cover containing a mix of species such as may be found in Tropical Evergreen, Dry Dipterocarp and Mixed Deciduous forests all of which occur in Northern Thailand at various elevations. Karen recognition of this fact is undoubtedly based on a long history of swidden cultivation, but the Palokhi Karen also point to the generally thin, dry layer of pine needles on the ground as evidence that such areas are unsuitable for swiddening compared to other forested areas which have a more mixed and thicker layer of litter. The Karen are, of course, entirely correct in their assessment.

[16] Palokhi Karen axioms and proverbs almost invariably consist of a couplet distinguished by semantic parallelism which is also a feature of their ritual texts. The essence of these axioms and proverbs is their ambiguity. While ambiguity is, indeed, a feature of a great many traditions of proverbs and sayings in the sense that they may be interpreted either positively or negatively (see, for example, Milner [1969] and a comment by Wijeyewardene [1974:101–2]), Palokhi Karen proverbs, on the other hand, frequently attempt to capture the paradoxes, contradictions, and dilemmas of life and human situations which, it might be said, also form the basis of much of their humour which thrives on such ironies. They are, therefore, really vehicles for expressing opinions which are formed by other considerations and interests. I should, perhaps, add that if or when the Palokhi **sa' pgha** expressed their opinions through their virtuosity in handling proverbs and axioms, both were probably lost on Tamu', the headman of Palokhi, who was partially deaf in both ears.

[17] This history of the events and considerations which led to the eventual resettlement of Palokhi in its present location is based on accounts provided by Nae' Kha (Tamu''s son) and Rae'. The principal actors in this particular scenario in the history of Palokhi, that is, Tamu', Chwi' and Lauy, were all unwilling to discuss these developments.

[18] The ideal of a harmonious state of affairs, much valued by the Palokhi Karen, is also consistently re-iterated in their agricultural ritual texts (see Chapter VI). Mischung (1980:30) also states that the role of the headman is to establish such a state of affairs for the community. It is interesting to note, as well, that Lewis and Lewis (1984:10, 96) in their excellent compilation of broad, general facts on six ethnic minority groups in the "Golden Triangle" (accompanied by remarkable photographs of their material culture and artefacts) for a general, non-academic audience, have used the term "harmony" in an attempt to capture the ethos of Karen societies.

[19] In the Karen settlement of Mae Muang Luang on which I have some, but admittedly scanty, data, the Head Rite is performed by the headman with the participation of all male heads of households. In Mae Muang Luang, the rite is held once every three years and each household contributes to the cost of purchasing a large pig which is sacrificed to the Lord of the Water, Lord of the Land of Mae Muang Luang. In another ritual which is said to have been performed when landslips occurred around a large

cliff consisting of felspathic rock, called Lekoepau (the "Shining Cliff"), a buffalo was offered as a propitiatory offering to the "Lord of the Shining Cliff" which was also paid for by contributions from all households in Mae Muang Luang, because the cliff lies within the domain of Mae Muang Luang. This ritual is no longer performed in the present because it is believed that the Lord of Lekoepau has been appeased after the two ritual offerings.

[20] Semantic parallelism in Karen ritual texts has not been particularly commented upon although its existence is recognised. It is usually referred to by the term "couplets" (Marshall [1922:177ff.]; Mischung [1980:34, 111ff.]). Mischung does remark on the fact that this is a feature of Karen prayers and poetry in discussing the appellation given to the tutelary spirit of the domain, that is, the Lord of the Water, Lord of the Land. He takes the view that the primary meaning of the term is that the spirit is the tutelary spirit of land while the reference to "water" in the term for the spirit is, essentially, the product of a device in oral literature. It is clear, however, from Palokhi ritual texts that the elements which make up the dyadic sets in the semantic parallelism of these texts are not without intrinsic meaning. That is to say, they are not merely verbal embellishments though aesthetic considerations are nevertheless important. Furthermore, the occurrence of elements in dyadic sets and their parallel juxtapositions, with their primary meanings, produce what might best be called "semantic agglutination", expressing meanings otherwise inexpressible by these terms individually or by their mere juxtaposition through grammatical conjunctions. Thus, as it seems to me, translating the term "Lord of the Water, Lord of the Land" to mean that the spirit is the spirit of land is to restrict the meaning of the term without giving sufficient consideration to the way in which semantic fields are enlarged in the form that Karen oral literature and ritual texts take. Although this may appear to be a relatively trivial problem of translation, nevertheless, it is of some consequence for our understanding of the significance of certain dyadic sets which recur frequently in **different** ritual contexts, one of which is **ghe** and **gwa** which I discuss shortly in this chapter. This suggests that the enlarged semantic fields of these dyadic sets may contain hierarchies of meaning which, in turn, have implications for an understanding of religious conceptions and ritual activities as they are cognitively organised. In other societies, such as the Rotinese as Fox has amply demonstrated (1971, 1974, 1975, 1983), these implications extend to the very nature of systems of social classification. In the case of the term "Lord of the Water, Lord of the Land", it is probably a mistake to see it in terms of a simple opposition between "land" and "water" (that is, **kau** and **thi**). The reason is that "land" is an encompassing category within which "water" (that is, streams and rivers) is to be found; thus, while the term recognises the difference in the properties of these two categories (undoubtedly based on an appreciation of their importance in agriculture), it also places, as it were, "water" within "land", so that the term "Lord of the Water, Lord of the Land" really means "Lord of 'land in which there is water'". The term "domain", therefore, seems far more preferable as a short-hand term for translating this rather unwieldy phrase. It also has the advantage, first, of conveying the idea that **kau** also contain human habitations and, second, of having a certain degree of latitude in translating **kau** which, for many Karen along the Thai-Burmese border has now taken a distinct political meaning, namely, "state". The independent state which the Karen National Union and Karen National Liberation Army have been attempting to establish (since 1948) through insurgency is known as "Kawthoolei", that is, **kau Ou le,** the "Land of Lilies" (Thra Pu Tamoo, pers. comm.).

[21] According to Palokhi Karen custom, the liquor prepared for this and other ritual occasions (such as marriage ceremonies) must be prepared within the same month when these rituals take place. There is another custom, and belief, that the yeast needed to prepare the rice liquor should be made by **unmarried** women. Although the preparation of liquor may be done by married women, the production of the yeast has to be done by unmarried women who should not be observed doing so, or else the yeast will not rise. According to the Palokhi Karen, the yeast "becomes shy" or "becomes ashamed" (**mae' chgha'**) and the rice-and-water substrate of the yeast will not, therefore, ferment to produce the liquor. The yeast in this particular ritual was, in fact, purchased from a Northern Thai in Ban Thung Choa.

[22] Iijima (1979:113–4) has reported the use of **Eugenia** leaves in a ritual performed by the Sgaw Karen whom he studied but it is likely that the use of **Eugenia** leaves which he describes is the product of Northern Thai or Shan Buddhist practices. In Palokhi, however, the presence of the **Eugenia** tree is not related to Buddhist or syncretised Buddhist ritual practices. Many Karen communities in Mae Hong Son which have come under Buddhist influence erect an altar in their houses which they then decorate with **Eugenia** leaves, but this is a practice which is not found in Palokhi or, for that matter, in other Karen settlements in the Mae Muang Luang-Huai Thung Choa basin.

[23] Soul calling rituals, in Palokhi, are categorised according to what may best be described as a very general age-grading system, which makes distinctions between infants and children, adults, and old people. In the rite of calling back the souls of old people, a nail is truck into the tree and a thread is tied to the nail and laid over a tray laden with food which is supposed to entice the wandering souls

of old people to return to their bodies. The thread is considered to be the route which these souls take on their return; but it is essentially an extension of the tree directed towards the offerings and, hence, the person concerned.

[24] Note again the occurrence of the term **kho** in the way that this soul is described. The evidence for this soul, which is adduced by the Palokhi Karen, is the palpitating fontanelles of infants in whom the cranial sutures have not yet grown together and calcified. The soul is regarded as being so important that when children have their heads shaved to de-louse them, a tuft of hair is left to "protect" the **koela kho thi'**. Similar to the Northern Thai and many other societies in Northern Thailand, the Palokhi Karen believe that an individual possesses several souls. The number varies from informant to informant, and from place to place amongst the Karen (Kunstadter, pers. comm.). In Palokhi, the range is usually between thirty-three and thirty-seven and they correspond to parts of the body. The variation in the number of souls seems to be related to the fact of whether or not informants are willing to enumerate parts of the genitalia when they enumerate parts of the body which are attributed with souls. The Palokhi Karen are generally extremely reluctant or embarrassed to talk about matters pertaining to sexual intercourse and sexual functions, yet at the same time they do have a small corpus of what we might call "obscenities" in English which are sexually based and which, as I found, it was not impossible to obtain information on. The difference is probably to be explained by a difference in social and linguistic contexts, a discussion of which need not detain us here.

[25] **Ba'** (with the same tonal value) has two meanings: "to affect" and "correct". In Sgaw Karen, this tone may be called a low falling tone. **Ba,** that is, without a final glottal stop with a mid-level tone, on the other hand, means "to believe", "to worship" to "to pray to" but it means more than what is implied by these terms. The Palokhi Karen themselves translate the term by the Northern Thai **thya** which, as Davis has pointed out (1984:17), is best rendered as "to abide by". In this particular prayer (as with some other ritual texts which I discuss in Chapter VI), there is a strong likelihood that tonal values and the presence or absence of the glottal stop are being "played" with on the basis of the phonological similarities of these two terms as is sometimes the case with Northern Thai terms (Davis [1984:156, 164]). The result is a composition of **meaning** which is arrived at, at least in the context of ritual texts, through a certain degree of inarticulation not otherwise possible if terms were clearly and unambiguously articulated. It is also possible that where ritual texts are generally accessible to everyone, as it is in Malay communities for instance, ritual language may in fact be **mystified** for a number of reasons through improper articulation (Endicott [1970:20]; Rajah [1975:11, 80–1]). Perhaps the most important reason is to maintain the esoteric nature of ritual language. In Palokhi, ritual texts and language are available to anyone although their recitations are essentially individual performances, as I discuss in Chapter VI. Thus, in transcribing and translating this particular text with the assistance of Chi Choe, I was told that it means Tamu' was "cooling" the tutelary spirit of the domain according to what was ritually "correct", that it also meant the lustral water was "touching" (that is, in contact with) the spirit, and that Tamu' was "worshipping" the Lord of the Water, Lord of the Land.

Chapter III

Kinship, Marriage, and Domestic Social Organisation

In this chapter, I describe the kinship system of the Palokhi Karen and its role in the formation, existence and interrelationships of domestic groups which are the cornerstone of social organisation in the community. Kinship, marriage, and domestic social organisation, however, do not exist merely in relation to one another. They are linked to a system of naming individuals, and a system of sex differentiation. Furthermore, the ritual life of domestic groups includes a ritual, 'au' ma xae, which is an integral part of the religious system of the Palokhi Karen, a system that is inextricably bound to agriculture.

I therefore propose to examine kinship, marriage, and domestic social organisation as well as ritual from several perspectives suggested by the occurrence of the systems of naming individuals and sex differentiation in relation to the kinship system. I also explore the implications of the relationships amongst these systems, and 'au' ma xae, a full description of which may be found in Appendix A. It is my contention that these implications are of critical importance for an understanding of Palokhi Karen social organisation, agriculture and religion. More specifically, I argue that these systems are structurally unified within an overarching indigenous symbolic and ideological system. The unity of these systems at symbolic and ideological levels may be found in a paradigm which may well be described as a "procreative model" of society in Palokhi. The elements of this paradigm in the context of kinship, domestic social organisation, and marriage and domestic rituals are central to the major theme of this study, that is, the reproduction of a cultural ideology and the maintenance of identity in Palokhi.

Kinship Terminology

When Lewis Henry Morgan first described and classified Karen kinship on the basis of Sgaw, Pwo and "Karen" kin terms provided by the Reverends Mason, Wade and Van Meter respectively (1871:441ff.; 518), he categorically labelled them as "classificatory" systems. Morgan, however, acknowledged that they also shared in some of the features which he took as the hallmarks of "descriptive" systems. Morgan's classification of kinship systems has, of course, since undergone considerable re-evaluation and many of the systems which he called "descriptive" have now come to be known as "cognatic" systems.

Following these changes and more particularly following Murdock's assessment of Southeast Asian kinship (1960), the systems of the Sgaw and Pwo are now paradoxically recognised as "cognatic" or "bilateral" (Lebar, Hickey and Musgrave [1964:61]; Hinton [1975:44]; Hamilton [1976:93]; Marlowe [1979: 177–78]; Mischung [1980:97]; Madha [1980:60–1]). It is clear from the lists of kin terms provided by Mason, Wade and Van Meter and those available in the contemporary ethnography of the Karen that these terminological systems are remarkably similar, despite the fact that they have been drawn from communities widely separated in time and space. Palokhi Karen kinship terms are no exception to this apparent general stability in Karen terminological systems; specifically, they resemble the Sgaw systems of Mason, Madha and Marshall (1922:135–6). Although the inventories of terms provided by these writers are somewhat abbreviated where affinal terms are concerned, the overall concordance in consanguineal and the few affinal terms between these inventories and Palokhi kin terms is sufficient to demonstrate the existence of fundamental similarities. I present below a list of Palokhi Karen kin terms, in Table 3.1, and some observations on their general applications in address and reference.

A number of these terms are modified in order to specify more precisely who is being addressed or to whom reference is being made. Thus, the term **phy** may be modified by **phado'** ("big", "great") to refer to, or address, male lineal kin traced bilaterally in the third ascending generation as there is no specific term for these categories of kin. The term **phi** is similarly modified for female kin in these generations. The terms **phy** and **phi** are also applied to collateral kin and non-kin in the second ascending generation, but only in direct address. When referred to, they are identified teknonymously where the terms **phy** and **phi** are prefixed by the names of their eldest grandchildren if they have grandchildren; if they only have children and no grandchildren, then they are referred to teknonymously where the terms **pa** and **mo** are prefixed by the names of their eldest children. Teknonymy in either of these forms may also be used in address but this is associated with a certain degree of formality which is rare in Palokhi. In the same way, collateral kin and non-kin in the first ascending generation are addressed by the terms **phati** or **mygha**, depending on their sex, and referred to teknonymously in which case the referential terms would take the form **pa** and **mo** prefixed by the names of their eldest children. As a general rule, then, kin and non-kin in ascending generations are usually never referred to, much less addressed, by their own names.

Table 3.1. Palokhi Karen Kin Terms

G + 2	phy	: FF, MF (address and reference); FFB, FMB, MFB, MMB, etc. (address); other male collaterals and non-kin of same generation (address).
	phi	: FM, MM (address and reference); FMZ, FFZ, MMZ, MFZ, etc. (address); other female collaterals and non-kin of same generation (address).
G + 1	pa	: F (address and reference); also term of address for spouse's F.
	mo	: M (address and reference); also term of address for spouse's M.
	phati	: FB, MB, FZH, MZH (address, sometimes reference); other male collaterals and non-kin of same generation (address).
	mygha	: FZ, MZ, FBW, MBW (address, sometimes reference); other female collaterals and non-kin of same generation (address).
	mipgha	: Spouse's F and M (reference).
G O	waecau'	: Elder male sibling (address and reference); parents' elder siblings' male children (address); elder female sibling's spouse (address); spouse's elder male sibling (address).
	waenau	: Elder female sibling (address and reference); parents' siblings' female children (address); elder male sibling's spouse (reference and address); spouse's elder female sibling (reference and address).
	waeko'	: Eldest sibling (reference).
	wae	: WeB, HeB (reference); elder female sibling's spouse (reference).
	py	: Younger sibling (address and reference); parents' younger siblings' children (address).
	pysoeda	: Youngest sibling (reference).
	pyde	: WyB, WyZ, HyB, HyZ (address and reference).
	ca'li	: yZH, HyZH, WyZH (address and reference).
	demy	: yBW, WyBW, HyBW (address and reference).
	tapypgha	: Spouse (general reference).
	phau'khwapgha	: H (general reference).
	phau'mypgha	: W (general reference).
	pghaghane	: Spouse (reference only, by spouses).
	wa	: H (general reference, also address by spouse).
	ma	: W (general reference, also address by spouse).
G-1	phokhwa	: S (address and reference); DH (address).
	phomy	: D (address and reference); SW (address).
	phoko'	: Eldest child (reference).
	ma'	: DH (reference).
	dae'	: SW (reference).
	phodo'	: Siblings' children (address and reference); other collaterals and non-kin of same generation (address).
G-2	li	: Children's children (address and reference); other collaterals and non-kin of same generation (address).
G-3	lo	: Children's children's children (address and reference); other collaterals and non-kin of same generation.
G-4	la	: Childrens' children's children (address and reference); other collaterals and non-kin of same generation (address).

In contrast to the terms for kin in ascending generations (and in descending generations), there are comparatively far more terms for kin within ego's own generation and this is a feature common to virtually all terminological systems whether cognatic or non-cognatic. These terms deserve special attention because together with associated generic kin terms they denote certain classes of kin which are an important consideration in the way that the Palokhi Karen formulate their marriage rules.

As with other Sgaw Karen, the Palokhi Karen have a term which specifically distinguishes the members of a sibling set from all other kin, **dau'pywae**. It is a compound term derived from the terms for elder male and female sibling, **waecau'** and **waenau**, reduced to **wae**, and the single term for younger sibling, **py**, which does not make a distinction between the sexes as do the terms **waecau'** and **waenau**. The term **dau'** is a grammatical conjunction meaning "and", "together" or "with". When it occurs preposed before two nouns, the compound term so formed denotes a group or set whose attributes are defined by the postposed categories. The term **dau'pywae** means "elder and younger siblings".[1] It does not include the parents of the siblings. Indeed there is no term for the nuclear or stem family although the members of a household are collectively called **doe' pho**, **xau' pho** which literally means "children of the house, children of the steps", where "steps" is a common synecdoche in Karen for house and household. Where it has been reported, the term **dau'pywae** has generally been glossed as "siblings" or "brothers and sisters" (Hamilton [1976:98]; Marlowe [1979:169]; Madha [1980:202]), but Iijima (1970:31) states that the "**Dopuweh** … is almost identical with a family although it is based on a matrilineage" (see also Iijima [1979:107]). This very singular interpretation which Iijima places on the term **dau'pywae** is supported neither in other accounts of Karen kinship (Mischung [1980:97 n. 47]; Madha [1980:203–4]) nor, indeed, by my informants.

Within the **dau'pywae**, the two principal features of the kin terms used by siblings are, first, a distinction in relative age and, second, a sex distinction in the terms for elder siblings and an absence of such a distinction in the terms for younger siblings. Younger siblings, regardless of sex, are called **py**, although where it is necessary to indicate the sex of younger siblings, the term **py** may then be qualified by the sex categories **phau'khwa** ("male") and **phau'my** ("female"). The terms **waecau'**, **waenau** and **py** are used in reference and address although it is not uncommon to hear siblings using their names in addressing, or referring to each other. There are two other terms, in addition to these, which distinguish first and last born siblings, and these are **waeko'** and **pysoeda**.[2] The terms **ko'** and **soeda** are also used by parents to refer to their eldest and youngest children in which case the respective terms are **phoko'** and **phosoeda**.[3]

The Palokhi Karen also have a term, **dau'takhwa**, which defines groups of consanguines consisting of related **dau'pywae**, that is, groups of parallel or cross cousins.[4] This term is applied bilaterally. The general term **dau'takhwa** is usually modified by an ordinal number which indicates the degree of removal between ego and his, or her, cousins, for example **toetakhwa** ("first cousins"), **khitakhwa** ("second cousins") and **soe'takhwa** ("third cousins"). It is rare, however, for the Palokhi Karen to indicate degrees of removal beyond that of third cousins (although in theory this system of indicating degrees of removal could be extended indefinitely), thus suggesting that for all practical purposes this is the "cut-off" point in the recognition of cousinship. The terms of address for ego's **dau'takhwa**, of whatever degree, are the same as the terms used within the **dau'pywae**, except that the use of the appropriate terms (**waecau'/waenau** or **py**, that is, elder or younger) depends — at least in theory — not on the relative ages of the persons concerned, but on the relative ages of their respective parents or grandparents. In practice, however, relative age more often than not overrides what in theory is the generational basis on which the address system for **dau'takhwa** rests. Thus, those of "senior" or "elder" **dau'takhwa** will often be addressed by name or even the term **py** if they are younger than ego. Nevertheless, as with members of a **dau'pywae**, ego is as likely to refer to members of his, or her, **dau'takhwa** by name as he or she is likely to do so by kin terms.

I come now to affinal kin terms in Palokhi kinship nomenclature. Affines in general are termed **do'** or **dau'do'** (see also Marshall [1922:315]), but there are also specific terms for certain categories of affinal kin just as there are for consanguineal kin. As the list of kin terms shows, there are two general terms for "spouse" and a set of specific terms for "husband" and for "wife". The differentiation or elaboration in spouse terms, including those for "husband" and "wife" are striking, to say the least, when compared with all other kin terms which do not show such elaboration. The two paired terms **phau'mypgha** and **phau'khwapgha** are terms which denote the married status of women and men, and as such they contrast with the paired terms **mykoe'nau** and **phau'khwa** which mean "unmarried" women and men. **Pgha** in both terms (and in the generic term **tapypgha**) means "mature" or "old" and it is the same lexeme in the term for "to marry", **thau pgha**. **Thau**, itself, means "to rise", "to ascend" or "to raise up"; it also has a specific connotation of "to grow" and is invariably used to refer to the growth of rice and other swidden crops in agricultural ritual texts. The term **thau pgha** and the various spouse terms containing **pgha**, therefore, mean rather more than "to marry" or "married". These terms imply the achievement of adult status at marriage or, perhaps, even a "growing" into this status through marriage. The terms **phau'mypgha** and **phau'khwapgha**, thus, are not merely kin terms. They are also terms which encode the idea of a socially recognised adult status. These two terms are used as general terms of reference. The terms **ma** and **wa**, on the other hand, are both terms of address and reference. **Pghaghane**, however, is a term of reference that is said to be used in a very specific context — when one's spouse is present. It literally means "that person".

The Palokhi Karen say that they do not use the names of their spouses, or spouse terms, in reference or address (although names are used when courting) if others are present because they feel "embarrassed" or "ashamed" (**mae'chgha'**) to do so, and that they therefore use the term **pghaghane**. In general, however, it appears to be used by newly married spouses who may, indeed, be embarrassed to use proper spouse terms in public, at least initially, while the use of proper names (by which they are known to others) seems to be inappropriate or incongruous in the context of marriage. It is worth noting that the term **pghaghane** is not the third person singular pronoun which is **'oe'wae** in Sgaw Karen (see also Jones [1961:18]); it is a fully deictic term. **Pgha** (tonally different from **pgha**, "old", "mature") means "people" in a generic sense and **gha** refers to "person" of indefinite number, while **ne** is the locative "there". It would appear, therefore, that the use of the deictic **pghaghane** represents a means of interposing a certain distance between newly-wed spouses in public situations before they have become accustomed to, or comfortable with, behaving as a "couple" according to social expectations.

If indeed newly-wed spouses are concerned with maintaining a certain "social distance" in public, as a result of an ambivalence experienced in the transition between unmarried to married statuses and roles, then the use of the term **pghaghane** as part of a particular repertoire in sociolinguistic behaviour is entirely appropriate. Quite apart from the social expectations attaching to the condition of being unmarried or married, the logic of the kinship system and its terminology, as I argue later, in fact stresses as it were the conjunctiveness of the conjugal bond in opposition to other kin ties and social relationships. The term **pghaghane**, from this perspective, may well be regarded therefore as a linguistic solution to an ambivalence in the transitional situation experienced by newly married spouses.

When a child is born, however, spouses then refer to each other in one of two ways. The first is by referring to each other as "male child's mother" (**phokhwa mo**), "male child's father" (**phokhwa pa**) or "female child's mother" (**phomy mo**), "female child's father" (**phomy pa**), according to the sex of the child. This form of teknonymy also constitutes the form of address used by spouses and, thus, supersedes those used prior to the birth of a child, that is **ma** and **wa**. Alternatively, spouses may refer to each other teknonymously through the use of the name of the child. The basis of teknonymous reference (which is also used by others with respect to the two spouses) in this form is always the name of the eldest surviving child. If there is only one child, and the child dies, then the referential and addressive system employed by spouses reverts back to that used before the child was born. Where others are concerned, the spouses would then be addressed and referred to by their proper names.

The term for the parents of both spouses is **mipgha** and this is used only in reference. The terms of address for the parents of one's spouse are **pa** and **mo**, the same terms used for one's own parents. The reciprocals of the referential term, **mipgha**, are **ma'** (daughter's husband or "son-in-law") and **dae'** (son's wife or "daughter-in-law"). The corresponding terms of address are **phokhwa** and **phomy** (or, more generally, **pho**) which are also used for one's own children.

Perhaps the most interesting set of kin terms, apart from spouse terms, are the terms for affines within ego's generation. These terms may be categorised according to whether the kin they describe are related to ego by an affinal link (the marital tie) and a consanguineal link, in that order (that is, working outwards from an ego-centric point of view), or by a consanguineal link followed by an affinal link.

In the first category are the siblings of one's spouse. This category of affines is not fully distinguished, terminologically, from ego's own siblings and it follows the set of sibling terms in the distinction that is drawn between the sexes for elder siblings but not for younger siblings. Thus, the referential term for a spouse's elder male sibling is **wae**, as against **waecau'** for one's own elder male sibling. However, the terms of address for both are the same, that is **waecau'**. In the case of one's spouse's elder female sibling, the referential and addressive terms are identical to that for one's own elder female sibling, namely, **waenau**. Younger siblings of one's spouse, regardless of sex, are called **pyde** in reference and address. As with the term for younger siblings, this term may be modified to indicate the sex of the younger sibling of one's spouse, in which case the terms would be **pydekhwa** and **pydemy**. There is, however, one important difference between the use of these terms as affinal and consanguineal kin terms. Whereas their use as consanguineal terms hinges upon the fact of relative age differences between siblings, their use as affinal terms over-rides these very differences between ego and ego's spouse's siblings. Thus, if a man were older than his wife's elder siblings, he would use the terms **waecau'** and **waenau** in address; similarly, even if he were younger than the siblings of his wife, he would address them by the term **pyde**.

In the second category of affines, the spouses of one's younger siblings are sex distinguished. The husband of a younger sister is called **ca'li**, and the wife of a younger brother is called **demy**. The reciprocals of these terms are, of course, **wae** and **waenau** in reference, and **waecau'** and **waenau** in address as I have already described above. It is worth noting that ego's spouse refers to, and addresses, this second category of affines by the same terms as ego. That is, terminologically, ego's spouse's affines are equated with ego's own affines in this category.

Sociologically, however, there are no significant differences in the relations that exist between a person and his, or her, affines in both categories and those between his, or her, spouse's affines — beyond that which is conditioned by residential arrangements, which I discuss in the section on marriage and residential patterns. The significance of this feature of affinal kin terms, therefore, lies not so much in what is revealed about affinal relations but, rather, in what is revealed about the conjugal bond within the Palokhi kinship system.

The homology between the terms for siblings-in-law and the terms for siblings is not an altogether unusual feature of cognatic systems. In the Palokhi system, this homology in itself is not necessarily significant however. What is significant is the congruence in the use of affinal kin terms by spouses on the basis of this homology. The use of affinal kin terms rather than names (which contrasts with the more open choice between the use of names and kin terms within the **dau'pywae**) for siblings-in-law, the fact that the use of these terms overrides relative age differences, and the equation of spouse's affines with own affines all point to the "assimilation" of spouses to each other's position **vis-a-vis** their respective **dau'pywae** and affines. This "assimilation" of spouses in fact is no other than what Burling has called "zero degree genealogical distance" in discussing the nature of the marital tie in the context of English kinship terminology (1970:29). Alternatively, we may say that the terminological system for affines of both categories, which turns on ego's spouse's position relative to ego's spouse's siblings and affines "marks" out the distinctiveness of the conjugal bond in opposition to all other kin links in the kinship system.

While the evidence from the terminological system is sufficient, in itself, to warrant this conclusion, nevertheless, we shall see that the naming system and teknonymy in Palokhi lend further support to this conclusion.

The Naming System: "Event" Names and Teknonymy

The essential feature of the naming system in Palokhi is a fortuitous event which occurs in the village and which usually (though not always) concerns the conjugal family or stem family if one or both of the parents of the wife are still alive at, or close to, the time a new-born infant is given its name. This takes place when the stub of the baby's umbilical cord drops off after it has been ligatured at birth.[5] These events are drawn upon in a variety of ways to form the names of children.

These names, therefore, may well be regarded as "event" names. The names which parents give to their children, on the basis of such events, may be nouns, adjectives or verbs, or compounds of these. For example, the name Mi' Zo is a compound of the Thai word **miit**, "knife", (though not a loan word) and **zo** the Karen word for Northern Thai and Shan or, as Marlowe (1979:196) suggests, for all Tai speakers. This name was given to a boy when some Northern Thai came to Palokhi and asked the boy's father, the blacksmith-cum-gunsmith in the village, to repair some bush knives. Another name, Khae' By, is a compound of two terms: **khae'**, a loan word from the Thai **khaek** ("stranger", "guest", "foreigner") which the karen use ethnonymically to designate non-Karen and non-Thai as in **Khae' Lisau** (the Lisu) and **Khae' Hau** (Haw or Yunnanese Chinese); **by,** on the other hand, is the generic term in Karen for "rice". This name was given to a girl because some Lisu from Ban Lum had come to buy rice in Palokhi.[6] A further example is Ty We, where **ty** means "to arrive" and **we** means "town", possibly derived from the Northern Thai **wiang** which means the same thing although its original meaning was "fortified city" (but cf. Jones [1961:26]). This name was given to a girl when her father was accidentally shot by his eldest son and had to be sent to Chiang Mai for medical treatment.

While these examples serve to describe the essential aspects of the naming of individuals, there is however more to the way in which the naming system operates in Palokhi. Most Palokhi Karen retain the names given to them at childhood until, of course, they become parents after which they are known teknonymously. Nevertheless, it sometimes happens that individuals do have more than one name bestowed upon them by grandparents, siblings or age-mates on the basis of some personal idiosyncrasy or other. These names are more in the nature of nicknames and they generally do not replace the names given to them at birth. Names may, nevertheless, be changed for specific reasons such as prolonged illness. For instance, a girl by the name of Ti Ka was sick for several months and when her parents consulted a ritual specialist, he said that apart from his ritual ministrations, her successful recovery would also depend on changing her name to a new one. Her parents renamed her Mi Sau meaning, literally, "new name".

What is important in the Palokhi naming system is that the names, and the social identities which they represent, are formed on the basis of events which are **unique** or non-replicable; thus, the proper names created from such events are themselves also unique.

In an illuminating discussion on the significance of naming systems in **The Savage Mind,** Levi-Strauss has pointed out that proper names, or autonyms, possess an individuating function and also imply a distinction between "self" and "other" (1966:192). The discussion is instructive and the distinction is wholly appropriate in approaching the significance of the relationship between the naming system and certain kin terms in Palokhi.

In the Palokhi naming system, this individuating function of autonyms, and the "self-other" distinction is carried to the extreme. The autonyms are not drawn from a common pool of names available to all members of the society but, on the contrary, are formed from unique events. The "self-other" distinction and the distinctiveness of individual social identities in Palokhi is, therefore, highlighted by the very uniqueness of all autonyms which, incidentally, accords with a high degree of personal or individual autonomy in Palokhi. It also suggests a reason for the practice of naming children when the stub of the umbilical cord drops off: children are given names only when the last vestige of their connection with their mothers is lost, and hence acquire an identity separate from that of their mothers.

As I have mentioned before, there are two instances when autonyms are relinquished in Palokhi. The first is when a man and woman marry, and commence using the various spouse terms described. The second is the advent of parenthood, when teknonymy is used. There is an important difference in the two. In the first case, although a married couple do not use their autonyms, they are nevertheless known by their autonyms as far as others are concerned. In the second case, teknonyms replace the autonyms by which they are known to others. These two cases should, therefore, be examined separately.

If autonyms and their use, stress the individuality and the distinctiveness of social identities — the "self-other" distinction — then the abrogation of the use of autonyms upon marriage by husband and wife must be seen to stress the opposite relation, namely, a down-playing of such a distinction between spouses, as opposed to others who, nevertheless, continue to use their autonyms. In other words, the relinquishment of personal names in favour of spouse terms marks the conjunctiveness of spouse relations and the conjugal bond as against all other relations. The logic of the naming system, thus, leads us to exactly the same conclusion which was arrived at from an examination of the terminological system.

We can now turn to the question of teknonymy in Palokhi. Levi-Strauss has observed that whereas autonyms stress the individuality of persons, teknonyms and necronyms, on the other hand, are "relational" terms where the definition of "self" is derived from an "other" whose autonym forms the teknonym while necronyms effect this definition "negatively" since the names of the dead are never mentioned. Teknonymy in Palokhi is no different. The relations expressed in teknonyms are links of affiliation which are evident in teknonyms such as De' Chaj Pa ("Father of De' Chaj") and De' Chaj Mo ("Mother of De' Chaj"). In Palokhi, however, teknonymy is extended into the second ascending generation as well (on a matrilateral basis because of uxorilocal residence at marriage), so that the parents of De' Chaj's mother would be known, after the birth of De' Chaj, as De' Chaj Phy ("Grandfather of De' Chaj") and De' Chaj Phi ("Grandmother of De' Chaj"). The point of reference in the system of teknonymy in Palokhi is, therefore, the eldest surviving child in the last descending generation.

In Palokhi, however, necronymy does not exist, so that unlike the Penan system which Levi-Strauss discusses, and which he describes as possessing three types of "periodicity" (necronym necronym, autonym necronym, teknonym necronym), the Palokhi system possesses only a single "periodicity": autonym teknonym. Levi-Strauss has proposed that in systems characterised by these three types of "periodicity", "teknonymy and necronymy are a single problem and amenable to one and the same solution" and that as far as teknonymy is concerned, "the reason why parents may no longer be called by their name when a child is born is that they are 'dead' and that procreation is conceived not as the addition of a new being to those who already exist but as the substitution of the one for the others" (1966:194-5). In a system such as that in Palokhi where teknonymy exists, but not necronymy, the significance of teknonymy is in fact otherwise. Parents revert to the system of reference and address employed prior to the birth of their first child if the child dies, and hence "avoid" the "negative" definition of "self" through necronymy. Moreover, if there are more than one child, the death of the eldest child does not mean the end of teknonymy; teknonymy then becomes based on the autonym of the next child. Furthermore, when there are three generations, the autonyms appropriated from the second generation to define the first generation teknonymously become replaced by autonyms appropriated from the third generation.

Teknonymy in Palokhi, therefore, stresses the "positive" definition of "self" in which procreation **is** conceived as the addition of a new being to those who already exist. The relational nature of teknonymy in Palokhi thus emphasises **continuity** of links of affiliation as part of an ideology which treats the conjugal bond as a reproductive association within the "continuous flux of generations" (cf. Levi-Strauss [1966:199]).

There are two other features in the naming system which are worth noting: sex differentiation and age-grading. As we have seen, autonyms or "event" names in Palokhi do not, of themselves, contain any distinction between sexes being made up, as they are, of simple verbs, adjectives or nouns. However, when they are used with respect to individuals, they are usually prefixed by sex markers in address or reference according to context. These markers are **pha,** for males, and **nau** for females.

Very generally, these markers are used together with autonyms when ego is addressing or referring to another person who is older than, or is an age-mate of, ego. Age mates of the same sex who are on intimate terms may, however, drop the marker in direct speech if they are speaking to the person concerned, or if they are referring to the person when speaking with other age-mates. The sex marker is, however, usually retained if ego is referring to an age-mate, notwithstanding the closeness of the relationship, if ego is speaking to an older person.

On the other hand, these markers are retained if ego is referring to a person who is either older than ego or an age-mate, when ego is speaking to someone younger. If, however, the person referred to is younger than ego but is of the same age as the person spoken to, or younger, then the sex marker may be dropped. The reason why relative age is a factor in these usages is that it is not uncommon for there to be wide disparities in the ages of individuals within any particular generation.

It is clear that these markers function as honorifics of sorts, but this does not obscure the fact that their **primary** function is to indicate the sex of the person bearing a particular autonym.

Sex marking also exists in the case of teknonyms where the kin terms **pa, mo, phy** and **phi** are prefixed to the autonyms of eldest children. These terms are, in themselves, sex-distinguished. Thus, teknonyms are not merely relational terms; they also identify the person bearing a particular teknonym by sex. At the same time, they also act as age-grade or generational markers by virtue of the fact that the kin terms express generational relationships.

It may be noted here that teknonymy is a naming system that depends on the availability of relevant genealogical information and the social field of the individuals concerned. In Palokhi, the necessary information is wholly available because the community is small. This is not necessarily the case when the Palokhi Karen deal with Karen from other villages in the area as local knowledge then tends to be less than perfect. In such circumstances, general kin terms such as **phati, mygha, phy** and **phi** would be used in address and reference. As terms of reference, they are of course extremely vague and other information would then be necessary if there is a need for precision in referring to the person concerned.

Male and Female: The System of Sex Differentiation

It will, I think, be evident that functioning within the systems of kin terms and naming there is another system: a system of sex differentiation. In kinship terminology, there is a consistent distinction between male and female kin. The only exceptions to this are the terms for younger siblings, spouse's younger siblings and parents-in-law. Nevertheless, even these terms may be distinguished accordingly by the use of the sex categories **phau'khwa** and **phau'my** as modifiers. Similarly, in the naming system, the distinction is established through the use of sex markers prefixed to autonyms. In the case of teknonyms, the sex distinction is made in the use of the kin terms **pa, mo, phy** and **phi**.

The entire corpus of linguistic categories which make distinctions between sexes, in Palokhi, is represented in these two systems. However, some categories which are used in these systems in the class "humans" are also used to make sex distinctions in the class "animals". These categories cannot, therefore, be examined independently because some of them are common to both classes.

If the corpus of terms which establish sex differences in their various usages is examined in its own right as a **system,** some intriguing features become apparent.

To begin with, there are only three basic contrastive pairs which express sex differences in the class "humans" and the class "animals". They are:

Humans:	phau'khwa/phau'my = male/female (-khwa/-my)
	pa/mo = father/mother
Animals:	pha/mo = male/female

The elements in these pairs may well be regarded as fundamental semantic units since they cannot be reduced further to any other constituent units of meaning. Furthermore, in their respective classes, they can only be defined semantically by their relationship to each other. As we have seen, **phau'khwa** and **phau'my** are general sex categories, while **pa** and **mo** are kin terms. The other kin terms **phy** and **phi,** which are also sex differentiated, cannot be regarded as fundamental terms because they can be represented in Karen by other forms such as "father's father", "father's mother" and so on. The term **mo,** on the other hand, is the same for "female animal" and "human mother". Similarly, the term **pha,** "male animal" and the male sex marker for autonyms is the same. They are, very clearly, polysemous terms.

Another important feature is the asymmetry between the categories "unmarried male" and "unmarried female" (**phau'khwa/phau'my),** and the sex markers (**pha/nau**) for the autonyms of males and females who are unmarried, and who are married but have no children. The term **phau'khwa** describes both the general sex category "male human" as well as "unmarried male human". The general sex category, "female human", on the other hand is **phau'my** while the category "unmarried female human" is different, that is, **mykoe'nau.** The term **mykoe'nau,** therefore, is a marked term.

It may be noted that the term **mykoe'nau** has the additional meaning of "pubertal" applied specifically to female humans (see also Jones [1961:123]) and that there is no equivalent term for males. Furthermore, although the term is partly derived from the general sex category (or, more accurately, its minimum free form —**my**—), **nau** itself presents every semblance of being a female marker of its own, serving the same functions as **my.** It occurs, for example, in the kin term **waenau** (elder female sibling). As we have seen, the complementary term for **waenau** is **waecau';** unlike **nau,** however, **cau'** does not appear elsewhere outside of kinship terminology.[7] **Nau,** therefore, is clearly also a marked term. Accordingly, the term **mykoe'nau** thus possesses a high degree of redundancy, as it were, in terms of markedness.

The asymmetry in the sex markers for autonyms (**pha/nau**) lies in the fact that **pha** also describes a sex category in a different class (namely, "animals") while **nau** is a marked term which is to be found only in the class "humans".

Another noteworthy feature in the system of sex categories is the distinction that is made between being unmarried and being married in the class "humans". This is to be seen in the terms for "unmarried human male", "unmarried human female" (**phau'khwa/phau'my**) and "married human male", "married human female" (**phau'khwapgha/phau'mypgha**). If we also consider the case of autonyms and teknonyms, it will be seen that this distinction is taken further. Autonyms and their sex markers are used only for males and females who are either unmarried or who are married but have no children. Teknonyms, on the other hand, indicate not only the sex of the person concerned but also the fact that they are married and have children.

Other than the major contrast animal/human which forms the two classes within which these sex terms are found, all these terms are organised according to a single **natural** dimension of contrast, namely, male/female. The symmetries and asymmetries between the various terms which correspond to this contrast suggest, however, that there is some other ordering characteristic or dimension of semantic contrast at work in the class "humans". This can be no other than the distinction between "unmarried" and "married" which appears consistently in the class. More precisely, the distinction is that between (umarried) + (married-without-children)/(married-with-children)   + (married-with-grandchildren) as the set of sex markers for autonyms and teknomyms indicate.

While this distinction is appropriate to the class "humans" and, indeed, essential to indicate the kinds of discriminations made in this class, it is clearly inappropriate to the class "animals". Yet, as I have noted above, there are some terms (**mo** and **pha**) which may be found in both classes. The unmarried/married distinction therefore introduces a somewhat false dichotomy because it restricts further comparisons and contrasts between the categories in both classes which is analytically necessary, given the occurrence of **mo** and **pha** in both classes. A more general contrast applicable to both classes which allows the distribution of these two terms to be represented, and which can also subsume the unmarried/married distinction, is thus required. The only logical contrast which permits   this   is   the   contrast   non-procreative/procreative   or non-reproductive/reproductive. Such a distinction, I suggest, is the other dimension of semantic contrast operating alongside the animal/human and male/female distinctions which together account for the particular configuration of sex categories and their uses in Palokhi. For present purposes, I shall use the terms "non-procreative" and "procreative" to express this distinction.

Table 3.2 shows the various sex terms organised according to the three dimensions of semantic contrast which underlie the various uses of these terms in Palokhi. The symbol (+) indicates marked categories, while **pha** and **mo** as applied to animals make no distinction between those which have offspring and those which do not.

When the terms are ordered in this way, it becomes immediately apparent that they do not simply constitute a system of sex and gender differentiation. They also form a system of **social classification** for humans based on a logic of sexual difference, generational difference and the difference between states of "non-procreativity" and "procreativity".[8] This classification is significant for what it establishes simultaneously. First, it isolates "non-procreative" female humans from all other categories, particularly the categories which share the feature "procreative" across classes. Second, it establishes, as it were, that the property "procreative" is common to animals, male humans (unmarried or married) and female humans with children, through the distribution of the polysemous terms **pha** and **mo.**

In the class "humans", the nature of the relationship between the set of marked terms (that is, non-procreative female) and all other terms is the most crucial aspect of the classificatory scheme. The categories **phy** and **phi,** as I have mentioned before, are not basic contrastive pairs according to the semantic differentiations which underlie this scheme; they may be regarded as extensions of the terms "father" and "mother" according to the logic of generational difference and they are, therefore, not a crucial feature of this scheme. Any significance they possess in the sub-class "procreative" derives from the term **pa** and **mo.**

Table 3.2. Sex Terms as Expressions of Non-procreative and Procreative Categories

	ANIMALS		HUMANS			
	Male	Female	Male		Female	
			phau'khwa		phau'my	
Non-procreative			phau'khwa	pha + autonym	mykoe'nau (+)	nau + autonym (+)
Procreative	pha	mo	phau'khwa + pgha	autonym of eldest child + pa	phau'my + pgha	autonym of eldest child + mo
				autonym of eldest grand-child + phy		autonym of eldest grand-child + phi

The relationship between the set of unmarked terms and the terms for non-procreative female humans are represented in Figure 3.1 which summarises the essential features of Table 3.2.

Figure 3.1 The Relationship Between Marked and Unmarked Categories

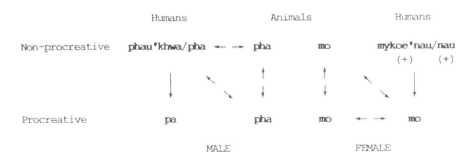

The bi-directional arrowed lines stand for "equivalent" relationships. The uni-directional arrowed lines stand for "non-equivalent" relationships and a substitution of terms in the direction of the lines according to sociolinguistic usage following the transition of individuals from "non-procreative" to "procreative" statuses.

These relationships lie at the core of the system of classification. In terms of the pragmatics of the uses of these terms, what is important is the regular **substitution** of terms as individuals go through their life cycles which recognises not only their sex at all times, but their change in "states of being", that is, from "non-procreative" to "procreative".

There is, however, a **further** significance to this cluster of terms. Much of the difficulty in apprehending it lies in the translation labels which may be used to represent the Karen terms. It will be more readily apparent if the Karen terms are rendered as follows:

phau'khwa	=	"male"
phau'my	=	"female"
mykoe'nau/nau	=	"maiden"/"maid"
pha	=	"non-genitor male"
mo	=	"mother-genetrix"
pa	=	"father-genitor"

Although somewhat clumsy, these labels serve to indicate the essential meanings and distinctions which are made by the Karen terms in their various uses. Other than the distinction between "non-procreativity" and "procreativity" and the singling out of non-procreative human females, it will be apparent that embedded in this group of terms is a distinction between the nature of reproduction in the two classes "animals" and "humans". Where animals are concerned, there is a general recognition of the procreative role of females (or "motherhood") but not that of males. In the case of humans, however, the roles of both males and females

are indeed recognised. As I show in my discussion of the domestic ritual **'au'**
ma xae (see Appendix A), the Palokhi Karen do indeed say that it is impossible
to establish the "paternity" of domesticated animals since any number of males
could copulate with a single female to produce offspring. This is not to say,
therefore, that the Palokhi Karen are unaware that males and females (whether
animal or human) are both equally necessary in sexual reproduction. They are
quite aware of this biological fact. The point I wish to stress is that this group
of terms, as cultural categories, carries with it **cultural definitions** of the nature
of animal and human reproductive processes. Central to these definitions is
"paternity" and "maternity" in human reproduction, and "non-paternity" and
"maternity" in animal reproduction.

To return to the system of sex differentiation: it will be noticed that while
the system is based on the logic of the differences discussed earlier, there is
nevertheless an apparently arbitrary distribution of terms as well as markedness
and non-markedness across classes.

This is a good illustration of the kinds of problems not uncommonly
encountered in componential analysis and the referential approach to the study
of semantics which Fox (1975:118–9) has noted. The reason, as Fox also points
out, is that "… it is not taxonomic generality but polysemy — the property of
a symbol to relate to a multiple range of other symbols — that becomes the
criterion for hierarchical inclusion". This is precisely the case with the Palokhi
classificatory system. Where Palokhi sex categories are concerned, polysemy or
"interlinkage" to use Frake's term (1969, cited in Fox [1975:119]) includes
relationships of homonymy, antinomy and shared semantic fields. It is this which
gives the system the appearance of having an arbitrary distribution of terms
and markedness.

The apparently arbitrary distribution of terms across and within classes,
therefore, is in fact simply the "surface" manifestation of an embedded system
of classification that rests on the semantic associations produced by a remarkable
parsimony in what can only be called a selective distribution of lexical items.
The system is, in other words, "motivated": it is not just a linguistic artefact; it
is sociologically meaningful.

As empirical systems, kinship terminology, naming systems and systems of
sex (and gender) differentiation may be — and indeed often are — treated as
linguistic systems in their own right as I have done here to some extent. The
principal value of investigating these systems as such rests in the contributions
which may be made toward an understanding of the human universals which
underlie their formulation. My purpose in examining these systems in Palokhi,
however, has been rather different, namely, to arrive at what is sociologically
meaningful about these systems in the particular context of Palokhi Karen society.
In this restricted context, it is not the features of these systems taken individually

which enable us to determine what is sociologically meaningful but, rather, those which emerge from their interdigitation. The classification of males and females in terms of "non-procreative" and "procreative" states of being is one such feature. The distinctiveness of "non-procreative" female humans, through redundant marking, is the other.

When, however, such emergent motivated features exhibit a demonstrable relation with features of the same order in a different, non-linguistic system, it can only be concluded that these features are not only sociologically meaningful but culturally **significant** as well. In Palokhi, such a relation of homology does indeed exist between the classification of males and females and a system of dress and colour symbolism.

Dress and Colour Symbolism

One of the most striking aspects of the attire of the Palokhi Karen, obvious even to the most casual observer, is the difference between the dress of unmarried women, including young girls, and that of married women. There is no difference, on the other hand, in the dress of young boys, unmarried men and married men.

Young girls and unmarried women wear a white, smock-like dress reaching to the ankles. The dress is usually decorated at the hem and sleeve-ends with a red band or two, or some embroidery. Married women, however, wear a black blouse, half of which is embroidered over with various designs and stitched-on beads made from Job's Tears **(Coix lachryma jobi),** which forms one part of their dress. The other part consists of a tubular, wrap-around skirt similar to a sarong. The skirt is conspicuous for its basic red, with narrow bands of black and white created by the **ikat** technique of dyeing yarn for the warp of the cloth with tie resists. Young boys, unmarried men, and married men wear a red pull-over shirt which is usually decorated with a dark, narrow band across the chest, tassles and a fringed hem. These shirts are worn short, ending at waist-level, with indigo-blue or black cotton Northern Thai-style trousers, or blue denim jeans. Both kinds of trousers are purchased from shops in the Northern Thai settlements of Ban Mae Lao or Ban Pa Pae.

In this system of dress, the primary opposition is white/red followed by a secondary opposition white/black according to chromatic distributions. That is, the costumes of young boys, unmarried men, married men and women are all characterised by the dominance of the colour red. The costumes of young girls and unmarried women, on the other hand, are distinguished by the colour white whereas the costumes of married women are conspicuous for the colour red and black. The distribution of the colour red, quite clearly, parallels the distribution of the feature "procreativity" amongst the sex terms discussed earlier. This concordance in the distribution of features, and their referents, in these two systems must be taken, at the very least, as **prima facie** evidence of a conceptual association between the colour red and "procreativity". Similarly, the distinctiveness of the terms **mykoe'nau** and **nau,** and the colour white, must indicate a similar association between the colour and the property or condition "non-procreativity". In other words, there is an isomorphism in the **iconicity** of these two systems. But, what then of the secondary opposition white/black? As this contrast appears only in the sub-class "female humans", its symbolic value must therefore lie in the further distinction that it establishes specifically between "non-procreative" and "procreative" female humans.

The overall significance of the concordance between the distribution of terms with the attributes "procreative" and "non-procreative" and colour symbolism in male and female dress must be that "procreativity" is a state or condition that is inherent in, or intrinsic to, animals both male and female, and male humans whatever their status, but not female humans. It is a state which women only enter into when they are married, that is, when their fecundability or "procreativity" is realised in them through a **cultural process,** that is, marriage.

It is worth noting here that apart from the symbolism of colour in the system of dress in Palokhi, there is also a practice associated with the use of married women's skirts which has nothing to do with dress as such. It consists of tying the used, worn or unserviceable skirts of married women to the base of fruit trees (usually papaya) in house gardens. It is not marked by any ritual activity nor is it the focus of any special attention. The practice is simply termed "dressing up (with) the skirt of the tree" **(ky' thau se ni).** The Palokhi Karen, however, state quite explicitly that this helps the tree to bear fruit. There is, in other words, a conceptual association between married women's skirts — and, hence, married women — with the notion of procreativity or fertility. It is significant, however, that swidden crops, the wet-rice crop and fruit trees in the forest are not similarly treated with married women's skirts. The implication of this is clear: women and their procreativity or powers of reproduction are linked with the domestic domain.

This examination of kinship terminology, the naming system and the system of sex and gender differentiation in Palokhi makes it evident that these systems do not exist in isolation. They are, in fact, interrelated in consistent and specific ways which may be summed up according to three considerations: the primacy of the conjugal bond or marital tie in the kinship system, continuity of links of affiliation in the naming system and teknonymy, and the classification of men and women as "non-procreative" and "procreative" in the system of sex differentiation. They hold together in — to use Sorokin's term (1957:7–19) — a "logico-meaningful" integration. I suggest that the interrelationships of these systems, in this manner, constitute a model or paradigm of social organisation in Palokhi. I consider, next, other aspects of this "procreative model" of society in Palokhi.

Marriage Rules

Marriages, in Palokhi, are not arranged in the sense that parents choose spouses for their children. Young men and women make the choices themselves after a period of courting that is initiated by men. Courting, which is idiomatically called "to go and visit young women" (**lae ha' mykoe'nau**), usually takes place during the planting and harvesting seasons when there is a great deal of co-operative labour exchange between households in Palokhi swiddens and wet-rice fields.[9] As there are no prohibitions on village endogamy or exogamy, this also applies to other villages where the Palokhi Karen go to assist in the work on a labour exchange basis.[10] Often, however, during the slack season in the agricultural calendar, visiting between households in Palokhi itself and between villages occurs, and young men also take such opportunities to woo young women they are interested in.

When a young man and woman are certain that they do want to get married, they then inform their respective parents who, by this time, usually have an inkling of their intentions. Parents in Palokhi say that they generally do not object to their children's choice of spouses unless these choices contravene the rules of marriage in Palokhi. Some Palokhi parents do say that, apart from this major consideration, they would object under two circumstances: opium addiction in the case of a prospective son-in-law and being an unmarried mother in the case of a prospective daughter-in-law. A potential son-in-law who is likely to be, or already is, an opium addict represents a liability as the Palokhi Karen know only too well from their experiences in Palokhi and other villages in the area. Not only is he likely to be incapable of contributing his labour to agricultural production, but he may well attempt to dispose of family possessions or livestock to obtain the wherewithal with which to buy opium.

A woman with an illegitimate child, however, represents a liability of quite another kind. Apart from the moral reprobation which her condition provokes, an unwed mother is an anomaly which forcibly confronts the ideas and beliefs which the Palokhi Karen hold about marriage and the status of offspring from a conjugal union.[11] Yet, at the same time, many Palokhi parents say that they feel a great reluctance to object to their children's choice of spouses (whatever the reasons and this includes matches which would contravene the rules which govern marriage in Palokhi) because they fear that the couple, especially if they are not susceptible to dissuasion, will commit suicide (**kha lau sa'**, literally, "to kill down [one's own] heart").

Some parents and elders, elaborating on this fear, express their concern in terms of the limited repertoire of Buddhist concepts which they have acquired through their on-going contacts with Northern Thai. Specifically, they say that they would be "affected by demerit (**ba' ba'**).[12] On the other hand, some also say that those who commit suicide become transformed into malevolent spirits (**tamyxa**) which would be a danger to the villagers. Thus, while parents and elders may feel an obligation to prevent, or at least object to, a match which they regard as undesirable, nevertheless, children who are bent on their choice of spouses can, even in such circumstances, have their own way, namely, by seeking recourse in the threat of suicide. This does not, by any means, imply that such threats are devoid of real intent. There have been sufficient precedents in Palokhi (and elsewhere) to justify the apprehensions of parents in this regard. Ultimately, of course, this means that parents and elders have no real means of enforcing their objections, which is of some consequence in the context of infringements of marriage rules in Palokhi.

If, however, parents feel that a match is acceptable, then the onus of initiating formal discussions lies with the parents of the man. This is done through a go-between (a man) appointed by the man's parents. He approaches the parents of the woman to ascertain that they consent to the marriage, after which various details of the marriage are worked out such as the time when the marriage ceremony should be held (which should not fall in an odd month), the size of the pigs to be slaughtered for the ceremony, the amount of rice liquor to be brewed and the time that this would take, and who should constitute the party of elders essential to the ceremony.

As there is no system of payments, apart from certain prestations made to the woman by the man and which are fixed by tradition, these discussions therefore do not entail bride-price or bride-wealth negotiations. Discussions can, however, stretch over a period of two or three months, mainly because of financial considerations, and whether or not the parties concerned are able to muster enough rice (for making the liquor and for feeding guests at the marriage ceremony) as well as money for the purchase of pigs if they do not have pigs available. One other important consideration in contracting marriages is whether the elder siblings of the man and women are married or not. The Palokhi Karen say that children should get married according to their birth order (see also Madha [1980:58]). If a person marries before his, or her, elder siblings, then he or she has to present them with a pig each before the marriage can take place. This, therefore, is a consideration which can also prolong the period of discussions initiated by the go-between before a marriage can take place.

While the foregoing are general considerations which attend marriages in Palokhi, the most important consideration is, of course, the rules which govern marriage in Palokhi.[13] These rules may all be subsumed under a general prohibition on "crooked marriages" (**thau pgha ke'ko**), as the Palokhi Karen call it.[14] The Palokhi Karen do not offer any categorical definitions of what would constitute "crooked marriages", though from the examples cited by them (see below) it is apparent that such unions are those which result in the superimposition of affinal kin links over consanguineal kin links. Some Palokhi

Karen, however, do say that "crooked marriages" are those where, metaphorically, "elder brothers become younger brothers, elder sisters become younger sisters" (**waecau' kae' py, waenau kae' py),** or where the parties to such unions "love (each other), mutually prying apart that which is closely bound together" (**'ae' khoekhae' lau sa').** The first formulation, or rationalisation, refers to the contradictory applications of kin terms which would result or, what Freeman has called, "dysnomia" (1960:74, 161 n. 17). The second, interestingly, refers to what are thought to be the divisive effects of such unions where not only is there a confusion in the application of kin terms but also in the order of commensalism in the **'au' ma xae** ritual which I discuss later. Such a blanket prohibition would, therefore, rule against virtually all inter- and intragenerational unions within the range of kin, recognised by the terminological system, who are genealogically traceable or "operative" kin to use Firth's term (1963).[15] While this may seem improbable — and it is certainly true that in some societies dysnomia may be no bar to the marriage itself — nevertheless, the fact of the matter is that the Palokhi Karen express the prohibition on "crooked" unions in just this manner. It is also believed that the families of the couple in a "crooked marriage" will be "affected by their xae" (**ba' xae;** see Appendix A on **'au' ma xae).**

At the same time, however, the Palokhi Karen also point out that "crooked marriages" are "destructive" (**tahaghau**) because they invite sanctions from the Lord of the Water, Lord of the Land. In general, these sanctions manifest themselves in ways where the natural order of things is upset or reversed, such as "tigers entering the village" (**bauso' ny' zi pu).**[16] It is significant, however, that the Palokhi Karen specifically say that "the village becomes hot, the land becomes hot" (**zi ko, hau ko** or **ko ba' zi, ko ba' hau,** "the village is affected by heat, the land is affected by heat") resulting in the "destruction of the rice crop" (**by haghau).** There is, clearly, a conceptual association between marriage and the cultivation of crops.

In practice, it would appear that three kinds of unions constitute "crooked marriages". These are: cousin marriages, marriages between traceable kin across generations and multiple marriages between two hitherto unrelated families where the relative birth orders of the siblings concerned cross-cut each other. The first two cases are shown in Figure 3.2, extracted from an actual genealogy in which two such "crooked" unions did occur in Palokhi.

Figure 3.2 An Intergenerational "Crooked" Union

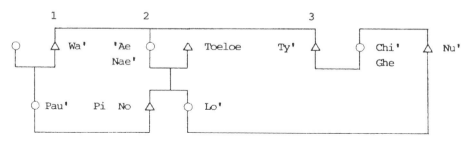

(Numerals indicate birth order)

When Ty' married Chi' Ghe, the situation was clear enough. 'Ae Nae' used the term **py** in respect of Ty' and the term for younger brother's wife, **demy,** in respect of Chi' Ghe. Nu' was **pyde** to Ty', and 'Ae Nae' was **waenau** to Ty', Chi' Ghe and Nu'. Lo', on the other hand, referred to and addressed Ty' and 'Nu' as **phati,** and Chi' Ghe was called **mygha,** while she herself was **phodo'** to all of them.

Although in different generations, the age difference between Lo' and Nu' was not great, and when they wanted to get married Lo''s parents and the village elders objected on the grounds that it would be a "crooked marriage". The reason adduced in this case was that the marriage would result in a variety of conflicting kin terms in use: Nu' being either **pyde** to Ty', or **phodo'** by virtue of being Lo''s husband, 'Ae Nae' would be **mipgha** and would have to be addressed as **mo** whereas she was **waenau** prior to the marriage, and so forth. When the intended marriage was opposed by the elders in Palokhi, Nu' and Lo' attempted suicide by drinking insecticide. Although the attempt was unsuccessful, the village elders remained adamant, despite considerable misgivings lest Nu' and Lo' should repeat the attempt. Nu' and Lo', however, presented the elders with a **fait accompli** by leaving the village for a nearby unit of the Royal Forestry Department where Nu' managed to find employment as a wage labourer. Their parents and the village elders were forced to acknowledge the **de facto** union, but the headman and elders demanded that an expiatory rite be performed to appease the Lord of the Water, Lord of the Land. This was done, and a simple wrist-tying ceremony followed in **lieu** of the marriage ceremony which could not be performed under the circumstances.

The second union in Figure 3.2 (Pi No'-Pau'), is clearly a union between first cousins. The general consensus of opinion among the Palokhi Karen seems to be that cousin marriages are not permissible. First cousin marriages are definitely prohibited but, nevertheless, there are some who say that cousin marriages, beyond the first cousin range, are permissible. Those who say that marriage between cousins of whatever degree is prohibited allude to the old saw:

Toetakhwa lau chghe, lau de
Khitakhwa hi' ke, phau' ke

which, roughly translated, means "first cousins fall (?) close together in the (same) navel, second cousins taken back (must be) caught back". The first line of this couplet quite unequivocally points to the closeness of first cousins who, therefore, are unmarriageable. The second line, however, gives rise to ambivalent interpretations in Palokhi. Those who regard all cousin marriages as prohibited unions interpret the second line to mean that the "catching" of second cousins is too difficult to achieve and, therefore, indicates that second cousin marriage is not permissible. Others who say that cousin marriage (beyond the first cousin range) is permissible take the second line to mean that "catching" a second cousin, although difficult, is possible and that, therefore, cousin marriage is permissible.

Even for those who say that cousin marriage is possible, there is however disagreement over whether this is possible at the second or third cousin range. It is interesting to note, in this regard, that some Palokhi Karen say this would depend on residential arrangements regardless of the range: they say that if physical proximity such as living in the same village or nearby lead to on-going intimate social relations, then cousin marriage under these circumstances should not be permitted. There is, nevertheless, a generally consistent agreement that cousin marriage (beyond the first cousin range) is possible only if the man belongs to an "elder" or "senior" **dau'takhwa**, and the woman to a "younger" or "junior" **dau'takhwa**, where "elder/senior" and "younger/junior" are defined in terms of the birth order of the parents or grandparents in the relevant connecting ascending generation. The rationale invoked to support the alleged permissibility of cousin marriage in this form is that when the couple perform the **'au' ma xae** rituals (as they will have to eventually), the man has to eat before the woman and this would at least be consistent with the rule that food in the ritual should be partaken of according to sibling order. According to this formulation of permissible cousin marriage, therefore, same sex siblings would only be able to marry cousins in **dau'takhwa** forbidden to their different sex siblings (see Figure 3.3). It must be stressed, however, that this is by no means a prescribed or even preferred form of marriage. All it implies is that **if** cousin marriage is at all allowed, then it should take this form.

Figure 3.3 Permissible Cousin Marriage in Palokhi

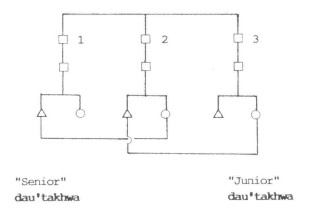

"Senior"
dau'takhwa

"Junior"
dau'takhwa

(Numerals indicate birth order)

The first cousin marriage shown in Figure 3.2, therefore, goes against all the views on cousin marriage in Palokhi because it is, first, a union between first cousins and, second, because Pau' belongs to a "senior" **dau'takhwa** since her father, Wa' is elder brother to 'Ae Nae', the mother of Pi No'. The circumstances leading to this "crooked" union were no less interesting than those surrounding the Nu'-Lo' union. Pau', though unmarried, became pregnant when she was living at a unit of the Royal Forestry Department several kilometres away where her father was working as a wage labourer. Pau' claimed that Pi No' was responsible for her condition which he apparently denied vehemently. Wa', however, pressed the matter with the parents of Pi No' (reasoning that a prohibited union for his daughter would be less shameful than her being an unmarried mother). The Palokhi elders decided that an expiatory rite should be performed and the two could then live as husband and wife after a wrist-tying ceremony similar to that for Nu' and Lo'. For reasons best known to himself, Pi No' consented to these arrangements while still protesting his innocence. He added, however, that as proof of his innocence, the child that Pau' was carrying would die on being born. As it turned out, the child did die but Pi No' did not carry the matter further. This union was, needless to say, regarded as a **ke'ko** union.

The third prohibited form of marriage is shown in Figure 3.4. If Ri' were younger than By Zo, or if La' were younger than Mau' Ghe, the use of kin terms before and after the two marriages would be clearly unambiguous. Ri' would address La' as **wae** by virtue of his being the husband of La''s younger sister Mau' Ghe, and this would also be the term he would use in respect of La' as his elder sister's husband. By the same token, the other members of the two marriages would have no difficulty in using the appropriate kin terms since these would all be consistent with one another if the two sibling orders were not crossed in marriage. As it is, Ri' is older than By Zo, and La' older than Mau' Ghe. Ri' married Mau' Ghe first and, some time later, La' and By Zo decided that they wanted to get married. This was met with objections by their respective parents and the village elders for the reasons I have already discussed, including the dysnomia which would result. For instance, La' could be either **wae** to Ri' as Mau' Ghe's elder brother, or **ca'li** as the husband of Ri''s younger sister, and so on. Moreover, the dysnomia would not be confined to these people (and their siblings) but would also extend into the next generation. Their children, Ki Da and Phan, could be either **waenau/waecau'** and **py** to each other, or neither. When it became clear that La' and By Zo were determined to get married, By Zo's father attempted to apply the maxim "Those who love each other prying apart that which is closely bound together, cannot drink water on the same steps" (**ae' khoekhae' lau sa', 'au thi toe tauxau toe' se**) literally by giving them a bag of rice and ordering them to leave the village. After three days, the hapless couple returned and begged to be taken in. Duty done, and after consultation with the village elders and headman, By Zo's father accepted them into his house when the appropriate rituals had been conducted for the Lord of the Water, Lord of the Land.[17]

Figure 3.4 An Intragenerational "Crooked" Union

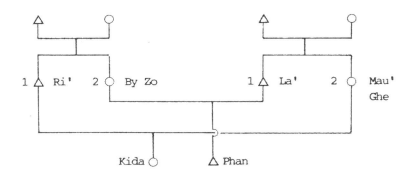

(Numerals indicate birth order)

It is obvious, from the cases which I have described above, that the rules which govern marriage as they are conceived by the Palokhi Karen are violated. Indeed, these cases were referred to by my informants in Palokhi to point out where the rules should not be contravened. This, however, raises two important issues in the operation of the kinship system in Palokhi: first, what is it about the structure of Palokhi kinship which would allow for the possibility of the contravention of these rules; second, what is there in the system of authority and social control which fails to prevent infringements of marriage rules, given the fact that "crooked marriages", as they are defined in Palokhi, are said to be prohibited.

To answer the first question: we have seen that the Palokhi Karen rationalise the prohibition on "crooked marriages" by referring to, amongst other things, the confusion arising from the contradictory application of kin terms — or what Tambiah has called, in dealing with a similar type of problem in Northeastern Thai ethnography, "an unacceptable linguistic asymmetry between husband and wife" (1973:131). There is, however, an important difference between the Thai and Karen cases. In the Thai case, husbands address their wives by the term **naung** ("younger sister") while wives use the reciprocal term **phii** ("elder brother"). The "unacceptable linguistic asymmetry" that Tambiah discusses arises, therefore, when a man is younger than his wife and thus pertains to relative age differences between husbands and wives.

In the Karen case at Palokhi, the kinds of terms employed by husbands and wives have nothing to do with sibling terms. Instead, they constitute a set of terms in their own right within the corpus of kin terms. The linguistic asymmetry, which is rather more of a contradiction as the Palokhi Karen see it, therefore does not concern spouse terms and relative age but, rather, the kinds of terms employed with respect to, and between, traceable kin connected with "crooked marriages". In other words, it is the result of the superimposition of affinal links on kin links prior to the unions which constitute the domain of difficulty. "Crooked marriages", moreover, are implicitly defined in terms of previous marital unions to which the parties in "crooked marriages" are linked either consanguineally or affinally. Furthermore, where there is a broad rule such as the Palokhi Karen have against the contradictory application of kin terms, then such a rule must logically rest on the kinds of kin recognised in the society through its kinship terminology. The conclusion which may be drawn from this, therefore, is that marriage with genealogically traceable kin is undesirable.

Given, then, a general preference for marriage with non-kin (however, obliquely this may be expressed in Palokhi), this nevertheless leaves the problem of cousin marriage unresolved. If we consider the logic of the restricted form of cousin marriage described earlier, in terms of dysnomia, it is apparent that even in such cousin marriages dysnomia would result. For instance, if a man marries a woman from a "junior" **dau'takhwa**, there would still be a situation where the use of affinal kin terms would clash with the system of address for cousins which, in theory, is based on sibling terms applied **per stirpes** from the connecting ascending generation. Apart from considerations which have to do with **'au' ma xae**, the explanation for this inconsistency lies in another aspect of Palokhi kinship.

In cognatic type systems, the application of kin terms may be extended indefinitely so long as genealogical connections may be traced. The way in which the Palokhi Karen recognise cousinship could, hypothetically, be applied **ad infinitum** but, as I have suggested, the notional limit to the reckoning of cousinship seems to lie at the third cousin range. There is a good reason for this: the Palokhi Karen do not have very deep genealogical memories. The use of kin terms for kin, and non-kin, in ascending generations, the strong social sanctions which actively discourage children from referring (much less addressing) kin and non-kin in ascending generations by name (if they happen to know them), and the practice of teknonymy all serve to produce "genealogical amnesia" (Geertz and Geertz [1964:101]). Most Palokhi Karen do not know the names of their parents or grandparents, so that for them to be able to trace third cousins to a common forebear by name is very unusual indeed. Of course, in the Palokhi system, to be able to classify someone as a second or third cousin, it does not require a person to know who the common ancestor was. All he or she would need to know is how his or her parents addressed, or referred to, the parents of the person concerned. Given, however, that relative age sometimes overrides this system of address for cousins, and teknonymy, cousinship beyond the first cousin range under these circumstances tends to be a vague relationship. This holds true especially when the appearance of new generations, the movement of households and the absence of prolonged social contacts lead to the gradual sloughing off of otherwise traceable genealogical connections. This, of course, would apply equally to kin other than second or third cousins.

Looked at from this perspective, the "problem" of cousin marriage takes on a quite different complexion. The ambiguities over cousin marriage arise because of difficulties in defining where cousins become sufficiently removed to be non-kin. And the restricted form of cousin marriage is just what it implies: it is a means, at least in a functional sense, of restricting marriages between cousins and reducing the superimposition of affinal links over consanguineal links to a minimum. In terms of the logic of the rationale of dysnomia, this is wholly consistent. But, note that this consistency is achieved by invoking a **different** principle; this principle, which underlies the restricted form of cousin marriage, is sibling order in the ascending connecting generation.

The rules of marriage and definitions of who constitute eligible and ineligible mates in Palokhi **do not**, therefore, form a neat or tidy set of proscriptions and prescriptions.

The foregoing also points to the significance of the role of parents and elders in determining whether prospective unions should be allowed or not. The reason for this is that they possess more genealogical information than those in descending generations. This is due to the general properties of the kinship system and teknonymy which lead to gradual losses of such information through successive generations.[18] This is not to say, however, that there is an absolute attrition of genealogical information over time. Each generation acquires a certain amount of information from existing operative kin links, but this is slowly lost with the appearance of successive generations where new information comes into existence; it is this which reproduces the continuities and discontinuities — of which the ambiguities over cousin marriage are a part — of the system.

We can now turn to the question of why the possibility of infringements of marriage rules occurring cannot be prevented with absolute certainty. Headmanship and the position of elders in Palokhi do not carry with them any capacity for social controls and punitive action. There are, consequently, no real means available for enforcing the rules of marriage in Palokhi, nor are there any effective sanctions which could act as deterrents to the infringement of these rules. In the final analysis, however, it is the fact that the Lord of the Water, Lord of the Land **may** be placated through propitiatory rites, as a last resort, which allows for the possible occurrence of "crooked marriages".

"Heat" and "Cooling": The Symbolic and Ideological Significance of Marriage

It is significant that the Palokhi Karen see the consequences of "crooked marriages" in terms of sanctions imposed by the Lord of the Water, Lord of the Land in the form of "hot land" and the "destruction of crops". Quite clearly, the sanctions fall on the community as a whole rather than on the offending couple. It is also significant that part of the consequences of "crooked marriages" concern the immediate kin of the couple in such prohibited unions. It is said that their kin may be "affected by **xae (ba' xae).** Here again, the consequences are transitive rather than reflexive, that is, they are "other" cathected. In both cases, the only secular sanctions which may be imposed are expulsion of the couple from the village, and a ban on participating in the **'au' ma xae** rituals of their respective families. Although expulsion is never pursued unremittingly, it is said that the ban is strictly applied. The consequences of "crooked marriages", therefore, are conceived of in terms of a disruption of the solidarity of the community and the domestic group.

What is noteworthy about the communal consequences of infringements of marriage rules, however, is that they are expressed in an idiom of "heat" and a breakdown of the cultivation system. "Heat" (**tako**) and its corollary in Palokhi, "cooling" (**takhy**), are idioms central to Palokhi Karen religious conceptions. As we have already seen, one aspect of the ritual significance of "heat" and "cooling" is the "cooling" of the Lord of the Water, Lord of the Land in the Head Rite through which harmonious and auspicious conditions necessary for the well-being of the community are established. This relationship is also of critical importance in agriculture; the simultaneous induction of a "cool" state in the rice crop and household members, for example, is a major theme of a rite called the "protection of swiddens". The essence of the relationship between "heat" and "cooling", which lies at the heart of these ritual performances, is quite simply the ritual management of "heat".

"Crooked marriages" and the "heat" that they generate are, therefore, part of a larger complex of religious conceptions in Palokhi. In the case of infringements of marriage rules, this "heat" is managed through a rite that propitiates the Lord of the Water, Lord of the Land. According to the Palokhi Karen, the rite entails the sacrifice of a pig or buffalo. The throat of the animal is slit and the resulting flow of blood is directed into a hole in the ground. The animal is then butchered and cooked to be eaten first by the headman and elders, followed by other villagers. The offending couple eat last after which a wrist-tying ceremony is conducted for them which, in effect, sanctions the union. Adultery is also said to require the performance of this ritual because the consequences are the same.

Here it is appropriate, indeed essential, to consider the symbolic significance of ordinary or correct marriages in Palokhi. Ordinary marriage rites are characterised by a multiplicity and density of symbolic representations as I show in the following section. I shall therefore examine here only those aspects of the symbolism of ordinary marriages which are of immediate interest.

One conspicuous feature of marriage rites is, interestingly enough, ritual "cooling". At various stages of marriage ceremonies, for example, water is used for "cooling" purposes and this is described by the same expression as that in the Head Rite, that is, "sprinkling with water to make cool" (**pghi thi ma takhy**). The Palokhi Karen claim that this has nothing to do with "hot" land. The evidence of ritual performances, however, indicates that there is a general, diffused state of "heat" with a specific source.

To follow the sequence of ritual performances, the bridegroom is first "cooled" as he begins his journey to the bride's house or village. Immediately after this, he and his escort are showered with water from bamboo water vessels (**thi toe**) to "cool" them. The musical instruments which are brought and played along the way are also "cooled" but this is done with libations of rice liquor which are also offered to the Lord of the Water, Lord of the Land as well. On arriving at the bride's house or village, the groom and escort are once again showered with water. Thereafter, on various occasions, the bride pours water over the feet of the groom as he crosses certain thresholds in making his way to the main room of the bride's parents' house. Significantly, the bride is not subjected to these "cooling" ministrations and showers at any stage. It is only after the final ceremony, when she has changed into the costume of a married woman and a formal sharing of rice liquor with the groom has been held, that she and her husband are jointly "cooled" by the officiating headman and elders.

The groom is, quite unmistakably, the primary focus of "cooling" and the reason, according to the Palokhi Karen, is that he is "hot" or is liable to be so. This is also said to be the case for his escort and the musical instruments. However, it is clear that as the principal focus of "cooling", the groom is the source or centre of "heat" which his escort and the instruments share through their association with him. On the other hand, the bride who is not the focus of "cooling" cannot therefore be regarded as "hot". It is only when the final ceremony is over, when she has become a married woman, that she shares in the state of "heat" which distinguishes the groom.

The inevitable conclusion that we are led to about a more general, abstract level of conceptualisation within the system of religious ideas in Palokhi can only be this: men are inherently "hot" while women are "cool" until they have gone through the ritual process of marriage.

It becomes immediately apparent that the "distribution" of "heat" parallels the distribution of the colour red in the Palokhi dress system, and the way in which men and women are distinguished according to the "procreative"/"non-procreative" dichotomy. As we have seen, there is a demonstrable isomorphism in the iconicity of these two systems resting on an identity between the colour red and "procreativity". In the case of "heat" and "cooling", the Palokhi Karen do indeed establish at a certain cognitive level an identity between the colour and "heat". In the rite called "the protection of swiddens" (which is specifically concerned with "cooling"), there is a ritual text which places the metaphors for fire — "heat" (**tako**) and "redness' (**taghau**) — in a metonymical relationship through semantic parallelism. In short, if the religious terminology of the Palokhi Karen is taken as a semiotic system at the levels of the terms "heat", "cooling", and "redness", then we have yet another set of symbolic representations which express the **same** set of structural relations contained in the systems of dress and sex and gender differentiation.

The symbolism of marriage, however, is more complex than is indicated by the distribution of "heat". In their everyday life, the Palokhi Karen are by no means concerned to manage the "heat" inherent in men and married women. It is only in marriage ceremonies that the ritual management of "heat" becomes critical. In other words, what is there in marriage ceremonies which makes "cooling" necessary that is not present in the normal course of events? I suggest that it is none other than what marriage ceremonies are all about: the conjoining of men and women or, more generally, the ritual conjunction of male and female in a process that actualises the fecundability or "procreativity" of females and thus increases the general state of "heat" which, therefore, requires its management.

This brings us to the crucial question: if "heat" is also present in ordinary marriages, in what sense then are ordinary or correct marriages different from the union of men and women in "crooked marriages" and adultery? The answer very much depends on what we understand by "crooked marriages" and, for that matter, adultery. I have already described, through various examples, what constitutes "crooked marriages" as the Palokhi Karen see it. Essentially, they involve unions between men and women in violation of untidy but, for all that, customary definitions of eligible mates. There are, therefore, two concerns here which need to be kept analytically separate: first, unions between men and women; second, the definitions of eligible or ineligible mates. It is important to bear in mind that the fact of **wishing** to marry someone who is considered ineligible does not of itself result in "hot" land or a state of "heat". It is through the attempt to establish unsanctioned conjugal relations, or by actually controverting established relations as in adultery, that these consequences come about. Of course, given culturally held notions about marriage and the attitudes they predispose to, the community — or, more precisely, the headman and elders — not unexpectedly attempts to pre-empt such consequences by threats of expulsion, bans on participation in **'au' ma xae,** and indeed by the propitiatory rite itself.

The heart of the matter, however, seems to be **uncontrolled or unregulated sexual relations** (or procreative behaviour) between men and women, however their eligibility as mates may be defined. This is, of course, the issue which stands out more starkly in adultery. To take the perspective of the Palokhi Karen, what they have are certain untidy definitions of who constitute appropriate marital partners; given this, the system of social controls, however imperfect it happens to be, is brought to bear on those who threaten the established cultural order. It is an order in which marriage not only has an important part but, indeed, plays a crucial role in maintaining as the belief in "hot" land and the breakdown of the cultivation system clearly shows.

It is here that the symbolism of marriage becomes "ideological". For it is the headman and elders, acting on the impulses, values and attitudes fostered by the cultural order to which the symbolism of marriage is integral, who ritually manage "heat". They are the mediators between the community and the Lord of the Water, Lord of the Land; in effect, they are the custodians of this order which is established in the Head Rite and, for all practical purposes, the system of social controls lies in their hands. Their role in marriage, therefore, is no other than the management of procreation or reproduction in younger generations by males in senior generations.

But, as we have seen, the cultivation of crops is also implicated in the symbolism of marriage in the form of the infertility of land, represented as it were by "hot" land. Thus, if the role of older men is the management of reproduction in younger generations, it is also concerned with the management of land and crops. To put it another way, the symbolic management of crops and agricultural production is effected through the management of marriages. It is in this sense that marriage and its symbolism are **ideological** as I defined it earlier. While the symbolism of marriage consists of a certain array of conceptual relations, its extension into the domain of crop cultivation constitutes a further level of relations which form an important part of what may be called the cultural ideology of the Palokhi Karen.

Marriage: The Ritual Process

In view of the importance placed on correct marriages in the maintenance of a harmonious relationship with the Lord of the Water, Lord of the Land from which devolves the well-being of people and crops, it is not surprising, therefore, that marriage ceremonies in Palokhi consist essentially of informing the Lord of the Water, Lord of the Land that a man and woman are being married and asking for the spirit's blessing. Because the Karen have a rule of uxorilocal residence at marriage, these ceremonies and the rituals entailed in them not only mark the union of the man and woman, but also the incorporation of the man into the household of the woman's parents. These ceremonies, like most Palokhi rituals, are not elaborate or complex, but it is evident that they also mark out symbolically two things: the liminal condition of the man as he moves from single to married status, and the separate integrity of the union between the man and woman, apart from that of the woman's parents. A brief description of marriage ceremonies as they are conducted in Palokhi will suffice to elucidate these points. The overall structure of marriage ceremonies in general, in terms of the use of time and space, is represented schematically in Figures 3.5 and 3.6. The description which follows concerns marriage between a man from Palokhi and a woman from another village. If, however, marriage is between two people from Palokhi, then there is of course no movement outside the village, and the structure of the ceremony is essentially that shown in Figure 3.6.

The ritual begins prior to the man's departure for the village where the woman lives. A boar is killed in the morning and part of it is cooked for a meal which the man, his parents and siblings, the headman, village elders, and members of the escort, including the go-between, eat. Before the meal is eaten, the headman and elders are given small cups of rice liquor (**si'**) which they use for making libations (**khwae' si'**) as they say prayers (**thupata**) to the Lord of the Water, Lord of the Land and other tutelary spirits of the area. They do this by facing the walls of the house to which they happen to be nearest, and as they crouch here, they use their index or middle fingers to cause the rice liquor to drip slowly down the cups, which is how the libations are made. At the same time, they pray to the Lord of the Water, Lord of the Land and other spirits, informing them that the man is about to be married, and request them to "look after" (**koe'tau**) the married couple, the villagers, their crops and their livestock. When this is done, the headman and elders then tie the wrists (**ki cy'**) of the man with lengths of cotton thread. The purpose of this is to bind his souls (**koela**) to his body. It is also believed that the man and his escort are susceptible to becoming "hot" and, consequently, as the man and his escort leave the house of his parents, water is thrown over them from bamboo water containers (**thi toe**) by other villagers to "cool" (**pghi thi ma takhy**) them. At the same time, the prestations for the bride are given to a woman in the escort to take to the bride's parents. These consist of a winnowing tray, two headcloths, a married woman's blouse and wrap-around skirt, a packet of betel nut, a packet of salt, and four 25 **sataang** pieces (= 1 Baht). The head of the pig which was killed for the meal, and pieces of fat are also given to a man in the escort to take along for the parents of the bride. The man and his escort are then accompanied by his parents, the headman, and village elders to the boundaries of the village just before the forest, and here a mat is placed on the ground. On this mat are placed the gongs, drums, and cymbals played by the escort. The headman, the go-between, and village elders then squat around the mat and the father of the groom hands them a bottle of rice liquor and cups. The rice liquor is poured into the cups and they repeat their prayers to the Lord of the Water, Lord of the Land and the other spirits while making libations to them. This time, however, the rice liquor is dropped onto the musical instruments to "cool" them. When this is done, the liquor is drunk by the headman, go-between, and village elders after which more liquor is poured out and passed around for the groom and the members of his escort to drink. The headman, an elder, or a ritual specialist then tears three leaves from a nearby bush in random fashion, and the pieces are then counted in pairs. This is a divinatory procedure to determine if it is safe for the groom and his escort to proceed with their journey to the bride's village. If there is an even number of pairs of leaf pieces, then it is an indication that the party may leave the village. If, however, there is an odd number of pairs, the process of praying and making libations to the Lord of the Water, Lord of the Land and other spirits is repeated, followed by further divination until a favourable omen presents itself. With the appearance of such a sign, the groom's party then departs, amidst further showers of water, along the track leading from the village into the forest.

Figure 3.5 Schematic Representation of the Ritual Process in Marriage Ceremonies Involving a Man and Woman from Different Villages

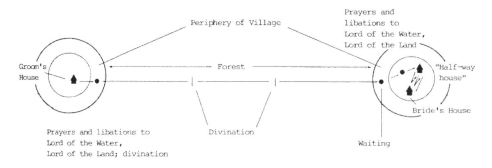

Figure 3.6 Sequence of Movements when a Groom enters the House of the Bride's Parents in Marriage Ceremonies

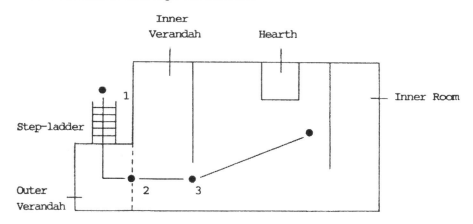

● Position of whet-stone on which the groom steps when his feet are washed by the bride

At various stages of the journey through the forest, the go-between, an elder or the ritual specialist if he is also in the party, will perform further divinations (usually after traversing one stream valley into another) to determine whether it is safe for the party to continue with its journey. This may be done with leaves, or all the people in the escort may be instructed to pick up twigs from the ground and break them into small pieces and cast them onto a cloth laid out on the ground. The diviner then counts them in pairs and, as with the other method of divination, if there is an even number of pairs, the party proceeds with its journey. Apart from the time spent on divination, the procession usually moves along at a brisk pace to the clashing of cymbals and the beating of gongs and drums. This is undoubtedly part of the festive nature of marriage ceremonies, but according to the ritual specialist in Palokhi, the din made with all these instruments keeps away malevolent spirits (**tamyxa**) from the groom and his escort.

On arriving at the periphery of the bride's village, the party waits while the go-between and an elder go to the house of the bride's parents. Here, they are offered rice liquor, and together with the elders and headman of the village, say prayers to the Lord of the Water, Lord of the Land and other spirits along with the mandatory libations. During this time, the groom and other members of his party wait at the outskirts of the village. When the prayers and libations have all been completed, the go-between then goes to bring the groom and his party into the village. From this point onwards, everything proceeds in slow, measured stages. As the groom approaches the house of the bride, he is met by elders of the vilage, and the precentor in the bride's party. A mat is laid out on the ground and the village elders, the precentors from both parties, the go-between and elders in the groom's escort squat around the mat on which the bride's father places a bottle of rice liquor and small cups. The go-between also places a bottle of rice liquor on the mat and the liquor is then exchanged between the two parties — those in the bride's party pouring out the liquor into the cups and offering them to those from the groom's party and vice versa. Prayers and libations are again made to the Lord of the Water, Lord of the Land and other spirits, after which the liquor is drunk. More liquor is then poured out and passed around to those present.

When this stage of the ceremony is completed, a sword dance is then performed by men from each party to the accompaniment of cymbals, gongs and drums. When this is done, the groom is then led to a "half-way house" in which he stays for two days before he finally moves into the bride's house. As he commences walking to the house, the people in the host village immediately shower him and his escort with water thrown from water containers (**thi toe**). While he remains in the house, the members of his escort are invited into the bride's house. As they file up the step-ladder and step on the outer verandah of the house, a brother or sister of the bride will pour water over their feet after which they enter the main room of the house where they are offered tea and pickled tea leaves.

Towards the evening, the elders of the bride's village, the headman, the go-between and elders from the groom's party assemble in the bride's parents' house, and they are given rice liquor and cups with which to make further libations and prayers to the Lord of the Water, Lord of the Land and the other tutelary spirits of the area. They then go to the house where the groom has been staying, and repeat their prayers and libations to these spirits. During this time, a sow is killed and cooked for the ritual meal of the evening which the groom and bride share. When the prayers and offerings of rice liquor to the Lord of the Water, Lord of the Land have been completed in the house where the groom stays, the groom is then led by the go-between to the bride's parents' house. At the foot of the step-ladder leading up to the house, a whet-stone is placed on the ground. Here the bride waits for the groom with a bamboo water container filled with water. As the groom approaches the step-ladder, he places both feet on the whet-stone, and the bride pours water over his feet. From here, he is led into the house and sits at the back of the main room (see Figure 3.6) which is usually where the parents of the bride sleep. The bride joins him here, and a wooden eating tray (**soebi'**) in which rice and pork stew have been placed is set before them. The headman, elders, and go-between sit near them and, again, make their prayers and libations to the Lord of the Water, Lord of the Land after which the couple are given the cups of liquor to sip from. The cups are returned to the men who said the prayers, and they sip from the cups passing them around to each other until all the liquor in the cups have been drunk.

The couple are then told to eat the meal placed before them. They usually eat sparingly of this meal, and when it is judged that they have had enough, the headman, elders and the go-between repeat their prayers to the Lord of the Water, Lord of the Land and the other spirits. The cups of rice liquor are then passed around again, and when this is done the groom is led back to the house where he was staying. The headman, elders and go-between remain in the house of the bride and continue drinking. At this stage, the precentors of both parties begin singing traditional poem-songs (**tha**) usually about love and courtship. Young males from the groom's escort and from the bride's village will, at this point, usually go to the house where the groom is staying and here they do the same thing.

The next day, this process is repeated, but with two differences. First, a boar is killed for the ritual meal and, secondly, when the groom is led to the bride's house, the whet-stone is placed at the top of the step-ladder where the outer verandah adjoins the inner verandah, at which place his feet are again "washed" by the bride. Some variations in practice do occur with regard to the latter. In some cases, after the ritual meal has been eaten by the couple and when the prayers and libations have been made, the groom is led back to the "half-way house" where he stays for several hours. He is then led back to the bride's house for another meal and, on this occasion, the whet-stone is placed where the inner verandah joins the main room of the house, that is, in the doorway. Alternatively, the whet-stone may be placed, first, at the place where the outer verandah joins the inner verandah and then, immediately, in the doorway in which case only one ritual meal is, of course, eaten by the couple on the second day. These variations seem to be dictated, primarily, by whether there is sufficient food because the ritual meals eaten by the couple are invariably followed by the provision of food for the guests and other villagers.

On the third and last day of the ceremony, the groom goes to the bride's house for the final time. On this occasion, he is led directly through the verandahs and enters the room where he again sits at the back facing the door. Here he changes into a new suit of clothes, while the woman changes from her white shift (which young girls and unmarried women wear) into the black blouse and red wrap-around skirt that only married women may wear. The man changes in front of the guests while the woman changes in the small back room after which she joins the man in the main room. This time, however, they are not given a meal to eat. Instead, the man is given a bottle of rice liquor and a cup. He pours a measure of the liquor into the cup which he drinks, and this is followed by a second measure which he offers to his wife. This cup is put aside, and other cups are then set before him which he fills and he then proceeds to offer them to the father of his wife, the elders from his wife's village and to the go-between and elders in his escort. They then pray to the Lord of the Water, Lord of the Land and the other spirits, making their libations at the same time, after which the cups of liquor are passed around to be sipped by the couple and the ritual officiants at the ceremony.

The first bottle of rice liquor which, by now, is usually half empty, is set aside and other bottles are brought out by the father of the bride. The man then pours out more cups of liquor and these are offered by them to the other people present. This continues until all the bottles of rice liquor are exhausted. Then the man pours out the liquor remaining in the first bottle and offers this to the ritual officiants who proceed to pray to the Lord of the Water, Lord of the Land and the other spirits. When this is completed, the cups of liquor are passed around again to be sipped by the couple and the ritual officiants. This marks the end of the marriage ceremony, after which the headman and elders of the village pour water over the heads of the now married couple while the members of the man's escort prepare themselves to return to their village. Before they do so, they try to "take the man back" with them by pulling on one of his arms. At this stage, the young men of his wife's village seize his other arm and try to detain him. While this may begin in a jocular fashion, it can sometimes become very earnest indeed, but after a while the groom's escort relinquish their hold on the man and leave in a shower of water thrown at them by members of the bride's village.

As a rite of passage, the symbolism of the ritual performances and the use of time and space throughout the marriage ceremony quite clearly mark the incorporation of the man into the household of the woman's parents. What may not be so obvious, but which is nonetheless "stated" in the rituals, is the **separate integrity** of the union apart from but yet within the stem family that is formed. The evidence for this comes, of course, from the slaughtering of the sow and boar (which some informants quite explicitly say stand for the man and woman), and the drinking of rice liquor from a common cup which is, then, set aside and not put to general use at that particular stage of the marriage ceremony. But it is also to be seen in the serving of liquor by the man, on the last day of the ceremony, which **a fortiori** points to the couple as a unit distinct from the stem family, even though they reside in the house of the woman's parents.

Under ordinary circumstances any ritual observed in a family which entails the use of rice liquor (in libations to the Lord of the Water, Lord of the Land) or, indeed, when liquor is drunk merely for enjoyment, the head of the family (that is, the father in a nuclear family, or the father of a married daughter in a stem family) is required to serve the liquor in just this manner to the headman and village elders. It is a duty and obligation which no one else may assume. It is significant, then, that instead of the father of a daughter, it is the newly married husband of the daughter who is required to perform the act of serving liquor in this manner (which is a ritual in its own right no matter how trivial it may appear to be) in the house of his wife's parents. For, during the period in which he and his wife are resident in his wife's parents' house, and as long as his father-in-law is alive, it is his father-in-law who serves liquor in the rituals which entail libations to the Lord of the Water, Lord of the Land. The performance of this particular ritual by a newly married husband, therefore, signifies the assumption of responsibilities, on the part of the man, that have no context other than within the nuclear family (and stem family) of which he **will** eventually become the head and ritual leader when the stem family fissions. The marriage ceremony, thus, reverses the priority as regards who should serve liquor in a stem family in ritual situations, marking out the distinctiveness of the new conjugal bond that is constituted by the ceremony. Palokhi marriage rituals, therefore, express precisely the same thing found in the terminological system, and teknonymy, described earlier.

Marriage, Residence, and Domestic Group Formation and Fission

Despite the general rule on uxorilocal residence upon marriage, in Palokhi, this rule does not lead to the formation of extended families consisting of parents, married daughters and their husbands and children. The reason for this is that the Palokhi Karen stipulate that a house should not contain more than two married couples on a permanent basis. Thus, if in a two generation family with one married daughter, another daughter marries, then the daughter who married first and her husband (and children if any) must make way for the second daughter by moving out of the natal family and building a separate house for themselves. On the other hand, if it is a three generation family to begin with, then even the first daughter who marries and her husband cannot expect to remain indefinitely in the house of her natal family. She and her husband would usually move out within a year of being married. Married daughters who move out of their parents' houses usually build houses near their parental homes, although virilocal and neolocal residence have been known to occur. The reasons have been mainly economic, having to do with wage labour opportunities available at the various units of the Royal Forestry Department in the area, and personal preferences as well.

The Palokhi Karen offer no satisfactory reasons for the limitation on the composition of stem family households beyond saying that "it must be done so" (**ba' ma di' ne**), although some informants say that the reason for the limitation is that otherwise there would be "too many people" for the **'au' ma xae ritual**.[19] In fact, however, the reason for the limitation on household composition becomes readily apparent when we examine the sleeping arrangements of households in Palokhi. Houses have one main room, and this room is roughly divided in half by a hearth, as Figure 3.6 shows. In a nuclear family household, the parents and children would sleep in the rear half of the room. As their children grow older, pubertal daughters sleep in the front half of the room, while pubertal sons sleep either on the inner verandah or the rice barn, or in other rice barns along with their age-mates.

In traditional times, "communal houses" (**blau**) served the purpose of accommodating young men who were expected to sleep on their own, as well as other ritual functions (Marshall [1922:139]); but, in Palokhi, there is no such communal house, hence the practice of young men sleeping in rice barns or inner verandahs. When a daughter in a nuclear family marries, the front half of the room is given to her and her husband to sleep in, thus maintaining a spatial, and therefore **symbolic**, separation of the two married couples in the stem family that is formed. With the marriage of a second daughter, such a separation of all the couples would be impossible to maintain if the second daughter and her husband were to reside in the house as well, given the structure of Palokhi houses. In the same way, in a three generation (stem) family, such a separation would not be possible to maintain when a woman married, because her grandparents would occupy the rear half of the room, and her parents would occupy the front half of the room.[20]

This is not to say that house form in Palokhi determines the composition of households by any means, but, rather, that sleeping arrangements which are conditioned by house form are taken into account in an ideology of kinship which emphasises the discreteness of conjugal pairs, even within stem families.

Palokhi residence customs, however, are a little more complicated than I have indicated in the foregoing. If a mother dies, the house is taken apart and burnt, and the father then builds a new house in which he and his children live. The Palokhi Karen say that the reason for this is that "the house belongs to the wife" (**phau'mypgha 'a' doe'**), at least, initially. The house which a widower builds, however, "belongs" to him, so that when he dies the house is likewise destroyed. If, on the other hand, a father dies before the mother, the house is not destroyed, and the mother and her children may continue to live in the house.[21] In either case, the rule that there may not be more than two married couples living in the same house still applies, with the surviving parent and deceased parent regarded as constituting a "union" nonetheless.

This condition on residential arrangements, the stipulation that there should not be more than two couples in a house, may in practice be circumvented in either of two ways. The first, a long term one and one which was resorted to on only one occasion in Palokhi, entails building a separate hearth (which, in effect, means extending the house) for the couple not ordinarily supposed to live in the house. This also requires the construction of separate step-ladders so that, for all practical purposes, the separate hearths and steps represent separate houses.[22] The second device which is a short term one, and customary practice in Palokhi, involves one or the other couple sleeping on the inner verandah of the house until the new house for the first married daughter and her husband has been built and is ready for occupation.

In the event that both father and mother die, the house is destroyed and alternative arrangements are made. If there are any children who are married, then the unmarried children may live with either the married sister or married brother, although the former is more usual given the fact that the brother moves away to live with his wife. If there are no married children, then the children are fostered out to patrilateral, or matrilateral, kin depending on the circumstances: that is, whether they can be located easily or not, whether they can afford the upkeep of the children, and so forth.[23] Whatever the resulting arrangements, married siblings cannot live in the same house when their parents are dead, and the reason for this lies in the way **'au' ma xae** rituals are structured, as the Palokhi Karen conceive it, and which I discuss later. In sociological terms, however, this is understandable. First, the rule on uxorilocal residence at marriage which leads to brothers marrying out would act to prevent the formation of households consisting of co-resident married brothers, or married brothers and sisters. Second, the **succession** of married sisters resident in their natal homes, according to the condition on uxorilocal residence described above, would itself act to prevent the formation of households composed of co-resident married sisters.

Residential arrangements are, of course, part of the total process of household formation and household fission within the overall developmental cycle of domestic groups. This cycle, in ideal type terms, spans three generations. During the cycle, brothers marry out, and as sisters marry successively, nuclear family households are formed, while the natal family at any point in time retains a fixed structure, consisting of two conjugal pairs, regardless of whether it is a two or three generation stem family. The cycle ends with the death of grandparents, followed by parents, and what is left are siblings with independent nuclear family households which then repeat the process. This cycle in the family sociology of Palokhi, and its residential concomitants, are fully reflected in the structure and organisation of the **'au' ma xae** ritual.

A full account of the **'au' ma xae** ritual may be found in Appendix A. It is a quintessentially domestic ritual and it is an integral part of the religious life of the Palokhi Karen. As I show in my discussion of the ritual, it is relevant to a further understanding of the institution and rituals of marriage, the family sociology of the Palokhi Karen, as well as the issues which I consider next.

Divorce: Throwing Away Marital Partners, Pots, and Pans

In the foregoing sections, I have attempted to draw out the main features of Palokhi Karen kinship and the symbolic aspects of marriage as well as to show how these are linked together. The discussion would not be complete, however, without a consideration of divorce and remarriage, both of which have occurred in Palokhi, although not frequently.

Divorce, which is termed "to throw away mutually" (**cu khi' lau sa'**), may occur for a variety of reasons. These include infidelity and adultery (which has happened, despite the fact that this is said to give offence to the Water, Lord of the Land), dissatisfaction with a spouse's handling of marital responsibilities, and a desire for children not possible to fulfil because of a spouse's presumed barrenness or sterility. As with "crooked marriages", the Palokhi Karen believe that adultery results in sanctions imposed by the Lord of the Water, Lord of the Land and, consequently, an important feature where adultery has been committed is the expiatory rite performed for the Lord of the Water, Lord of the Land, as discussed before. For this rite, a pig must be supplied by the persons party to adultery. Divorce, if it is sought, in the case of adultery is called "to throw away the husband" (**cu khi' 'a' wa**) or "to throw away the wife" (**cu khi' 'a' ma**), depending on who is guilty of infidelity. In circumstances where divorce is desired by mutual consent, there is, however, no need to perform the expiatory rite. Divorces in either case are effected by a version of **'au' ma xae** which is called "to finish eating the pig, to finish eating the chicken" (**'au' lau thu' thau'**, **'au' lau thu' chau**) which, of course, refers to the **kho thi'** animals reared for **'au' ma xae**. Unlike "big" **'au' ma xae**, where four nights are required for the performance of the ritual, this requires only two nights. When the couple have decided when they wish to perform the ritual, they have to sell off all but the oldest **'au' ma xae** pigs and chickens so that they do, in fact, eat the last pig and chicken. All other pigs and poultry may be shared out between the two, or sold off and the proceeds divided between them.[24] This also applies to buffaloes and rice in the barn.

When all this is done, and it has to be done before the ritual, then the couple may conduct the **'au' ma xae** which dissolves their marriage. On the first day, the last chicken is killed and served in the same way as that for ordinary **'au' ma xae**. Before they eat, both the husband and wife take out pieces of the **kho thi'** and wrap these up in banana leaves, with some rice. As they do so, they pray to the souls of their respective parents (if they are deceased) informing them that this is the last meal that they will eat together as it is the last **kho thi'** chicken. This done, they shove the wrappings through the floor of the house and eat the food in the tray. If their parents are alive, however, they attend this ritual and they, instead of the couple, will then say the prayers to their deceased parents' souls. The eating of the last **kho thi'** is done in the same manner as that in ordinary **'au' ma xae**, that is, the husband eats first, followed by the wife, and then their children according to birth order. The eating of the last pig is also carried out in the same fashion. When this is completed, the wooden eating tray, cooking pots, the bamboo spoons for stirring rice and stews, the bamboo water vessels, and the three hearth stones are all thrown away in the bush outside the village. For one day, after the eating of the last **kho thi'**, the couple must not do any work, and on the following day the man leaves the village.

There can be no doubt that these cooking utensils stand, symbolically, for the domestic household. This symbolism is by no means confined to the Palokhi Karen. Although it has not been reported in the contemporary ethnography of the Karen, Marshall (1922:260) has observed, however, that Karen families in Burma who renounce their traditional religion and **'au' ma xae** in favour of Christianity, throw away these utensils.[25] This alone suggests a symbolic link between household cooking utensils, the marital tie and the domestic group, as well as the traditional religion of the Karen. The practice of disposing these utensils in the context of the last **'au' ma xae** which dissolves a marital union, however, is indisputable evidence that the three are inextricably linked.

When the ritual is completed, the children of the couple are given the choice of remaining with their mother or accompanying their father. Whichever the choice they make, they may not, thereafter, have anything to do with the parent they did not elect to be with which, in practical terms, means that they do not sleep in the house of that parent. For children in such situations, any **'au' ma xae** performed for them will be by the parent they have chosen to live with. When they eventually marry, however, they do call upon the souls of both parents in the **'au' ma xae** they conduct if both parents are dead. Otherwise, the parent with whom they chose to live with would, of course, attend the ritual in person. It is well worth noting in this connection that children are given a **choice** as to which parent they wish to live with following the divorce. Although a variety of factors may operate to influence the choice, it is significant that in theory there is a choice. It is a reflection of an ethos of individual autonomy here extended to children.

A Note on Remarriage

Remarriage for divorced men or women is a relatively simple matter. But, here again the marriage ritual would depend on the status of their new spouses-to-be. If, for instance, a hitherto unmarried man marries a divorcee, then the ritual recognises his unmarried status in the killing of a boar, and the two are then married by a simple wrist-tying ceremony. The same applies to a divorced man who marries a woman who has never been married before, but in this case a sow is killed for the wrist-tying ceremony.

Remarriage, as with first marriages, also results in the formation of **xae** by the married couple and the birth of their children. This **xae**, however, is regarded as separate from that which a divorcee shares with his or her spouse and children from a previous marriage. This is also extended, of course, to the children from the second union. Thus, in these circumstances, two distinct **'au' ma xae** must be performed according to the two **xae** which exist in such situations of remarriage. If the children of a divorcee are **ba' xae**, for example, the ritual may only be performed by their parent. Their stepparent and stepsiblings may not participate in the ritual. Conversely, **'au' ma xae** for their stepsiblings will be performed by their parent and stepparent; they themselves can have no part in the ritual.

These sociological and ritual arrangements are fully reflected in the kin terms which are employed in such circumstances. It is interesting to note that although the Palokhi Karen have no terms for "stepfather" and "stepmother", the terms **pa** and **mo** are not used in reference or address for stepparents. Instead, the terms **phati** and **mygha** are used. If further specification of the nature of the relationships is necessary, then these collateral kin terms may be modified by the terms **pa** and **mo** as suffixes. By the same token, stepchildren are referred to and addressed as **phodo'**. Stepsiblings, however, use real sibling terms in both reference and address. It is also worth noting that step-relationships, where they are recognised (that is, stepparent/stepchildren) are sloughed off with the appearance of a further generation: thus, a person's stepchildren's children will refer to and address him, or her, as **phy** or **phi**. This is what we might expect in view of the observations made earlier about the terminological system. The structure of **'au' ma xae** and the use of kin terms in situations characterised by divorce and remarriage, thus, recognise the separateness of marital unions and the offspring from these unions just as it is in the case of first marriages, and evident in the rest of the kinship system and the ritual.

I have in this chapter described the kinship system in Palokhi, the naming system, the system of sex differenttiation, marriage, and residence and the formation and fissioning of domestic groups. These three systems and **'au' ma xae** are interrelated at several levels to form a complex whole in which there is a discernible ideology linking key features in these systems and the sociology of marriage and domestic groups. Central to this is a logic of sexual difference, the primacy of the conjugal bond as a procreative union and the role of males in senior generations in managing reproduction in younger generations.

In the next chapter, I consider the broader sociological implications of the kinship system in Palokhi for subsistence production which were left unexplored in this chapter.

ENDNOTES

[1] Madha (1980:202), however, says that the term for younger siblings, **"pu"**, may be modified by the suffixes **"de khwa"** and **"de Moo"** to indicate the sex of younger siblings. I believe Madha is mistaken in this having probably confused the terms for younger affinal kin with the terms for younger siblings, as I indicate later.

[2] It has been reported for the Pwo (Hamilton [1976:116–7]) that terms for intermediate children also exist, similar to the Roman system. The Palokhi Karen, however, do not have such terms.

[3] For the term **phosoeda,** see also Jones (1961:201). Madha (1980:202) reports the term **"weh-ko"** which he says is a general term for "elder brother" and "elder sister". Madha is again mistaken in this; the term refers to eldest brother or sister.

[4] The etymology of the term **dau'takhwa** is unclear to me. Although its meaning is clear, the form that it takes varies from place to place as it has been reported in the literature. **Dau'** is the same co-ordinate as in **dau'pywae,** while **ta** is a nominalising prefix, and **khwa,** "male". This does not, of course fit in with the way the term is used, that is, bilaterally. Jones (1961:201), however, provides a Moulmein Sgaw term for cousin which is bilateral in form, namely, **khwamy'.** Hamilton makes similar observations with regard to the cognate Pwo term **dang the khwae,** where **the** is the nominalising particle in Pwo, of which the cognate in Sgaw is **ta** (Hamilton [1976: 117]; Jones [1961:25]). Morgan (1871:445) says, on the basis of information provided by Wade, Mason and Van Meter, that male cousins are known as **ta-khwa** and female cousins as **ta-khwa-mu.** Hamilton notes that there is an alternative term in Pwo for cousins, namely, **dang myng dang khwae** which he glosses as "related female related male". He suggests that the term **dang the khwae** represents a shortening of the term **dang myng dang khwae.** This would, indeed, seem to be the only reasonable explanation for the variations in the term and the fact that it is applied bilaterally.

[5] See also Smeaton (1887:81–2) and Marshall (1922:170).

[6] The word for rice seems to be reserved exclusively for female names suggesting an association between "femaleness" and rice. This association is also to be found specifically in the cultivation of rice where a small crop of rice, which is grown solely for ritual purposes, is called **By Mo Pgha** or "Old Mother Rice".

[7] Jones (1961:179) notes that whereas in most Sgaw dialects in Burma, **s** (cognate to **cau'** in Palokhi Karen) means "Mr", nevertheless, in Moulmein Sgaw, it has the additional meaning of "elder brother". Jones offers no further comment, but it is by no means unlikely that the original meaning of the term was "elder brother" and that it was at some later stage employed as an honorific, perhaps, beginning in an urban setting. **Nau** along with **pa, pha** and **mo** would appear to form a related set of terms, in

themselves, of some antiquity, if Benedict's historical reconstructions for Tibeto-Burman (1972) and Jones' reconstructions for Proto-Karen are accepted. From terms in various Tibeto-Burman languages (but not Karen) "sister", "maiden", "cousin", "daughter-in-law", and so forth, Benedict reconstructs the root ˙s-nam (1972:35). Jones reconstructs ˙nam in Proto-Karen for various cognates of **mykoe'nau** (1961:123). For "mother", Benedict offers ˙ma in Tibeto-Burman (1972:148), but Jones does not provide any reconstruction for the term in Proto-Karen. Benedict also gives ˙mow for "woman" (1972:66). For **pha** and **pa,** Benedict gives ˙-pa (1972:134), whereas Jones has only ˙phah for **pha** (1961:124). It is clear from these, and other related terms in present-day Tibeto-Burman languages (Benedict [1972:35, 63]) that the relations amongst these terms are highly complex. I refer to these reconstructions, however, to indicate that in these related languages there is a conspicuous, if not a consistent, differentiation in the female terms which is not the case with the male terms. The differentiation of these terms in Palokhi, therefore, is not some linguistic oddity peculiar to Palokhi Sgaw Karen (or Karen dialects), but to the family of languages to which it belongs even though the cultural meanings of these differentiations may not necessarily be the same.

[8] There is a certain irony in this. With the exception of the Pa-O or Thaungsu whose kinship system exhibits very clear Dravidian features (Wijeyewardene, pers. comm.), developments in kinship studies since Morgan would now lead us to place most, if not all, other Karen kinship systems outside the category "classificatory" in Morgan's nomenclatural sense. Yet, these Karen systems (if the Palokhi data is anything to go by) are undoubtedly classificatory, though in a sense that Morgan did not perhaps quite appreciate. It is clear, I think, that the Palokhi terminological system — or at least parts of it — functions together with the systems of naming and sex and gender differentiation to establish what is, for all practical purposes, a classificatory system that is sociologically significant.

[9] In common with what has been reported on courting patterns in other Karen communities, the Palokhi Karen also treat funerals as occasions for courting. The common denominator in planting, harvesting and funerals is that these are all occasions when singing or chanting takes place. For the Palokhi Karen, singing is one of the ways employed by young men and women to express obliquely their interest in each other.

[10] The Karen have a saying containing that brand of ironic humour, much appreciated by them, about the business of seeking wives. It runs as follows:

'Ae' ma kau zi, mae' blau'
'Ae' ma zi pu, kau'ka'

Roughly translated, it means "To love a wife in a distant domain, is to be blind; to love a wife within the village, is to be lame".

[11] I am not suggesting that these objections are necessarily shared cultural attitudes. However, they do certainly reflect the concern of many Palokhi Karen parents. In Palokhi, there were seven confirmed opium addicts and one unmarried mother (who lived with her parents), so the parents who expressed their views on the undesirable qualities of potential spouses were undoubtedly doing so on the basis of their experiences of life in Palokhi.

[12] See Chapter II, p. 106, n. 25, for a comment on **ba'**. The use of the term in this context suggests interesting insights into Palokhi Karen religious conceptions in relation to Buddhist concepts. The Palokhi Karen cannot be considered Buddhist in any real sense of the term and, indeed, their acquaintance with Buddhism is superficial. Though familiar with the common Thai expression, **tham bun daj bun, tham baab daj baab** ("to perform meritorious acts is to receive merit, to perform demeritorious acts is to receive demerit"), nevertheless, the Palokhi Karen do not use the literally more accurate Karen gloss for **daj** which would be **ne** ("can", "to acquire", "to receive" through one's own efforts or fortuitously). The use of the auxilliary verb **ba'** suggests "being acted upon", a common feature in Palokhi conceptions of illness which is generally thought of as being the product of some external agent.

[13] Karen marriage preferences have sometimes been described as preferences for "kindred exogamy" (see, for example, Hinton [1975: 55]; Marlowe [1979:178]) but I would prefer not to use such a term (see n. 15, below).

[14] In a preliminary description of Palokhi Karen domestic ritual and the "ideology of kinship", I referred to these marriages as "crossed" (1984:355). I wish, here, to correct that error in translation. The literally more accurate translation of the term **ke'ko** is "crooked". The term is used in a generic sense, but cousin marriages of the kind where the birth orders of the siblings involved are not followed are sometimes described as "crossed".

[15] Firth's term is particularly appropriate to the Palokhi data as it accords more closely with the nature of the constitution of kin groups which, in large part, depend on the traceability of genealogical

connections. This is an important consideration in understanding why the Palokhi Karen express their marriage prohibitions in such elliptical ways, as I discuss later.

[16] The Palokhi Karen interpret "tigers" metaphorically, taking it to mean wild animals. Many, however, are convinced that in the past, when there were tigers, this did in fact happen.

[17] About a year later, after this had happened, an ethnic Karen Seventh-Day Adventist missionary came to Palokhi to convert the villagers. By Zo's father took the opportunity to convert to Christianity including his whole family and the couple. They were the only people who became Christians in Palokhi. Duang, By Zo's father, told me that he did so because he was afraid that the rites to placate the Lord of the Water, Lord of the Land might not have been entirely successful leading to supernatural sanctions being imposed on the village. He was also apprehensive that the family would have to perform the **'au' ma xae** rituals frequently (see Appendix A) which would have too onerous to bear. Moreover, Duang was also concerned that if, indeed, the crops in Palokhi failed, he and his family might be forced to leave the village and either abandon the wet-rice fields which he had acquired, or sell them at a loss.

[18] I am, here, of course drawing out the operative principles at work in the Palokhi kinship system. This does not necessarily explain the individual cases of "crooked marriages" which provided not only insights into how the Palokhi Karen conceive of their marriage rules, but the point of departure for this analysis of the system itself. The people involved in these cases of "crooked" unions, unfortunately, were reluctant to discuss the personal facts of their unions. If anything, however, I would suggest that these cases do lend support to my argument that people in descending generations tend to disregard what in ascending generations are seen as significant kin links, much more than is stated in my argument.

[19] It is significant that **'au' ma xae** is so readily adduced as a rationale for various arrangements having to do with kinship and domestic organisation. One reason for this is that the ritual itself contains a complex of ideas based on kinship (as I discuss later in the Appendix on **'au' ma xae**) and religious beliefs, and in this sense these ideas could well be regarded as an "ideological" system, as conventionally if loosely understood, quite apart from the sociological arrangements which I describe here.

[20] There are, however, ways by which these can be circumvented — through temporary sleeping arrangements or a restructuring of the house itself while yet maintaining the spatial and symbolic separation of the couples involved.

[21] Almost all houses in Palokhi are built of bamboo, but four are built of more durable materials, namely, wooden planks. Some informants say that it would be a waste to destroy these houses built from wooden planks, in which case — should the necessity arise — the houses can be taken apart and rebuilt.

[22] In Palokhi, a very attenuated long-house of this kind did exist some ten or fifteen years ago consisting of a single structure with two hearths. It was built to accommodate a married couple and the aged mother of the husband.

[23] Adoption does not seem to be practised in Palokhi. In April 1981, a woman with an only daughter died, and no one in Palokhi was able to trace any of her kin to whom the thirteen year old daughter could be sent. The elders in Palokhi finally enquired in the nearby Northern Thai village of Ban Mae Lao to see if there were any Northern Thai families prepared to adopt the girl. A family was eventually found and the girl left Palokhi to live with the family in Ban Mae Lao.

[24] Whoever buys these **'au' ma xae** animals cannot use them in their own **'au' ma xae** rituals. These animals would be reared for use in other sacrifices, or for feeding helpers during the planting and harvesting seasons. The orginal owners of these animals, however, cannot eat the flesh of these animals after they have been sold, regardless of the circumstances.

[25] This was in fact done by the one family (H3) in Palokhi which converted to Christianity.

Chapter IV

Village Organisation and the Sociology of Production and Consumption

Kinship in Palokhi, as we have seen, is inextricably linked to systems of naming, sex categories, and customary rules on residence at marriage as well as ritual. It is a central part of social organisation in Palokhi and, as I have shown, it also possesses symbolic and ideological elements. In this chapter, I turn to a consideration of yet another important aspect of the community life of the Palokhi Karen, namely, the socio-economic relations in subsistence production and consumption which, for all practical purposes, may well be regarded as constituting the other major substantive aspect of social organisation in the community.

In broad, general terms, all subsistence production and consumption in Palokhi is organised at the level of house-holds or domestic groups. This is a general characteristic of economic organisation which the Palokhi Karen share with other Karen communities (Hinton [1975:54ff.]; Mischung [1980:21–4]; Madha [1980:58]; Hamilton [1976:119]). Domestic groups, however, do not exist in isolation of one another, nor do they remain constant in composition over time. They exist with other domestic groups with which they are related through kinship links of one kind or another, although the significance attached to these links varies, as I noted in Chapter II. They also change in composition in their developmental cycles. Yet, at any point in time, they retain a certain "corporateness" and identity of their own which, as I emphasised in the last chapter, is also a primary feature of the symbolic and ideological aspects of kinship in Palokhi. These considerations are directly relevant to the sociology of subsistence production and consumption in Palokhi.

First, the fact of household formation and fission implies that the organisation of production and consumption must necessarily undergo some re-arrangement as domestic group composition changes over time and as different sets of kinship relationships come into play.

Second, at a more general level, certain agricultural tasks demand some form of co-operative organisation of labour. For example, planting in swiddens requires large labour inputs within a relatively short period of time to ensure that swiddens are ready before the onset of the rains. Similarly, harvesting needs to be completed without undue delay lest the crop suffers from unseasonal rains, the predations of pests and theft. Most Palokhi households, however, have high dependency ratios and therefore cannot supply all the labour required for such intensive tasks. The variable emphasis placed on different kinds of kin relations between households is thus an important consideration in the organisation of co-operative labour. As I have pointed out before, this is best seen in terms of the interplay between genealogical relations and non-genealogical factors.

Finally, there are the symbolic and ritual aspects of kinship which express, and through which are constituted (or reconstituted), the ideological importance of the domestic group in Palokhi Karen culture. Allowing for changes in domestic organisation over time and the interdependence of households which are demanded by the recurrent necessities of certain agricultural tasks, in what sense then is the ideological significance of the domestic group maintained? This concerns the relationship between social organisation in the broader context of the economics of subsistence, the way in which this is symbolically represented, and the place it occupies in the cultural ideology of the Palokhi Karen. It is a question which requires some consideration because it is relevant to the major concerns of this study.

In this chapter, I propose to examine these issues by focussing on several case studies, paying close attention to the pragmatics of domestic economic organisation, and the symbolic aspects of eating and familial commensalism in Palokhi. My purpose is two-fold: first, to describe the various sociological arrangements which make up the organisation of economic activities in Palokhi, within and outside the context of kinship; second, to show how domestic and community organisation is symbolically represented and maintained in the cultural ideology of the Palokhi Karen.

The Domestic Organisation of Production and Consumption: Some Case Studies[1]

Taking a general perspective, it is useful to view the array of socio-economic arrangements in the domestic economy of Palokhi in terms of degrees of relative household autonomy and areas of sharing within and between households in production and consumption. The nature of the economic functions of households and the variations in their associated sociological arrangements, which are not only features of domestic economics in Palokhi but of village economic organisation in general, requires this descriptive and analytical approach. As White, for example, observes in his introduction to a collection of papers in the volume

Rural Household Studies in Asia:

> ... there is no clear-cut distinction between 'sharing' and 'not-sharing', but rather a **range** of possible domestic arrangements in any society in which there are different **areas** of sharing ... It is in fact their degree of **autonomy** of internal economic organization relative to one another

rather than any particular uniformity in that organization which marks off 'household' units from each other. (1980:14–6).

These observations are equally applicable to Palokhi.

Case 1: H1a, H1b

H1a consists of the headman, Tamu', his wife, their daughter, her husband Gwa and their two children. H1b consists of Tamu''s son, Nae' Kha, his wife and their four children. The economically active people in these two households were Tamu', his daughter Poeloe, Gwa and Nae' Kha. Tamu''s wife was too infirm for the more arduous tasks in agricultural work while Nae' Kha's wife was for much of 1981 house-bound as she was nursing a new-born son.

Figure 4.1 The Genealogical Relations between H1a and H1b

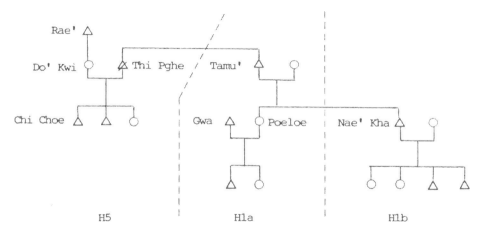

Nae' Kha married his wife in 1975 and went to live with her in her parents' house at Huai Dua, following the customary rule on uxorilocal residence. In Huai Dua, he worked his father-in-law's wet-rice field but, at the same time, opened up a plot of wet-rice terraces by himself. After three years, however, he returned to Palokhi with his wife and, at that time, their two children. The wet-rice field that he opened was left for his father-in-law to use. There were two reasons why he returned to Palokhi. The principal reason was the expectation that he would eventually succeed his father as headman. For this, residence in Palokhi was mandatory. He also needed to familiarise himself with the various ritual performances and prayers required of a headman, although in the years when he was resident in Huai Dua he returned to participate in the Head Rite described in Chapter II. The second reason was that he found much of the burden of agricultural work fell upon him at Huai Dua because his father-in-law, an opium addict, left most of it to him.

Upon his return to Palokhi, he built a house next to Tamu''s and a number of arrangements between the two households came into being which, in 1981–82, were still in the process of working themselves out. Prior to Nae' Kha's return, Hla cultivated swiddens and a wet-rice field owned by Tamu'.[2] When Nae' Kha returned to Palokhi, Tamu' and Gwa assumed responsibility for cultivating the swiddens of their household, whilst Tamu' and Nae' Kha were, on the other hand, responsible for cultivating Tamu''s wet-rice field. However, in early 1981 Nae' Kha also rented a plot of wet-rice terraces from Chwi' (one of the former co-founders of Palokhi with Tamu') who had moved to Huai Dua in 1977 after divorcing his wife. The field was rented on a share-cropping basis. When Chwi' died later in the year, Nae' Kha exchanged his field in Huai Dua for Chwi''s field in Palokhi with Chwi''s second wife at Huai Dua. In addition, a small sum of money was paid over to her because Chwi''s field was a little larger than Nae' Kha's. At the same time, he also began to open up his own plot of terraces near Tamu''s wet-rice field. This marked the establishment of a certain independence in subsistence farming for Nae' Kha and his family. Although they were not under any undue pressure to do so, there was nevertheless a general expectation that they would eventually cultivate fields of their own whether they were swiddens or wet-rice terraces.

It may be noted here that the separation of responsibilities in working Tamu''s swiddens and wet-rice fields between the two brothers-in-law was essentially dictated by ritual considerations (see Chapter VI).[3] As far as the sharing of labour in Tamu''s swiddens and wet-rice field were concerned, there was in fact no real division of labour, at least in theory. In practice, however, Nae' Kha was unable to contribute substantially to the cultivation of Tamu''s swiddens because he was committed to working his rented field and opening the plot of terraces for his family's use. Gwa, however, assisted Nae' Kha in cultivating the latter's rented field and, occasionally, in the work on the new terraces.

Certain distinctions, however, were made in the sharing of the rice from the fields of H1a and H1b. While the crops from Tamu''s swidden and wet-rice field were shared between the two households, the harvest from Nae' Kha's rented field was retained by him for his family's use in 1982.

The somewhat fluid arrangements in the sharing of labour and rice between the two households undoubtedly reflected the fact that the situation was a transitional one for H1b. There are, however, two important points to note about these arrangements. First, the expectation that Nae' Kha would eventually farm his own fields (which he was determined to do); second, the "non-accountable" nature of labour between the two households where it was provided freely (instead of being on strict reciprocal terms) subject to the exigencies faced by the two households. The farming of independently owned fields is significant because it reflects a general attitude that households should have their own fields. The generally free exchange of labour, on the other hand, reflected the inability of both households to provide all the labour necessary for the cultivation of their own fields. It also shows the importance of primary kin ties and male affinal ties in such "non-accountable" labour exchanges.

In non-agricultural spheres, however, the separation of economic functions and the management of domestic budgets between the two households were decidedly marked. For example, the earnings of the two households from the sale of tea leaves collected in Tamu''s garden were managed independently. Thus, although both households had free access to the garden, the incomes from the sale of leaves were earned according to the labour that each expended instead of being pooled for common use. The use of money incomes were similarly decided upon separately. In other words, as far as cash incomes and expenditures were concerned, the two households operated quite independently. The only exception to this were rice purchases when rice stocks were near depletion in late 1981. Both households contributed to the purchase of rice but there was no strict accounting of their contributions. They also made additional purchases on their own from time to time according to their respective immediate needs.

Case 2: H2, H13a, H13b, H13c

The households which are of immediate interest here are H13a and H13b, but I have included H2 and H13c to illustrate other related features of domestic economic organisation which are not fully apparent from H13a and H13b.

Figure 4.2 The Genealogical Relations between H2, H13a, H13b, and H13c

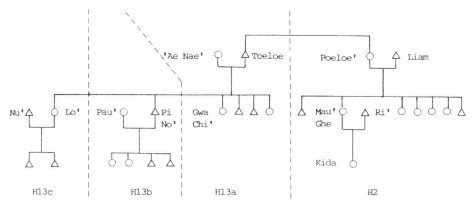

H13a consists of Toeloe, his wife, four children and a grandchild. The grandchild is the daughter of Toeloe's eldest daughter, Gwa Chi', who was not married. There were only three members of the household who were economically active, namely, Toeloe, his wife and Gwa Chi'. Cha Pghe, the eldest after Gwa Chi', was fifteen years old (in 1981) and did a considerable amount of agricultural work but according to technical definitions may not be properly regarded as being part of the labour force.

The household cultivated only swiddens and did not own any wet-rice fields in 1981. A variable cash income was also earned by Toeloe who was Palokhi's blacksmith and gunsmith. The main source of this income came from gunsmithing for which Toeloe had a considerable reputation even beyond Palokhi and, indeed, a great many of his customers were Northern Thai from surrounding settlements. Toeloe, however, was an opium addict and much of this income was spent on opium. Because of his addiction and smithing work, Toeloe was rarely involved in swidden cultivation, his participation being confined more often than not to agrarian rites. Most of the agricultural work was done by his wife, Gwa Chi' and Cha Pghe. At various times, prior to 1981, Toeloe's eldest sons (Nu' and Pi No') who had moved away when they married came to assist in the more labour intensive tasks of swiddening, namely, planting and harvesting.

Early in 1981, however, Pi No' returned to Palokhi with his wife and children from the Flower Plantation of the Royal Forestry Department's Watershed Development Unit 1, where he had been working for about three years.[4] Their intention was to settle permanently in Palokhi. Throughout 1981, they lived in Toeloe's house (their sleeping quarters being the outer verandah) and during this time Pi No' assisted the household in cultivating their swidden. This assistance, however, was only partial because he devoted a considerable amount of time to wage work in the Northern Thai settlement of Ban Mae Lao, the picking and sale of **miang** and tea leaves as well as other forest products. He also used Toeloe's smithy for work of his own of a similar nature such as making and repairing muzzle-loading caplock guns, bush knives, and so on.

For the most part of 1981, Toeloe's family and that of his son formed, for all practical purposes, a single household. This was particularly evident where the consumption of rice was concerned. The two families shared the rice from the previous agricultural season. The harvest from 1980, however, was small (as it was in 1981 as well) because the family had insufficient domestic supplies of labour to farm larger swiddens which would have been more appropriate to their needs. Thus, for most of 1981, they had to rely on rice purchased with money earned in the cash sector. Both families contributed to the purchase of rice which was pooled for common consumption.

Notwithstanding these arrangements in the sharing of rice, certain distinctions were nonetheless made in the management of the domestic budgets of the two families. The incomes earned by them in the cash sector were used to purchase items other than rice on the basis of quite independent decisions. Although these expenditures (on consumer durables, clothing, footwear, and so on) were small, they were distinctly separate reflecting the separate needs of the two families.

Despite the fact that H13a and H13b functioned more or less as a single household, it was clear in the latter part of 1981 that Pi No' had every intention of setting up his own household. He began to open up a plot of wet-rice terraces for his family's use in 1982. It is interesting to note that in doing so, he entered into a specific short-term labour exchange arrangement with Nae' Kha who was also opening a plot of terraces nearby. One reason why he did not seek any assistance from H13a was that the parental household was constrained by limited supplies of domestic labour. An equally important reason was the fact that he and Nae' Kha were in essentially the same situation. Both were able-bodied men who were the only full-time workers in their families; the arrangement, therefore, was to their mutual advantage. It is important point to note, however, that despite their on-going association with their parental households, both were acting to establish an independent subsistence base for themselves.

H13c consists of Nu' and Lo' (whose marriage was regarded as a "crooked" union as discussed in Chapter III) and their two children. In September 1981, they returned to Palokhi from the sub-unit of the Royal Forestry Department where they had eloped, with the intention of settling permanently in the village. Between September 1981 and February 1982 (when Nu' built a house for the family), the couple stayed with Toeloe with Lo' assisting H13a in various agricultural tasks. Nu', on the other hand, occasionally assisted H12, his parental household (see Case 4), but contributed little to the subsistence activities of H13a. Nu', who was an opium addict, spent most of his time picking and selling **miang** in order to earn money for buying opium. Some of his income was spent on the purchase of rice, but the rice was given to his mother in H12 where he took most of his meals. The reason why Nu' and Lo' took their meals in their respective parental homes was simply that H13a had insufficient rice to meet the needs of everyone. After Nu' and his family moved into their new house in 1982, Nu''s declared intention was to cultivate a swidden to meet, if not all, then part of his family's needs for the following year.

The case of H13c is, again, a transitional one but it shows that considerable flexibility is possible within the framework of domestic economic arrangements in Palokhi. The relative poverty of all the three households undoubtedly demanded various accommodations if they were to meet their very minimal consumption requirements in the transitional periods that they were going through. What is important, however, is that such accommodations are possible in the context of Palokhi kinship, familial sociology and their concomitant economic arrangements.

H2 is included, in this case, as an example of how households of siblings tend to assume a high degree of independence in economic functions especially when they are in the later stages of their domestic life cycle. That the the households of the two siblings, Toeloe and Poeloe', were well advanced in their developmental cycle is, of course, evident from the fact that they had married daughters and sons. H2 cultivated swiddens and owned two plots of wet-rice fields and, in 1981, had the largest surpluses from agricultural production. Although Toeloe "borrowed" rice from Poeloe' (which was never repaid) on one occasion in 1981, the two households were for all practical purposes quite independent of each other in subsistence production and other economic activities. H2 was, perhaps, the wealthiest household in Palokhi but there was no feeling of obligation, nor was there any expectation, that the household should assist H13a with rice or labour although Toeloe and Poeloe' were brother and sister.

Case 3: H4, H5, H8, H9, H10

Figure 4.3 The Genealogical Relations between H4, H8, H9, and H10

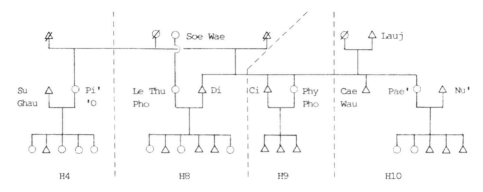

Case 3 illustrates a variety of domestic arrangements which may come into existence over a long period of time. Some of these arrangements are described in the two cases above, but this particular case shows the further directions that they may take as domestic groups proceed further along their developmental cycle. It also illustrates how choice is a factor in whether or not kin links are activated in domestic economic functions as the network of kin becomes extended.

As the genealogical relations between households in the figure above show, Di and Ci, both full brothers, have a half-sister Pi' 'O by the same mother. When their mother and the father of the two brothers died, the three of them went to live with 'Ae', the sister of their mother (see Case 4) at Huai Khon Kha. When Su Ghau married Pi' 'O, in 1955, he moved into 'Ae''s house for a short period of time, after which he, Pi' 'O and Ci moved to Pang Ung where they lived as a single household cultivating only swiddens.

Di later married Le Thu Pho and went to live with her family at Mae Lak. For twelve years, apart from occasional visits, Di had little to do with his brother and half-sister's family. In 1969, Su Ghau, Pi' 'O, their children and Ci settled in Palokhi, followed later by Di and his family. Di's decision to do so was guided by the availability of the wet-rice fields in Palokhi (news of which he had learnt from 'Ae' and Su Ghau), as it was in the case of Su Ghau. By the time Di arrived in Palokhi, both his family and that of Pi' 'O were fully independent and functioned quite autonomously of each other. Although they assisted each other in agricultural tasks, this did not entail cultivating the same fields or the sharing of rice.

Ci married Phy Pho in 1970 and moved into her parents' house, her father (Lauj) being the former headman of Palokhi. When Ci married Phy Pho, her elder sister Pae' was already married to Nu'. Pae' and Nu', therefore, had to move out of Lauj's house into a house of their own, following the custom on the succession of married daughters being co-resident with their parental families.

In the time that Nu' was living in Lauj's house, he assisted Lauj in the cultivation of Lauj's wet-rice field together with Cae Wau, Lauj's son. When he and his family lived on their own, however, he commenced swiddening on his own, although the rice from the two households was occasionally shared in times of need. Lauj, as I noted in Chapter I, was an opium addict and as he became older, eventually lost interest in farming leaving the work to Cae Wau and Ci. The two brothers-in-law, who began smoking opium with Lauj, became addicted in turn, so that the burden of cultivating Lauj's wet-rice field finally fell upon Nu', despite the fact that he was no longer a part of Lauj's household.

When Lauj's wife died in 1979, the family house was destroyed according to custom. Lauj and Cae Wau built a hut for themselves, while Ci (who preferred to disengage himself entirely from farming) built another house for his family. From then on, Ci committed himself to wage work in Northern Thai settlements and at sub-units of the Royal Forestry Department. Lauj and Cae Wau cooked and ate together, drawing upon rice from Lauj's wet-rice field which was stored in Nu''s house.

In early 1981, however, when Nu' built a new house, Lauj and Cae Wau moved into that house and, for all practical purposes lived as dependents of Nu' and his wife. Ci's household was virtually independent although his wife, Phy Pho, often obtained rice from Pae' of which no account was kept.

It will be recalled, from Chapter II, that Thi Pghe of H5 died in 1978 thus leaving behind his aged father-in-law, wife and three young children. As a result of Thi Pghe's death, the family encountered difficulties in cultivating their wet-rice fields primarily because of a shortage of labour and they rented out the field.[5] The mainstay of their subsistence activities was tea and **miang** picking for a Northern Thai from Ban Mae Lao from which they derived a cash as well as rice income to meet their needs. Although they received some assistance within Palokhi, it is interesting to note, however, that this came from Su Ghau (H4) rather than Tamu' (H1a) who was Thi Pghe's brother. The assistance from

Su Ghau consisted of a work arrangement between him and Chi Choe (Thi Pghe's son) in which Chi Choe assisted Su Ghau in working his swidden; in return for this, Chi Choe was allowed to share in part of the harvest from the swidden. While the arrangement was mutually advantageous (though it perhaps worked out rather more in Su Ghau's favour than Chi Choe's), what is significant here is that Tamu' and his family felt no obligation to assist H5. It might be added, on the other hand, that no one in H5 expected H1 to assist them either.

This very clearly illustrates that collateral kin links are, by no means, **necessarily** important in guiding the sociological arrangements in the subsistence activities of related households. Indeed, if anything, it serves to show that very pragmatic — if not calculated — considerations of mutual advantage inform the decisions on the basis of which such arrangements come into being. More generally, it also shows that as households of siblings (or, in this case, siblings and step-siblings) assume a greater autonomy as they get older, this may be matched by other forms of organising subsistence activities which are not predicated on kin links. The possibility of this happening is related, of course, to the growth of the village and hence the availability of a wider range of related and unrelated households for co-operation in which choice then becomes a significant factor.

Figure 4.4 The Genealogical Relations between H11a, H11b, and H12

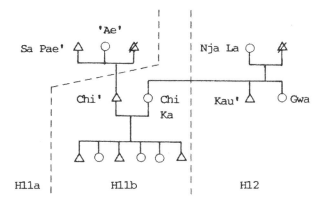

Case 4: H11a, H11b, H12

H11a consists of only two people, a sixty-three year old woman, 'Ae', and her fourth husband, Sa Pae', a Yunnanese Chinese deserter from a Kuomintang garrison in Chiengrai. 'Ae' first settled in Palokhi in 1955 with her second husband. When they came to Palokhi, they bought a wet-rice field which became 'Ae''s when her second husband died. 'Ae' subsequently married Chwi' but they were divorced in 1976, the grounds allegedly being adultery between 'Ae' and Sa Pae'. Sa Pae', who came to Palokhi in 1974, had been taken in by the couple as part of the household which meant, in effect, that they provided him with board and lodging in exchange for help in their fields.

H11b consists of Chi' ('Ae''s only son), his wife Chi Ka and their seven children. H12 (see Case 2) consists of an eighty year old widow Nja La (Chi Ka's mother) and her two unmarried children, Kau' and Gwa.

The association of these households over a period of approximately nineteen years is interesting because it illustrates how the patterns in domestic economic arrangements may change through time, and how general statements about Karen kinship and residential patterns can often disguise the variety, complexity and fluidity in such arrangements among related households.

Chi' married Chi Ka in 1953, when his mother 'Ae' was still living in Huai Sai Luang. He went to live with Chi Ka and her family (at Huai Khon Kha) and, thereafter, had little to do with his mother apart from occasional visits. When Chi Ka's younger sister married, he and Chi Ka set up house of their own and continued to remain in Huai Khon Kha for a number of years after which they moved to various other places. After 'Ae' settled in Palokhi, however, he also moved to Palokhi in 1959 with the intention of opening up wet-rice fields for cultivation.[6] This he failed to do; instead, he cultivated swiddens and assisted 'Ae' and her husbands in working the wet-rice field which was originally acquired by 'Ae' and her second husband, but which became her's on his death.[7] Three years after Chi' moved to Palokhi (that is, in 1962), Nja La, her husband and their four children also settled in Palokhi. This, however, did not affect the arrangements which existed between H11a and H11b which consisted, essentially, of sharing in the cultivation and crops of Chi''s swiddens and 'Ae''s wet-rice field. H12 functioned virtually independently cultivating only swiddens.

The close co-operation between H11a and H11b in agricultural cultivation existed for two main reasons. First, H11a comprised only two people and was therefore unable to provide all the labour in wet-rice cultivation which made assistance necessary. That this was provided by Chi', his wife and two children of working age was, undoubtedly, because of the primary relationship between the two families. Second, the cultivation of fields in Palokhi, whether swiddens or wet-rice terraces, entails a series of ritual performances throughout the agricultural calendar and the role of men in these performances is of primary importance. As Sa Pae' was unfamiliar with these rituals, the responsibility for them devolved on Chi'.[8]

The domestic budgets of H11a and H11b, on the other hand, were managed separately following the pattern common in Palokhi. The separation of the budgets was very clear because the harvests from their fields were more than sufficient to meet their consumption needs.[9] Thus, unlike some of the other households discussed before, H11a and H11b were under no pressure to purchase rice which could be pooled for common consumption following the arrangements in agricultural cultivation.

In terms of the residential patterns associated with marriage and the family sociology of the Palokhi Karen, what is interesting in this case is that customary practice does not preclude an out-married son (and his family) from reestablishing links in subsistence activities with his parental household after being an integral part of his wife's parental household in accordance with the rule on uxorilocal residence at marriage. It is significant because it is not a special case — namely, succession to headmanship — in which there are **institutional** factors at work which require a son and his family to return creating conditions under which co-operation with the parental family might then become a necessity, albeit for an interim period. This is also significant because it once again demonstrates the importance of choice or preference (and their attendant advantages) in how kin links may be activated or ignored in the sharing of economic functions between related households.

Some General Patterns

The case studies discussed above show a great deal of variation in the way in which individual households manage domestic production. Nevertheless, some general patterns may be discerned.

First, an important factor in the variability of domestic economic arrangements is the life cycle of domestic groups and its associated processes of household formation and fission. I have shown in the preceding chapter that the features of household formation and fission in Palokhi are related to the custom of uxorilocal residence at marriage, the belief that a house should not contain more than two married couples (and their offspring), and the succession of married daughters, their spouses and children who are co-resident with their parental families as they get married. In general, the various arrangements in subsistence and other activities between households related by primary kin ties reflect adjustments which are made in response to changes which occur in their composition and residential patterns over time. Accordingly, households as production and consumption units are not organisationally fixed over time; however, at any point in time, they may consist of either stem families or nuclear families.

Second, the rule on uxorilocal residence at marriage by no means precludes the return of sons who have married out. They may, and indeed do, return to set up households of their own. In such circumstances, there exists a certain amount of sharing in agricultural tasks and crops. However, in contrast to married daughters and their families who are co-resident with their parental families, the degree of sharing is more restricted reflecting the primary importance of the household as an integral unit of production and consumption. Furthermore, there is a general expectation that sons (and indeed daughters) and their families who establish separate households should assume responsibility (at least in theory) for their own production and consumption. This is, in fact, an ideal which rarely manifests itself in practice because of the exigencies (for example, limited domestic supplies of labour) often faced by such households. The ideal is also rarely translated into practice because of attachments between such related households. Thus, the economic association between parental households and the separate households of married children is never broken off entirely. When the parents of married siblings are dead, however, there is a greater autonomy in the management of agricultural production among married siblings especially if they have enough children of working age. Nevertheless, it is also possible for brothers-in-law to establish close working relationships especially if their households are marked by limited supplies of labour.

Third, at any given stage of the developmental cycle of domestic groups (whether they consist of stem or nuclear families), the likelihood of related households working together and sharing the returns to work (on a "non-accountable" basis) is greater in agricultural production than non-agricultural production. Indeed, where the management of domestic incomes and expenditures is concerned, such sharing is very limited even within stem family households reflecting the different or specific needs of their constituent units rather than the larger domestic group. In this area of economic activity, the separation is clear with conjugal or nuclear families being the operative socio-economic unit. Exceptions, however, occur. When domestic groups suffer a shortage of rice and need to buy it, their constituent units (that is, nuclear or conjugal families) usually do not maintain strictly separate budgets.

Finally, the kinds of arrangements between related (and unrelated) domestic groups may also be guided by wholly pragmatic considerations which, as we have seen, are by no means unimportant in informing the decisions made by a household to work with a particular household rather than another. In other words, beyond primary kin links (between households), kinship is not necessarily a factor of over-riding importance in determining the way in which households co-operate in subsistence production, nor is it necessarily a significant factor in distribution.

Contractual and Non-contractual Arrangements in the Organisation of Agricultural Production

Apart from the various ways in which domestic production and consumption is organised as described above, the Palokhi Karen recognise a number of arrangements which form a part of the organisation of agricultural production. In general, these arrangements may be distinguished according to whether they are contractual or non-contractual, loosely defined—that is, binding agreements which recognise certain terms or conditions as against informal non-binding agreements, between two or more people. There are, essentially, four kinds of arrangements which may be regarded as contractual: they are "partnerships" and various forms of share-cropping or rent contracts. The only important non-contractual arrangement is co-operative labour exchange.

Partnerships

Partnerships, the most general type of contractual agreement between two or more people, are termed **ma 'au' soekau'**. It literally means "to work-eat in association". **Ma** means "to work" and **'au'** "to eat". **Soekau'** can refer to a companion, an associate or a partner, that is, someone who is rather less than a friend (**ghomau'**). Friends and kin, however, can of course be **soekau'**. In essence, the term **ma 'au' soekau'** describes any binding agreement between two or more people to work together and to share the proceeds of their effort, on the basis of some criterion or principle of equity. More often than not, it relates to agricultural work though it can also be used with respect to non-agricultural income earning activity in which case the term is used rather more loosely.

In 1980–81, there was only one instance of a **ma 'au' soekau'** arrangement in Palokhi. This was the arrangement between Su Ghau (H4) and Chi Choe (H5) described earlier.

Share-cropping

There are three kinds of share-cropping arrangements which the Palokhi Karen distinguish and they are similar to Northern Thai share-cropping arrangements. Indeed, given that these arrangements pertain to the cultivation of wetrice and not swidden farming, it is altogether likely that the arrangements recognised by the Palokhi Karen are derived from Northern Thai practices.

The first kind of share-cropping arrangement is called **ma 'au' pha' phau** which means "to work-eat divided in half". It is similar to the Northern Thai **baeng koeng** or **baeng koeng kan** which means "dividing in half". The contracting parties in such an arrangement would be a cultivator and an owner of a field. As the term implies, payment is made in the form of an equal share in the rice crop. In some cases, there may be additional payments if, for example, the use of a buffalo for ploughing is also made available by the owner of the field. Alternatively, the cultivator may rent the use of a buffalo from someone else, in which case the payment (in rice or cash) would then constitute a separate contractual agreement. In 1980, there was only one case of such a **ma 'au' pha' phau** agreement; it was entered into between Duang (H3) and Chwi' (one of the co-founders of Palokhi along with Tamu') who owned a field in Palokhi and left to settle in Huai Dua in 1974, as discussed in Chapter II. In 1981, Nae' Kha took over the cultivation of the field under a similar arrangement with Chwi'. This particular contract and the consequences of Chwi''s death are discussed in more detail, in the next chapter, in the context of the ownership of land in Palokhi.

The second type of share-cropping arrangement is called **'au' kho pghe** which means "eating the price of the head". It is similar to, and indeed is the literal equivalent of, the Northern Thai **kin kha hua** ("eating the cost of the head"). As with **ma 'au' pha' phau,** rent payments are made in the form of rice. However, the payments are much less with the cultivator retaining more than half of the crop. In 1980 and 1981, there were no **'au' kho pghe** contracts in Palokhi.

The third contractual arrangement is termed **'au' chi' 'a' khloe xi.** The term means "to eat the back of the wetrice field". It is a wholly Karen term but it refers to a practice which is also found among the Northern Thai who call it **syy** or "buying" (Wijeyewardene [1966:48]). The arrangement consists essentially of the sale of use rights to a field for a particular period of time. As the Palokhi Karen conceive it, it is the owner of the field who "eats the back of the field". In Palokhi, there was one **'au' chi' 'a' khloe xi** contract which lasted from 1979 to 1981. In this case, the use rights to a plot of wet-rice terraces (of 0.51 ha) were sold by H5 to a Northern Thai in Ban Mae Lao for a fee of Bht 1,200. Further details of the circumstances surrounding this agreement are discussed in the following chapter in relation to land use, ownership and inheritance in Palokhi.

The various contractual arrangements described above are not commonly practised by the Palokhi Karen. The norm in swidden and wet-rice cultivation is owner-cultivation of fields. One reason for this is that there is no excess capacity in the form of wet-rice land which may, therefore, be rented out to individuals or households which require land. A more important reason, however, is that in general there are sufficient tracts of land in the Huai Thung Choa valley which can be brought under both swidden and wet-rice cultivation thus eliminating the need to rent land. The existence of these contractual arrangements is nevertheless important. It shows that they constitute mechanisms which may be resorted to in the short term, according to the exigencies of the circumstances of households, as a means of meeting their subsistence requirements until a more permanent solution—in the form of ownership of wet-rice land—is found.

It will be noticed that the contracts entered into by the Palokhi Karen happen to involve non-kin. It is worth noting, however, that the Palokhi Karen say that these kinds of contractual arrangements may be entered into by kin and non-kin. In other words, such contractual agreements do not necessarily apply to non-kin only. One area where such contractual agreements between kin are potentially important in Palokhi is the inheritance of wet-rice fields. As I discuss the inheritance of land in the next chapter, it will be sufficient to point out here that the Palokhi Karen say that some of these agreements may be entered into by siblings who inherit wet-rice fields. The reason why inheritance and such agreements are not yet an an issue of major importance in Palokhi lies in the fact that only two of the male heads of households who opened up wet-rice fields have died.

Co-operative Labour Exchange

As with most if not all agrarian societies, there is in Palokhi an informal, non-contractual system for organising agricultural work on the basis of co-operative labour exchange. The underlying principle in this system is reciprocity in the provision of labour. In Palokhi, such work arrangements are called **ma dau' lau (poe') sa'** which may be taken to mean "working together" or "working mutually". The literal translation of this expression is "to work with (our) hearts falling together" where the essential sense of the term is conveyed by **lau sa'**, a phrase that functions as a simulfactive denoting mutual, reciprocal action or common activity.

Co-operative labour exchanges are most commonly found in clearing, planting, weeding, and harvesting in swidden cultivation. In wet-rice farming, it is found in the preparation of fields (ploughing, harrowing and levelling), planting, and harvesting. The main reason why labour exchange usually takes place in these tasks is that they either require large inputs of labour over a short period of time, or because they are tedious, time consuming tasks in which the presence of others helps to reduce the drudgery of the work as in weeding.

An examination of labour expended by Palokhi households on agricultural work and co-operative labour exchange (see Appendix B) reveals some interesting patterns which bear out some of the conclusions from the case studies.

First, the data show very clearly that despite the general principle of reciprocity which guides the exchange of labour there is, nevertheless, an imbalance in the labour supplied and received by all households in both swidden and wet-rice cultivation (see especially Tables B.2 and B.3). Much of the variation in the lack of full reciprocity in labour exchanges may be explained by the operation of contingent factors. These include differentials in the size of swiddens or wet-rice fields which affect the amount of labour required for the performance of related tasks, the size of domestic supplies of labour and domestic dependency ratios, competing demands on labour faced by households in non-agricultural activities, and so on. Other very human considerations also affect the amount of labour which may be contributed by households in co-operative labour exchanges. These include the degree of amity between members of different households, the expectation that good food will be provided for the labour gangs, the presence of marriageable young women who invariably attract a larger number of young men, and so forth.

Second, following some of the patterns discernible in the case studies, households related by collateral kin links by no means consistently work together. Indeed, in some cases, the level of exchange labour is greater between non-related households than that between related households.

The Sociology of Production and Consumption in Palokhi

In examining the social organisation of production and consumption in Palokhi—through the examples of various households as well as general arrangements, both contractual and non-contractual—I wish to establish the importance of four considerations.

First, the operative socio-economic units in Palokhi are households. As we have seen in the last chapter, this follows from the fact that households are constituted according to the operation of the kinship system and, specifically, marriage and customs on residence.

Second, given that the household is the fundamental unit of production and consumption in Palokhi, there are nevertheless a variety of possible socio-economic arrangements within and between households. The significance of this is that kinship does not necessarily provide all the guiding principles in social organisation especially in the area of subsistence production in Palokhi.

Third, the variety of possible socio-economic arrangements show that there is considerable flexibility, in terms of available options, in the organisation of subsistence production in Palokhi. Indeed, adaptability might better describe this essential feature of production and consumption in the community. It is this flexibility or adaptability which allows the Palokhi Karen to maintain a certain level of subsistence production, in the agricultural and non-agricultural sectors of their economy, by which they attempt to meet either part or all of their basic needs.[10]

Fourth, it will be noticed that despite the variety and flexibility in socio-economic arrangements none of these includes an institutionalised system of redistribution. Apart from the contractual arrangements described earlier, most if not all socio-economic arrangements have an **ad hoc** character and they do not, strictly speaking, constitute redistributive mechanisms. This has a direct bearing on the central theme of this study. Domestic groups or households which do not produce enough for their subsistence needs cannot make up these deficits by relying on the "internal" economy of Palokhi. They must seek recourse in an "external" cash or market economy which, for all practical purposes, firmly anchors Palokhi within a network of economic links in the Pa Pae hills which, in turn, is linked to the lowland economy of Chiang Mai. And they do so as independent households.

In sum, therefore, kinship provides the basic organising framework for social organisation. Within this framework, various possibilities are provided for on the basis of kinship relations in some cases, and non-kin relations in others, which enable the Palokhi Karen to organise themselves in subsistence production and consumption. We might say, then, that while kinship structures social organisation in certain ways, it also does not preclude the interplay of other factors through which households seek to meet their basic needs. In Palokhi therefore, social organisation in general, and the organisation of production and consumption in particular, are constituted through the operation of the kinship system and **practical** social relations among households.

In terms of the cultural ideology of the Palokhi Karen, however, there is a specific set of behaviour which links— in the sense of a "relation between relations"—the operation of the kinship system, the household as the fundamental socio-economic unit in the community and the practical relations associated with it, as well as the larger organisation of the community. The behaviour in question is the actual consumption of food, eating, which functions as an operative, symbolic activity that establishes these links through the symbolic meanings it expresses in the contexts of day-to-day household routines and community rituals.

Eating: The Consumption of Food as Practical Symbol and Symbolic Practice

The consumption of food for sustenance forms the most fundamental goal of productive activity in Palokhi. Besides this, or indeed perhaps because of this, eating as an activity and idiom in verbal expressions appears to be a pervasive means of expressing and communicating ideas, concepts and cultural meanings about social relations. Some of these we have already seen.

In Chapter II, for example, I described the Head Rite and its sequel, and showed how the ritual commensalism among the co-founders of Palokhi and the rest of the community may be interpreted as a symbolic expression of certain social and ritual relationships which also involve the Lord of the Water, Lord of the Land. Other examples of the symbolic significance of eating were also described in Chapter III, namely, the joint consumption of a meal by the bride and groom in public view on the final day of marriage ceremonies, followed by the drinking of liquor from a common cup. In the **'au' ma xae** ritual, which is a quintessentially domestic ritual, as discussed in Appendix A, commensalism is the principal ritual activity; along with other considerations, it establishes the cultural meanings of various social relationships. And, in this chapter, we have seen how a number of contractual arrangements are described through the idiom of eating.

These examples are by no means the only ones to be found in Palokhi. There are many others which attest to the pervasiveness and power of eating as a polyvalent idiom in the symbolic representation of a host of cultural meanings in the social life of the Palokhi Karen, ranging from the seemingly trivial to the highly complex and significant.

Not unlike the Northern Thai, the Palokhi Karen often point to the number of times a day that people eat to make distinctions between ethnic groups. Indeed, because they eat three meals a day — as do the Northern Thai — this is taken as an indication of some similarity as against the Lisu, for example, who are said to eat five times a day. Again, similar to the Northern Thai, and a great many other Southeast Asian societies, a commonplace greeting in Palokhi has, as its subject matter, eating. The greeting, which is shared by the Pwo Karen (Hinton [1975:76]), is simply "Have you eaten yet?" (**na 'au' me wi li**). And, if the answer is in the affirmative, the next question could then be "What did you eat with rice?" (**na 'au' me dau' ca' lau**). The response is almost invariably "(I) had rice with pounded chillies" (**'au' me dau' mysa tho**).[11]

In ritual and non-ritual meals where chicken or pork is prepared, children (especially if they are very young) are not permitted to eat parts of the head. The reason given by parents is that the children will go hither and thither, heedless of parental instruction. Or, as we might say it in English, they would become "headstrong". There is, perhaps, another unarticulated reason, namely, that the eating of the head is only appropriate to those who are mature or "old" because they are less vulnerable to the effects of what is consumed. In quite another context, healing rituals in cases of "soul loss" and "spirit invasion" entail the eating of a meal not only by the patient, but by all members of the household as well. The patient, however, is also given lustral water which has been chanted over with prayers or, more properly, spells, thus consuming the restorative power of the spells through the medium of water.

Furthermore, in all important rites which feature commensalism in one form or another, the accompanying ritual texts contain the words "eat" (**'au'**) and "drink" (**'au'**) as a key dyadic set stating explicitly the fact of commensalism which takes place. And, not unlike many societies in which eating is associated with sex (see, for example, Goody [1982: 11]), the Palokhi Karen have a formula for verbal abuse which makes a similar association. It translates as "eat your mother's vagina" (**'au' noe' mo 'a' li**).

As an idiom and activity, eating very clearly has the capacity to express a wide variety of meanings in Palokhi. One of these, of particular relevance to the present discussion, is the "corporateness" of the household and the relations between households which generally make up the community life and organisation of the Palokhi Karen. This is to be found in two contrasting modes of eating behaviour. The first is routine eating behaviour; the second is a generalised commensalism which takes place in one of the most important community rituals in the village, that is, the rites of the New Year (**lyta thau ni sau**).

In analysing the significance of these two modes of behaviour it is necessary to consider commensalism as a form of behaviour which can take place in a variety of contexts (as indeed it does in Palokhi) in which the symbolic meaning of the activity may vary, but which nonetheless possesses some common symbolic property, feature or value. The analysis, in other words, must take into account the fact that eating does indeed occur in different contexts, that there is at least some common meaning attributable to the fact that the activity is the same in different contexts, and that there may also be **other** meanings present which are derived from the particular circumstances of the different situations in which the activity takes place. Thus, although I am specifically interested in interpreting two contrasting modes of eating behaviour in Palokhi — routine domestic commensalism and feasting in the rites of the New Year — the interpretation should nevertheless be generally applicable to other instances of commensalism, some of which have already been described and some of which will be discussed later (see Chapter VI).

The analysis which I present below draws on Kapferer's essay (1979) on ritual as a transformative process which is primarily concerned with the form and organisation of rituals as performances (rather than their content), and how transformations in meaning and action may be effected. In essence, the meaning of a ritual is the product of its context which is composed of its constituent elements (such as objects, actions, symbols and identities) and their particular configuration. Thus any change in the relation between these elements, for example, leads to a change in meaning. Following Grathoff (1970) and Handelman (1979) on the concept of "symbolic types", Kapferer argues that:

> ... specific symbolic elements or forms have properties, often culturally encoded within them, which effect transformations in other symbolic elements and in the organization of the context which they enter. (1979:10)

Such elements or symbolic types, then, have their own internal consistency which may transform the contexts in which they appear, thus, effecting transformations in meaning. Symbolic types also have the property of "summarising" symbols (Ortner [1973]; Kapferer [1979:12]). That is, they can contain aspects of meaning which they carry with them from one context to another.

In terms of the organisation of rituals, symbolic types, furthermore, can be of two kinds. They can themselves be altered as a consequence of the transformations they bring about; or they can remain unaltered despite the changes in meaning that they effect. The former kind are best exemplified in rites of transition, the latter in "affirmatory" rites.

Although Kapferer is essentially concerned with ritual in its "religious" or "sacred" sense as conventionally understood, it is clear that the definitions of "symbolic type" and "context" permit their wider application.[12] Indeed, they must. Symbolic entities and, by implication and extension, the contexts in which they appear are not symbols and not necessarily "ritual" **sui generis.** They are appropriated from the context of everyday life and are, as it were, constructed symbols and situations. Accordingly, a consideration of an entity or element that is symbolic in ritual contexts must require at least some consideration of its relation to what it is when it is not symbolic or when it exists in a non-ritual context. Or as Firth has pointed out in an essay specifically concerned with food symbolism (1973:245–6), it is the conceptualisation of the object in a given relationship that is significant and that where food is concerned, the symbolic and non-symbolic relationships are in fact intertwined.

In more general terms, the critical issue here is whether or not a clear-cut distinction can be established between what is ritual and what is not. As Leach has suggested (1964:12–3), this is not always so easy to determine and a far more useful approach lies in taking the view that human actions may be placed on a continuum ranging from the purely technical to the highly sacred. What is symbolically meaningful and not symbolically meaningful, ritual and non-ritual, can therefore only be determined by a consideration of the objects, elements or entities **and** their contexts simultaneously. It is here that the nature and composition of what constitutes a "symbolic type" become important.

I suggest that as a practical activity, commensalism, may be regarded as a "symbolic type", the typical property of which is the "constitutive" in the sense that social relations are symbolically constituted by it. This is a view of commensalism which is by no means new in anthropology. Commensal behaviour, as it is well-acknowledged in the anthropological literature, symbolically expresses a solidarity, commonality (or, indeed, communality) and shared identity of those who participate in it. Furthermore, I suggest that it is this property of commensalism as a symbolic type which effects transformations in meaning and, at the same time, allows it to remain unaltered despite these changes which it may bring about. In terms of the transformative aspect of ritual, therefore, we may consider commensalism as a symbolic type that transforms the context in which it appears through its "constitutive" property such that the essential meaning of the context lies in the process of the constitution of social relations or identities. The kinds of social relations or identities that are constituted, however, are defined by other elements in the context in which commensalism features. At the same time, the symbolic value of commensalism, in each context, remains the same notwithstanding the transformation in meaning that it brings about. Commensalism, in other words, is essentially "affirmatory" symbolic activity.

Domestic Commensalism in Palokhi

The Palokhi Karen eat three meals a day, and of these meals the early morning and evening meals are consumed in their homes while the mid-day meal is usually

125

consumed in their fields. There is not a great deal of symbolic meaning attaching to the kinds of food that they eat, but there are certainly symbolic aspects to how food is domestically prepared and the utensils which are used for this purpose. Cooking utensils, for example, are used in ways which establish very broad distinctions between food that is cultivated or domesticated and food that is not. The cooking of rice, for example, is done in a pot that is reserved specifically for this function. Similarly, stews consisting of the flesh of domestically reared animals and cultivated crops are cooked in a separate pot. For each kind of pot, there is also a spoon or ladle which can only be used together with it. On the other hand, game must be cooked in a different vessel. The pots and spoons, therefore, are not interchangeable insofar as their uses are concerned. I have also noted in the previous chapter, for example, that the cooking utensils of a married couple are thrown away when spouses are divorced and when families convert to Christianity. Much of the general symbolic significance of food in Palokhi occurs, therefore, in domestic contexts.

It is, however, mundane social behaviour associated with the eating of food at domestic levels that throws into relief the importance of domestic commensalism as a practical symbol through which social relations are expressed. Such behaviour might be dismissed as trivial were it not for the fact that it occurs consistently and is always predictable. It is behaviour of a kind that is so much a part of everyday social life, to which little thought is given, that it eludes explicit exegesis or formulation of its motivation or rationale except within its own frame of reference. For this very reason, however, it is I believe a good example of the kinds of "taken for granted" social interaction or behaviour which constitutes much of the praxis of what we choose to call, by way of abstraction, social organisation — in the same way that we might describe social organisation through an observation of the activities of production and consumption. It is, in other words, yet another aspect of social interaction in which social organisation is, as we might say, "immanent" as praxis.

When the Palokhi Karen eat at home, they almost invariably shut the doors of their houses. In some houses, the meal is eaten from a large, circular wooden tray (made from a cross-section of a tree trunk) which is placed on the floor near the fire-place. Rice is spooned from the cooking pot all around the tray. A dish or two of food accompaniments and chilli relish is placed amidst the rice in the centre of the tray. In other houses, large enamel dishes (purchased from shops) are used instead of the wooden trays. The meal is eaten by members of the household as they squat, or sit, around the tray. They use their fingers to pick up the rice and other food. Soup or gravy is eaten with common spoons shared by all. There is no particular order which dictates the eating of the meal. Where households are small, all members of the family eat together while in the case of large families, household members may be broken up into two groups which eat consecutively because they cannot all sit around the tray.

Domestic commensalism in Palokhi is, by its very nature, clearly "inclusive" and "exclusive" at the same time, for it includes only household members and excludes non-household members. This is, of course, symbolically established by shutting the door of the house, but it is also to be seen in the behaviour of non-household members during meal times. In general, doors are shut only during the night when the household sleeps and during meals. Shut doors, thus, can only have two meanings in Palokhi; outside of sleeping hours, they indicate that a meal is in progress. At such times, it is understood that visits should not be made.

On the other hand, if the Palokhi Karen visit one another, and they then notice that a meal is being prepared or is about to be served, they invariably leave the house and return later when the meal is over. As a matter of courtesy, they are usually asked to stay and eat, but such invitations are always declined (see also Hinton [1975:183]). The implicit rule, therefore, is that the members of a household do not generally eat in other households.

Feasting in the Rites of the New Year

There are a number of important features in the rites of the New Year in Palokhi. Some of these I consider in Chapter VI where I discuss the annual ritual cycle in the community. Here, therefore, I shall consider only the commensalism that takes place in what is the most important ritual in the community.

The New Year celebrations are held over two consecutive days, the first of which is given to final preparations for the feasting that takes place on the second day, and an evening meal eaten only by members of the domestic group. Before this meal is eaten, the oldest married woman in the household performs a "soul calling" (**kau' koela**) ritual in which the souls of all household members are called back to the home. The meal is eaten in much the same way as ordinary meals, the only difference being that a richer repast is prepared in the form of chicken or pork. What marks the eating of this meal from other meals and the annual **'au' ma xae**, however, is the fact that it occurs in the context of the New Year celebrations thus distinguishing it as an activity of special significance to the Palokhi Karen as a community.

On the next day, the household has its early morning meal which is immediately followed by a wrist-tying ceremony for all members of the domestic group. Their wrists are tied by the head of the household and his wife with lengths of cotton yarn. The purpose of the ceremony is to bind the souls of household members to their bodies. Thereafter, members of the household (usually children) go to other houses in the village, beginning with the headman's and that of the elders, inviting the occupants to "come and eat, come and eat". As every household does this, the scene in the village eventually becomes one of people bustling to and fro, either issuing invitations to eat or entering houses for a meal and emerging only to be faced with another barrage of invitations. And so it goes on through the day.

The headman and elders are usually invited together as a group. The reason for this is that when they have finished eating the meal, they are asked to make offerings of rice liquor to the Lord of the Water, Lord of the Land as well as to pray for blessings on the household. They are, in other words, invited as ritual officiants inasmuch as they are members of the community like all others who are invited.

As visitors arrive at each house, food is placed before them in the eating tray for them to eat. They are usually joined by a member of the host family who, under the circumstances, eats as a token gesture. Needless to say, as visitors make their rounds, they too are only able to eat in token fashion. After the meal is eaten, rice liquor is served along with tobacco and fermented tea (**miang**). Feasting in the New Year celebrations of the Palokhi Karen is, to use a more familiar idiom, an "open house" affair.

The Constitutive and Transformative Aspects of Commensalism

It will be apparent from the accounts above where the essential area of contrast lies between routine domestic commensalism and the generalised commensalism of the rites of the New Year. Domestic commensalism is very much confined to members of the household with a corresponding exclusion of non-household members. The commensalism in the rites of the New Year, on the other hand, reverses this norm where the Palokhi Karen eat in every house contrary to everyday practice.

Although everyday household commensalism may not be regarded as a "ritual" activity, its primary significance lies in — to use Firth's phrase — its "conceptualization in a given relationship", that is, as an activity that is associated with, and identifies, those who live, work, and consume the products of their labour together. It is in this relational sense that domestic commensalism may be regarded as "constitutive". But if commensalism is so, at the level of the mundane or quotidian, it is undoubtedly elevated to the symbolic in the meals taken by the domestic group on the evening of the first day and morning of the second day in the New Year celebrations. At this time, the conceptual and relational aspects of domestic commensalism are, quite unambiguously, symbolically "constitutive" of the "corporateness" or solidarity and identity of the domestic group or household.

However, the second day of the celebrations is also given to commensalism as the principal activity of the community as a whole. It is during this generalised commensalism that the activity of eating becomes "transformative" and "constitutive" at the same time. The rites of the New Year effect a transformation in terms of what is being constituted through commensalism in a different context, a context that is now defined by the general participation of all members of the community as opposed to participation in commensalism at the strictly domestic level. Here, it is the "corporateness" of the community in its entirety that is affirmed through commensalism, following that of the domestic group. In other words, the process of transformation lies in the change from the affirmation of domestic group identity to community identity.

This is important for what it reveals of the ideological status of the household or domestic group, both individually and collectively. In strictly practical terms, the household is as we have seen the fundamental operative social and economic unit in Palokhi while general social organisation and the organisation of subsistence production and consumption consist of a variety of arrangements which make up the relations among households. It is, however, the representation of this fact through routine domestic commensalism **and** the generalised commensalism in the rites of the New Year, as symbolic or ritualised activity, which is indicative of the place which the household and general social organisation, effectively, occupy in the cultural ideology of the Palokhi Karen. At a general level, this is consonant with the family sociology of the Palokhi Karen as well as features of the ideology of the kinship system, marriage and residence discussed in the previous chapter. It is also totally consistent with the way in which households function as ritual units in the cultivation of crops (see Chapter VI). Although ideologies, at their most general, do not necessarily consistently reflect practical social arrangements, in Palokhi this is indeed the case. It implies a degree of internal consistency in the cultural ideology of the Palokhi Karen which is relevant to an understanding of the maintenance of a social and cultural order that is distinctively their own. It is this very internal consistency, along with other considerations discussed in the concluding chapter, which ensures a certain continuity in the cultural ideology of the Palokhi Karen if only because there are fewer areas of tension or contradiction which would, ultimately, require resolution thus rendering it open to restructuring or change.

In this chapter, I have attempted to describe the general social organisation of Palokhi in microsociological terms by examining a variety of practical social arrangements in subsistence production which form, in large part, the substantive aspects of this social organisation. I have also attempted to show that the cultural ideology of the Palokhi Karen reflects this organisation in ways which are consistent with other aspects of social organisation, namely, kinship, marriage and residence and that this is effected through commensalism, as practical and symbolic activity, which "summarises" (or abstracts from social reality) the social relations within and among households in which much of social organisation in Palokhi exists as praxis. These considerations are directly relevant to an understanding of the subsistence economy of the Palokhi Karen which I discuss in detail in the next chapter.

ENDNOTES

[1] I have chosen to approach Palokhi social organisation and the organisation of production and consumption through an examination of case studies for a number of reasons. First, it is only through an assessment of the **details** of how the Palokhi Karen actually work out the arrangements in subsistence production that we may then usefully draw conclusions about social organisation in general and about the organisation of production and consumption in particular. Second, I wish to further substantiate as fully as I can, through this micro-sociological approach, my views on kinship expressed in Chapter II: namely, that kinship principles (as they might conventionally be understood) do not necessarily operate independently in determining the particular configurations that characterise various forms of social organisation in Palokhi, beyond domestic group formation and fission. Third, in so doing, it is also my intention to present an alternative interpretation of Karen kinship and social organisation, especially in the domain of economic activities, to that contained in some contemporary anthropological writings on the Karen. A number of these interpretations are, I believe, over-formalised and as such misleading in many respects. Of the Pwo Karen, Hinton says, for example, that

> ... a network of cognatic ties linked all households in the village. It is further useful to regard a community as being composed of three levels of personnel: firstly, a large nucleus of close cognates; secondly, a category of people whose links with the first group were of greater genealogical distance, and third, men and women who had married people from the first or second categories, but who had no cognatic ties with one another, nor with any other village member. (1975:44).

As an attempt to depict social organisation in terms of kinship, there is nothing particularly problematic in this. However, it is in relation to specific sociological arrangements that difficulties arise. Immediately following this account, Hinton says it is noticeable that "the greater an individual's genealogical distance from the cognatic nucleus, the greater his social disadvantage". This, apparently, manifests itself in heavier fines, the inability to influence the opinions of others, and in "obtaining cooperation in the economic sphere". In a more modest description of cooperative labour exchange however, Hinton has this to say:

> No kinship or other principle applied to the recruitment of cooperative work groups. Members of a village community helped one another on an arbitrary basis. Except at planting time, little effort was made to formally coordinate work. As the number of people involved was relatively small, **ad hoc** arrangements sufficed. (1975:153).

As far as this goes, it is true for the Palokhi Karen as it is for the Dong Luang Karen studied by Hinton. While I have no wish to quibble over the facts that Hinton adduces, I would nevertheless claim that Hinton's depiction of Dong Luang social organisation in terms of kinship is clearly inadequate in terms of the different and, indeed, apparently contradictory kinds of behaviour that may take place. The difficulty arises because of an implicit assumption which attributes too much explanatory power to kinship and some notion that the strength of affective sentiments, influence, etc. is inversely proportional to genealogical distance — for that is what Hinton's depiction amounts to. He is not alone in this. Madha asserts that among the Sgaw Karen he studied, "As the degree of kinship-distance increases, loans take on a more business-like aspect" (1980:157). Yet he also tells us in his discussion of sibling ties (which are central to his analysis of social organisation and kinship) that there is considerable variation in the nature of economic arrangements between siblings in the two villages he studied (1980:181–92). Hamilton's discussion of Pwo Karen social organisation represents perhaps the most earnest attempt at a formalised account but it is, in my view, highly unsatisfactory because it raises more questions than it attempts to answer. In his account of kinship, he says:

> An obvious and major function of the kinship network is that of linkage. Through the network individuals are able to interact in predetermined, predictable ways, and the kinship system is extended to Karen who are nonkin in order to allow interaction.

> The network of bilateral kin terms is focused through the recognition of the relationship between a man, a woman, and their children, as well as the surrounding set of relatives of the husband and wife. The bilateral kinship network ... leads ... to a system of filiation, consisting of set statuses with correlative behaviour patterns for structuring relationships ... (1976:97).

The implication here is that interaction is not possible without the kinship system which "predetermines" behaviour and makes it "predictable". This must surely be an overstatement. For one thing, it raises the question as to what exactly is the difference in behaviour between kin and non-kin? Second, the only possible kinds of behaviour which could be spoken of in these terms are, in fact, avoidance and joking relationships (at least in the context of cognatic systems) such as those found in certain societies in Peninsular Malaya (Benjamin [1980]) where certain types of behaviour are deemed appropriate, indeed obligatory, between **specified** kin. Hamilton also sets out what he calls the "social structural organisation of economic activities" in terms of the "subsistence economy", which he says may be called the "kinship economy", and the "market economy". His observations on the former are that

> The kinship economy is based upon cooperation, reciprocity, mutual aid, and sharing within and between Karen social units. Individuals cooperate in fishing endeavours; they help each other in preparing, planting, caring for, and harvesting crops; they go hunting together, and they cooperate in other ways as well. People may or may not share crops equally, but if one family is in need, it may borrow from another family, and return the favour at some later time; in some cases, however, there may be no return at all. This subsistence economy has behaviour patterns based on kin, lineage, friendship, and village relations. There is a discernible structure, with rules, in these economic inter-relations. (1976:195).

It is difficult to see how this can be a "kinship economy" if it has "behaviour patterns" which run the gamut that Hamilton mentions. I might add that his argument that "lineages" exist among the Ban Hong Pwo Karen is far from convincing. They are, if anything, rather like Northern Thai matrilineal descent groups (see Cohen and Wijeyewardene [1984]) constituted solely for ritual purposes. **There** hangs an intriguing anthropological tale but it is best left for discussion elsewhere. Furthermore, it is not at all evident that there is a "discernible structure" nor what the "rules" are. While it is true that Hamilton presents this "kinship economy" as an ideal type of sorts, contrasting with the "market economy", he also claims that actual economic organisation consists of "mixtures of relations and rules between the extremes". But as he does not indicate what this "mixture" specifically involves, the heuristic value of the "kinship economy" is, to say the least, highly doubtful. Hamilton's general sociological observations in fact tell us very little. The central issue in these accounts of Karen social organisation, kinship, and economic activities is whether or not cognatic kinship systems can be talked about in terms of statuses, roles, or indeed some notion of "morality" or an "axiom of amity" (Fortes 1969:231–2) beyond primary kin relationships. The issue is by no means confined to the Karen ethnography but as it concerns questions which lie outside the scope of the present discussion, I shall not, therefore, go into them here. However, I should at least point out that there are a number of papers (most of which are unfortunately as yet unpublished), of considerable importance, which challenge (with, in my opinion, good reason) the kinds of assumptions often found in discussions of Southeast Asian cognatic societies of which those in the Karen case are examples. The first is **Kinship: An Essay in its Logic and Antecedents** by Wijeyewardene (1974), which is very much concerned with theory and addresses a wide range of issues. One of these issues concerns assumptions of the kind mentioned above which Wijeyewardene argues constitute a "sociological fallacy" because, along with other considerations, kin behaviour in cognatic societies cannot be regarded as role behaviour in any formulable sense. Nor can such behaviour necessarily be spoken of in terms of rights and obligations beyond primary kin relations. There are also a series of papers on the prehistory and comparative ethnography and ethnology of Aslian societies in Peninsular Malaya by Benjamin (1980, 1985a, 1985b). One of Benjamin's major arguments is that in these societies (all of which are cognatic), kinship may actually be manipulated, that is employed to establish certain kinds of organisational differences, as part of a process of selective adaptation to, and the creation of, ecological niches. This concerns a particular set of issues which are, quite possibly, related to those which Wijeyewardene deals with briefly in his discussion of the different terminological systems employed by the Eskimo in different contexts (1974:174). As a last comment, it goes without saying that there are different kinds of cognatic systems in so far as their terminologies are concerned. Accordingly, the broad generalisations which have, in some ways, grown uncritically since contemporary rethinking of these systems by Murdock (1960) and Freeman (1958, 1960, 1961) among others, are often of limited value. The point I wish to make in all of this is that there is much that cannot be taken for granted in the analysis of Southeast Asian cognatic systems generally, and Karen kinship specifically. For these reasons, and also because I am of course concerned with somewhat different issues in this thesis, I have chosen to approach the analysis of Palokhi social organisation as I have done here.

[2] The ownership of fields in Palokhi is an interesting and, indeed, important aspect of the cultivation system involving kinship, gender considerations, inheritance as well as certain ritual concepts which are relevant to an understanding of the cultural ideology of the Palokhi Karen where it concerns the use of land. This is discussed in the next chapter.

[3] The ritual considerations concern the ritual ownership of fields as opposed to non-ritual ownership. I discuss the ritual ownership of fields at some length in Chapter VI.

4 The marriage between Pi No' and his wife, it will be recalled, was a "crooked" union as discussed in Chapter III. As the wife, Pau', was living in the Flower Plantation where her father was a wage-worker, Pi No' thus went to live with her according to the custom on uxorilocal residence at marriage once the appropriate rituals had been conducted. After fulfilling the requirement on residence dictated by custom, and after saving up some money, Pi No' decided to return to Palokhi to take up farming because he found the work at the Flower Plantation "not enjoyable" (**toe' my'**).

5 I discuss this rent arrangement as well as some others later in this chapter in the section on contractual and non-contractual arrangements. Further details concerning land transactions in Palokhi may be found in the next chapter.

6 As discussed in Chapter II, a major reason for the migration of households to the Huai Thung Choa valley was the prospect of reclaiming the abandoned Hmong wet-rice fields. Chi''s decision not to cultivate wet-rice fields eventually was partly due to the fact that it was possible for his family to share in the cultivation and the crops of 'Ae''s field. It was also partly because the reclamation of fields required labour inputs which his family could not supply as his children were still young. In short, it was a decision based on several considerations. Nevertheless, this did not prevent Chi' from **claiming** ownership to a number of plots of land although he had no intention to open them up for cultivation. As I discuss in the following chapter, this appears to have been nothing but a scheme to profit from the sale of these plots to subsequent migrants to Palokhi. One reason for this was that Chi' was an opium addict and needed money to buy the drug. The other was that he was, quite simply, an opportunist and a rogue though a likeable one, a fact which the Palokhi Karen recognised and which perhaps explains why he did not earn much opprobrium, at least overtly.

7 The ownership of fields by women is very unusual indeed in Palokhi and this was, in fact, the only case. I discuss the reasons for this in Chapter V.

8 Some of these rituals and the central role of men in their performance are dealt with in Chapter VI where I describe and discuss the cycle of agrarian rites in Palokhi.

9 I might point out here that the harvests from 'Ae''s wet-rice field were far in excess of what was required by her and Sa Pae'. This was not the case with the harvests from Chi''s swidden as his family was large. The fact that there were surpluses from both fields, however, indicates that the deficits in Chi''s household were being made up by rice from 'Ae''s field.

10 That is, where households cannot produce enough for their consumption requirements, they have to obtain rice by other means in the non-agricultural or cash sector. As I show later and in Chapter V, this is done by households on an individual basis. The flexibility or adaptability, in other words, lies in the variety of arrangements which households can enter into either together or on their own in both sectors. It is this which enables them to meet their subsistence requirements.

11 There is, in fact, more to these greetings and they deserve to be examined in their own right. Very briefly, they appear to encode certain ideas about — for lack of a better term — the "offensiveness" of repletion, and suggest a reluctance to establish or assert (however perfunctorily) differences in well-being. I have on a number of occasions heard Palokhi parents check their children who, with little care for social niceties and with obvious relish, informed their friends of some dish of meat which they enjoyed at home in response to precisely these kinds of alimentary greetings. It is true that the Palokhi Karen almost invariably have a chilli-based relish with their rice. However, while it is the commonest fare, it is also the most basic. "Pounded chillies", however, is a generic term which covers a wide variety of preparations which, I might add, by no means compare unfavourably with many equivalent relishes in Northern Thai cuisine. I suspect that an important reason why "pounded chillies" is a standard response is that the Palokhi Karen experience a certain degree of embarrassment in indicating that they have eaten well when they know that others may not have done so. While this makes sense in terms of social interaction, what makes this kind of verbal behaviour culturally significant is that it is yet another manifestation of an ethos of egalitarian social relations. Though there are disparities in wealth among Palokhi households, wealth is generally never ostentatiously displayed. The avoidance of assertions of socio-economic differences is, thus, effected through the use of metaphors of shared poverty — in this case "pounded chillies" — in order to assert that all are equal in what people are compelled to eat in lean times. However, I might add that Palokhi Karen cuisine is not as impoverished as is often believed by the Northern Thai many of whom in fact are convinced that all that the Karen eat is rice and "pounded chillies".

12 Though Kapferer does not deal with this, it is clear from his review of the papers to which his essay is an introduction, that he accepts that the most fundamental definition of a symbol lies in the relationship between a signifier and what is signified and that symbols are not symbolic objects, elements or identities

in themselves. In the same way, rituals are not **ipso facto** rituals but are constructed situations with symbolic meaning.

Chapter V

The Economy of Palokhi: Subsistence in a Regional Context

The Palokhi Karen are best regarded as subsistence-oriented or, to use Penny's term (1969:152), "subsistence-minded" producers. They are subsistence-oriented rather than pure subsistence cultivators in the sense that virtually all productive activity, agricultural as well as non-agricultural, is directed towards the satisfaction of basic food requirements. Of these requirements, the consumption of rice is by far the most important as it is their staple food.

The economy of Palokhi consists of two sectors: an agricultural sector which is based on swiddening and wet-rice cultivation, and a cash or market economy which links Palokhi with other communities in the Pa Pae hills and the lowlands of Chiang Mai. Although the cash sector is not directly concerned with agricultural production, it is nonetheless as important as the agricultural sector in enabling the Palokhi Karen to meet their rice requirements. The reason, as I noted in the introductory chapter, is that agricultural production in Palokhi fails to satisfy these requirements and that the cash sector provides a cash income, from various activities, which allows the Palokhi Karen to purchase rice from stores in Northern Thai settlements to make up the deficits incurred in their dual system of swiddening and wet-rice cultivation.

Notwithstanding this, the Palokhi Karen by and large regard swiddening as the dominant mode of agricultural production in their lives, although they are fully aware that wet-rice cultivation is more productive than swiddening, and that they are dependent on an external, market economy for rice to make up shortfalls in their own agricultural system. This view of swiddening, as I show in the next chapter, is very much an ideological one based on their historical experience. The Palokhi Karen say that the Karen have always practised swiddening and that wet-rice agriculture is but a recent development. Indeed, the relationship between these two systems of rice agriculture is expressed in terms of a metaphor of siblingship: "the swidden is the elder sibling, the wet-rice field is the younger sibling" (**hy' kae' wae, chi' kae' py**).[1]

Although there is an implicit identification of swiddening rice with the Karen as a people, in an ethnohistorical sense, in the way that the Palokhi Karen express these matters, they are really talking about a development in their known history which is ultimately based on Karen migration and occupation of the Mae Muang Luang-Huai Thung Choa area or, as in some instances, other areas prior to settling in the area. This is because virtually all Karen communities in the area and, indeed, elsewhere so far as I have been able to ascertain, have taken up wet-rice agriculture within living memory, or one generation ago. The only exception appears to be the Huai Dua Karen whose agricultural system rests almost exclusively on wet-rice cultivation; but even they acknowledge that this has come about gradually from a time when their parents or grand-parents practised swiddening.

The perception of swiddening as a dominant form of agriculture, at least in Palokhi, is also related to the fact that the religious life of the Palokhi Karen continues to revolve around swidden agriculture, although some swidden rites have been transferred to wet-rice fields along with some wet-rice agricultural rituals which have been adopted from the Northern Thai. Thus, the annual ceremonial cycle in Palokhi remains oriented about rites associated with the growth cycle of swidden rice despite the fact that the agricultural sector is based on the two systems of rice cultivation. The on-going cultivation of swiddens has, in other words, ensured the persistence of religious conceptions and a ritual life which continue to structure the way in which swidden agriculture is perceived. This perception, regardless of the economic realities in Palokhi is an important one. It accounts for, amongst other things, attitudes towards "work" and "wage labour" between which the Palokhi Karen make a certain distinction, and a sense that they live in an agricultural and social context of their own in which their relations with their neighbours, however much determined by economic necessity, are nevertheless peripheral to an essentially "Karen" way of life.

In this chapter, I show how rice production fails to meet the needs of the Palokhi Karen and how they make up their rice deficits by recourse to a cash economy. Because of limitations of space, and because there are general similarities between the agricultural system of the Palokhi Karen and those of other Karen described in existing studies (Hinton [1975], Hamilton [1976], Kunstadter [1978], Madha [1980]) which make an extended description somewhat unnecessary — at least as far as my major argument is concerned — I shall confine my discussion of subsistence agriculture to the following: an overview of the cycle of agricultural activities in Palokhi; land use in swidden and wet-rice cultivation; and an analysis of swidden and wet-rice production in relation to consumption requirements. Further details (for example, perceptions of the nature of work and wage work, the technical aspects of swiddening and wet-rice cultivation, the terminology of wet-rice cultivation in Palokhi Karen which actually consists of Karen-Northern Thai macaronics, and a list of crops grown in Palokhi swiddens) may be found in Appendices C, D, E, and F (see also Rajah [1983]).

In this chapter, however, I also take the opportunity to discuss the relationship between land use, the inheritance of wet-rice fields, and the role of men in these areas because this is of some importance to my argument regarding the cultural ideology of the Palokhi Karen and religion and ritual activities in which men are dominant as managers of the "symbolic capital" of the community.

My discussion of the cash sector, especially the part played by tea and **miang** (fermented tea) in the economic system of the Palokhi Karen is rather more extensive as this is an aspect of Karen economic systems which has not been documented before. A fuller discussion of the cash sector is also necessary as I wish to draw out rather more clearly than I have done in Chapter I, the ways in which the Palokhi Karen are integrated into a larger economic system through their need for rice from external sources.

I leave to the next chapter a discussion of the rites of swidden cultivation which form the major component of the ceremonial system in the community, a system which sustains in large part the cultural ideology of the Palokhi Karen.

The Agricultural Calendar

The rice cultivated in Palokhi swiddens and wet-rice fields grows and matures at different rates because of the different water regimes in these two systems of cultivation. Since the growth cycle of swidden rice is not dependent on the accumulation of water in fields, but on sufficient moisture for seed germination and growth, it is of course planted earlier in the wet season, that is April-May, whereas wet-rice is transplanted only in July. The overall agricultural calendar, however, is based on the longer growth cycle of swidden rice within which the shorter growth cycle of wet-rice is articulated. The year itself has three main seasons — a cool dry season lasting from November to February, a hot dry season which extends from March to April, and a wet season brought about by the south-west monsoons from April or May to October.

The wet season is clearly the most important in swidden cultivation as the rains are necessary for the germination and growth of rice and other crops. The swidden cycle is consequently oriented around this season. Wet-rice cultivation on the other hand, is less dependent on week-by-week rainfall in the wet season, but nevertheless it is not as independent of rainfall as it is in the Chiang Mai plains where extensive irrigation systems fed from up stream storages help to offset the effect of dry spells in the May-October rainy season. At Palokhi, irrigation for wet-rice cultivation is only feasible later in the rainy season (June-July) when the Huai Thung Choa increases in volume. This and the climatic changes in the region also explains why only an annual crop of wet-rice is possible in Palokhi. The occurrence of the wet season, its variable beginning and end is thus the single most important factor in structuring agricultural activities in Palokhi. It also influences the growth cycle of another economically important crop, tea (**Camellia sinensis),** which the Palokhi Karen pick and sell in order to obtain money with which to buy rice to make up shortfalls in their harvests. Tea cropping, however, is subordinate to the cultivation of rice and I therefore leave discussion of it to later in this chapter.

The cultivation of rice in swiddens and wet-rice fields entails several activities, for example the preparation of fields, planting (and transplanting in the case of wet-rice), weeding, reaping, threshing, and storing of the harvest in each agricultural season. A summary of these activities in the agricultural calendar of Palokhi, approximated to the solar calendar, may be found in Table 5.1 and Figure 5.1, while more detailed descriptions may be found in Appendices D, E, and F.

Table 5.1. The Calendar of Agricultural Activities in Palokhi (1980)

Month	Karen Month	Activities in Swidden Cultivation	Activities in Wet-rice Cultivation
January	**La Talae**[*] (6 Jan – 4 Feb)	Transporting and storing of harvest	Transporting and storing of harvest
February	**La Thi Phae'** "The month of clearing" (5 Feb – 5 Mar)	Clearing	
March	**La Thi Khu'** "The month of felling" (6 Mar – 4 Apr)	Clearing, building fire-breaks	
April	**La Soe**[*] (5 Apr – 3 May)	Burning, building field-huts, planting, fencing, setting traps	Opening new terraces
May	**La De' Nja** "The frog, fish month" (4 May – 2 Jun)	Weeding	Opening new terraces, repairing irrigation canals
June	**La Nwi** "The seventh month" (3 Jun – 1 Jul)	Weeding, collecting cultigens	Planting of dry-bed nurseries, building dams, flooding of fields
July	**La Xau'** "The eighth month" (2 Jul – 31 Jul)	Weeding, collecting cultigens	Repairing bunds, ploughing, harrowing, transplanting seedlings
August	**La Ku'**[*] (1 Aug – 29 Aug)	Weeding, collecting	Weeding terraces maintaining irrigation canals and water sluices in terraces
September	**La Ci My** "The month of little rain" (30 Aug – 28 Sep)	Collecting cultigens	Weeding terraces, maintaining irrigation canals and water sluices in terraces
October	**La Ci Cha** "The month of few stars" (29 Sep – 27 Oct)	Reaping, stooking	Breaching dams, draining fields
November	**La Nau** "The month of weeds" (28 Oct – 25 Nov)	Threshing	Reaping, stooking
December	**La Ply** "The month of the dead" (27 Nov – 25 Dec)	Transporting and storing of harvest	Threshing, transporting and storing of harvest

[*] These month names were not given any meanings by the Palokhi Karen.

While the agricultural cycle is dependent on seasonal changes, the calendrical system of the Palokhi Karen itself reflects the importance of swiddening in the past and in their present life. There are also certain significant features about the system and associated beliefs which play a role in determining the availability of labour for agricultural activities in Palokhi. Although the full workings of the Palokhi calendar are still unclear to me, it is nevertheless possible to pick out aspects of the system which are relevant to this discussion.[2]

Figure 5.1 The Cycle of Agricultural Activities in Palokhi

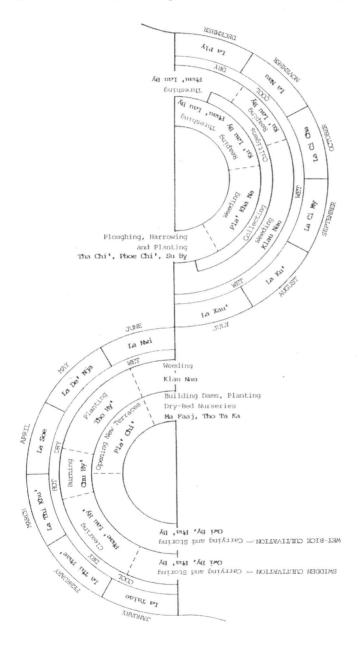

The calendar is a lunar one and the lunar year (**ni**) is divided into twelve months or "moons" (**la**). Each month is reckoned from when the new moon appears, which is spoken of as "the rising of the new moon" (**thau la sau**), to when there is no moon which is called "the moon dies" (**la si**). The month is divided into two halves, corresponding to the waxing and waning phases of the moon, which are marked by the full moon (**la pghe**) and no moon (**la si**). In the first half, the moon is thought to "rise" (**thau**) while in the second half it is thought to "descend" (**lau**). These two terms, **thau** and **lau**, which reflect the cyclic nature of the moon's appearance provide a good indication of how time is conceived of in Palokhi Karen thought, with agricultural processes as a central consideration.

In various agricultural rituals (see Chapter VI), the cyclic nature of agricultural seasons is implicitly described in terms of metaphors of "rising" and "descending". The transition between the old and new agricultural seasons (between wet-rice harvesting in November-January and swidden planting in April-May) is also described in these terms: this transition, which is marked by the rites of the New Year, is called "the descent of the land" (**kau lau we**) and "the rising of the new year" (**thau ni sau**). Although these expressions do not constitute symmetrically paired oppositions, it is significant that the transition from one year to another should be described in terms of two different processes, one of which is seen as a descent while the other is seen as an ascent, or a rising. The first expression has to do with a belief that the land itself "rises" towards the end of the rainy season along with the rice crop. As we have already seen (Chapter III), the growth of the rice crop is in fact described by the same term, **thau**, which is an idiom central to "marriage" and the attainment of adult or reproductive status.

It is clear that in Palokhi usage (and perhaps more generally among the Karen) "rising" is a powerful metaphor with wide applications, all of which are concerned with process or development. After the rainy season, the land "descends". The "rising of the new year", however, parallels the description of the waxing moon, but it is significant that the year is never spoken of as "dying" unlike the moon. The Karen use of **thau** and **lau** in describing temporal phenomena points to a conceptualisation of time in terms of **dynamic** rather than static oppositions. It indicates that (similar to the Head Rite) agricultural seasons, as they are conceived of by the Palokhi Karen, repeat themselves in their constituent features and succeed one another through a renewal according to what might best be described as an idiom of natural "organic" rythms rather than as a simple return to a previous state.

The waxing and waning phases of the moon are again divided in half by the quarter phases of the moon, called **la dau'pha'**. The Palokhi Karen believe that work — which refers essentially to agricultural work — should not be done on

la si, la pghe, and **la dau'pha'**. The prohibition on work is, however, by far the more important on **la si** and **la pghe** than on **la dau'pha**. The reason is that the Palokhi Karen have acquired from the Northern Thai the idea that the eighth and fifteenth days of the two phases of the lunar month (**pet kham**) are Buddhist holy days (**wan sin**), when in fact their own tradition recognises the fifteenth days as significant days through the prohibition on work. The ban on work on the eighth days, therefore, is derived from the Northern Thai. Although this is given some cognisance, the ban on work on the eighth days is not rigidly adhered to, and it explains why the Palokhi Karen (who are not Buddhist in any real sense of the term) do not observe it. The prohibition on work which is more strictly observed on **la si** and **la pghe** is important is determining the amount of labour time available in Palokhi: it means that in each agricultural year, at least 24 days (that is, almost one lunar month) are not given to agricultural work.

Very generally, bans on work in Palokhi appear to be part of the process of the symbolic management of time associated with ritual transformations in individual statuses or social states. For example, when a man and woman marry, they may not work for three days after the completion of their marriage ceremonies. Divorced couples are also not supposed to work for one day after the final **'au' ma xae'** which dissolves their marriage, while households which perform the ritual in the normal course of events do not work on the day or days when the ritual is held. Similarly, when a child is born in the village, all work ceases on that day (Chapter VI, pp. 395–6). Bans on work are thus integral to the way in which time is organised and structured in Palokhi. The bans on work on **la si** and **la pghe** are, similarly, a part of this process. Indeed, there could be no more suitable way of representing time in Palokhi. Work is something that is done "all the time" in the agricultural cycle and its prohibition, particularly when it is enjoined upon all members of the community, could not be more experientially disjunctive of the flow of time and life. The existence of this prohibition at those points of the lunar cycle — the very means by which time is measured — when the moon's phases undergo a change, and the absence of any ritual activity whatsoever (unlike those I have mentioned) suggest that it is indeed a key feature in the representation of time in Palokhi.

I turn now to a brief discussion of the months in the Palokhi calendar in order to show that it is essentially based on the swidden cycle, even though individual households depend heavily on wet-rice cultivation and their earnings from wage labour outside the village.

The first month of the year is called La Talae but the Palokhi Karen were unable to provide a meaning for this month name. Marshall (1922:49–50), who records a similar name (Th' Le), says that it means "the searching month, when the villagers hunt for a new village site". This, however, cannot be the meaning in Palokhi, although the Palokhi Karen do indeed begin their preparations for house-building in this month which corresponds approximately to January. The second and third months, however, offer positive evidence that the calendar is associated with the round of swiddening activities. According to the Palokhi Karen, the second month, La Thi Phae', is "the month of clearing" (which Marshall also claims is the meaning of this month), while the third is called La Khu' which means "the month of chopping" or "the month of felling". These two months correspond roughly to February and March when the Palokhi Karen do, in fact, commence clearing their swiddens. The remaining months of the year do not, however, pertain to swiddening activities and appear to describe seasonal phenomena. The month La De' Nja (May-June), for instance, is said to be "the frog, fish month" because they abound at this time of the year, following the onset of the rains which usually appear in mid-April. Marshall, however, who gives the same month name says that it means "the lily month, when the wild lilies bloom" but this is a meaning which the Palokhi Karen do not appear to have any knowledge of. The months which fall roughly in September and October are named La Ci My and La Ci Cha and are said to mean "the month of little rain" and "the month of few stars" respectively. The latter has the same meaning as that given by Marshall, while the former according to Marshall means "the month of a little sunshine, when after the heaviest rain there is a little fair weather". "Little sun" is, in fact, the literal meaning of the month name, but the Palokhi rendering of this name derives from a folk etymology relying upon the expression for rain **my kho chu**, which means "the sky (literally, "the sun's head") rains". La Nau (October-November) contains an oblique reference to the final stages in the cycle of swidden cultivation, according to Palokhi explanations; it means "the month of weeds" which begin to appear in swiddens once the rice has been reaped.

Swidden Agriculture: Land Use

The systems of land use and rights in the Karen communities described by Kunstadter (1978), Hinton (1975) and Madha (1980) all share certain common features. The most important are fallow cycles, ranging from four to ten years (or slightly more), which are closely observed, and usufructuary rights to swiddens and fallow swiddens which are inalienable and inheritable but which may be voluntarily transferred from an owner (or household head) to another household by surrendering the rights, or by sale. Both these features are essentially mechanisms which regulate access to forest resources for swiddening purposes in conditions which are characterised by ecological deterioration as a result of population increases.

In Palokhi, however, neither of these features exist as part of a system of land use and rights regulating access to forests and swidden land. Because of the generally stable ecological conditions in the Huai Thung Choa valley and the relative abundance of forests, there are few, if any, ecological constraints which would demand some form of regulation of access to resources. Furthermore, although the population of Palokhi has increased steadily since the founding of the settlement, population growth has yet to reach a level where the resources of the Huai Thung Choa valley would be inadequate for the swiddening needs of the Palokhi Karen. Another reason why ecological conditions have tended to remain favourable and, indeed, improve over the last ten years (Prayad and Chapman [1983]), is because the Palokhi Karen have diversified their resource base by taking up wet-rice cultivation thus reducing pressure on the forests of the Huai Thung Choa valley as a resource for swidden cultivation. All these factors explain the absence of institutionalised regulation of access to land for swiddening in the form of a thorough-going system of land use and rights in Palokhi. I might add, however, that the Palokhi Karen are not altogether unfamiliar with land use-rights systems having themselves migrated to Palokhi from areas where there were shortages of swiddening land, as I noted in Chapter II.

Swidden sites are selected freely by individual households — except when, of course, households may have decided to swidden a particular area without knowing that some other household had already chosen the same location. This, however, is a very rare occurrence because households in Palokhi are usually well-informed about such matters. Information about site selection is not made known through formal or institutionalised means such as "meetings of elders" and so on; it is made known in the course of conversation in the day or, more usually, in the evenings after meals when the Palokhi Karen visit one another for pleasure and to organise labour for some task or other. Where use rights are concerned, households retain residual rights to swiddens which they have cultivated before but this takes the form of having access to some of the cultigens which continue to grow when the swiddens are left fallow and it is an access that is by no means restricted to others in most instances. Because swidden land is readily available, households for all practical purposes do not hold on to usufructuary rights to fallow swiddens.

The existence of ample forest reserves for swiddening in the Huai Thung Choa valley has two important implications for an understanding of swidden production in Palokhi. First, the fallow periods of cultivated land are very long. Many households in Palokhi have never returned to swiddens which they previously cultivated. In some cases, a few households have cultivated land previously swiddened by other households, but this has been the exception rather than the rule. The shortest fallow period in these isolated cases, reported by the Palokhi Karen, is twelve years. In one highly exceptional case, one household (H2) cultivated a swidden in 1981 which it had cultivated in 1980 although the members of the household were fully aware of the fact that the rice harvest in 1981 would be drastically smaller than that in 1980. The reason why they did so was because they had considerable surpluses from the 1980 harvest and wished to take advantage of this by committing a greater proportion of their labour to opening up an additional plot of rice terraces. They expected that the previous year's surpluses and the harvest from the additional plot would offset the decline in swidden production for the year which, as it turned out, proved to be the case.

The second important implication is that shortfalls in rice production in Palokhi are not associated with poor swiddening conditions in the form of short fallow cycles along with low levels of organic fertilisers which are the result of burning regenerated forest cover with a low biomass. The shortfalls are associated with insufficient domestic supplies of labour for a more extensive cultivation of rice to meet the needs of a relatively larger non-economically active population. In short, rice deficits in swidden (and wet-rice) cultivation are related to the generally high dependency ratios of households resulting from the fairly rapid increase in the population of Palokhi since it was first settled.

Wet-rice Agriculture: Land Use, Inheritance, and the "Management" of Agricultural Land

The history of wet-rice agriculture in Palokhi, although a short one, is nonetheless interesting from several points of view. Palokhi Karen entry into wet-rice cultivation may be regarded as pioneer activity of sorts because they had not practised this system of rice cultivation before, although they were not unfamiliar with the general techniques and principles of the system, having come from villages which in some cases did have such a system of cultivation. The acquisition of wet-rice terraces, by the Palokhi Karen, was not always by means of clearing the vegetation which had grown over the fields abandoned by the Hmong. In certain instances, the Palokhi Karen actually purchased the fields, fully or partially cleared by Northern Thai who had preceded them or from Karen who had done so but who could not cultivate all the plots of terraces which they had laid claim to. Entry into wet-rice cultivation has also meant the development of new systems of land use and tenure which are significantly different from that in swidden agriculture. It has also resulted in the gradual evolution of an inheritance system which is still in the process of working itself out, with the death of a few men who initially laid claim to the Hmong terraces. Wet-rice cultivation has also led to an elaboration of the ritual life of the Palokhi Karen, as I noted before, and this has taken the form of adapting some swidden rituals to the wet-rice cycle, and adopting some Northern Thai rituals wholesale along with some agricultural techniques learnt from the Northern Thai.

Land use

The history of wet-rice cultivation in Palokhi is best traced through an examination of the ways in which the abandoned Hmong terraces have been acquired and brought under cultivation as well as the numerous transactions in these terraces that have taken place.

The original means by which these terraces were reclaimed for cultivation involved clearing the secondary growth in the fields, burning the slashed vegetation after it had dried, and hoeing out the terraces again. It is a method which the Palokhi Karen still use in opening up new terraces. Because the terraces were cut before, the work of reclamation is less onerous than the opening up of terraces from the forest which some Palokhi households are, in fact, now doing as the last Hmong terraces have all been reclaimed. As the accompanying table (Table 5.2) shows, the Palokhi Karen were preceded by two Northern Thai households and one Burmese household in the reclamation of the wet-rice plots. Subsequent in-migration of Karen and the departure of the Northern Thai and Burmese households changed the pattern of land acquisition somewhat with the Karen either reclaiming the Hmong terraces or purchasing them.[3] Purchases have been made from those who had opened up the terraces (partially or fully) for cultivation or, as it happened in some cases, from those who laid claim to plots of land but did not clear these plots for cultivation. The Palokhi Karen who purchased wet-rice fields have done so either from non-Karen who had preceded them in the Huai Thung Choa valley, or from Karen who for one reason or another left Palokhi after reclaiming, or purchasing, plots of wet-rice fields. The nature of purchases of wet-rice fields have consisted of various arrangements ranging from straight-forward cash payments to payments in kind (notably in buffaloes, the largest form of capital in Palokhi after, of course, wet-rice fields) which are essentially exchange transactions, to share-cropping, that is, rice payments, or a combination of share-cropping and cash payments. As the details of the various forms of land acquisition for the purpose of wet-rice farming are presented in the table, I shall therefore confine my discussion here to drawing out the more significant aspects of the process as it has taken place in Palokhi.

Table 5.2. Land Transactions in Palokhi (c. 1950–1981)

Plot	Area[*]	Year	Nature of Transactions and Principals[**]	Terms[***]
A	2	c.1950	Di Wo(NT) reclaimed	
		1953	Di Wo(NT) sold to Lauj	Half-share of first year's harvest + Bht 800
B	4	c.1951	Mauchwaelu(B) reclaimed partially	
		1953	Mauchwaelu(B) sold to Lauj	1 buffalo (NA)
		1955	Lauj reclaimed further	
		1965	Lauj sold to Kasa	1 buffalo (Bht 1,500)
		1975	Kasa sold to Di	Bht 1,500
B1	1	1981	Di opened	
C	2	1952	Taa 'Yyng(NT) reclaimed partially	
		1954	Taa 'Yyng(NT) left unused	
		1960	Taa 'Yyng(NT) sold to Liam	Half-share of first year's harvest + Bht 640
C1	0.5	1981	Liam opened	
D	6	1952	Lu Sa reclaimed partially	
		1962	Lu Sa sold to Kasa	Bht 1,200
		1971	Kasa died; inherited by 'Ae'	
E	2	1953	Nila Phy reclaimed	
		1968	Nila Phy sold to Puu Taa(NT)	4 **taaj** unhusked rice + Bht 200
		1972	Puu Taa(NT) sold to Chwi'	2 buffaloes (Bht 3,000)
		1974–77	Chwi' leased to Taaj(NT)	As payment for re-building an irrigation system (including a wooden aqueduct) for the field
		1978	Chwi' leased to Soet(NT)	Share-cropping
		1979	Chwi' let out to step-son (Chi')	Share in harvest
		1980	Chwi' leased to Duang	50 **pip** unhusked rice
		1981	Chwi' leased to Nae' Kha	50 **pip** unhusked rice
			Chwi' died; plot inherited by wife and son in Huai Dua and made over to Nae' Kha	Exchanged for a plot owned by Nae' Kha in Huai Dua
F	2	1954	Tamu' reclaimed	
G	5	c.1950	NT reclaimed partially	
		1955	NT abandoned	
		1965	Mauchwaelu(B) reclaimed partially	
		1972	Mauchwaelu(B) sold to Thi Pghe	Bht 1,500
		1978	Thi Pghe died; inherited by wife and children	
		1979–81	Leased to Taan(NT)	Bht 1,200
		1980–81	Taan(NT) sub-let to Chwi	Bht 800
H	2	1961	Lu Sa reclaimed	
		1977	Lu Sa died; inherited by wife and children	
I	6	1968	Taa 'Yyng(NT) reclaimed partially	
		1971	Taa 'Yyng(NT) sold to Puu Taa(NT)	NA
		1972–79	Puu Taa(NT) leased to various NT	Share-cropping
		1980	Puu Taa(NT) sold to Kino	Bht 20,000 — inclusive of price of **miang** gardens and a house also purchased by Kino
J	2	1969	Chi' claimed; "sold" to Toeloe	Bht 60
		1973	Chi' sold to NT	Bht 800
		1980	NT sold to La Zi	Bht 3,025

K	4	1971	Chwi' reclaimed partially	
		1972	Chwi' sold to Duang	Bht 2,000
K1	2	1979	Duang opened	
L	2	1974	Chi' claimed; sold to Su Ghau	Bht 1,600
M	3	1979	Chi' claimed; sold to Thi'	Bht 1,800
N	2	1979	Chi' claimed; acquired by Thaun(NT)	Nil
O	1	1981	Nae' Kha opened	
P	2	1980	Duang claimed	
		1981	Duang relinquished claim; turned over to Pi No'	Nil

' This is given in Thai units of measurement, that is, **raj** (1 **raj** = 0.16 ha), and the figures were obtained from the present owners of the fields. The figures in this column tally with those stated in receipts held by the owners for a tax (**phasii bamrung thaung thii 6**) paid by them (see text). These are estimates declared by the owners themselves as no cadastral surveys were conducted by the Department of Lands. More accurate measurements of the areas of these plots are given in Table 5.3 of this chapter where I discuss returns to land and labour in Palokhi.

" The initials in brackets after the names that appear in this column indicate non-Karen owners: NT — Northern Thai; B — Burmese. All last named owners are Palokhi Karen with the exception of Kino, a Karen merchant resident in the large Northern Thai settlement of Ban Pa Pae, and Thaun, a Northern Thai living in the village of Ban Mae Lao.

" As discussed in Chapter IV, there are various share-cropping arrangements which are recognised by the Palokhi Karen and they are derived from the Northern Thai. The cash transactions are given according to their value when the transactions took place. The money value of buffaloes (in brackets), however, are given in terms of 1980–81 prices prevailing in Palokhi and Northern Thai villages in the area which would be, roughly, twice that in the years 1965–68. The rice measures **taaj** and **pip**, are Northern Thai units which the Palokhi Karen have adopted from the Northern Thai. A **taaj** is a jute sack (also known as **kasaub**) and 1 **taaj** is equivalent to 6 **pip** (which is otherwise called **taang**). In the highlands of Northern Thailand, 1 **pip** or **taang** is, usually, eqivalent to 22 litres rather than 20 litres as in the lowlands (Thannarong, **et al.**, n.d.). The **pip** or **taang** actually refers to the large tins in which kerosene is commercially sold. It is now not uncommon, however, to find **pip** or **taang** defined in terms of 20 litres. In the Pa Pae hills area and the Mae Muang Luang-Huai Thung Choa area a **pip** is generally equivalent to 22 litres.

Figure 5.2 Sketch map showing Palokhi Karen Wet-rice Fields and Swiddens (1981) in the Huai Thung Choa Valley nearest the village

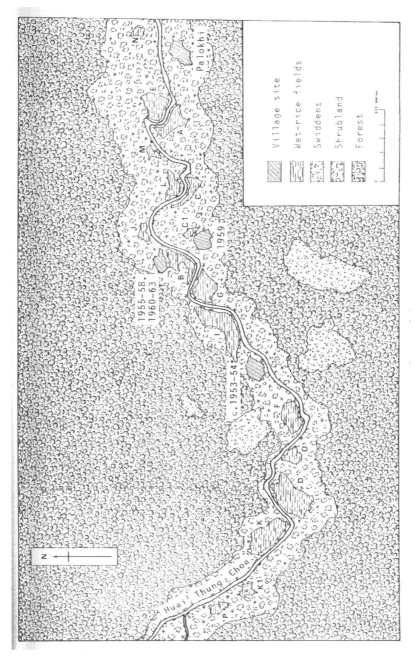

Note: About one third of the area used for swiddens lay further from the village.

Perhaps the most immediately obvious features of the general pattern of land acquisition in Palokhi are the increase in ownership of fields by the Karen, and the recurrent presence of Northern Thai in reclaiming and cultivating fields.[4] It is clear that as the Karen migrated into the Huai Thung Choa valley, they actively opened up wet-rice fields in the area. This, however, was a gradual process in which the fields (where they were reclaimed or purchased, partially cleared, by the Karen) were brought under cultivation through small increments, during which time swidden cultivation was also practised just as it is up the present time. It should also be noted that not all the fields that were brought under cultivation in this manner were abandoned Hmong wet-rice fields; plots B1, C1, J, L, M, N, O and P were all cleared from the forest along the banks of the Huai Thung Choa. In other words, wet-rice cultivation through the years has now reached a stage when wholly new wet-rice terraces are being cut, and it is a process that will continue into the future as several households owning these new plots intend to do so in order to enlarge their fields. It may be noted, too, that in some instances, Karen families on moving into the area tended to "over claim" fields by acquiring more than they could cultivate with their domestic supplies of labour. As we have seen (Chapter II), most of the families that migrated to Palokhi, especially in the early part of the settlement's history, were all young families with high dependency ratios. This was the case, for example, with plot B purchased by Lauy from Mauchwaelu in 1953. This also happened with plots B and D where D was worked, while B was left virtually uncultivated. The same happened in the case of plots E and K although under slightly different circumstances. Chwi' acquired these plots when he was married to 'Ae' who owned D which was one of the largest plots in Palokhi, and which was able to support them to a large extent. The ownership of wet-rice fields by women is highly exceptional in the village (for reasons which I discuss later) and this was the only case. The plot was inherited by 'Ae' when her first husband, Kasa, died (see p. 344, n. 11). As can be seen, these "excess" plots were eventually disposed of by sale (the normal pattern of land transfers involving Karen principals) with Lauy selling plot B to Kasa, and Kasa selling it subsequently to Di, while Chwi' sold plot K to Duang.

The transactions involving plot E, however, are unusual in that they entailed lease which is not typical of Palokhi land transactions in general. This was because of Chwi''s special situation. As I mentioned in the preceding chapter, Chwi' and 'Ae' were divorced in 1976. By that time, Chwi' had already leased out the plot to Taay for the period 1974–77 having found the labour commitments in 'Ae''s field too great to allow him to also cultivate plot E as well. Although this is an exceptional occurrence in Palokhi, nevertheless, it indicates that it is only those households which already own sufficient wet-rice fields which can acquire more. When Chwi' left Palokhi for Huai Dua after the divorce, he continued to lease out the field as an absentee landlord as a means of obtaining rice to supplement the rice from a wet-rice field which he acquired there.

The transactions involving plots J, L, M and N however, do not represent "over claiming". They were all schemes thought up by Chi' (the son of 'Ae') who was an opium addict, to obtain money in order to support his habit. None of these plots were actually cleared for cultivation at the time of sale. They were merely claimed by Chi' who then sold them off when other Karen arrived in Palokhi and wanted to acquire wet-rice fields.

Nevertheless, this reveals an important aspect of land acquisition in Palokhi which characterises the acquisition of land by other Karen in Palokhi: the fact of claim immediately confers rights to fields.

This explains why Su Ghau and Thi', for instance, who were vaguely aware that they were probably being taken advantage of, nevertheless, parted with their money.[5] The only case of a dispute over land in Palokhi, however, concerns plot J. According to Toeloe, Chi' agreed to sell the plot to him for Bht 60, but Chi' claimed that he was only renting it out to Toeloe. Toeloe did pay Chi' the money, and opened up a small part of the plot for cultivation. A few years later, however, Chi' arranged to sell the plot to a Northern Thai of his own accord. When Toeloe learned of this, he attempted to stop the sale of the plot but the Northern Thai was not prepared to forego the use of the land. Eventually, the Northern Thai paid the money to Toeloe instead of Chi' and the matter was left at that.[6] Where plot N is concerned, however, Thaun a Northern Thai from the village of Ban Mae Lao was not convinced that Chi' had any rights to the plot at all, despite Chi''s insistence to the contrary. After several attempts to induce Thaun to pay him something for the plot, Chi' eventually gave up all hope of obtaining money from Thaun, who began cultivating the plot in 1981.

The Northern Thai (and Burmese) presence in the Huai Thung Choa valley is to be explained, according to Palokhi Karen accounts, by the fact that they, like the Palokhi Karen, were attracted by the prospects of acquiring wet-rice fields with the advantage of bringing them under cultivation with relatively low inputs of labour. Yet, the Northern Thai presence has not been a permanent one. With the exception of the two Northern Thai and Burmese cultivators who were actually resident in the area in the early fifties, all the Northern Thai who owned, or leased, wet-rice fields in Palokhi (that is, from 1968 onwards) only stayed to cultivate these fields during the wet season. So while they were interested in cultivating the wet-rice fields in Palokhi, nevertheless they were not interested in settling in the area, preferring to remain in their own settlements (Ban Pha Taek and Ban Mae Lao) along the Mae Malai-Pai road and cultivating these fields on a part-time basis. With the exception of Taan, who owned a small plot of terraces in Ban Tung Choa (the Northern Thai village nearest Palokhi), and Puu Taa a merchant in the village of Ban Mae Lao, all the other Northern Thai are said by the Palokhi Karen to have been landless in their own settlements.

Why, then, did they not settle in the Huai Thung Choa valley? I doubt very much if the reason is that they were displaced and later pre-empted by Karen in-migration as Karen movement into the area was in small numbers and then again only gradually, as I have shown in Chapter II. The reason is most likely to be found in Northern Thai attitudes towards the habitation of forests and nature. The Northern Thai, as Davis explains (1984:79–85), view the forest as being outside of "civilisation", the epitome of which is the city, an extremely important feature in their cultural topography. In between are human settlements which are regarded as being more, or less, civilised according to their proximity to cities or roads which are the evidence of civilisation. In these terms, the Huai Thung Choa, at least from its middle section upwards, would most certainly be beyond the pale as far as the Northern Thai are concerned and it would account for their reluctance to settle in the area.

Nonetheless the Northern Thai presence in the valley is significant because it provides some indication of what socio-economic conditions were probably like in Northern Thai communities in the wider area. The fact that most of them who acquired land were landless suggests that even in their own communities resources were relatively scarce. By this, I am not however referring to a scarcity resulting from environmental deterioration.

Although some Northern Thai in the area do practise swiddening (for example, around Mae Lao), most of them seem to prefer wet-rice cultivation. In the Pa Pae hills, however, land suitable for such cultivation occurs in small pockets in little stream valleys such as the Huai Thung Choa. With the gradual increase in Northern Thai populations in the area, as a result of upland migration and natural growth, and with the Karen, and even Hmong in some cases (see Cooper [1984:77]), turning increasingly to wet-rice cultivation, there can be little doubt that land for wet-rice cultivation was gradually becoming scarce from the Northern Thai point of view. It is altogether likely that the number of Northern Thai not engaged in rice cultivation has been increasing despite the fact that the Northern Thai have migrated upland in order to seek out opportunities for wet-rice farming. A good indication of the availability of Northern Thai for labour employment may be seen in Kunzel's study (1983) which shows relatively large numbers of Northern Thai being employed by units of the Royal Forestry Department compared to the Karen and Lisu in the Mae Muang Luang-Huai Thung Choa area. Similar reasons very probably account for the recurrent presence of the Northern Thai in the Huai Thung Choa valley: apart from cultural attitudes which would explain why they did not (and still do not) settle there, their off-and-on presence is related to alternative economic opportunities elsewhere, even before the units of the Royal Forestry Department offered employment for the surplus labour in Northern Thai settlements.

There is one other point to note about the presence of Northern Thai in the Huai Thung Choa valley. Northern Thai contribution to the development of Karen wet-rice farming systems in the form of irrigation technology has been widely reported (see, for example, Iijima [1979:104]; Hinton [1975:122]), although in at least one case the Lua' have also assisted in the process (Kunstadter [1978:92]). In Palokhi, however, this has not been strictly the case because when the Palokhi Karen arrived and began to cultivate wet-rice fields, they were already familiar with the methods of irrigating wet-rice fields by building dams, irrigation canals, and so on. In a more general, historical sense however there is no doubt that the original source of this technology has been the Northern Thai. The terminology of wet-rice cultivation in Palokhi is essentially Northern Thai (see Appendix F), as is the case with the Pwo Karen studied by Hinton.

An important feature of the various transactions that have taken place from 1950–81 is the increasing costs of wet-rice fields. Although the increases have not been regular, the general trend has been for the price of wet-rice fields to increase over time. There are two reasons for this. First, the increases, and their irregularity, reflect the cost of labour in bringing the fields under cultivation through reclamation. Thus, the prices of fields have increased as the fields were progressively cleared. In other words, the fields have become more valuable according to the amount of labour put in to make them cultivable. The second reason has to do, of course, with general inflationary trends in the wider economy particularly with the construction of the Mae Taeng-Pai road which reached Ban Mae Lao in 1980.

It is also worth noting, in connection with the terms of transactions, that cash payments have played a part from the time when the first Karen settlers arrived, with the exception of the payments in rice and buffaloes. The significance of this is clear: the Palokhi Karen are no strangers to a cash economy and were able to raise to some extent the cash necessary to purchase land from their Northern Thai, Burmese and, subsequently, Karen predecessors. The cash payments, however, were rarely made in one transfer. In most cases, payments were made in instalments because insufficient cash was available. Indeed, the sharecropping arrangements that also include cash payments, and the payments in the form of buffaloes, all represent negotiated settlements because of insufficient cash. So, although the Palokhi Karen were no strangers to a cash economy they, nevertheless, lacked large supplies of cash to handle transactions which require it. This is still a feature of the economy of Palokhi.

This brings us to a consideration of land tenure and ownership in Palokhi. We have seen that ownership in its most general sense is established by the mere fact of claim. The claim to land for wet-rice cultivation is essentially no different from the claim to land for swiddening. As far as the Palokhi Karen are concerned, claims to land confer full rights of ownership and disposal as long as one wishes to use the land.[7] There is, however, one obvious difference between ownership of land for swiddening and land for wet-rice cultivation. While land, in general, is a "free good" in both cases, the ownership of swiddens is relinquished after cultivation because of the availability of forests for further cultivation (see also Grandstaff [1976:157]), whereas this is not the case with land for wet-rice cultivation because the land may be re-used continuously, so to speak.

From a Palokhi perspective, we might say that the ownership of wet-rice land is the possession of usufructuary rights held in perpetuity as it were. From this point of view, however, the ownership of land for wet-rice cultivation is clearly an important one in terms of the ownership of personal property which is the only other kind of ownership recognised in Palokhi and this is the reason why land is transacted in the way it is, that is, by being bought and sold. When such land is claimed, cleared and cultivated it is withdrawn from the pool of land available to others in the community "permanently" unlike swiddening land which is withdrawn only for a year although, effectively, this would be for as long as it takes for the forest to regenerate sufficiently for swiddening to be viable again. In **principle**, therefore, ownership in a Karen context means absolute rights of use which may be voluntarily deferred, transfered or relinquished and it underlies all forms of land rights and tenure whether this concerns access to swiddens in ecologically degraded areas, ecologically favourable areas (such as the Huai Thung Choa valley), or wet-rice fields.

Legally, however, the Palokhi Karen do not in fact own or even possess their wet-rice fields. Under the Land Code which came into effect on 1 December 1954, with the Promulgation of Land Code Act B.E. 2947, a distinction now exists between land ownership and land possession.[8] The former is recognised by a document of title (**canood**) which includes a land title deed with a map, a pre-emption title deed, and a pre-emption certificate (**baj caung**). Land possession, on the other hand, is recognised by the pre-emption certificate which is an "authorization of temporary occupation of land". There is also a "certificate of use" in addition to these two documents which is merely a document by a "competent official certifying that land has already been put to use". The Palokhi Karen possess none of these certificates or documents. All that they have are receipts acknowledging that they have paid a tax, the **phasii bamrung thaungthii 6** which is a "tax for maintaining the upkeep of a locality no. 6", similar to a conservancy fee. It does not specify the nature of the land or the use to which it is put.[9] The tax is assessed at Bht 5 per **raj** and was first levied in 1977 when officials from the Mae Taeng District Office came to Pa Pae to register people in the area for the purposes of issuing them with identity cards. As far as the Palokhi Karen are concerned, however, they believe that the tax is paid specifically for their wet-rice fields. Indeed, some of them believe that these receipts, which they are instructed to "keep safely", indicate that they own their fields. Others, however, are vaguely aware that the receipts do not do this but they believe that eventually they will be given documents which will certify ownership of their fields.

Although they are ignorant of the complexities surrounding the legal ownership of land, nevertheless, the Palokhi Karen are conscious of the importance of having their rights to wet-rice fields officially recognised and they are very conscientious indeed when it comes to paying the tax. They are also extremely concerned about having any land transfers officially witnessed. Given, however, the fact that in the eyes of the law they are only occupants of land who do not even possess pre-emption certificates or certificates of use, this means that the land transfers and transactions in Palokhi have no legal status whatsoever. Nevertheless, they make attempts to obtain "official recognition" of their land transactions by having the **kamnan** (the officially recognised headman of a cluster of villages) of Ban Mae Lao write up, on a sheet of exercise-book paper, a statement to the effect that a certain plot of terraces has been sold by one person to another (identified by name) at a certain price or according to certain terms, and which the **kamnan** himself witnesses by appending his signature along with that of two other witnesses. The Palokhi Karen themselves place their thumb-prints on the paper. These pieces of paper are kept as carefully as the tax receipts.

There is one further point to note about the ownership of wet-rice fields in Palokhi. With the exception of 'Ae', they are all "owned" by men. The explanation for this is that as men have opened up these fields for cultivation they, therefore, own it although of course the crops are shared by the household and in this sense the fields may be said to belong to all members of the household. There are, however, other reasons why wet-rice fields are seen to be essentially owned by men. Although most tasks in wet-rice farming are not marked by a sexual division of labour, as in swiddening, nevertheless the areas where such a division is far more conspicuous than in swiddening are tasks such as ploughing, harrowing and the construction and maintainance of irrigation systems. Furthermore, the performance of rituals — as in swiddens — is very much the prerogative of men. The identification of men as the owners of wet-rice fields in Palokhi is, therefore, very marked at the present time.

It follows from the foregoing that, in Palokhi, inheritance is an issue which has no legal status in the sense that it is not legally documented, nor does it follow Thai law.[10] The inheritance of wet-rice fields — to the extent that it may be said to follow any semblance of formulable rules — is based on traditional custom and precedents set in longer established villages but, as I noted earlier, it is an issue that is still in the process of working itself out.

Inheritance

According to the Palokhi Karen, inheritable property, that is, wet-rice fields, buffaloes and cattle, should be equally shared by the surviving spouse and children of a person when he, or she, dies. This, at any rate is the theory in Palokhi, and it is a rule or custom that is reported for other Karen as well (see, for example, Hinton [1975:62–3]; Madha [1980:68]; but cf. Hamilton [1976:61]). In practice, however, there is considerable ambiguity surrounding what the Palokhi Karen actually do, suggesting that the "rule" which they enunciate is very much an ideal one. To understand why this is so, it should be noted that traditionally the Karen probably did not have immovable property that could be inherited in the first place, although they may have had livestock. Most property was, and still is, property for personal use, for example, bush knives, smoking pipes, muzzle-loading guns, looms, sling bags, silver bangles and earrings, and so on. In Palokhi custom as with that of other Karen, such personal effects are buried (or burnt in some other communities) along with the body on the person's death. In other words, such property was not inherited.

In Palokhi, they do admit however that objects such as silver ornaments and Northern Thai muzzle-loaders (which are superior in construction and beauty to those made by the Karen) are too valuable to be destroyed in this way (cf. Hinton [1975:63]). What is usually done in such cases is that all the objects which are supposed to be buried with the corpse are taken along with the corpse to the burial ground; the objects which are regarded as being too valuable to be interred are then deposited just outside the ground while the body and other objects are buried. The next day, the objects are retrieved and they may then be shared by the spouse and children of the deceased.

It will be noted that most of these objects are sex specific, for example, guns, bangles, earrings, and so forth and they are, therefore, taken by wives or husbands, sons or daughters, accordingly. Alternatively they may be sold off and the proceeds divided among the inheritors. This underlies the elaboration to the rule that if non-partible property such as cattle, buffaloes and land cannot be shared equally, then they may be sold off and the money divided equally among the inheritors. In practice, however, a variety of arrangements may be entered into which allow inheritors to have a share in their inheritance without resorting to sale, namely, agistment of livestock, and sharecropping of wet-rice fields. These arrangements are, of course, conditional on practical considerations such as willingness to assume the responsibility of rearing the livestock, residence which would make cultivating the fields feasible and worthwhile, and so on.

These arrangements are all entirely sensible, rational and pragmatic given that the rule of inheritance, as an ideal, attempts to ensure an equal distribution of property and it is wholly consistent with, as Hinton has noted, the fundamentally egalitarian ethos of Karen societies. The problem about inheritance in Palokhi, however, is not what is (said should be) done to effect an equitable settlement among inheritors. The problem is what actually happens to land, specifically wet-rice fields, when a man dies and is survived by a wife and children, because it appears — from the three instances of inheritance that have occurred in Palokhi — that wives "inherit" but do not "own" such fields (see also Stern [1965]).[11] Although I have been using the term "inheritance" thus far, I wish to make the suggestion at this point that it is not, perhaps, very useful in describing what seem to be fluid, or variable, sociological arrangements pertaining to the transmission and sharing of property rights where wet-rice fields are concerned. This will be self-evident from the three cases of inheritance that I consider now.

The first case of a death involving the transfer of property (Plot H) occurred when Lu Sa died in 1977. He was survived by a wife and five adult children. Of these children, two sons were resident in Palokhi with their mother, while the other children (two daughters and a son) were resident elsewhere. All of the children were said to have a share in the plot of terraces which Lu Sa had opened up, as did their mother. The plot was cultivated by Can Ta' and La who were resident in Palokhi. Their siblings resident elsewhere retained their rights to the plot but at no point in time did they exercise them, nor did they ask that they be paid money as part of the share from Can Ta', La, or their mother. Neither were share-cropping arrangements entered into. The plot was left as it was and cultivated by Can Ta' and La, although in the end Can Ta' became the principal cultivator because La lost interest in working the wet-rice field. According to Can Ta', the field belonged to all of them, but clearly the field was being worked for the members of the household resident in Palokhi. For all practical purposes, however, Can Ta' made all the decisions concerning the field. In terms of domestic arrangements and household economics, all of this makes sense. The point to note, however, is that Can Ta' was the **de facto** "owner" and that his mother had little, or no, say in the use of the land. Undoubtedly, if his other siblings had wished to obtain their share of the plot, arrangements would have been made as I have already described so that this could be effected. This was not the case, however, because the plot was a small one and it was felt that the needs of the household left in Palokhi were great enough that they should continue to cultivate it for themselves. Besides, it would also have been difficult for Can Ta' (let alone La, who was an opium addict) to raise the money to buy his other siblings out.

The second instance of inheritance in Palokhi occurred with the death of Thi Pghe in 1978. He was survived by his wife, his three children (the eldest of whom was sixteen years old), and his wife's father Rae', the ritual specialist in Palokhi. It was felt that Chi Choe, the eldest son, was still not old enough to work the field and, therefore, the land was leased out to Taan, a Northern Thai from Ban Thung Choa. Rae' himself was too old to work the field, but in any case there was no doubt that he did not have any rights to the land. Nonetheless, he was responsible, in the main, for making the decision to lease out the field, although this was done in consultation with two other older men in the village who, along with Rae', usually officiated at various agricultural rituals, that is, Su Ghau and, of course, the headman Tamu'. Here, again, the role of Thi Pghe's wife, was marginal. Chi Choe's younger brother and sister were far too young to merit consideration insofar as working the field was concerned, although their rights to the land, as well as that of their mother, were acknowledged.

The third case of inheritance arose with the death of Chwi' who had gone to live in Huai Dua after his divorce as discussed earlier. The circumstances pertaining to the land transactions of plot E are outlined in Table 5.2 and I shall therefore mention only those aspects of this case which show something of how this property was disposed of.

In Huai Dua, Chwi' left behind a wife and a three year old son. They were said to own his fields at his death. As Nae' Kha wished to make an exchange of fields, Su Ghau was sent to Huai Dua to arrange the transaction. This transaction is very revealing indeed of how surviving wives may "inherit" land from their husbands but not "own" it. It was decided by the elders in Huai Dua that as Chwi''s son was far too young to work the field, and as it would be a very long time before he would be able to do so, short term arrangements such as leasing out the land (as in Chi Choe's case) were impracticable. Chwi''s plot in Palokhi was exchanged for Nae' Kha's plot in Huai Dua, and this latter plot was eventually sold off and the money handed to Chwi''s wife. She was, of course, consulted in these matters.

These three cases do not, however, cover the range of possibilities in inheritance which can be generated by the kinship system of the Palokhi Karen and concomitant residential patterns described in Chapter III. They have also occurred at a relatively early stage in the history of Palokhi when marriage, residence and death have yet to throw up these possibilities as real issues which the Palokhi Karen have to consider in deciding how to apply their rule on inheritance. For instance, in none of these cases is to be found a situation where there is a married daughter and her husband resident in the household of the dead person. Given the workings of the kinship system, and the norm that married daughters and their husbands stay in the parental house in succession, this is obviously a situation that will arise eventually in the future. This sort of situation, according to the Palokhi Karen, is not very different from those I have already described. The only difference would be the presence of a son-in-law who would, then, be able to cultivate the field if he and his wife wish to do so, and if the wife's siblings are agreeable. As far as ensuring equitable shares in the land is concerned, the elaboration to the inheritance rule would still hold. Competing claims to cultivate the field may, of course, arise if there is a brother or brother-in-law also resident in the village, but this would have to be decided upon through negotiations and pragmatic considerations. Accommodations, therefore, can always be worked out. Indeed, such accommodations or arrangements may be worked out before the death of the owner of the field — not necessarily deliberately with a view to settling the issue of inheritance, but because of the exigencies of household members' life circumstances.

A good example of this may be seen in the case of Lauj and plot A. Lauj has two daughters, both of whom are married and live in Palokhi with their husbands, and an unmarried son also resident in the village. Lauj himself stopped working his field for several years because of his age and addiction to opium. When his first daughter married Nu', the field was worked by Nu' and Chae Wo, the son, and the crop was shared by all members of the household. When his second daughter married Ci, Nu' and his first daughter set up house of their own and cultivated swiddens, although Nu' continued to contribute his labour to the cultivation of the wet-rice field which was then cultivated by Ci and Chae Wo. Lauj however continued to perform the agricultural rituals associated with the cultivation of the field.

When Lauj's wife died, the house was destroyed, and Ci and his wife built their own house, while Lauj and Chae Wo built a small hut for themselves. The field was, at this time, still cultivated by Ci and Chae Wo, but Nu' began to assume a more dominant role in its cultivation as Ci and Chae Wo gradually became addicted to opium in turn. The year after Lauj's wife died, Nu' built a larger house into which Lauj and Chae Wo moved as well, and from that time onwards Nu' took over the cultivation of the field, although Lauj still performed the necessary rites. Ci, on the other hand, did not cultivate a swidden or wet-rice field (although he assisted Nu' occasionally) and supported his family and habit almost entirely through wage labour. In 1980–1, it was evident that Nu' was, for all practical purposes, the "owner" of the field. There can be no doubt that this succession of events and the accompanying arrangements in residence and household economics will greatly influence the inheritance of Lauj's field; it is almost certain that Nu' will take over the field through his wife's claim in the field.

Although these arrangements have been conditioned by the fact that three out of four men are opium addicts, nevertheless one significant feature relevant to inheritance issues clearly emerges: household composition and the presence of a man — whether he is a son or son-in-law — are extremely important in the development of conditions which would need to be taken into account in inheritance, because the cultivation of fields, where the Palokhi Karen are concerned, is dependent on a man.

The Role of Men as Managers of Land

Notwithstanding the particular circumstances of the four cases above, and the variability in arrangements that attended the three instances of inheritance, there is one prominent feature about inheritance in Palokhi: the relationship between men and land is all important, and it affects the application of the rule on inheritance in two ways. First, it is men who determine what is done with land, as in ritual life. Second, the presence of a man among inheritors who may cultivate the land is an important factor in determining the outcome of how land is disposed of under the terms that guide the application of the inheritance rule. These are the fundamental aspects of inheritance in Palokhi, regardless of the workings of the kinship system and associated residential patterns. Thus, while we may expect different outcomes in how land is finally disposed of, that is, according to whether or not there are resident sons and daughters, or married daughters and sons-in-law, and how sharing arrangements or sales of shares are worked out, the common denominator in the final analysis is the presence of a man who, then, becomes the **de facto** owner. The reason (as I discuss below) is that men are necessary for the ritual management of cultivated land.

Looked at in this light, perhaps it does not matter very much whether the transmission of land, or rights to land is talked about in terms of "inheritance" or "ownership" or not at all, in so far as **individuals** are concerned. It would be more accurate to speak of the "ownership" by **households** (that is, domestic groups), and where the death of a man occurs, a re-allocation of shares or rights to land must take place because a man is required to cultivate the land. Given the sociology of agricultural production and domestic arrangements, such a re-allocation would in general result in another household assuming the "ownership" of the land through the share of one person whether that person is a son, a daughter, or even a wife — but only if she has a son, or son-in-law, resident with her who could undertake the cultivation of the field.[12] To put this another way, households "own" land, and "ownership" is transmitted through individuals, male or female, by their rights or shares in the land, to the new households that are formed at the death of men in the original households. But, in all cases, men are the "managers" (which women never are or can be) of the land, whether they happen to be sons or sons-in-law.

The importance of men in conditioning the outcome of the inheritance of land undoubtedly lies in certain conceptualisations of sex roles and gender relations integral to the ideology of agricultural production, which is itself an essential part of the ideology of Palokhi Karen religion. In wet-rice agriculture, the construction of irrigation systems, and ploughing, harrowing and smoothening wet-rice fields — all of which require the driving of buffaloes — are seen as distinctly male tasks and these tasks are, needless to say, fundamental to wet-rice cultivation. While women may assist in clearing or repairing irrigation canals, they never construct dams (the completion of which requires the performance of a ritual by the men who constructed it and share in its use) and it is inconceivable in Palokhi that women may drive buffaloes in order to plough, harrow and level wet-rice fields.[13] Furthermore, with only one exception (which I discuss in the following chapter), all agricultural rituals are performed by men.

As we have also seen elsewhere, only men (the village elders and the headman) perform the Head Rite (**talykho**) which is specifically concerned with territorial spirits, and the tutelary spirit of the domain — the Lord of the Water, Lord of the Land. They are also the ones who attempt to impose the rules of marriage and officiate at marriage ceremonies. As I have shown however, an important part of the symbolic and ideological significance of marriage in Palokhi consists of the ritual management of "heat" and the infertility of land in the form of "hot" land. Land, in other words, is an **essential** feature or aspect of the "symbolic capital" of the Palokhi Karen. The inheritance of wet-rice fields in Palokhi, therefore, is not only concerned with the transmission of land for agricultural purposes to surviving kin. It is also concerned with religion and the dominance of men in the ritual life of the community, both of which are inseparable from agricultural production in the cultural ideology of the Palokhi Karen.

This, I might add, is one justification for a view which I expressed in Chapter I: that swidden agriculture has exerted a "priority" through which wet-rice agriculture has been subsumed within an existing ideological system. To the extent that wet-rice agriculture is a later historical development, where the Palokhi Karen are concerned, the ideological relationship between men and land embedded in the inheritance of wet-rice fields may be taken as a structural extension of a pre-existing relationship into a new form of land use.

Rice Production and Consumption Requirements

In Table 5.3 may be found data on land use, rice production, and consumption requirements in Palokhi. The data on the size of swiddens were obtained by a method commonly known as the field-book-and-compass-traverse method, while the size of wet-rice fields were determined through the use of aerial photographs. The data on rice production and consumption are based on reported figures and are given in litres.

Table 5.3. Rice Production and Consumption in Palokhi (1980–81)

Household No.	Household Size	Swiddens			Wet-rice Fields			Total Production		Consumption Requirements (litres)	Surpluses/Deficits	
		Area (ha)	Production Non-glutinous (litres)	Glutinous (litres)	Area (ha)	Production Non-glutinous (litres)	Glutinous (litres)	Non-glutinous (litres)	Glutinous (litres)		Non-glutinous (litres)	Glutinous (litres)
H1a	4	1.05	1,100	220	0.36	4,400	—	>3,036	>97	>2,555	>+481	>+97
H1b	6	—	—	—	—	—	—	—	—	—	—	—
H2	12	2.46	7,700	660	0.37	2,600	—	5,708	290	2,190	+3,518	+290
H3	11	—	—	—	0.62	6,600	—	3,643	—	2,555	+1,088	—
H4	6	1.84	220	176	0.14	2,640	—	1,579	77	1,643	[-64]	+7
H5	5	—	—	—	—	—	—	—	—	1,095	[-1,095]	-1,460
H6	7	—	—	—	—	1,100	—	607	—	1,278	[-670]	-766
H7	5	—	—	—	—	—	—	—	—	1,095	[-1,095]	-1,460
H8	9	0.91	1,760	—	0.36	1,826	—	1,980	—	2,555	[-576]	-741
H9	8	—	—	—	0.37	2,640	1,100	1,458	484	2,008	[-550]	+484
H10	5	—	—	—	—	—	—	—	—	1,095	[-1,095]	-1,460
H11a	2	1.11	1,320	—	0.9	4,400	2,200	—	—	—	—	—
H11b	8	0.49	660	—	—	—	—	>3,522	>968	>3,285	>+237	>+968
H12	3	1.02	1,320	—	—	—	—	729	—	1,643	[-914]	-1,015
H13a	7	0.46	1,320	—	—	—	—	—	—	—	—	—
H13b	4	—	—	—	—	—	—	>729	>—	>2,555	>[-1,826]	>-1,565
H14	3	0.09	440	—	0.33	1,188	—	899	—	1,095	[-196]	-262
H15	2	—	—	—	—	—	—	—	—	NA	NA	NA
H16	5	—	—	—	—	—	—	—	—	1,825	[-1,825]	-2,190
H17	4	—	—	—	—	—	—	NA	NA	NA	NA	NA
Total	116	9.43	15,840	1056	2.64	27,434	3,300	23,890	1,916	28,470	+5,874	+1,019
Mean	5.8	1.18	1,760	352	0.33	3,048	1,100	NA	NA	NA	NA	NA

* Production of rice from swiddens and wet-rice fields are given in litres of unmilled rice.

** Total production is given in litres of milled rice. The conversion factors for non-glutinous and glutinous rice, unmilled to milled, are 0.55 and 0.44 respectively. These factors were obtained from a series of samples based on rice milling for household consumption in Palokhi. The sampling was conducted in the middle of 1981.

*** In Palokhi, all deficits are made up through the purchase of glutinous rice. Thus, the figures in brackets indicate deficits in non-glutinous rice from under or non-production of rice, while the deficits in glutinous rice show the actual amounts of glutinous rice required to meet consumption requirements. Where H4 is concerned, although non-glutinous rice production was insufficient to meet its needs, glutinous rice production was sufficient to make up the resulting deficit with a small surplus, hence the surplus of 7 litres.

The Palokhi Karen invariably measure their rice harvests in swiddens and wet-rice fields, using as their standard unit of measurement a 22 litre kerosene tin called a **pip.** It is a measure which they have adopted from the Northern Thai. The estimates of the size of harvests brought in by households are generally reliable, although the Palokhi Karen usually round off their reported figures to the nearest 10 **pip.** The annual consumption requirements of households in Table 5.3 are based on the amounts of rice required per day, as reported by each household. As far as domestic consumption requirements are concerned, the amounts required by households per day tend to be constant, unless there are visitors or when there are village celebrations. The figures on annual rice consumption requirements do not take into account the extra demand for rice on these occasions.

In the table, rice production from swiddens and wet-rice fields is given in litres of unmilled rice, while total production is given in litres of milled rice, in order to render the table a little more concise, and for purposes of comparison with consumption requirements. The conversion factors for glutinous and ordinary rice (unmilled to milled, by volume) are 0.55 and 0.44 respectively. These factors were obtained from a series of samples based on rice milling (or husking) for household consumption. The method of milling in Palokhi, which is employed by all rice-growing households, consists of pounding rice in a foot-powered mortar. The consumption requirements of households are given in litres of milled ordinary rice, which is generally consumed in preference to glutinous rice. Glutinous rice is usually used for making liquor and rice cakes on ceremonial occasions and households will only eat this kind of rice on occasion, for variety, or when their stocks of ordinary rice are exhausted.

Rice surpluses and deficits are also given in milled rice. The crucial data in the table, for this analysis of rice production and consumption in Palokhi, are the data on rice deficits, expressed as deficits in **glutinous** rice, experienced by individual households. All surpluses are given in litres of glutinous and non-glutinous rice where applicable. The deficits in non-glutinous rice (in brackets) have, however, been converted to deficits in glutinous rice which are the key indicators of the extent to which households are dependent on an external economy for their rice to make up their deficits. The reason is that the Palokhi Karen invariably buy glutinous rice from shops in Northern Thai settlements as this is cheaper. It is also, generally, rice that is more commonly available as it is the preferred form of rice among the Northern Thai in these settlements who also purchase it to meet their own requirements. The deficits in ordinary rice have been converted into deficits in glutinous rice for each deficit household in the table. The conversions were arrived at on the basis of reported figures on how much glutinous rice would be required for each household's daily requirements if there was no ordinary rice. For those households which did not produce any rice at all, the glutinous rice deficits represent absolute rice requirements for the year. For those households which cultivated one or both kinds of rice, the deficits in glutinous rice represent glutinous rice requirements only after their stocks of ordinary and glutinous rice were used to meet their consumption needs.

I have already noted in the previous chapter that there is no redistributive system as such in Palokhi where rice from surplus households may be channelled to households with deficits. It may also be pointed out here that in Palokhi, the Karen generally do not make it a practice to buy or sell rice which they produce themselves, although occasionally rice may be exchanged for some commodity or other.[14] Such transactions are limited in nature and are resorted to when there may be a lack of ready cash. Furthermore, rice is usually only exchanged in this way by households with rice surpluses so that the initiative and willingness to utilise rice in this manner lies with them. As most goods in these transactions are available through easily accessible sources (within or around Palokhi, and in shops in Northern Thai settlements), the use of rice in such exchange transactions is the exception rather than the rule. Within Palokhi, therefore, rice is only circulated or "redistributed" in very small amounts. Accordingly, deficit households can only obtain rice from external sources, namely, shops in nearby Northern Thai settlements such as Ban Mae Lao and Ban Pa Pae.

As may be seen from Table 5.3, total consumption requirements, in Palokhi, in non-glutinous rice was 28,470 litres, while total production, also in non-glutinous rice, was 23,890 litres, thus giving an overall shortage of rice amounting to 4,580 litres or 16 per cent of consumption requirements. The deficit would in fact have been somewhat less, as some households could make up part if not all of their shortages with the glutinous rice they grew. The actual rice deficits in Palokhi are best indicated by the amounts of glutinous rice which deficit households have to purchase. As shown in the table, the total glutinous rice requirements of all 10 deficit households in 1981 was 10,919 litres. At the prevailing price of glutinous rice in Northern Thai shops in the area, which was 4.5 Baht per litre in 1981, these requirements represented a total cost of Bht 49,135.5 to the households concerned.

There was no evidence in 1981 to indicate that any of the households were eating considerably less rice than they required daily, at least in general, although there were occasions when a few households (notably H5, H10, H13a, and H13b) reduced their consumption by having two meals a day (rather than three which is the norm in Palokhi) as and when it became necessary. Despite the straitened circumstances which these households occasionally faced, this indicates that the Palokhi Karen were generally able to meet their rice deficits through purchases of rice. It is probable that the amounts of rice purchased were greater than the estimates of the deficits given in Table 5.3. The reason is that these estimates represent basic consumption requirements, and do not take into account the fact that some of these deficit households were under some obligation to make rice liquor and rice cakes on various occasions, as well as to feed visitors and helpers in their fields. Nevertheless, the estimates of rice deficits in terms of glutinous rice will be sufficient to show the extent to which the Palokhi Karen as a whole depend on external sources for rice to meet their consumption requirements.

Subsistence in a Regional Context: Miang, Tea, and the Cash Sector of the Palokhi Economy

From a general historical perspective, it would appear that the Karen have been associated with a cash economy in one form or another for a long time, and with trade relationships (which need not necessarily have depended on the use of money) with neighbouring communities for even longer. For instance, some Palokhi households possess objects of considerable antiquity (see Chapter VII) not manufactured by the Karen themselves, and this alone suggests that some form of trade existed in the past in which the Karen were involved. While most accounts of Northern Thailand and Burma, written by British colonial administrators, from the latter part of the last century have tended to depict Karen communities as self-contained, isolated societies, nevertheless there are scanty but suggestive reports of Karen involvement in economic exchanges with their neighbours. In a description of Mae Sariang in the 1880's, for example, Hallett (1890:40–1) says that most of the elephants employed in the teak industry there were rented out by the Karen to foresters. Bock, on the other hand, noticed on his journey north of Phetchaburi in the 1870's, that "the Karen used to come down to buy rice" (1884:87). Evidence still to be found in the present, of Karen involvement in a cash economy or trading networks, in past times may be seen in British Indian Empire rupees and annas that are worn by Karen women to this day as ornaments—either intact as pendants or necklaces, or as earrings and bangles beaten from the silver rupees.

Contemporary research, however, very clearly indicates the existence of a cash component in the subsistence economies of various Karen communities, but the extent and characteristics of this component vary markedly from community to community. The accounts themselves show considerable differences in the attention given to the details of the operation of this component in Karen subsistence systems. The differences in scale, configurations, and importance of the cash component in the subsistence economies of the Karen reported on appear to be the result of a variety of factors: proximity to neighbouring communities, especially Northern Thai, the size of rice deficits incurred in the agricultural sector, the availability of alternative means for making up such deficits, internal demands for commodities ranging from "necessities" to "luxury goods", and the extent of opium addiction and associated indebtedness in these Karen communities. Hinton (1975:211–30), for instance, describes what amounts to a complex cash sector involving capital accummulation in the form of rearing buffaloes and cattle, and the realisation of profits through the sale of the livestock to Northern Thai, occasional wage labour in Mae Sariang, the renting out of elephants to Thai and Chinese timber contractors, and the sale of forest products. Interestingly enough, Hinton says that rice purchases were small with rice deficits being managed (by those households which suffered them) through the supplementation of rice with maize for domestic consumption. Kunstadter (1978:116–20), on the other hand, says that most of the money in circulation among the Karen (and Lua') came from the lowlands through wage labour. Agricultural land, however, was mortgaged for rice (or, sometimes, cash) in some cases in order to meet consumption demands that could not be met by domestic agricultural production. No less interesting is the fact that most mortgages were held by the Karen from the Lua', because the Karen were comparatively better off as they had only small deficits in agricultural production and, then too, these deficits were experienced by only a few households. Where the purchase of commodities is concerned, this was confined to obtaining a few manufactured necessities and luxury items. Hamilton, however, describes in greater detail a more thorough-going participation of Karen in what he calls a "bazaar economy" or "market economy" (1976:184ff.). He does say that this economy has always seen Karen participation and that this has grown increasingly in recent times because of the inability of the Karen subsistence system to meet rice consumption requirements as a result of population increase and a commensurate reduction in the availability of agricultural land. Madha's account of the workings of the cash sector among the Karen he studied (1980:160ff.) is essentially similar to that by Hamilton. It is clear from both these accounts of Karen subsistence economies that the use of money dominates in the functioning of the cash sector. In contrast to these two descriptions, Cohen's analysis of Karen indebtedness (1984) shows that opium is widely used as a means of paying for Karen labour in Hmong opium fields, and that opium and rice constitute a major part of the structure of credit arrangments and indebtedness between the Karen and Northern Thai, Shan and Chinese merchants in Karen communities.

Regardless of the extent to which the Karen may have been engaged in a cash economy and trade in past times, it is wholly evident from recent descriptions of Karen subsistence systems that the Karen are very much a part of a cash economy involving economic relations with their neighbours, particularly the Northern Thai; but their participation, and the operation of the cash economies that they are involved in, exhibit considerable variation in the kinds of arrangements which make up this sector of their subsistence systems.

The cash sector in the subsistence economy of Palokhi represents yet another variation in the set of possible economic arrangements and relations, and it is further evidence of the diversity in the symbiotic ties which may exist between the Karen and their Northern Thai neighbours. There is, however, one significant difference between the cash sector in Palokhi and those of the other Karen communities, and it is one which reflects a regional (though by no means a thorough-going) differentiation, or specialisation, of economic systems in which the Northern Thai dominate. This lies in the **miang** (or steamed fermented tea) industry which the Palokhi Karen are a part of, and which does not appear to play an important role in the subsistence economies of the Karen found to the west in Mae Hong Sorn (Hinton [1975], Kunstadter [1978], Madha [1980]), Hod (Hamilton [1976]) or just south-west of the city of Chiang Mai (Cohen [1984]).

This regional difference in the prominence of **miang** as an economically important crop is, very probably, not of recent provenance although it may be noted that even in Chiang Mai itself the importance of the crop varies (see, for example, Van Roy [1971] and Wijeyewardene [1971]). While the tea plant (**Camellia sinensis**) is to be found over most of Northern Thailand, it is noteworthy that its economic significance was not commented upon by early travellers such as Hallett, whereas McCarthy (1900:62) who observed its presence in its wild state everywhere in the north was, nevertheless, struck by the extensive **miang** gardens on the slopes of Doi Suthep close to Chiang Mai. More recent studies, however, show very conclusively the considerable importance of the crop in Chiang Dao involving Northern Thai, Hmong and Lahu (Van Roy [1971], Keen [1978]) not only in the **miang** industry but in the tea (that is, dry-leaf) industry as well (see also Pendleton [1963:40]) which appears to have been started in the 1950's as a deliberate Thai entrepreneurial attempt to break into the Bangkok-based Chinese monopoly of the tea trade in Thailand (Van Roy [1971 158–81]). Although these studies have focussed on Chiang Dao, it would seem from the accounts of some Northern Thai, and Palokhi Karen, that the Pa Pae hills area has been part of a **miang** network (Durrenberger [1974]) leading down to Mae Malai, in Mae Taeng, for some time. And, as with Chiang Dao, the Pa Pae area has been drawn within the ambit of the Chiang Mai-based Raming Tea Company, the largest manufacturer of this kind of tea in Thailand (Donner [1978: 714]), which has plantations in Mae Taeng.

Although a part of the **miang** and tea industry centred at Mae Taeng, the Palokhi Karen and the Northern Thai in the Pa Pae hills are only linked with the industry indirectly, that is, through **miang** merchants and tea buyers. Where the Palokhi economy is specifically concerned, this association is nevertheless a very important one because it provides a considerable income for the Palokhi Karen with which rice purchases may be made when their own stocks of rice are low or exhausted. Apart from **miang** and tea related activities, however, there is a wide range of income generating activities which the Palokhi Karen engage in — within Palokhi itself, as well as outside in Northern Thai settlements, Lisu villages and units of the Royal Forestry Department in the Mae Muang Luang-Huai Thung Choa watershed. Similarly, the Palokhi Karen also purchase a diversity of commodities, other than rice, from one another in Palokhi and in these other places. The range and diversity of transactions in the cash sector of Palokhi's subsistence economy defy easy classification or categorisation because they are numerous and involve small sums of money at any point in time, and often they are made on the basis of **ad hoc** needs and opportunities.

I should also point out that an important feature of the cash sector in the economy of Palokhi is the autonomy of households and it is this very autonomy which integrates the "internal" economy of Palokhi with the wider economy. The reason is that all transactions which occur in the cash sector of the economy are undertaken by households acting on their own as units of production and consumption, and by individuals. Palokhi, as a village or community, does not act as a corporate group in the economic relations which exist between it and other communities. This, of course, follows from the nature of social organisation in Palokhi and the way that production and consumption is organised according to households. The integration of the subsistence economy of Palokhi with the wider economy, thus, lies in the cash flows generated by non-agricultural production within, and outside, Palokhi through income earning activities, as well as concomitant expenditures on various commodities, and to some extent services, within Palokhi and elsewhere, by households.

In the rest of this section, I present an outline of the more significant features of the cash sector in Palokhi according to general patterns of income earning activities and expenditures.

Income Earning Activities

The most important external sources of income, for the Palokhi Karen, lie in activities associated with the **miang** and tea industries which constitute an integrated, complex, structure not characteristic of other income earning activities undertaken by the Palokhi Karen. Despite the general decline of the **miang** economy in Northern Thailand (Keen [1978:267]; Thannarong, pers. comm.) in recent times, this economy nevertheless continues to provide the Palokhi Karen with the greater part of their income obtained from related activities followed, secondarily, by the income derived from the sale of the crop specifically for use in the tea industry.[15] In Palokhi, **miang** and tea cropping are the major form of subsistence production, second only to the cultivation of rice, in terms of the amount of labour expended and rice obtained (through the cash nexus) from this expenditure of labour. As a type of cash cropping integral to the subsistence system of the Palokhi Karen, it is thus extremely important indeed to the way in which subsistence requirements are met in Palokhi. And, as this particular pattern in Karen subsistence economies, in general, has not been hitherto described, it is therefore worthwhile for comparative purposes to examine, in some detail, the functions of this aspect of the subsistence system in Palokhi.

In Northern Thailand, the growth cycle of the **miang** or tea plant is, as I have noted before, influenced to some extent by the occurrence of the wet season which, in turn, affects when the leaves of the plant may be harvested. In the traditional **miang** cropping cycle, leaf-picking takes place four times a year but the duration of cropping at each time, or season, varies because of the effect that the wet season has on the rate of regeneration of new leaf.

In a typical cycle, which Van Roy describes (1971:94), the first harvest (called **muuj**) takes place in December. This harvest season lasts only for about two weeks, but it provides leaf which is highly prized in **miang** processing. The second cropping season (**hua pii**) takes place from March to April, after new leaves have grown during the cool dry and then hot dry seasons. After another month for further growth to occur, comes the third cropping season (**klaang**) which lasts from approximately July to August. The fourth season (**sauj**) occurs from about September-October to November. The third and fourth seasons are usually not well separated because during the wet season leaf growth is fairly rapid. These four cropping seasons are to be found in the Pa Pae hills where they are generally closely observed by the Northern Thai involved in the **miang** economy but they are not as closely followed by the Palokhi Karen for the simple reason that this **miang** cropping cycle is largely in conflict with the two growth cycles of rice in swidden and wet-rice cultivation. In December, for instance, the Palokhi Karen are still engaged in harvesting and storing their rice from swiddens and wet-rice fields. And, again, in March and April, they are busy clearing, burning and planting their swiddens, while from May to July they are involved in the preparation of their wet-rice terraces and the planting of wet-rice. Even in the **klaang** and **sauj** seasons (July to November) a conflict exists because of the need to weed swiddens leading up to the time when the first harvesting of rice must be carried out; but during this period, the stocks of rice in Palokhi have already begun to run down (if they have not been exhausted) and the Palokhi Karen are faced with the competing demands for labour in weeding their swiddens to ensure satisfactory rice harvests and in obtaining rice for the satisfaction of their immediate needs. There is, in fact, hardly an option in this and the Palokhi Karen thus give greater priority to the latter and unreservedly take advantage of the opportunities offered in the **klaang** and **sauj** seasons. Many households, however, attempt to anticipate this problem in the allocation of their domestic supplies of labour by working in the **hua pii** season in between attending to the tasks in swidden and wet-rice cultivation. But, when the harvest season is in full-swing in their swiddens and wet-rice fields, there is a total halt on **miang** and tea associated activities.

The structure and organisation of the **miang** economy in the Pa Pae hills is probably similar to that described by Van Roy and Keen especially around the Northern Thai settlements of Ban Pa Pae and Ban Pha Daeng where **miang** merchants or wholesalers are to be found in the area.[16] Further upland, around the Pang Luang, however, conditions are a little different. In the two Northern Thai settlements nearest Palokhi, that is, Ban Tung Choa and Ban Mae Lao, and Toeloekhi (the closest Karen village) as well as Palokhi itself, the Northern Thai and Karen own **miang** or tea gardens and are, therefore, independent producers of the leaf.[17] In the Northern Thai villages, however, some **miang** processing is done but not in the two Karen villages except for domestic consumption.[18] The Northern Thai sell both raw leaf and processed **miang** to a Yunnanese Chinese wholesaler (who is also a buyer of leaf for the tea industry) based at Ban Pha Daeng. The Karen, on the other hand, sell only the raw leaf which is also bought by the same wholesaler for processing into **miang** or for resale to the Raming Tea Company. The Palokhi Karen (and, for that matter, the Toeloekhi Karen) generally do not sell their raw leaf to the Northern Thai **miang** producers in Ban Mae Lao although they do work for them in related activities. This is because the Northern Thai producers lack large supplies of cash, or stocks of rice, to pay for the leaf.[19] The Northern Thai at Ban Mae Lao do not act as intermediaries between the Palokhi Karen and the Pha Daeng wholesaler because the wholesaler comes up to Ban Mae Lao to buy the **miang** and raw leaf directly from both the Northern Thai and Karen. The Palokhi Karen and, very probably, most of the Northern Thai in Ban Thung Choa and Ban Mae Lao, therefore, are not bound into the socio-economic relationships characteristic of the "entourage" or **pau liang,** that is, patron-client, systems which Van Roy (1971:101ff.) and Keen (1978:257–8) — following Hanks (1966:55–63) — see as the principal institutional framework of the **miang** economy of Chiang Dao.[20] There is also no system of renting gardens from **miang** wholesalers or merchants, with rents being paid in **miang,** nor is there a cycle of credit and indebtedness (but see below) carried over from year to year — at least as far as the Palokhi Karen in general are concerned. Another related difference is that the raw leaf is sold to the Pha Daeng merchant by the Palokhi Karen, and most Northern Thai growers in Ban Thung Choa and Ban Mae Lao, according to weight rather than bundles (**kam**) which is the normal practice in Chiang Dao, and payments are usually made in cash, although rice payments may also be made depending on whether or not this is specifically asked for.

The selling and buying of **miang** and raw leaf is held in Ban Mae Lao and payments are made immediately by the Pha Daeng merchant. During the **klaang** and **sauj** seasons, the merchant comes to Ban Mae Lao almost everyday, but generally the frequency of his buying trips depends on the intensity of picking through the **hua pii** to **sauj** seasons. The price paid by the merchant for raw leaf is the same whether it is sold by Northern Thai or Karen but they vary depending on the quality of the leaf and the end use of the leaf, that is, as **miang** or as tea. In April of 1981 (that is, towards the end of the **hua pii** season), when several Palokhi households picked and sold leaf from their gardens after planting their swiddens, the price of raw leaf for **miang** was Bht 2 per kilogram. During the **klaang** and **sauj** seasons, however, the price increased by as much as two and a half times, with the leaf being bought at the rate of Bht 4.5 and Bht 5 per kilogram, the difference depending on whether the leaf was bought at Ban Mae Lao itself, or Ban Thung Choa which was closer to Palokhi. The Bht 0.5, thus, was a reflection of transportation costs incurred by the Pha Daeng wholesaler. Leaf for tea, however, commands a much lower price but the price is stable throughout the year. In 1981, this was Bht 1.5 per kilogram. Despite the growing tea industry in Chiang Dao and Mae Taeng, the reason why the raw leaf for this industry does not command premium prices in the Pa Pae hills is that the leaf here is used as "filler" for the better quality leaf from the tea plantations in Chiang Dao and Mae Taeng in blending. This kind of leaf is, in fact, called "old tea" or "old leaf" (**saa kae** or **baj kae** in Ban Mae Lao and Ban Thung Choa, and **la pgha** in Palokhi) and it is not used in **miang** processing. Nevertheless, the fact that it is purchased and used in the tea industry means that the Northern Thai and Karen have an additional source of income from their gardens which has, to some extent, offset the progressive loss in incomes resulting from a gradually declining **miang** industry.

Where the Palokhi Karen are specifically concerned, the urgency of the need for rice during the growing season of rice in their swiddens and terraces, and the considerable importance of the **miang** and tea industries in enabling them to meet this need, may be gauged from the fact that a large proportion — if not all — of the income derived from the sale of raw leaf, each time, is immediately converted into rice at the point of sale, that is, at Mae Lao. As soon as they are paid for their leaf, they purchase rice from either of the two Northern Thai shops in the village.

However, not all of the income earned by the Palokhi Karen outside of Palokhi, in **miang** and tea related activities, comes from the sale of leaf. The Palokhi Karen also earn money from wage labour for the Northern Thai in clearing **miang** gardens, chopping firewood which is required in the process of steaming **miang** and portage because some Northern Thai own **miang** gardens near Palokhi. There is a regular demand for Karen labour, especially in the **klaang** and **sauj** seasons, in Northern Thai settlements because there is a shortage of young adult males to perform the heavier tasks associated with the cropping of **miang.**

Notwithstanding the lack of any demographic data on the Northern Thai in the area, it seems clear that this shortage of young men in Northern Thai settlements has been due to their migration as a result of two principal factors. The first is the activities and projects (for example, road construction, house-building, reforestation, the growing of pine and coffee seedlings, horticulture of ornamental flowers, and so forth) of the Royal Forestry Department's Watershed Unit which have created opportunities for employment within the Mae Muang Luang-Huai Thung Choa area well away from these

Northern Thai settlements (Kunzel [1983], n.d.). The second, paradoxically, is highland-lowland or, more specifically, urban migration representing a reversal of the trend which originally brought the Northern Thai to the Pa Pae hills. This has undoubtedly been caused by the construction of the Mae Malai-Pai all-weather road which began in 1979 and reached Ban Mae Lao in 1980–81. The construction of the road itself provided employment opportunities in the labour gangs working on the road for young men in the area. The most significant effects of the road, however, were the vastly increased ease and frequency of communications and transportation between the highlands and lowlands, and their lower costs. When the road reached Ban Pa Pae, for instance, there were **at least** five privately operated "four wheelers" (**sii lau,** that is, modified pick-up trucks with a roof and two, or sometimes three, rows of benches) making daily runs between Mae Malai (in Mae Taeng) and Ban Pa Pae, which was extended to Ban Mae Lao as construction of the road progressed. The one-way fare between Ban Pa Pae and Mae Malai was Bht 15 in 1981, and Bht 20 between Ban Mae Lao and Mae Malai. In mid–1981, even before road construction had reached Pai, a twice daily privately operated bus service was started, plying between Pai and Chiang Mai (though less regularly in the wet season) charging Bht 20 for a one way fare.[21] Thus, while young Northern Thai men have found employment opportunities else-where away from their villages, similar opportunities have opened up in these villages for the Palokhi Karen.

The average wage rate for manual labour prevailing in Northern Thai settlements (and in units and sections of the Royal Forestry Department) in 1981 was Bht 30 per day for men, and Bht 25 per day for women. These rates applied to the Karen as well, but it may be noted here that Palokhi women do not go out to do wage work in Northern Thai villages. The work of clearing **miang** gardens, however, commanded higher rates (Bht 40 per day) because it is hard work and it also requires a great deal of care in order not to damage the **miang** bushes as the undergrowth is slashed away.

Within Palokhi, however, **miang** and tea is picked and sold on a household basis (from household owned gardens which average 2 **raj** in size) similar to the organisation of rice production in the village. Nevertheless, in 1981, a form of employment by one household of other Karen in Palokhi was organised because of the special circumstances of the household. This is so exceptional that it deserves some comment.

It is unusual on two counts. First, the Palokhi Karen as a rule do not work for one another for remuneration of any kind and this, I think, is to be explained by the egalitarian nature of their society in which the asymmetric social relations implicit in the structure of wage work would be a contradiction or inconsistency. Wage work would also highlight differentials in wealth which are usually played down in the community. Second, the employment of several people by this household was in itself unusual given that the Palokhi Karen do not generally engage one another in wage labour.

This household was one of the two which had moved to Palokhi in 1980 after working for several years in the Flower Plantation of the Royal Forestry Department's Watershed Unit. The plot of terraces which the household had opened in 1980 was still too small to meet the rice needs of the household by a very large margin and so La Zi, the head of the household, decided to organise **miang** picking on as large a scale as possible not only as an attempt to make up the household's very considerable rice shortage in 1981 (which was evident even when the 1980 harvest was brought in), but also with the hope of making some profit as well. As the household did not own a **miang** garden, La Zi therefore rented two gardens (totalling approximately 5 **raj**) from Kino the Karen merchant in Ban Pa Pae (which the latter had bought from Puu Taa along with plot I, noted earlier); the rent was set at a flat fee of Bht 1,500 payable at the end of the year. Given the conditions of the **miang** and tea economy in the area, that is, generally stable, if low, prices and direct access to a buyer, the viability and success of the enterprise obviously hinged upon the volume of leaf sales that could be attained which depended, in turn, on the availability of extra-household labour for leaf-picking, especially as the household's own supply of labour was made up of La Zi and his thirteen year old son, his wife being for all practical purposes house-bound as she was nursing a child she had given birth to in that year. Although most of the households in Palokhi had their own gardens to crop, La Zi was nonetheless able to "employ" several people in his enterprise because of the additional income that thus became available through working for him. It is worth noting that this was not regarded as "wage work" but as "help" — an indication of how the inconsistency between the asymmetry of wage labour relations and the ethos of egalitarian social relations may be overcome by semantics. The inconsistency, or contradiction, was perhaps not as great as we might imagine it to be because the wage work arrangements could hardly be said to constitute institutionalised relationships. Nor were there credit arrangements (or indebtedness) as payments for the leaf picked by La Zi's Karen "employees" were made immediately the leaf was sold at Ban Mae Lao or Ban Tung Choa. This, of course, was only possible because the Pha Daeng merchant made spot payments for the **miang** and tea leaf sold at these two villages.

It is worth noting that the system of payments for the work done in this enterprise was essentially similar to that of the Northern Thai. La Zi's "workers" (who included his sister and, occasionally, some of her children) were paid according to the amount of leaf that they brought in, namely, Bht 2 per kilogram. The leaf was **miang** as this fetched a higher selling price than leaf for tea. Towards the end of the **klaang** season, however, rice payments were made in addition to cash at an appropriate exchange rate according to the price of milled glutinous rice (in the Ban Mae Lao shops) which varied between Bht 99 and Bht

110 per **taang** of broken rice, the cheapest kind available in these shops. Rice payments, however, were usually made in smaller quantities, that is, litres (of which there are 22 to a **taang** in the highlands), and the corresponding prices were Bht 4.5 and Bht 5 per litre.

Given the clear comparative advantage of picking and selling leaf directly to the Pha Daeng merchant, we may well ask the question why the Karen worked for La Zi. The reason is that even if they had wished to pick and sell more leaf, they could not do so because of the small size of their own gardens (for those who owned them) and to increase the area of their gardens would have required additional expenditures of labour in clearing these gardens to begin with. From their point of view then, the work for La Zi was supplementary to cropping their own gardens.

I should also point out here that there was, in fact, one household in Palokhi which was employed in **miang** picking virtually throughout the whole of the **klaang** and **sauj** seasons by a Northern Thai to whom they were indebted from the previous year (1980) for rice that they had obtained on credit. This was H5 the household whose head, Thi Pghe, had died in 1978 and which rented out plot G because the eldest son Chi Choe was still not old enough to cultivate the wet-rice field. The debt was paid gradually (but not completely even by January 1982) in the form of **miang** leaf picked in the gardens of the Northern Thai, Thaun, near Palokhi calculated at the rate of Bht 2 per kilogram, the standard rate paid for leaf-picking by owners of **miang** gardens as was the case with La Zi's enterprise. This, however, was an exceptional case of indebtedness associated with **miang** cropping in Palokhi.

Apart from **miang** and tea related activities, however, the Palokhi Karen also earn a substantial cash income (though not as much) from external sources through other economic activities. Unlike the sale of leaf, or **miang** connected wage labour, these activities are not linked with the wider economy of the Pa Pae hills in a systematic manner. These activities are diverse and they are performed on an **ad hoc** basis as, and when, the opportunities for them arise and, of course, when the Karen themselves are able to take advantage of these opportunities. The income earning activities are, very broadly, wage labour, and the sale of goods, livestock and services.

The main forms of wage work in 1981 were clearing of compounds and house-building for the Northern Thai of Ban Mae Lao, clearing of **miang** gardens, chopping of firewood (for **miang** steaming) in various Northern Thai settlements, planting, harvesting and portage work for the Karen merchant from Pa Pae during these two seasons when he came to stay and overseer the cultivation of his wet-rice field by a share-cropper, portage work for some Northern Thai engaged in collecting rattan from the forests around Palokhi, and carrying stores for a section of the Royal Forestry Department's Watershed Unit.

The goods sold by the Palokhi Karen included forest products and certain items made by a few households in the village. There were only three types of forest products which were of any economic significance for the Palokhi Karen in 1981. These were pine wood (**Pinus kesiya**) and the bark of two trees, known by their Northern Thai names, **kaj** and **kae** (**Ternstroemia spp.** and **Combretum spp.** respectively). The sale of pine wood constituted the most important source of income of these three forest products. Indeed, a large part of the cash income of households with no wet-rice fields and only small swiddens, and households with opium addicts, was derived from this source. The reason is that the demand for pine wood (as fire starters and torches) in Northern Thai villages where the people have no access to pine trees is generally consistent throughout the year. The Palokhi Karen also use the pine wood for these two purposes and they obtain the wood by chopping mature pine trees (which are found in stands in parts of the forest around Palokhi) and then chopping up the felled trees into large splinters for use whenever their supplies in their homes run out. The pine wood is sold at a price of Bht 2 per kilogram in Ban Thung Choa and Ban Mae Lao when the wood is fresh, but the price drops to Bht 1.5 per kilogram if the trees have been left on the ground for some time because the inflammable resin dries up to some extent under these conditions. The bark of **Ternstroemia** and **Combretum** are sold to a Northern Thai in Mae Lao and another Northern Thai in Ban Mae Lak. According to the buyer in Mae Lao (who purchased only **Ternstroemia**), the two kinds of bark are resold in Pai for the manufacture of incense sticks.[22] The selling price of **Ternstroemia** bark was Bht 4 per kilogram and that of **Combretum**, Bht 1.5 per kilogram.

One other source of income, though an irregular one, obtained from the exploitation of the forests around Palokhi is the sale of barking deer (**Cervulus muntjac**) meat which is highly esteemed by both the Palokhi Karen and Northern Thai. Hunting of the deer is done individually, or in pairs, at night with muzzle-loading caplock guns and the aid of modified flashlights bound to the head (somewhat like miners' head-lamps) and operated by a rudimentary switch device strapped to the waist. If the game is brought in by a pair of hunters, it is shared between the two of them regardless of who actually shot the deer. Households which bring in barking deer usually cook as much of it as possible, and sell the rest of the meat, organs and entrails to other households and in the two Northern Thai settlements. In Palokhi, prime meat is sold between Bht 30 to Bht 40 per kilogram, as in the Northern Thai villages. Most households in Palokhi, however, would buy cheaper cuts. When the meat is sold in the Northern Thai villages, usually a whole haunch is taken for sale at a price varying between Bht 100 to Bht 120 and it may be bought by one household or by several who then divide the meat amongst themselves.

The sale of livestock also provides an occasional source of income for the Palokhi Karen. The most commonly sold livestock are chickens and pigs which

Northern Thai from the two nearby villages, workers from sections of the Watershed Unit, and Lisu from Ban Lum come to buy in Palokhi. The Northern Thai villagers and forestry workers usually buy chickens and pigs to rear, while the Lisu buy mainly chickens for certain curing rites which are said to require large numbers of chicken offerings. Some Palokhi households also obtained an income in 1981 from the sale of cattle and buffaloes reared on agistment and the buyers of these animals were either Karen or Northern Thai.

The manufactured articles sold by the Palokhi Karen were essentially of two kinds. The first was winnowing trays which one household made in 1981 specifically for sale to Northern Thai and Karen in other villages as a means of obtaining some extra cash for purchasing mainly "luxury" goods as the rice obtained from its wet-rice field was almost sufficient for the needs of the household. The second was muzzle-loading caplock guns and associated repairs and blacksmithing work. One household (H13a) specialised in this and, in fact, gunsmithing and black-smithing was the economic mainstay of this household. Toeloe, the head of the household enjoyed a considerable reputation for the guns he made and his customers were Palokhi and other Karen, as well as Northern Thai from various villages in the area. The household cultivated swiddens but these were invariably small because their domestic supply of labour was limited to Toeloe's wife, Gwa Chi' his daughter, and Cha Pghe his fourteen year old son. This was augmented when his son and family came to live in Palokhi, but only to a limited extent as this son was more interested in opening up wet-rice fields to support his own family. Despite the lucrative business of making and repairing guns and iron tools, the income thus obtained failed to enable the household to successfully supplement the rice from its swiddens because Toeloe was an opium addict and a large proportion of this income was spent on opium. Indeed, in several instances, he was in fact paid in opium. The price of a gun varied between Bht 100 and Bht 120 (if cash payments were made) depending on the length and thickness of the iron barrels. Payments could also be made in kind in the form of barrels where a buyer would bring in two barrels (which are actually common plumbing pipes about a metre in length) purchased at Ban Pa Pae; one of the pipes would be turned into a gun, while Toeloe would keep the other to be used later as a barrel or a source of iron in repair work, or for turning into bush knives, sickles, and so on. Repair work, on the other hand, was charged lower rates depending on the nature of the repairs involved. The replacement of a hammer, for instance, cost only Bht 15, but the total replacement of the trigger mechanisms would cost Bht 30 or Bht 40 depending on whether some of the old parts could be refashioned or re-used. The sale of services by Palokhi Karen was confined to two people, Rae' the ritual specialist and Chi' the tattooist (whose services were much sought after by the Karen in the area) who also claimed to be a ritual expert of sorts. Their clients were Northern Thai and Karen (from Palokhi and elsewhere) but their earnings were irregular throughout 1981.

As I have noted in the foregoing description of the various forms of income earned from external sources, the Palokhi Karen also do earn cash (or rice) incomes within the village as well. It follows from this that if households earn incomes in this way, then these incomes at the same time represent expenditures on the part of other households. The array of goods (but not services) bought and sold in Palokhi are, however, more limited than that in the transactions between Palokhi and other communities because a number of items which some households sell to people from other communities are either available to all (for example, pine wood) or are, in any case, owned by households (for example, livestock). Those items which are transacted generally represent items which are manufactured through a specialisation of labour in Palokhi, specifically, guns and iron tools made by Toeloe, or various commodities "retailed" by some household or other which happens to have a stock of these commodities purchased from stores in Northern Thai villages or from Karen from elsewhere, which other households lack at a particular point in time and are, for one reason or another, unable to go and purchase them outside Palokhi. Ritual services and tattooing also represent a form of specialised "production" from this point of view, and are similarly sought after, when illness strikes, and are likewise paid for.

It is, however, worth noting that in the early months of 1981 (approximately January to March), the two households which settled in Palokhi (from the Flower Plantation), "set up shop", as it were, and earned some money from other households in Palokhi by selling on a small scale various goods which were, nevertheless, obtainable in Ban Mae Lao. When these two households moved to Palokhi, they brought with them considerable stocks of rice (which was not sold) as well as tinned food, biscuits and preserved fish and shrimp paste. They were primarily for their own use, but because they existed in Palokhi, several households purchased these items from these two households. Their profit margins were very small, but the two heads of these households (La Zi and Thi') were encouraged enough to purchase, in bulk, more of such items at Ban Pa Pae (for which they got discounts) and which they continued to sell in Palokhi. This, however, was discontinued when the need for cash to buy rice became more urgent. It is interesting to note that this set an example which another household followed on two occasions in the year. This household, and Thi' as well, purchased large stocks of corn whisky in anticipation of a marriage between a man in Palokhi and a woman in Pong Thong and the round of rites protecting swiddens (**bghau hy'**) in the growing season of swidden rice. The profit margins in this enterprise were very good indeed by Palokhi standards, but it also involved considerable effort as well. The corn whisky was purchased from a Lahu—the only Lahu in the area whose sole activity was manufacturing the whisky—in Mae Muang Luang at a price of Bht 11 per 375 ml. bottle and sold in Palokhi at Bht 18 per bottle.

Expenditures

From the foregoing, it should be evident that households in Palokhi are quite firmly linked to an "external" cash economy which provides them with various sources of income. The Palokhi Karen, however, also purchase many items outside Palokhi, mainly in the Northern Thai settlements of Ban Mae Lao and Ban Pa Pae. The largest expenditures incurred by households, on any single item, are rice purchases. These purchases by households with rice deficits, as I have shown, lie in the region of approximately Bht 49,135. All rice is purchased in stores and not from Northern Thai cultivators of rice. The reason for this is that the Northern Thai themselves are not self-sufficient in rice and therefore do not have surpluses which the Palokhi Karen may buy. Thus, all the rice that goes into making up the shortages of rice in swidden and wet-rice cultivation in Palokhi (and, for that matter, in Ban Tung Choa and Ban Mae Lao) comes from the Chiang Mai plains. As the rice from the lowlands is made available in the Pa Pae hills by store-keepers and merchants in Pa Pae and Mae Lao, their role in the integration of what, for convenience, we may call the highland and lowland economies of the region is, therefore, a significant one.

In Pa Pae, there are three main stores, and in Mae Lao there are two stores which sell rice. All these stores or shops operate in very much the same manner and the principal store in Mae Lao may be taken as being representative of their functions as far as the Palokhi Karen are concerned.[23] The store is owned by a Northern Thai family but it is, effectively, run by the eldest daughter in the family. The family migrated upland to Mae Lao from Mae Rim in the plains in 1967 to join some relatives who had moved to Mae Lao earlier. The family did not acquire wet-rice fields but went directly into merchandising on a small scale. The store holds stocks of a large variety of goods typical of bigger stores in the rural areas. All the stocks are purchased in Chiang Mai from two markets, Wororot Market and Lam Yai Market. The rice which the Palokhi Karen buy at the shop comes from Chiang Mai where it is bought in bulk, that is, jute sacks (**kasaub** or **taaj**); in 1981, rice bought by the store) cost Bht 430 per sack. Although Wilaj, the daughter, occasionally made buying trips to Chiang Mai, most of the goods from Chiang Mai were usually brought in by **sii lau** operators who were "entrusted to do the buying" (**faak syy**) though, in fact, this arrangement amounted to hiring the services of these operators. The rice that was bought in Chiang Mai in this manner was transported to Mae Lao at a cost of Bht 30 per sack and the total cost of a sack of rice to the store was, therefore, Bht 460. In Mae Lao, the rice is sold, as I have mentioned earlier, in smaller measures or units, namely, **taang** or litres. In these smaller units, the price of rice was set by the store at Bht 120 per **taang,** and given that there are 6 **taang** to a sack, the profit on one sack of rice was thus Bht 260. These rates and profit margins apply generally to all the shops in the area, although the retail price of rice in Ban Pa Pae was slightly lower than in Mae Lao. From the point of view of the Palokhi Karen there is, however, little advantage in buying rice in Pa Pae because they have to pay Bht 10 for a return trip by **sii lau** as it is too far away for them to walk there.

Besides rice, the Palokhi Karen also purchase a range of goods which may be roughly categorised as food and non-food items. Most of the food items are items which are not available in Palokhi swiddens, for example, shrimp paste, pork crackle, dried, salted and occasionally fresh fish, sardines, noodles and biscuits and sundry confections much favoured Palokhi children and which parents rarely fail to indulge them with. Some food items which are grown in Palokhi swiddens are, nevertheless, purchased because supplies have run out, for example, chillies, eggplant, and tomatoes. Tobacco is also bought frequently although this is grown in swiddens but the amount thus obtained never meets the demand for it in Palokhi.

Non-food items include batteries (for flashlights and radios which some households possess), clothes, plastic sheets, cotton yarn (because cotton is not grown in Palokhi swiddens), needles, thread, footwear, kerosene (for lighters which are also purchased along with flints), bush knives, sickles, ploughshares, caps and lead shot (for the caplock guns), sulphur and potassium chlorate (for making gunpowder with domestically produced charcoal), aluminium buckets or pails, plastic scoops, enammelled metal dishes, and so on. Some of these items, particularly food, are also bought from a woman from Ban Thung Choa who regularly makes trips to Palokhi to sell her wares. An important aspect of the purchase of non-food items is that many of these items can by no means be regarded as necessities since the Palokhi Karen could easily produce them using wood and bamboo (for example, domestic utensils and houseware). They are, nevertheless, purchased for their "aesthetic" or "luxury" value and this suggests that insofar as these items are concerned, their supply in Northern Thai shops creates their own demand.

One important category of purchases in terms of the proportion of domestic income spent by a few households is opium and items related to its consumption, namely, oil or candles which are needed to warm up the opium preparatory to smoking, and aspirin powder (known by the Thai term, **jaa kae puat,** "pain relievers") which is used to "cut", or dilute, the opium in order to stretch out consumption of the drug as much as for the analgesic properties of the patent medicine. Opium is purchased from a variety of sources: Wilaj's shop (which obtains the opium from Lisu growers further up the Mae Malai-Pai road), the Lisu of Ban Lum or Mae Muang Luang, and other Karen who obtain it from these, or other similar, sources. The opium is usually sold in its smallest commercial unit called **tua** in Northern Thai (meaning "body" and also a classifier for animals) which is equivalent to the weight of an old **sataang** called **sataang daeng** ("red **sataang**") which is now no longer in circulation. The weight of the coin is approximately 4.8 grammes. Half units, however, are also sold and purchased. The price of opium in 1981 remained stable at Bht 40 but fell to Bht 30 per **tua** in January-February 1982 when the harvest season began.[24] Palokhi Karen opium addicts tend to buy opium in small quantities because they lack enough ready cash to buy the drug, but as with many other commodities, the purchases are generally regular and frequent.[25]

Household Economics in Palokhi: Some Examples

The considerable importance of the cash sector in the economy of Palokhi in enabling the Palokhi Karen to meet most if not all of their rice needs is best illustrated by household budgets. An examination of household budgets also serves to show the importance of the **miang** and tea industries in the cash sector and, more generally, the degree to which Palokhi is integrated in a regional economy. Tables 5.4 and 5.5 illustrate this in the case of seven households in Palokhi on the basis of aggregate data on incomes and expenditures for 1981 (but see also Appendix H).

Overall, it should be clear from the examples of household budgets presented in these tables that the Palokhi economy is highly monetised. While the cash sector is essential to the way in which the Palokhi Karen attempt to make up shortfalls in the agricultural system, it also allows them to acquire a great many commodities which they do not produce. In order to make use of the cash sector in this way, the Palokhi Karen are obliged to offer products to which they have access as well as their own labour. Despite the economic symbiosis between Palokhi and the external economy with which it is linked, the Palokhi Karen nevertheless are not locked into structured socio-economic relationships with the Northern Thai and others who also participate in this larger economy.

In this chapter, I have attempted to show that there is a regional context to the subsistence economy of Palokhi and that the Palokhi Karen are firmly linked to this larger economy through economic necessity, namely, the need for rice to make up deficits experienced in their own agricultural system. Although significantly dependent on a regional economy in order to meet their subsistence needs, the Palokhi Karen nevertheless maintain an autonomy in their community life for they cannot by any means be regarded as being structurally integrated into the larger social (and political) system which is dominated by the Northern Thai (and Thai) and which is, in this broader context, part of the regional economy.

In examining the economic system of the Palokhi Karen, I have also sought to show that even in their dual system of agriculture there are certain features (for example, land use, the inheritance of wet-rice fields, and the management of land) which possess cultural significance understandable only in terms of what I have called their cultural ideology. In the next chapter, I consider other aspects of the cultural ideology of the Palokhi Karen as it relates to agriculture, namely, the ceremonial cycle in the community which is based essentially on the rites of swiddening.

Table 5.4. Examples of Household Budgets: Income Earned (21 January 1981–31 December 1981)

| Household | Miang and Tea Related Activities | | | | Wage Labour | | Sales Income | | Total Income Earned | | Gross Income (in Baht) per capita |
| | Wages Earned (In and Outside Palokhi) | | Income from Sale of Leaf | | Wages Earned | | Sale of Food, Goods, Services, Livestock, Poultry, Ritual Services, etc. | | | | |
	Cash (Baht)	Rice (Baht)*	Cash (Baht)	Rice (Baht)*	Cash (Baht)	Rice (Baht)*	Cash (Baht)	Rice (Baht)*	Cash (Baht)	Rice (Baht)*	
Hla	218.0	108.0 [24.0]	1,164.2	—	—	—	1,837.0	504.0	3,219.2	612.0 [136.0]	638.5
H1b	203.0	45.0 [10.0]	947.0	—	—	—	152.0	387.0 [86.0]	1,302.0	432.0 [96.0]	289.0
H2	351.0	—	465.0	—	323.0	—	3,334.0	—	4,473.0	—	406.6
H3	1,891.0	242.25 [56.5]	24.0	—	662.0	38.25 [8.5]	2,665.0	—	5,242.0	280.5 [65.0]	552.3
H5	1,315.0	537.75 [119.5]	219.5	—	219.0	180.0 [40.0]	645.25	108.0 [24.0]	2,398.75	825.75 [183.5]	644.9
H6	16.0	—	4,433.5	2,704.5 [601.0]	40.0	54.0 [12.0]	4,123.5	171.0 [38.0]	8,613.0	2,929.5 [651.0]	1,923.75
H13b	798.5	166.5 [37.0]	153.0	—	398.0	243.0 [54.0]	521.5	126.0 [28.0]	1,871.0	535.5 [119.0]	481.3

* Rice incomes are given in terms of their cash value, that is, in Baht; the figures in brackets show their corresponding amounts in litres.

Table 5.5. Examples of Household Budgets: Expenditures (21 January 1981–31 December 1981)

| Household | Wages | | Rice Cash (Baht)** | Opium Cash (Baht)*** | Food, Goods, Services, Livestock, Poultry, Ritual/Medical Services, etc. | | Rent Cash (Baht) | Transport Cash (Baht) | Taxes Cash (Baht) | Total Expenditure***** | |
	Cash (Baht)	Rice (Baht)*			Cash (Baht)	Rice (Baht)****				Cash (Baht)	Rice (Baht)
H1a	—	NA	1,150.5	—	1,359.0	—	—	35.0	10.0	2,554.5 [1,150.5]	NA [44.0]
H1B	—	NA [35.0]	1,248.5 [290.0]	—	1,395.0	NA [4.0]	—	68.0	—	2,711.5 [1,248.5]	NA [39.0]
H2	56.0	NA [14.0]	—	10.0 [0.25]	3,713.75	—	—	71.0	10.0	3,850.75	NA [14.0]
H3	15.0	NA [4.0]	420.0 [89.0]	5.0 [0.125]	3,694.0	—	—	180.0	10.0	4,324.0 [420.0]	NA [4.0]
H5	—	NA [11.0]	403.5 [82.0]	5.0 [0.125]	1,325.5	99.0 [22.0]	—	227.0	25.0	1,986.0 [403.5]	NA/99.0 [11.0/22.0]
H6	943.0	1,478.25 [328.0]	1,527.5 [313.0]	165.0 [4.0]	2,673.5	—	1,500.0	87.0	10.0	6,906.0 [1,527.5]	1,478.25 [328.0]
H13b*****	—	—	666.0 [167.0]	—	165.0	—	—	10.0	—	841.0 [666.0]	—

* In this column, rice wages are given in terms of their cash value while the actual amounts of rice are given in brackets in litres. Where the rice used was glutinous rice purchased from shops in Northern Thai settlements, I have taken the cash value of such rice to be 4.5 baht per litre, the prevailing price in the Pa Pae hills area. I have not, however, indicated the cash value of rice wages where the rice used was rice grown in Palokhi. The reason is that as the Palokhi Karen generally do not buy or sell their own rice, it is therefore difficult to impute a cash value to the rice. In 1981, wage work was mainly done by a young girl (an only daughter) to earn some money and rice to support her sick mother. Her work consisted primarily of milling rice for some of the wealthier households in Palokhi (for example, H1a, H1b, H2, and H3) as well as child-minding. The work that she did was hardly essential to these households as they could quite easily do it themselves. Her employment, therefore, was motivated by a charitable concern for her and her mother's welfare. When her mother died in April, she was fostered out to a Northern Thai family in Ban Mae Lao, as I have noted before (Chapter III, p. 196, n. 23). She was paid rice wages in the form of milled non-glutinous rice grown by these households.

** The expenditures on rice are given in terms of their cash values, that is in Baht; the figures in brackets show the actual amounts of rice purchased in litres.

*** In this table, the expenditures on opium are given in Baht while the quantities of opium are given in tua in brackets. The purchases shown in the table are small and were bought essentially for medicinal purposes. They do not represent purchases by addicts (whose households are not reflected in the table) which were substantial but proved difficult to determine or estimate.

**** Rice is sometimes used to "purchase" other items in Palokhi. Such transactions are therefore exchange transactions in reality. In the table, the rice used in this way is indicated in terms of their cash values where it is possible to impute a cash value to the rice. The actual amounts of rice exchanged are given in litres in brackets.

***** Total expenditures are given here as cash expenditures on purchases including rice, and expenditures in which rice has been used as a medium of exchange. In the case of cash expenditures, I have also indicated in brackets the actual sums of money spent on the purchase of rice. Where rice expenditures are concerned, these are indicated in terms of their Baht values where applicable while the actual amounts of rice are given in brackets.

***** The data for H13b in this table are not as reliable as those for other households and this explains to some extent why its expenditures appear somewhat small in comparison. It should be noted, however, that H13b shared a number of economic functions with H13a (as discussed in Chapter IV, pp. 205–10) and several items (for example, tobacco) were obtained from the parental household without having to buy them from other households. As I have also pointed out, H13a and H13b were relatively poor and this also explains the lower levels of expenditures of the household in this table.

ENDNOTES

[1] In most, if not all accounts, of Karen agricultural systems characterised by a dual system of swidden and wet-rice cultivation, wet-rice agriculture is supplementary to swiddening and has come about as a later development. Hinton does however offer the suggestion (1973:249) that the Karen in the Mae Sariang area may have been wet-rice cultivators in Burma but on migrating into Northern Thailand (to escape Burmese oppression in the last century) took up swiddening because there was a shortage of land for wet-rice farming. Hinton acknowledges that this is speculative, however, because there is insufficient data from Burma to substantiate this. Grandstaff (1976:162, n. 7) argues against this and says that there was in fact no shortage of land for wet-rice agriculture in Northern Thailand because of low population densities in the region in the last century. I think Grandstaff is correct in this because there is sufficient evidence to show that Northern Thai populations were indeed small in the last century and that it is only within the last one hundred years or so that population growth has increased tremendously making land for wet-rice cultivation a scarce resource (see, for example, Wijeyewardene, **in press).** Further evidence may also be found in the nature of warfare in Northern Thailand and Burma where local populations in conquered territories were forcibly relocated in plains areas in order to cultivate rice to support urban populations — the "put vegetables in baskets, people in cities" formula (Kraisri [1965:6–9]). This has been the case with at least one Karen community still to be found in Hang Dong whose ancestors were taken prisoner in Burma and resettled there (Renard [1980:132]).

[2] I cannot, unfortunately, present a detailed description of how the calendrical system operates in Palokhi because of insufficient data. Although I have, for instance, a full list of the names of months in the Palokhi calendar, the Palokhi Karen were unable to supply the meanings of some month names. It is interesting to note, however, that there is a fair degree of concordance in month names between the Palokhi calendar and the list of months (in Sgaw Karen) supplied by Marshall (1922:49–50) and Iijima (1970:15–6). Only Marshall offers the meanings of month names (some of which I discuss in this chapter) but they do not all agree with those in Palokhi that are available to me. The following is a list of month names (approximated to the solar calendar) as they are found in Palokhi, and as they have been recorded by Marshall and Iijima.

	The calendar in Palokhi	The calendar according to Marshall	The calendar according to Iijima
January	La Tale	Th' le	La Plu
February	La Thi Phae'	Hte ku	Tha Le
March	La Khu	Thwe Kaw	Te Peh
April	La Soe	La khli	Te Li
May	La De' Nja	De nya	La Sa
June	La Nwi	La nwi	Dei Nya
July	La Xau'	La xo	
August	La Ku'	La hku	La New
September	La Ci My	Hsi mu	La Ku
October	La Ci Cha	Hsi hsa	
November	La Nau	La naw	Chi Mu
December	La Ply	La plu	Chi Sah

With the exception of the two months, Thwe kaw and La hkli given by Marshall and the omission of two months by Iijima, the general agreement in months names is remarkable. The current "official" Karen calendar, that is, the calendar published by the Karen National Union in Karen State of Burma or Kawthoolei, as they call it, is identical to Marshall's calendar. Month names, particularly in lunar calendars, can be useful in helping to ascertain how such calendars may be brought into phase with the solar, or sidereal, year (apart from other means such as observations of stellar shifts) as they may indicate a relationship between months and regularly occurring seasonal phenomena (see, for example, Fox [1979]). Often, the months may be named to coincide with such phenomena. In Palokhi, some of the months which are named after seasonally occurring phenomena, are slightly out of phase with these phenomena and there is no indication that the months are named, or that the calendar is adjusted specifically to coincide with such phenomena as a means by which the lunar calendar is phased in with the solar calendar, each year. Where Palokhi is concerned, the question of how the calendar is adjusted to the solar or sidereal year is, obviously, an important one as this has a direct bearing on when decisions are made to clear, burn and plant swiddens before the onset of the rainy season which is a regularly occurring annual phenomenon. I do not know how this is done, but it is likely that it involves observations on the movements of the stars. In a rite that is performed on the first day of planting (which I discuss in the next chapter), for instance, the position of the Great Bear or Big Dipper (**Cha Koechau,** literally, the "Elephant Stars") is taken into account. No one could explain the significance of the star in this ritual. Marshall (1922:53) however says that it indicates north for the Karen. Whether or not this is important in the calendrical system of the Palokhi Karen is not clear to me. It may be noted that for the Northern Thai the commencement of the agricultural season in April (which is roughly when the Palokhi Karen plant their swiddens) is indicated by a shift in the sun from the sign of Pisces to Aries (Davis [1984:99]). A problem related to the question of how the lunar year is brought into phase with the solar or sidereal year is, of course, intercalation. Intercalation itself is simple enough as all it entails is the addition of an extra month at appropriate intervals, and it is possessed by most if not all lunar calendrical systems. The real problem, however, lies in determining when this is to be done and this depends on the considerations that I have mentioned above. However, I failed to obtain any information on this in Palokhi. In the official Karen calendar of the Karen National Union, intercalation is done by means of repeating the month of Ci My and the two months are designated "First Ci My" and "Second Ci My". 1980 was an intercalary year in this official calendar. This calendar, however, should not be regarded as being necessarily representative of traditional Karen calendrical reckoning and calculations. Marshall, in his description of the Karen calendar, found it impossible to determine how intercalation was arrived at by the Karen.

[3] From the table, it will be noticed that the years in which wet-rice fields were acquired by some households do not correspond with the years in which they settled in Palokhi as described in Chapter II. The reason for this is that some households acquired the fields before actually settling in Palokhi, and some after doing so.

[4] I use the term "ownership" here only in its most general sense. I discuss in more detail, later, the issues involved in the ownership of wet-rice fields in Palokhi according to Karen ideas and the legal status of such ownership as it is defined in Thai law.

[5] Neither of these men were strangers to Palokhi when they arrived and, indeed, as with all other settlers they frequently visited Palokhi before settling in. They undoubtedly knew of the circumstances surrounding the "sale" of plot J (as I discuss shortly) or, if they did not they would certainly have had some idea that all was not right. On the other hand, they could not be **sure** (in each case) that Chi' might not have gone ahead and actually cleared and cultivated these plots. They could, of course, have claimed and cleared other areas (if their doubts had been strong enough) but what mitigated against this was the advantageous locations of the fields concerned. They are all situated near the village below the three dams erected by other cultivators and this offered the benefit of sharing the dams with the other cultivators, and shorter irrigation canals to construct — both of which, obviously, represent lower labour requirements in making these plots cultivable.

[6] This is also a good instance to show how tensions are managed in Palokhi. I have already mentioned that there is no council of elders, or any institutionalised mechanism to resolve problematic issues of mutual or common interest in Palokhi. The Palokhi Karen, instead tend to avoid such issues in public confrontations or, for that matter, in private between aggrieved parties. The resentments and grievances, however, eventually surface in the form of gossip. Even in this, they do not appear overtly and the mechanics are very subtle. A person may allude to an incident in a vague manner, or mention a detail which is unattributable to anyone, and round it all off by saying "but I don't know". The message, nonetheless, is communicated however unclear. It does mean, however, that as far as others are concerned, there is very little to go on by way of ascertainable facts so village opinion can never be mustered to a point where grievances eventually break out into the open. It also explains, partly, why there are no effective forms of social control in Palokhi. Within the confines of their homes, however, people are less constrained about discussing the iniquities of others (imagined or real). This was how I was, finally, able to obtain something of the background to the transactions in which Chi' was involved — from Mi' Zo, Toeloe's eleven year old son when no one else was prepared to say anything about these transactions beyond vague and mystifying remarks.

[7] In Palokhi, the term for "owner" is **koe'ca,** that is, "lord" and it is the same term used to refer to tutelary spirits of domains, as we have seen in Chapter II.

[8] A summary of relevant aspects of the Land Code and its implications for swiddening communities in Thailand may be found in a very useful paper by Justice (now Chief Justice) Sophon Ratanakhon (1978). The descriptions of the various certificates which I discuss here are taken from Section 1 of the Land

Code. From the Code, it would seem that Thai concepts of land use (on the basis of which it was drawn up) are not unlike those of the Palokhi Karen, at least in their fundamentals. The ranking of certificates which make distinctions among kinds of possession (as against ownership), despite the legal terminology, is clearly concerned with use rights. The Palokhi Karen and the Northern Thai with whom they have had dealings over land, appear to share similar ideas about the ownership of land and the transactions that I have described are all regarded as **bona fide** ones by both the Palokhi Karen and the Northern Thai.

[9] One household, however, has a certificate called **sau khau** 1 which is lowest in the series of graded documents which are taken into account in the recognition of possession of land.

[10] Under Section 41 of the Code, possessory rights (that is, as certified by the **baj caung**) to land may be inherited.

[11] I cannot resist making the observation that if "all men are equal in the eyes of the law", as Dicey once expressed it, then in Palokhi as far as the rule on inheritance goes, all men and women are equal — except when they are wives or unmarried women. Dicey's axiom in its literal sense is probably more true in Palokhi. As I go on to argue later, the key feature of inheritance in Palokhi is whether or not there is a **man** present who can control, or manage, that is, **cultivate** inherited wet-rice fields. From the table of land transactions, however, it will be seen that there is in fact one woman, 'Ae', who does own a plot of terraces by way of inheritance. In this case, she came to own the field although she did have a son (Chi') because she only came to live in Palokhi some time after her husband had died.

[12] In the case of 'Ae', the field was cultivated by her husband Chwi' and Sa Pae', and her son Chi'. Where the rituals entailed in the cultivation of the plot are concerned, they were performed by Chwi', and after their divorce, by her son. Her Yunnanese Chinese husband, Sa Pae', did not perform these rituals in any real sense because he did not know the prayers associated with them.

[13] Gender marking of work with buffaloes is also to be seen in a "wrist-tying" ritual conducted for buffaloes at the end of the planting season in wet-rice fields. It is a ritual that the Karen have very probably borrowed from the Northern Thai and the officiants are all **men**. In this ritual, it is actually the horns of the buffaloes that are tied with lengths of cotton yarn. This sort of gender marking is, in fact, to be found in Northern Thai agricultural communities as well (Davis [1984:152]), and it is interesting to note that in at least one such community, the symbolic reversal of sex roles — in certain rites which are held in relation to "matrilineal cults" — is expressed through the idiom of agricultural tasks and buffaloes. Potter (1976:145) says that in these rites, women act out ploughing with a man playing the part of a buffalo, and that a woman even mounts the man from the rear, suggesting that he is being "impregnated" by her. Although I cannot go into a discussion of this here, I suggest that the point is not "impregnation" as Potter seems to think but, rather, **agentivity** of the male in sexual intercourse which provides another idiom by which the reversal of roles is expressed, and which is conflated with the symbolism of buffaloes and ploughing. I do not wish by these observations that the predominant role of men in wet-rice agriculture in Palokhi is, therefore, the consequence of the adoption of wet-rice agriculture from the Northern Thai. If men appear to dominate wet-rice cultivation in certain tasks which entail the use of buffaloes and so on, it is because their dominant role in swiddening (in the form of appropriating land from territorial spirits, and so forth) has been extended into wet-rice cultivation which has permitted a more marked expression of this role.

[14] As I show later (pp. 337–42), cash transactions are certainly not uncommon in Palokhi; indeed, there is great deal of buying and selling that goes on in Palokhi. Rice, especially rice that is cultivated by households in Palokhi, rarely features in these kinds of transactions within the community. The Palokhi Karen give eminently pragmatic reasons why rice is not sold as a commodity in the community. They say that households with surpluses do not sell their rice because they can never be certain that forthcoming harvests would be sufficient for their needs, and that therefore the rice should be kept to meet contingencies. They also say, however, that if they did not have enough rice, they would be embarrassed or ashamed (**mae' chgha'**) to approach those with surpluses to sell rice. It is, however, the **attitude** that is intriguing. Part of the reason is that while they may indeed be embarrassed to approach households with surpluses to sell their rice, they are also at the same time concerned that they do not want to embarrass those with surpluses by placing them in a position of having to refuse to sell rice. These attitudes, I would argue, are reflective of a certain symbolic value or ideological weight that is placed on rice cultivated in Palokhi which makes it an essentially "non-transactable" commodity. Or, to borrow a term from marxist anthropology, rice is "fetishised" in the community.

[15] Around 1975, the selling price of raw leaf was approximately Bht 8 to Bht 10 per kilogram, according to the Palokhi Karen. The price in 1980–1 was about half this.

[16] In Ban Pa Pae, there were at least two Northern Thai merchants or wholesalers, and the Karen merchant mentioned earlier. In Ban Pha Daeng, there were two merchants — one a Northern Thai and the other a Yunnanese Chinese. Their participation in the **miang** economy appears to be only one of a number of activities that they are involved in some, for example, were also shopkeepers. In a socio-economic study of the Mae Muang Luang-Huai Thung Choa river system Thannarong **et al.** estimate that 3.9 per cent of the 254 Karen, Lisu and Northern Thai households (that is, 10) were engaged in **miang** production. Almost all these households were Northern Thai. Although the study does not bring this out, there can be no doubt that a far greater number of households in the watershed are also involved in the **miang** economy, if not as producers, then most certainly as occasional pickers and sellers of raw leaf for these 10 households, similar to the Palokhi Karen. Durrenberger (1974), in his short paper on economic networks and interrelationships in the area (based on his 1968–70 fieldwork on the Lisu at Ban Lum, now the site of the headquarters of the Royal Forestry Department's Watershed Unit) notes the importance of **miang** in the area. He says specifically that the Karen of Huai Pha Chao, that is, Huai Phra Chao (the Karen village nearest Ban Lum) produced **miang** which was also produced in Ban Pa Pae.

[17] In Palokhi, nine households owned **miang** or tea gardens and the mean size of these gardens was 1.9 **raj**. Most of these gardens were cleared from the forest for cropping, but some were sold to other Karen who migrated to Palokhi later in the history of the settlement. The ownership of these gardens is, in its principles, no different from that of wet-rice fields. The size of these gardens is not a reliable means of gauging their productivity, nor is it particularly useful for a description of how the Palokhi Karen crop the leaf. Some gardens have more, and some less, **miang** bushes. Furthermore, when the Palokhi Karen clear the undergrowth in their gardens, preparatory to picking the leaf, they may in fact clear more or less than the stated areas of these gardens. Those households which do not own gardens will often simply clear a part of the forest where **miang** bushes may be found in order to pick the leaf to sell, if they need money to buy rice. For these reasons, I therefore have not attempted to present a record of the ownership of these gardens and related transactions (since 1960) as I have done for wet-rice fields, nor do I give a breakdown of the areas of **miang** gardens owned by households in Palokhi.

[18] The Palokhi Karen produce **miang** for domestic consumption by the steaming method similar to that of the Northern Thai. Unlike the Northern Thai, however, they also drink tea as strong infusions with rock salt, especially after evening meals. The consumption of tea in this manner is greater than the fermented product. The tea is usually black tea, although some green tea (from the fermented leaf) is also prepared.

[19] The Northern Thai, by and large, and the Palokhi Karen are really in much the same position when it comes to **miang** and tea cropping. The Northern Thai, however, do employ the Palokhi Karen in certain tasks connected with **miang** and I discuss this later as well as the reasons for this.

[20] While not denying that the socio-economic relationships, which Van Roy describes, may be found in Chiang Dao and elsewhere in Northern Thailand, Wijeyewardene (1971) has, however, questioned Van Roy's use of the term **pau liang** to describe a "politico-economic role", that is, as an equivalent of the sociological concept "patron". Wijeyewardene suggests that the term is probably best viewed as one of address and a part of the complex of systems of address in Northern Thai society (see also Wijeyewardene [1968]). The evidence from Palokhi does, I think, lend some support to Wijeyewardene's interpretation of the use of the term **pau liang**. Any Northern Thai term which the Palokhi Karen use undoubtedly reflects its use in an essentially Northern Thai context and may be taken as a reasonably reliable indicator of the Northern Thai use of the term. It is indeed the case that the Palokhi Karen address the Pha Daeng merchant by the term **pau liang**, but when they reported their sales of leaf to me, he was usually referred to as "the **Cin Hau**", that is, "the Yunnanese Chinese".

[21] Even before the all-weather road was constructed, there was motorised traffic between Chiang Mai, Mae Malai, and Pai (see also Durrenberger [1974]) and there can be no doubt that the road has been an important part of the economic networks linking Pai and Chiang Mai, with the larger Northern Thai settlements in the area, such as Ban Pa Pae, acting as nodes in these networks for some time.

[22] **Combretum quadrangulare** is a host for the stick lac insect (Pendleton [1963:221]), but as the bark of **Combretum** collected in Palokhi does not have lac secretions, the bark is clearly not collected for lac.

[23] The stores all stock similar kinds of goods in general, but the two largest shops in Pa Pae (run by a Shan and a Yunnanese Chinese) have a greater variety. The stores in Mae Lao do not have the sort of creditor-debtor relationships with the Karen as described by Cohen (1984).

[24] According to the Palokhi Karen, the price of opium in 1979 was about Bht 50 per **tua**. Cooper (1984:155) reports that the price of opium in Homg villages per **sataang** measure (that is, **tua**) in 1974 was Bht 6 in February, Bht 15 in November, Bht 20 in mid-December, and Bht 10 in February 1975.

[25] There was one exception to this in 1981 when Chi' and two Karen elephant drivers from Mae Rim (who had come to Pa Pae to do logging work) devised a scheme to buy a large quantity of opium in Mae Hong Sorn for their own use as well as to earn money by selling the opium. This was an exception to the general pattern of opium purchases by the Palokhi Karen, but because it involved a considerable sum of money by Palokhi standards, some details of the scheme are worth noting here. One of the elephant drivers, Wa', knew of a Hmong village in Mae Hong Sorn where opium could be bought at a price of Bht 10 per **tua**. Initially, he and Chi' had agreed to go to Mae Hong Sorn to look for a certain type of dye (which Wa' knew could be found there and which was not available in Palokhi) for a particular tattoo which he wanted done by Chi'. Chi' had, in fact, a reputation for tattooing and the esoteric ritual knowledge associated with it. As they were going to Mae Hong Sorn for the dye, they also decided to take advantage of the opportunity to obtain the cheap opium and hence the scheme. Chi', however, had no money and Wa' therefore agreed to lend him some for the venture. As they conceived the plan originally, they had grandiose ideas of carrying out the project with a working capital of Bht 4,000 but eventually this was brought down to Bht 2,000 after incurring the expenses of travelling to Mae Hong Sorn by road. In Mae Hong Sorn, Chi' was able to earn about Bht 800 from tattooing alone, and he used this money to purchase the dye which cost him Bht 500. At the Hmong village, they bought Bht 2,000 worth of opium (that is, 200 **tua** or, approximately, 960 grammes) and they returned to Palokhi through forest tracks, passing various Karen villages, some three weeks later from the day they left (7 June). The market value of this amount of opium in the Mae Muang Luang-Huai Tung Choa watershed, at 1981 prices, was Bht 8,000. Wa' and Chi', however, sold 125 **tua** (840 grammes) for Bht 7,000 in one sale to a Northern Thai in Ban Tung Choa keeping the rest of the opium for their own use and for smaller sales. The Bht 5,000 profit was shared between the two of them. Chi', of course, had to repay the Bht 1,000 loan, but he was still left with Bht 1,500. His fee for tattooing **Wa'** with the dye (which gave birth to the whole enterprise) was Bht 200.

Chapter VI

Agricultural Rituals: The Ceremonial Cycle in Palokhi

We have seen in the last chapter that the Palokhi Karen are dependent on swiddening, wet-rice cultivation, and a cash economy for their subsistence needs. Indeed, for several households in Palokhi, the cash sector is crucial in enabling them to meet their subsistence needs. Notwithstanding the extent to which the Palokhi Karen are dependent on an external economy, swidden agriculture is regarded as the dominant form of subsistence production within the community. This particular perception of swiddening is based on two factors: first, an understanding that swidden agriculture predates wet-rice agriculture and is seen as a "Karen" system of cultivation; second, the continuing cultivation of swiddens which has ensured the persistence of a religious and ritual life that remains organised around the swidden cycle.

In this chapter, I present a description of several rites which form part of the cycle of ritual activities in Palokhi in order to show its crucial importance in the community and in relation to swidden agriculture, despite the fact that the Palokhi Karen possess a mixed subsistence system. As these swidden rites form the basis of rites performed in wet-rice fields, I shall not therefore deal with wet-rice agricultural rituals in Palokhi.[1]

The Ceremonial Cycle: An Overview

The ceremonial cycle in Palokhi consists of a large number of major and minor rites which are performed in swiddens and in the village, in the homes of households which cultivate swiddens. They are held at various times of the year according to various stages in the cycle of swidden cultivation beginning with the selection of swidden sites and culminating with the harvest celebration which marks the transition from one agricultural season to the next. These rites form a major part of a religious system which may well be regarded as a "totalizing" system, to borrow the use of the term from Levi-Strauss (1966:250–62), in which the larger significance of the Head Rite (**talykho**), certain features of kinship and **'au' ma xae,** for example, cannot be fully apprehended without reference to agricultural rituals and vice versa.

Figure 6.1

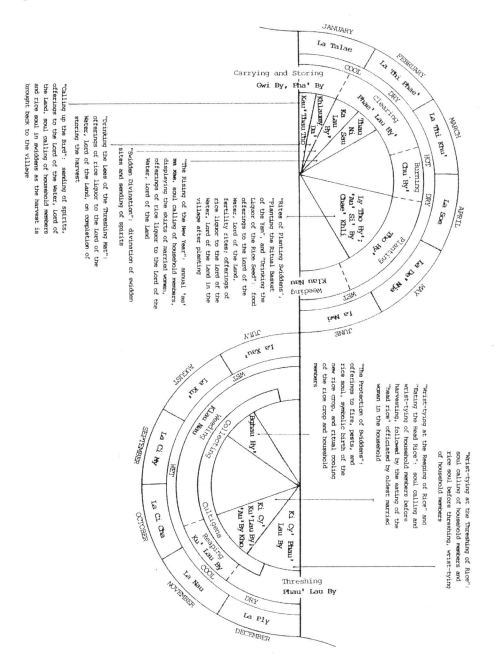

Figure 6.1 shows when these rites are held according to the cycle of swidden cultivation in Palokhi.

For convenience, these rites may be grouped as follows:

Table 6.1. The Rites of Swidden Cultivation in Palokhi

The Rites in the Ceremonial Cycle	Where Performed
The Rites of Clearing and Planting	
Swidden divination (**ka lau hy'**)	Swidden and village
The rite of clearing swiddens (no specific name)	Swidden
The rite of planting swiddens (**ly tho hy'**)	Swidden
Planting the ritual basket of the yam (**chae' lau nwae tasae'**)	Swidden
Drinking the liquor of the rice seed (**'au si' by chae' khli**)	Village
The Rite of Protection	
The rite protecting swiddens (**bghau hy'**)	Swidden
The Rites of Harvesting	
Wrist-tying at the reaping of rice (**ki cy' ku lau by**)	Village
Wrist-tying at the threshing of rice (**ki cy' phau' lau by**)	Village
Eating of the "Head Rice" (**'au' by kho**)	Village
Calling up the bird (**kau' thau tho**)	Swidden or village
Drinking the less of the threshing mat (**'au si' khlaumyda'**)	Village
The Rites of the New Year (The Descent of the Land, The Rising of the New Year)	
The annual **'au' ma xae** (no specific name)	Village
Calling back of souls (**phau' koela**)	Village
Wrist-tying at the descent of the land, the rising of the new year (**ki cy' kau lau wae, thau ni sau**)	Village

Although the annual **'au' ma xae** is not an agricultural ritual, nevertheless, it is an integral part of the yearly cycle of ritual activities and its performance needs to be viewed accordingly. That is, it is an essential element in the overall organisation of ritual activities, which are intimately linked with swidden agriculture, within the community.

The chief concern of these rites, with the exception of the annual **'au' ma xae,** readily apparent from their performances and accompanying ritual texts, is the successful growth of the rice crop. This is effected primarily through the propitiation of various spirits, the most important of which is the Lord of the Water, Lord of the Land. There are, however, other features embedded within these rites, and the overall structure of the ceremonial cycle, which are important. They are specifically: cultural definitions of a certain order which opposes settlement and forest, represented by relations with the Lord of the Water, Lord of the Land, within the domain; the complementary roles of male and female in reproduction symbolically applied to agricultural production; the importance of a "cool state" for the successful growth of rice; the identification of rice with humans; and a general aoristic and proleptic orientation which emphasises continuity through renewal.

As it will not be possible to examine here all the rites which make up the annual ceremonial cycle in Palokhi, I shall therefore consider only what is sufficient to illustrate these features. The rites which I focus on are those which make up the rites of planting, the rite of protection, "wrist tying at the reaping of rice" and "eating the 'head rice' " in the larger body of rites of harvesting, and the rites of the New Year.

In examining these agrarian rites in Palokhi, I take the view implicit in my earlier discussions of rituals that religion consists of a system of ideas and concepts, and an expressive or performative aspect, namely, ritual behaviour. As a general proposition, I think it would not be untenable to say that whatever else religion and ritual behaviour may involve, nevertheless, there is at least one level where they entail conceptual relations which represent some underlying schemata of cognition or cognitive models. As such, these conceptual relations are integrated, that is, coherent or patterned, and meaningful.

Ritual: Performance and Language

The conjunction of non-verbal and verbal performances in ritual is a phenomenon now well acknowledged in the anthropological literature. The prevalent view of these two aspects of ritual, it seems clear, is that they are both modes of symbolic expression analysable as communicative activity. In the 1968 Malinowski Memorial Lecture on "The Magical Power of Words", for instance, Tambiah has argued that the important feature of this conjunction of word and deed is the manipulation of metaphor and metonym, following Jakobson's discussion (1956) of these two linguistic forms. Specifically, he says that (Trobriand) ritual "actively exploits the expressive properties of language, the sensory qualities of objects, and the instrumental properties of action simultaneously in a number of ways" based on the principles of similarity and contiguity which underlie the construction of metaphors and metonyms (1968:189–90).

The idea of ritual as a **performative,** in Austin's sense (1962), is further developed by Tambiah in his 1979 Radcliffe-Brown Lecture. Here, Tambiah distinguishes two aspects of ritual as performative : the "constitutive" and the "regulative". The former "achieves the realization of the **performative** effect" while the latter "orientate(s) and regulate (s)a practical or technical activity" (1979:127–30).There are various implications of this view of ritual (which Tambiah explores) but we may note here that a key feature identified by Tambiah is the redundant social communication of meaning involving "interpersonal orchestration … social integration and continuity" (1979:133).

Fox (whose work Tambiah refers to amongst others) expresses a somewhat similar view. In a description of the ceremonial system of Savu in Eastern Indonesia, Fox (1979), drawing on a later study of Jakobson's (1970) on auditory and visual signs as semiotic systems distinguished respectively by time and space as structuring principles, has suggested that both ("oration" and "ostension") may be considered as different **modalities** in ritual. He then goes on to show that both modalities (at least in the case of the ritual systems of the

Savunese and Rotinese which he compares) exhibit the features of complementarity, markedness and parallelism more commonly associated with the analysis of linguistic phenomena.

Though concerned with the verbal and non-verbal aspects of ritual behaviour, Tambiah and Fox approach the subject from different but essentially complementary perspectives. Whilst Tambiah examines specific Trobriand rituals, Fox examines the entire ceremonial system of the Savunese. Yet, it is apparent in their analyses that the significance of specific rituals cannot be grasped without taking into account the totality of the symbolic systems of the societies they look at, and vice versa. In the literary analogy that Fox refers to (1979:171), we might say that in order to understand rituals, they need to be "read" as part of a single "text". The analogy is, in many respects, an apt one for the analyses that Tambiah and Fox advocate (despite differences in emphasis) both draw attention to the need to examine the ways in which meanings primarily associated with linguistic categories and forms may be expressed, similarly, in non-verbal performances which include the nature of the interaction of participants in ritual situations, the possibility that symbolic meaning may attach to the very participants themselves, and the manipulation of material objects in such contexts. They also establish the necessity to determine the range of contexts within which such symbolic expressions may take place and, thereby, guide the interpretation and analysis of the general and particular significance of these expressions.

These two discussions of the relation between act and language in ritual are instructive and provide a convenient starting point for this examination of Palokhi agrarian rites and, for that matter, the other rituals I have singled out for mention in earlier chapters. As we shall see, it will be necessary to re-examine the Head Rite and 'au' ma xae in the context of the ceremonial cycle in Palokhi.

Although there are certain features specific to Palokhi agrarian rites, they nevertheless share two essential generic characteristics which also distinguish the Head Rite and 'au' ma xae, namely, the recitation of formulaic prayers, and that most quotidian of activities — eating and drinking — as the focus of most non-verbal ritual performances. As with these two rituals, the prayers in agrarian rites are not impressive, public performances (though they are uttered in generally public situations), nor are the ritual acts highly colourful and dramatic events. They are best seen as falling in-between Fox's two modalities of ritual, "oration" and "ostension".

There is, however, one important difference between agrarian rites and the Head Rite and 'au' ma xae: agrarian rites are sequentially integrated following the cycle of swidden cultivation and they thus make up a cycle of ritual activities which are repeated annually. They are, therefore, not simply agricultural rituals but also calendrical rites articulated with certain key phases or stages in the agricultural calendar. Furthermore, these agricultural rituals taken as a whole, that is, as an annual complex, are performed individually by households at certain times and as a community with the headman and elders acting as ritual mediators between the community and the Lord of the Water, Lord of the Land. In other words, the ceremonial cycle in Palokhi brings together the two different themes of the Head Rite and **'au' ma xae** rituals — the interdependence of households as a ritual community in the former, and the separate identity and autonomy of domestic groups in the latter — within the overall structure of what is, substantially, a single corpus of annual ritual performances.

The Ritual Ownership of Swiddens

Palokhi agricultural rituals are, in the main, performed by individual households **qua** domestic groups wholly responsible for their own subsistence needs and a crucial aspect of this is the **ritual ownership** of swiddens as distinguished from general ownership in which all members of the household are regarded as owners of their swidden. Every household with a swidden has a ritual owner who may be **any** member of the family, and an officiant who is **always** the eldest male in the household, that is a father, a son or son-in-law. The two, therefore, are not necessarily the same person although in Palokhi it has generally been the case that the ritual owner has also been the ritual officiant.[2] The fact that the ritual officiant is always a male (with the exception of one ritual which I discuss later) has to do, of course, with the domination of ritual life by men and their primary association with the cultivation of land. The ritual ownership of swiddens, however, is related to certain conceptions in the religion of the Palokhi Karen where the successful growth of the rice crop is identified with the health and well-being of the ritual owner who, in effect, represents the entire household.

The Palokhi Karen have a term which is a compound of two elements which make up a dyadic set that is most often found in healing (soul calling) prayers. The first element is **tachu** which means "strength" and the second element is **takhle** which means "speed" or "fleetness of foot". Compounded, these two terms — **tachu takhle** — give us something like "good health" or "vitality". The Palokhi Karen say that if the ritual owner of a swidden is constantly plagued by sickness and ill-health, then his "vitality descends" (**lau tachu takhle**) and that as a consequence of this, the crops in the swidden will likewise suffer. On the other hand, although there may be no overt indication of ill-health on the part of the ritual owner, but if the harvests from swiddens are consistently poor, this too is taken as a sign that the "vitality" of the ritual owner has waned. Thus, the state of harvests are symptomatic of the condition of the ritual owner. The rationale for the practice of having a ritual owner, therefore, is that the "vitality" of the ritual owner is supposed to ensure a good harvest.

Ritual owners are usually also ritual officiants, but when it is deemed that the "vitality" of the officiant and owner has waned, then it becomes necessary to nominate a new ritual owner in order to ensure that subsequent harvests will be plentiful. It sometimes happens, however, that old men who are still in good health but are nevertheless unable to perform all the tasks required in agricultural pursuits may then decide to nominate a new ritual owner as a precaution against poor harvests which might result from the slow decline in their powers and abilities. The nomination of a new owner is usually decided at the discretion of the oldest male in the household and his wife. Not infrequently, however, this decision or choice of a new ritual owner may be arrived at through divination with the help of one of the two ritual specialists in Palokhi, or a Northern Thai ritual expert (called a **mau duu** in Northern Thai) in the nearby Northern Thai village of Ban Thung Choa. The new owner may be anyone in the household, male or female, but in general not children who have yet to reach an age when they can regularly perform a full day's work.[3]

If the new owner is a son or son-in-law, he will be taught how to conduct all the different rituals and their accompanying prayers as and when they become necessary to perform, that is on an **ad hoc** basis. This, it may be noted, is essentially how ritual knowledge is transmitted in Palokhi. Instruction in these matters is not carried out in any formal manner. It is thus not unusual to find a son or son-in-law forgetting parts of the prayers that he has been taught when he conducts agricultural rites in the swidden. Very often, he will perform the ritual acts and recite whatever he may remember of the prayers while his father or father-in-law stands by prompting him, or even reciting the entire text of the prayer himself.

If the ritual owner is a woman, however, the procedures are somewhat different. If a wife or daughter is the new owner, she performs only the ritual acts in **two** rites: those entailed in collecting soil samples for divination in order to decide on the final choice of a swidden site, and the harvesting of the rice grown solely for ritual purposes called the "Old Mother Rice" (**By Mo Pgha**). She may also be required to plant the Old Mother Rice. This, and the harvest of ritual rice are not structured performances nor do they involve the recitation of prayers unlike the collection of the soil samples which is conducted under the supervision or guidance of the father or husband. It is only in these circumstances that a woman actually performs rites in the swidden. She does not say the prayers which accompany the collection of soil samples; these are recited by the male ritual officiant of the household. From this, it is clear that despite the fact that women may sometimes participate in swidden rituals, this occurs in narrowly circumscribed contexts, and it is men who run the ritual life of domestic groups especially in relation to agriculture.

There are two aspects of the ritual ownership of swiddens worth noting which are relevant to an understanding of the symbolic meanings contained in the rites which make up the ceremonial cycle in Palokhi.

First, notwithstanding the fact that men are preeminent in managing the ritual activities of domestic groups, household members regardless of sex may become ritual owners of swiddens. The substitutability of household members as candidates for the role of ritual owner points to the "homogenous" or solidary nature of domestic groups since one member is as good as another regardless of generation or sex which are criteria that are otherwise important in the organisation, formation and fissioning of domestic groups and **'au' ma xae.** The practice of having a ritual owner itself indicates the close association between households, represented by the ritual owner, and the rice crop that they cultivate.

Second, although ritual owners may be seen to symbolise households or domestic groups in this particular sense, the relationship between ritual owners and the rice cultivated by their households is not merely a simple identification of person and crop; it is a **metonymical** relationship based on an implicit similarity and contiguity between what is best described as "life processes" in humans and rice evident in the perception that the successful growth of rice depends on the "vitality" of the ritual owner. Indeed, rice is in fact likened to humans in the number of souls that it is thought to possess, as held in common belief and explicitly expressed in certain agricultural ritual texts. It is not, however, attributed with "vitality" perhaps because it is not "animate" in the sense that humans (and animals) are. Nonetheless, its growth is spoken of as a "rising" (**thau** or **thau ghe,** "rising beautifully") similar to the way in which men and women are thought to "rise" into adulthood, maturity and procreativity as in the expression for "marriage", **thau pgha.** The verb **thau,** thus, expresses what are conceived of as processes of development in these two contexts, namely, the human and the agricultural, indicating a parallelism between the two.

The Rites of Clearing and Planting

Swidden Divination

The very first rite that is performed in association with swidden cultivation is the rite called **ka lau hy'**, or the "divining of swiddens". This is the simplest of all the rites performed in the agricultural cycle and it is held after the head of the household has decided on a number of potential swidden locations (as described in Chapter V, pp. 266–7). Divination is meant to establish the most favourable and, hence, the final choice of a swidden site. To do this, the ritual owner of the swidden-to-be has to go to each potential swidden location and, there, collect a handful of soil which is then wrapped up in banana leaf, the ubiquitous wrapping material of the Palokhi Karen. The samples of soil are then taken back to the house where a pair of chicken humeri (from chickens which have been eaten on previous occasions) are tied to each bundle of soil.

When all the households which intend to swidden in the year have collected all their samples of soil, the headman Tamu' then decides on a day most convenient for all when the divination of these chicken bones may be carried out. The divination is performed by Tamu', often with the assistance of the elders in the village.

On the day decided by Tamu', the various households present their bundles of soil with their accompanying chicken bones to him in the open space before his house. As with most if not all occasions of this nature, divination by the headman is an informal affair. He receives the bundles of soil and both he and the head of the household, or the ritual owner, unwrap the bundles placing the chicken bones on the samples of soil. Tamu' then picks up a pair of bones and scrapes away the dust, soot, grime and any left over flesh from them. Next, he cuts four fine slivers of bamboo about the length of toothpicks. Taking these one at a time, he searches out tiny holes in the humeri near their extremeties. These holes are the points of insertion of tendons in the bone and blood vessels leading to the marrow. The slivers of bamboo are inserted into these holes and examined for their orientation relative to the horizontal and vertical axes of the bones when they are held upright perpendicular to the ground. The principal criterion for a favourable outcome in this method of divination is symmetry in the orientation of the bamboo slivers along both axes.[4] If the outcome of this augury is favourable, this means that the site from which the sample of soil was collected may be swiddened without danger or mishap to the members because it is believed that the localised spirits which inhabit the area can be persuaded to leave.[5] There is also a general belief that the swidden will be farmed successfully. Even if divination of the first bundle of soil results in positive prognostications, Tamu' will nonetheless proceed to divine the other bones presented along with the other soil samples. If more than one location is suitable for swiddening, then the household can make a free choice as to which site it wishes to cultivate. On the other hand, if divination shows that not one of the sites is suitable for cultivation, then the household must proceed to seek out further alternative sites and repeat the procedure of divination on a future date with the headman all over again.

Once a household has a site determined as suitable for swiddening purposes, the ritual owner must then go to the site to claim it for the purposes of cultivation. This is done in the following way. The bundle of soil and the chicken bones, along with the slivers of bamboo, are taken to the place where the soil was obtained and the bundle is then placed in the fork of a branch of any tree in the area. The bundle may not be placed on the group or returned to the earth. The Palokhi Karen do not have a ready explanation for this practice but its symbolism is clear. The act of not returning the soil to the earth or ground represents symbolically the appropriation of the land for agricultural purposes. The prayer that is said when the bundle of soil and bones is thus deposited in the tree suggests that this is indeed the significance of this practice (see below), pointing to a concordance in the expressive meanings of the verbal and non-verbal aspects of this ritual. There is, as I argue later, also another aspect, namely, a high-low opposition implicit in this performance the significance of which is the imposition of a certain order along with the appropriation of land for cultivation. The soil samples and chicken bones with unfavourable portents, however, are thrown in the bush around the village. Although the soil samples are not returned to their original locations, there is nevertheless a certain symmetry in the symbolism of the disposal of these samples. The bush is not part of the settlement; it is a place where the Palokhi Karen defecate and where the detritus of their domestic lives are disposed including, as we have seen, the cooking vessels and utensils of divorced spouses.

The prayer which is said when the soil samples and bones are deposited in the tree is addressed to the spirits which are believed to inhabit the locality. The following is an example of the prayers said when the site is claimed for cultivation.

Coe' koe' phae' chghi, phae hy'	I will clear the fallow swidden, clear a swidden
Koe'zae tamy, koe'zae taxa	Spirit Lords
Koe'zae tatoe'ghe, tatoe'gwa	Lords of that which is not good, that which is not pure (literally, "white")
Ha' su thi soe'noe, Kau Su Ce'	Go to where the waters bend, (in) the Land of Black Silver
Coe' koe' ma chghi phi' 'i	I will work the fallow swidden here
Coe' koe' ma hy' phi' 'i	I will work a swidden here
Coe' koe' ma my phi' 'i	I will make the sun here[6]
Coe' koe' ma wae phi' 'i	I will do that here
Ma he loe' 'a' ghe	Doing all that is good
Ma he loe' 'a' gwa	Doing all that is pure
Coe' mae' toe' thi choe ba	My eyes (literally, "face") have not not noticed (you) with favour (literally, "sweetly")
Coe' na toe' thi choe ba	My ears have not noticed (you) with favour
He lau loe' tho xi' 'ylau, chau xi' 'ylau	Placing down all the auspicious bird bones, the auspicious chicken bones
Coe' koe' ma tatoethae', tatoekwau 'i	I will make a clearing, a circular space here
Coe' koe' ma me'u lau, phacha lau	I will bring fire down, ashes down
Koe'zae tamy, koe'zae taxa	Spirit Lords
Ha' su thi soe'noe, Kau Su Ce'	Go to where the waters bend, (in) the Land of Black Silver
'o' phi' 'i toe' ghe	To remain here is not good
Cho phi' 'i toe' ghe	To stay here is not good

The theme of this prayer (as with other similar prayers) is dispossession and appropriation. The spirits that inhabit the locality are told to leave and the ritual owner claims the land for agricultural purposes.

The expropriation of land from the spirits may be seen in the simple declarative sentences of intentionality which form part of the prayer. It is also expressed in certain tropological features of the prayer which also reveal other associated ideas. The contrast between "fallow swidden" (**chghi**) and "clearing" (**tatoethae'**), for example, is not merely one between regenerated forest and clearing; as their dyadic complements show, the contrast is also one between forest and a clearing that is a **circular** space. The underlying images of these contrasting metaphors are the disorder of naturally growing vegetation and a clearing marked by a regular, geometric shape which, in the order of things, is the product of **human** agency.

This contrast itself draws upon a more general distinction between forest and settlement akin to that made by the Northern Thai (Davis [1984:81—3]). It is also found in the Palokhi Karen belief that calamity would befall the village if wild animals (such as barking deer), which enter the village, are killed within the boundaries of the settlement.[7] The killing of such animals is described by the term **tahaghau,** that is, "destructive". The term, as we have seen, is used to explain the prohibition on "crooked" unions. The consequences of such "destructive" acts in both cases are that the land becomes "hot" and crops will be "destroyed". Although the Palokhi Karen themselves translate **tahaghau** by the Northern Thai term **khoet** or "taboo", it is clear that these consequences represent the infertility of land.

The forest and settlement, therefore, are important categories in Palokhi Karen thought. They establish a certain cognitive order in the lived-in world of the Palokhi Karen. The domains they represent also imply certain forms of appropriate behaviour and conduct; any inappropriate behaviour or action which transgresses the boundaries of these categorial domains results in "hot" land and the destruction of crops — the ultimate sanction that the community and its members can face.

Dispossession is also to be seen in that part of the prayer where the local spirits are told to "Go where the waters bend" in the "Land of Black Silver". These expressions reveal further conceptual associations which cohere with the distinction between forest and settlement. The meaning of these cryptic references rests on certain cosmological beliefs. According to one informant, the Land of Black Silver is a reference to the after-world inhabited by spirits (as against souls) of the dead. It is a world that is an inverted version of the here-and-now world of the living.[8] The Land of Black Silver, thus, contains an implicit contrast with the world of the living where silver is not black, that is, untarnished. In the larger context of the ritual, however, this elliptical cosmological reference cannot be restricted merely to drawing out this implicit dichotomy or else it would be meaningless. Its significance, therefore, must lie in the only possible (but unarticulated) distinction suggested by other features of the prayer, namely, the contrast between forest and settlement, wild and domesticated, and the non-living and the living contained in the implied dichotomy: that is, human activity in "non-human" (spirit) areas within the kau. In other words, the cultivation of the forest is conceived of in terms of a process produced by human agency in an environment which is not regarded as an area of human activity.

The meaning of "where the waters bend" is more obscure and I was unable to elicit any exegesis for this phrase other than that this is where spirits may be found. I would venture the suggestion, nonetheless, that it contains an implicit contrast paralleling that between "crooked" (**ke'**) and "straight" (**lo**) which have much the same metaphorical connotations in Palokhi Karen as do the English terms.[9] It would be consistent with the other distinctions made in the prayer.

The appropriation of land, on the other hand, is unequivocally stated in the prayer in which the ritual owner explicitly says that he intends to cultivate the area. It is significant that cultivating a swidden is said to be doing all that is "good" and "pure" while the spirits themselves are declared to be "lords of that which is not good, that which is not pure". The dyadic pair formed by the terms "good" and "pure" stands for "auspicious" conditions which, elsewhere as we have seen in the Head Rite, are obtained from the Lord of the Water, Lord of the Land. There are, thus, two senses in which "auspicious" conditions prevail with the appropriation of land from the local spirits. First, the departure of the spirits presents such conditions since the spirits are themselves "inauspicious". Second, the clearing and cultivation of forest represent conditions of an order which are one and the same as those obtained from the Lord of the Water, Lord of the Land. The creation of these conditions in the latter sense is reiterated consistently in agricultural ritual texts. Its recurrence in the next rite (the rite of clearing of swiddens) indicates, however, that there is yet another significant aspect to these conditions.

The Rite of Clearing Swiddens

The rite of clearing swiddens consists of a short prayer that is said by the head of the household as he first slashes the vegetation of the swidden site. It is performed on the first day of clearing by the household with the assistance of other villagers but it is an individualised performance. The outstanding feature of the rite, however, is that the ritual act is in fact a **technical** act accompanied by a prayer. The prayer is addressed to the Lord of the Water, Lord of the Land.

Sa, delau Thi Koe'ca, Kau Koe'ca	O, descend Lord of the Water, Lord of the Land
Coe' koe' phae' chghi phi' 'i	I will clear the fallow swidden here
Coe' koe' phae' hy' phi' 'i	I will clear a swidden here
Coe' koe' ma by phi' 'i	I will grow rice here
Coe' koe' ma 'a' phi' 'i	I will do much here
Ma he loe' 'a' ghe, 'a' gwa	Bestow all that is good, that is pure
Ma he coe' by to' kho, to' xau	Bestow upon my rice at the head, at the bottom
Ghe chae' pha',	Beautiful are the offerings
Ghe poe' khry'	Beautiful are our tributes
Ghe nju' pu,	Beautiful within (the swidden)
Ghe chghae' bo	Beautiful every stem

It is unmistakably clear that the rite is constituted by a perfect concordance of "performatives", namely, the technical ("ostension") and the verbal ("oration") where the technical becomes ritual by virtue of the recitation of the prayer. But, there is also a dialectical relation between the two. In the prayer previously described, the clearing of the forest is seen to result is auspicious conditions. In the context of this rite, however, the creation of these conditions is dependent on the actual clearing of the forest; the technical act is thus, also the operative analogue of the verbal performance.

It will be noticed that in this rite, these conditions are derived from the Lord of the Water, Lord of the Land which is called "down" (that is, from "above") to "bestow all that is good, that is pure" whereas in the previous prayer it is the clearing of the forest that is said to produce them. The phrase which expresses these meanings (**Ma he loe' 'a' ghe, 'a' gwa**) is the same in both prayers. Although an Agent is not specified in the phrase (which is a characteristic feature of such simple declarative sentences), the Agents in both cases are identifiable by context and confirmed by native exegesis. The occurrence of the phrase in both prayers and its recitation immediately after the head of the household states that he will clear the "fallow swidden" and "swidden" in the second prayer is, however, significant: it indicates a contiguity between the process of clearing the forest and the descent of the Lord of the Water, Lord of the Land according to which auspicious conditions are effected. This contiguity reveals a deeper meaning to the clearing of forest and the presence of the Lord of the Water, Lord of the Land, namely, that the tutelary spirit is part of the process by which order is established in natural disorder through the creation of boundaries. It also suggests that the state of auspiciousness is representative of this order. Thus, although the Lord of the Water, Lord of the Land is an overlord of a naturally defined domain (**kau**) in which may be found human settlements and areas occupied by non-human entities or spirits, it is nevertheless identified with a human and cultural order, an integral part of which is the cultivation of land.

It is this which underlies the dichotomous attributes of the tutelary spirit of the domain and the "inauspicious spirit lords". It also explains the particular symbolism of placing the soil samples and the "auspicious bird bones" and "auspicious chicken bones" in a tree above the ground (rather than returning them to the, as yet, unclaimed land) while the bones are nonetheless said to be "placed down" in the previous prayer.

The Rite of Planting Swiddens (Ly Tho Hy')

The planting of rice in swiddens is accompanied by the first major agricultural ritual performances of the season for swidden-cultivating households consisting of three related, but separate rites. The first is the rite of planting swiddens (**ly tho hy'**) which is held on the first day of planting in swiddens. It is followed by the rite called "planting the (ritual) basket of the yam" (**chae' lau nwae** tasae') which is also performed on the same day. The third is held several days later, in the house, and it is called "drinking the liquor of the rice seed" (**'au si' by chae' khli**). Unlike the rites entailed in divination and the clearing of swiddens, these three rites are not individualised performances. They are held in the presence of the labour gangs which are formed to assist the household and they involve the participation of village elders and the headman should he be present when a swidden is planted.

Planting begins early in the morning without any ritual performance. During this time, however, the head of the household or the ritual owner of the swidden plants the Old Mother Rice (**By Mo Pgha**). This is rice that is grown only for ritual purposes and it is never consumed. Its value is entirely symbolic and it is, in fact, rice that **symbolises** itself. When a household first swiddens on its own, it has to acquire rice seed. This may be obtained from a parental household or purchased from some other household. A small quantity of the seed is set aside to be the Old Mother Rice or, alternatively, some seed may be obtained from the Old Mother Rice of the parental household. The seed is planted in a small plot near the field hut in the swidden and it is harvested each year along with the principal rice crop. Thereafter, the Old Mother Rice is stored above the rice harvest in the household granary suspended from the rafters of the roof of the granary or of the house if the granary is built on the inner verandah of the house. It serves several symbolic functions but the most important is the representation of the continuity of the rice crop or the annual succession of rice from its own seed cultivated in swiddens.

The planting ritual takes place at about mid-day when the work party stops planting for the meal provided by the owners of the swidden. Food offerings consisting of rice, chicken or pork stew and chilli relishes are wrapped in banana leaves by the head of the household or his wife who then give the bundles of food to the headman and elders. The offerings are taken to any of the tree stumps that dot the swidden and the ritual officiants squat down before the tree stumps. Here, they hold up the offerings and pray to the Lord of the Water, Lord of the Land and other tutelary spirits of domains in an invocation similar, or identical, to the invocation which characterises the prayers of the Head Rite. The prayers said by the elders and headman are generally similar but variations in some details are not uncommon.

An example of the prayers said at this time is presented below. This particular prayer was recited by the head of the household (Chi' of Hllb) who was also the ritual owner of the swidden.

Sa, delau Thi Koe'ca, Kau Koe'ca   O, descend Lord of the Water, Lord of the
                                      Land

Koecoe Koe'ca, koelo Koe'ca	Lords of the mountain tops, Lords of the mountain ridges
Palaukhi, Palauklo' 'a' Koe'ca	Lord of the headwaters of Pang Luang, Pang Luang stream
Koecoe kho, koecoe lo	Mountain peaks, mountain ridges
Ce' Daw 'a' Koe'ca	Lord of Chiang Dao
Leke'pau 'a' Koe'ca	Lord of the Shining Cliff
Maungau' 'a' Koe'ca	Lord of Mau Ngau
Mauhauke 'a' Koe'ca	Lord of Mau Hau Ke
'Au' ky me kho, thi kho	Eat your fill of the first rice, the first water (literally, "head rice, head water")
'I thau; kwa lau	Here raised up; look down
Ha'sa, koetau	Look after, watch over[10]
Mycha toe ni nja 'i	(In) the morning of this day
Tho chghi, chae' hy'	(We) dibble the fallow swidden, tattoo the swidden
Ma 'e' coe' by ty 'a' ghe	Make my rice beautiful
Ty hy' kho, hy' xau	To the top of the swidden, the bottom of the swidden, (literally, "head of the swidden, steps of the swidden)
'Au' ky	Eat till you are full
'Au' pghe	Eat till you are replete

The supplicant then makes a series of requests which are punctuated by invitations to the tutelary spirits to eat the food offerings. The requests are varied:

Kae' 'e' by my koe'ca, by phau koe'ca	(Let me) be the lord of swidden rice the lord of rice granaries
'Au' pghe loe 'a' mynja	Eating fully into the future
Ha'sa, koetau kau' dy kau' gha	Look after, watch over each (domesticated) animal, each person
Wau' ke taghe	Bring back that which is good
Wau' ke taba'	Bring back that which is proper
Wau' ke ta'a'su koe'ca	Bring back the lordship of wealth
Wau' ke tapgho koe'ca	Bring back the lordship of things of power[11]
Nauzu Koe'ca, nauchau Koe'ca	(?)Ancient Lords, (?)Old Lords
Kae' 'e' ke koese koe'ca, koecau koe'ca	(Let me) be again the lord of horses, the lord of elephants
Xy, ne ta'a'ba', ne ta'a'ba'	Seeking, (let me) obtain that which is proper, (let me) obtain that which is right

Pghe, ba' ta'a'ba'	Buying, (let me) receive that which is cheap
Cha, ba' ta'a'xi'	Selling, (let me) receive that which is valuable

The prayer then ends with the standard formula for closing prayers addressed to the Lord of the Water, Lord of the Land and the other tutelary spirits.

Cy'noe (toe)chi ba thau Na	(My) ten fingers are raised up in prayer to You (literally, "praying up to You)
Ba thau Na	Raised up in prayer to You
Sa.	"Amen".

When the prayers end, the food offerings are then placed on the tree stumps and the ritual officiants return to the field hut where the work party commences on the mid-day meal.

In this particular prayer, there are only a few direct references to the rice that is being planted in the swidden and the plea for a bountiful harvest is condensed in the lines in which the supplicant asks to be "the lord of swidden rice, the lord of rice granaries". In other versions of the prayer, some of the supplicatory requests directed at the Lord of the Water, Lord of the Land and the other domain spirits are more elaborate in their references to the rice crop. There are, for instance, requests to the tutelary spirits to prevent felled trees from sliding down the slopes of swiddens and destroying the rice crop, or that a month's work will bring rice for a year, and so on. The tutelary spirits may also be asked for a bountiful harvest in hyperbolic terms where the supplicant or ritual officiant requests that each stalk of rice be made as big as the trees of the **Dipterocarp** species. Requests for a successful harvest may also be expressed in terms of an invitation (or, more correctly, a declaration) where the spirits are said to "sit in the swidden" and "rise up in the granary".

Aside from these differences in details, perhaps the most significant common feature in all prayers is the plea that the supplicants be owners ("lords") of wealth which is described either directly (as in the prayer above) or in terms of "exchangeables", "silver" (which is now also the term for the currency of Thailand), "bronze frog drums" and "horses and elephants" as stated in the foregoing prayer. Yet another characteristic feature of these prayers is the way in which these pleas for the "lordship" of swidden rice, granaries of rice and wealth in these various forms are framed in terms of a state, or condition, that comes into existence "again" (**ke**, literally, "return"). The state or condition therefore is expressed in an idiom of repetition or renewal.

For the Palokhi Karen and, indeed, most if not all Karen, the nineteenth century British Indian Empire silver rupees, silver ornaments made from these coins, elephants and bronze drums are wealth **par excellence**.[12] They are also symbols of wealth. However, while several households possess silver rupees, bracelets and earrings, none possesses elephants or bronze drums. Furthermore, as I have shown in the last chapter, only a few households achieve surpluses in rice cultivation and these surpluses are generally not traded or sold as a means of accumulating wealth. Thus, self-sufficiency or surplus production in agriculture does not generate wealth in any direct sense in Palokhi. Nor is rice seen as wealth **per se**. These references to wealth in its various forms, therefore, are of an entirely metaphorical order. What, then, underlies the pervasive occurrence of these metaphors for wealth?

The parallel juxtaposition of these metaphors following the references to "swidden rice" and "rice granaries" indicate that there is a relationship of metonymy between these metaphors and rice in swiddens and granaries. The metaphors in this relationship are, thus, expressions for increase and a bountiful harvest. But, if these condensed metaphors and metonyms represent a rich harvest and increase, they do not imply an absolute, progressive increase through time measured in terms of the agricultural calendar. The consistent use of the aoristic term **ke** in the constructions containing these metaphors points to a conceptualisation of the process of increase as an on-going, continuing one that repeats and renews itself.

I suggest, however, that there is also a sociological reality reflected in these metaphors which is masked by the ritual textual form that they take. The examples of household budgets in the last chapter demonstrate that it is the households which are self-sufficient in rice and which have rice surpluses that are also able to enjoy a better material standard of living. Their incomes and expenditures are much greater than that of other households. Furthermore, their varied expenditures are on non-subsistence commodities rather than rice. Most of them are also owners of buffaloes and cattle (see Appendix G). While it is true that these households do not indulge themselves in "conspicuous consumption", the myriad little unintended indicators of their better-off position and the size of their harvests are, on the other hand, not lost on others. This self-sufficiency in rice and the greater ability to purchase non-subsistence commodities are directly influenced by the larger domestic supplies of labour of these households. This is an economic and sociological relationship which the Palokhi Karen are by no means entirely unaware of. The easy equation, however, is that households with bountiful harvests are also those which have a greater access to non-subsistence commodities and are, therefore, "wealthy". It is this equation, I suggest, which lends these metaphors to the particular metonymical usage in the prayer. But, it also results in a certain misrepresentation, for the Palokhi Karen are unable to exegesise the meanings of these metaphors even in relation to "swidden rice" and "rice granaries" apart from saying that they are "similar" (**laugha'**).

They also say that these expressions are integral to "old prayers" (**thuphata loeploe**) which they undoubtedly are (but see below). These metaphors as with those in other ritual texts are not deliberately, or consciously, constructed. They are used because they are traditional formulae and because they are culturally appropriate. Their employment in the prayer, therefore, must also be regarded as the product — in part or in whole — of a certain "miscognition", in Bourdieu's sense ([1977]; see also Acciaioli [1981]), of sociological reality. Nevertheless, it is possible that for some individuals there is a muted awareness of at least one aspect of this reality in the prayers they use. For, as the last dyadic set in the series of metaphors suggests, the generation of wealth is expressed in terms of "buying cheap and selling dear". This is not typical of other similar prayers and it is, in fact, Chi''s own formulation.

Planting the Ritual Basket of the Yam (Chae' Lau Nwae Tasae')

The rite called **chae' lau nwae tasae'** (literally, "tattooing down the ritual basket of the yam") is performed at the end of the day when the work party has completed its task. It is a brief performance and the Palokhi Karen have virtually no explanation for the rite other than to say that it "makes the rice rise up" (**ma thau by**).

Nevertheless, this rite and the rite protecting swiddens (**bghau hy'**) when interpreted together (for reasons which I discuss later) are crucial for an understanding of how the agricultural process is conceived of in Palokhi Karen thought. They suggest that the symbolism of these two rites are expressions of the subliminal ideas and conceptual associations which make up what I called, in Chapter III, the procreative model of society in Palokhi, namely, the procreative roles of male and female, ritual heat and cooling, and the fecundation of land for cultivation.

The ritual owner first plants a yam tuber or a portion of it (of the species **Dioscorea**) in the ground next to a tree stump near the plot where the Old Mother Rice has been planted. A bamboo water vessel (**thi toe**) is next placed on the ground where the tuber was planted, and a long slim bamboo pole, split at its upper end, called a **kra' lau** ("descending pole" or "descending stick") is then placed in the water vessel with its upper end resting against a tree stump or on a forked stick. The bamboo pole is set in such way that it is oriented in the direction of the constellation Ursus Major (the Great Bear or Big Dipper) which is known to the Palokhi Karen as the "Elephant Stars" (**Cha Koe'cau**). When these preparations are completed, the ritual owner or head of the household pours water into the **thi toe** from another water vessel, saying as he does so:

By, 'oe, ma na ty do', na kau' do'	O, rice, (I) do this for you so that (literally, "until") you become great, each of you becomes great
By, 'oe, ghe kau' bo, ghe kau' zi	O, rice, beautiful on each stalk, beautiful in each village
Ghe ty loe' hy' kho	Beautiful to the top of the swidden
Ghe ty loe' hy' xau	Beautiful to the bottom of the swidden

As the water overflows from the **thi toe**, spilling on the ground, the members of the work party who have assembled around to watch the performance start shouting and hooting. As they do so, the ritual owner or head of the household splashes the water remaining in the water vessel that he is carrying over everyone. Usually, there are also men and women standing around with water vessels in hand waiting for this moment when they too then splash water over all those who are present.

The paucity of indigenous explanations for the performance of the ritual, the absence of myths which might suggest reasons for the role of yam in the ritual and the orientation of the **kra' lau** in the direction of the Great Bear, as well as the brevity of the prayer which makes no mention of the yam all make it difficult to interpret the symbolic meanings of the performance when taken merely within the specific context of the rite itself. When, however, the rite is viewed in terms of the features and "idioms" of ritual performances recurrent in other rites, the meanings embedded in the rite become clear.

The purpose or function of the rite is by no means obscure. The prayer, for example, is clearly addressed to rice itself and it unambiguously expresses what is considered to be the desired outcome of the rite. This and the proximity of the material appurtenances of the ritual to the plot where the Old Mother Rice is planted indicate that the Palokhi Karen are, at one level at any rate, indeed correct in saying that the ritual is designed to facilitate the growth of rice or to "make the rice rise up". In this respect, the ritual is consistent with the one performed at mid-day. The only difference is that in the mid-day ritual the conditions necessary for the successful growth of rice are obtained from the Lord of the Water, Lord of the Land, whereas in this ritual rice is directly ministered to. The expressions in the prayer are, thus, "performatives": but, they are not the most significant feature of the ritual.

Watering the Thi Toe and Kra' Lau in the Rite of Planting the Ritual Basket of the Yam.

The distinctive feature of the ritual is the production of a **cool** state that is brought about by the use of water — quite apart from its obvious function in agriculture — as a cooling medium for the successful cultivation of rice. Although this is not mentioned in the prayer, the ritual sequel that protects swiddens is wholly unambiguous on the necessity for this cool state. The use of water in this context, thus, possesses the same order of symbolic meaning as the showering of water on people and the application of lustral water on newly-married couples during marriage rites, as well as the lustrations to the Lord of the Water, Lord of the Land in the Head Rite. In all these cases, cooling is related to the creation of auspicious conditions. However, as I argued in Chapter III, cooling is none other than the management of "ritual heat" associated with the union of procreative males and females. In what sense, then, is "ritual heat" present in this rite?

The answer lies in the symbolism of the **kra' lau** and **thi toe**. Although there are no means of ascertaining the significance of the Elephant Stars (for the Palokhi Karen have no explanation or myth which would account for their role), the name of the **kra' lau** itself — **descending** pole or stick — is an important indication of the primary symbolism in the rite. It suggests that the **kra' lau** is oriented from the Elephant Stars towards or, more precisely, **into** the **thi toe**. When viewed in these terms, the imagery of the **kra' lau** and **thi toe** becomes transparent. They are an iconic representation of the quintessential conjunction of male and female in procreative mode, that is, sexual intercourse. And the heat that is implicitly managed in this rite is, thus, derived from this symbolic conjunction. Accordingly, the use of water takes on an added significance: it is as much a medium of cooling as it is a medium by which the fecundating properties of this iconic union are transferred to land. The rite therefore may well be regarded as a "fertility" or, more aptly, a fertilising rite. This, moreover, would explain why the rite is conducted when it is — after the rice has been planted in the swidden at which time the growth potential of rice may then be activated.

It is, however, more difficult to determine the significance of the yam in the rite. In the absence of Palokhi Karen explanations, myths and other ritual uses of yam which might inform an analysis of the role of the tuber in the rite, I therefore propose a deductive, rather than an inductive, interpretation.

In the context of the performance of the ritual, only two kinds of crops are planted which are directly relevant to the performance: rice and yam. Rice, as the term for the crop grown for ritual purposes ("Old Mother Rice") indicates, is "female". Given the primary symbolism of the rite in which male and female are conjoined, I would suggest that the yam is "male", representing the complementary, botanic "sex" (or "gender") category of rice.

It is important to note that the symbolism of the ritual is based on a logic of **human** sexual difference. It will also be recalled that when the Palokhi Karen wish to make their fruit trees (for example, papaya) bear fruit, they tie the skirts of married women to these trees. These are applications of conceptual associations derived from the human domain to the botanic domain. Although the Palokhi Karen may be aware of the fact of sexual dimorphism in certain plants (of which papaya is one), I have no reason to believe that this fact occupies an important place in their schemata of cognition beyond the attribution of female gender to rice which is, in any case, an extrapolation from the human domain. It is, on the contrary, human sexual difference that is important in the schemata of cognition of the Palokhi Karen. The point to note is that this difference and related processes in the human domain provide a **model** for processes in cultivated crops. The validity of this model in Palokhi — the procreative model of society extended to the cultivation of crops — is based, as we have seen in various other contexts, on a similarity and contiguity between the human and the botanic which is established through relationships of equivalence such as homology and analogy. In general belief and in the particular context of the rite of planting the ritual basket of the yam, "female" rice is such a relationship of equivalence. Given the primary symbolism of the rite and the logic of equivalences which guides the botanic extensions of the model of human society and processes, "male" yam therefore must be the other relationship of equivalence.

Drinking the Liquor of the Rice Seed ('Au' Si' By Chae' Khli)

The rite known as "drinking the liquor of the rice seed" is performed in the village but it is not a village-wide ritual. It is performed on a household basis with the headman and elders as officiants. The ritual consists of making offerings of rice liquor which, in theory, is made from the seed left over from planting. The left-over seed is often insufficient for making the liquor that is required (which is usually about three 750 ml beer bottles) and so it has to be supplemented with rice from the granary. In some cases, there may in fact be no left-over rice seed and the liquor is therefore made entirely from rice drawn from the granary. Depending on when and how long it takes to make the liquor, the rite may be held any time between two to three weeks from planting. When the liquor is ready, a day is set for the ritual which is held after the household has had its evening meal. It is usual for the household to invite other household members to attend.

The structure of the ritual is the same as that part of the Head Rite which is held in the headman's house. The symbolic meaning of the rite is essentially similar, namely, the expression of the communality of the village. There is, however, one important difference: the rite also expresses at the same time the autonomy of the household as a domestic unit of production because it is primarily a household ritual performed for the benefit of the household and its crop of rice. This is a concern that is fully expressed in the prayers that are said in the rite.

The use of left-over rice seed to make the liquor is also worth noting. It is a feature which appears in another ritual held later in the year called "drinking the lees of the threshing mat". The seed is rice which was put aside for planting and hence reserved for a specific purpose other than domestic consumption. What remains of the seed after planting (in actual practice or theory) is not returned for general consumption. Instead, it is consumed as Liquor in a performance which is part of a set of planting rituals. The seed, therefore, serves of a symbolic function appropriate only to a particular phase in the agricultural cycle. The ritual consumption of the left-over rice seed, thus, represents its total utilisation and marks the end of the planting season.

I present below an example of the kinds of prayers offered on behalf of households by the headman and elders. The prayer was recited by Su Ghau (H4) in his brother-in-law's house.

Sa, koecoe 'a' Koe'ca, koelo 'a' Koe'ca	O, Lords of the mountain tops, Lords of the mountain ridges
Phinja'i 'a' Koe'ca, Phinjapho 'a' Koe'ca	Lady Phinja'i, Lady Phinjapho
Tewabu', Tewada' 'a' Koe'ca	Celestial Lords and Ladies

Although the Lord of the Water, Lord of the Land of Palokhi and other tutelary spirits are not explicitly invoked in these opening lines, it is understood that they are being called upon in the first line of the prayer. The spirits or deities addressed in the following lines occur frequently in Palokhi Karen ritual texts but the Palokhi Karen are vague about the nature of these spirits or deities. While most of them are agreed on the fact that Phinja'i-Phinjapho is female and that she resides in the sky watching over the rice crop, some however say that Phinja'i and Phinjapho are two entities. The Palokhi Karen are equally vague about Tewabu'-Tewada', but they are clearly **devata** borrowed from the pantheon of Northern Thai Buddhism and, indeed, some Palokhi Karen admit as much. After invoking these various spirits or deities, the officiant continues with a series of requests on behalf of the household prefaced by a specific reference to his brother-in-law.

'I, pyde, 'au by chae' kho, by chae' khli	This, my wife's younger brother drinks the head of the rice seed, (the liquor of) the rice seed
My cha 'i, my ghe, la twae	This day, the sun is beautiful, the moon is bright

He lau 'au by chae' kho, by chae' khli	(We) place down for drinking the head of the rice seed, (the liquor of) the rice seed
Tho lau hy', pghe lau hy'	(We have) planted the swidden, (We have) filled the swidden
Pghe lau by, pghe lau me	Filled with rice, filled with cooked rice
Ma he lau 'a' 'au ba', 'au ba'	Bestow fullness in eating, fullness in drinking
'Au' ku', 'au' pghe	Eating replete, eating full
'Au' choe, mae' pghe	Eating sweetly, full of face
Kau' dy, kau' ghe	Each animal, each person
Poe' 'au' me kho pha' thau	We eat the first rice that is raised up (to you)
Poe' 'au thi kho khwae' lau	We drink the first water that is libated down
Ma he loe' 'a' ghe	Bestow all that is good
Ma he loe' 'a' gwa	Bestow all that is pure
Ma he loe' 'a' 'au ba', 'au ba'	Bestow fullness in eating, fullness in drinking

The prayer then continues with direct requests for blessings on the rice crop, some of which are:

Ghe 'a' si'so, 'a' la 'ae'	Beautiful be the (rice) sap, the spreading leaves
Ghe 'a' nju' pu	Beautiful within (the swidden)
Ghe chghae' bo, ghe kau' bo	Beautiful be every stem, Beautiful be each stem
Ghe kau' zi	Beautiful in each village
Ghe ty kho, ghe ty xau	Beautiful to the top, Beautiful to the bottom
Ghe	Beautiful
Si toe' lau xau, si toe lau xoe	So that (the rice) does not dwindle (literally, "descend the steps"), So that (the rice) does not diminish (literally, "descend to the bottom")
Ma he 'a' su ba', 'a' sa ba'	Make sure the livers, make sure the grains[13]
'A' thu ghe, 'a' dau' ghe	(Make sure) the shoots are beautiful, (Make sure all) together are beautiful
Chghae' tatoe'ghe, Chghae' tatoe'gwa	Disperse that which is not good, Disperse that which is not pure
Chghae' toe, chghae' plau	Disperse the ants, disperse (?) pests

Chghae' toexi, chghae' poe' 'u'	Disperse the ant grubs, disperse blights (literally, "afflictions")
Chghae' tamima', chghae' ta 'a' sa' pghi lau	Disperse the nightmares, disperse that which brings down light hearts

The Lord of the Water, Lord of the Land and the other spirits and deities are also asked to "watch over well, watch over purely" so that "our hands are not struck by knives, our feet are not tripped" and so on.

In the concluding section of the prayer, the ritual officiant re-iterates some of the requests contained in the prayers recited during planting.

Kae' ba' by my 'a' koe'ca	(Let us) be lords of swidden rice
Kae' ba' by phau 'a' koe'ca	(Let us) be lords of rice granaries
Kae' ba' talae' 'a' koe'ca	(Let us) be lords of wealth (literally, "exchangeables")
Kae' ba' taka' 'a' koe'ca	(Let us) be lords of riches[14]

The Rite of Protection

The Protection of Swiddens (Bghau Hy')

After the rites of planting, there are no further ritual activities until August when the rice crop has reached a height of approximately one metre and when rice grains begin to appear. When this happens, it is time to perform the rite that protects swiddens. This is individually held by households and does not require the presence of the headman or elders in Palokhi. It is performed by the head of the household.

The ritual has three purposes: first, to make an offering to pests and crop diseases in order to send them away; second, to induce a cool state in the swidden crop and household members; third, to make an offering to the rice itself so as to encourage its growth and maturation. In analytical terms, however, the overriding significance of the rite is the symbolism which it shares with the rite of planting the ritual basket of the yam and which it elaborates upon. The elaboration of this symbolism is based on logical extensions of the underlying processes reflected in the conceptual associations common to both rites. It is for these reasons that the analysis and interpretation of the meanings of the planting of the ritual basket of the yam and the protection of swiddens require the two to be taken together.

The description and discussion of the **bghau hy'** rite that follows is based on a performance in the swidden of the headman, Tamu'. It was conducted by Tamu' and his son-in-law, Gwa, who was the ritual owner of the swidden. Gwa prepared the various objects required for the ritual and made the chicken sacrifices integral to it while Tamu' confined himself to saying the accompanying prayers because Gwa was not, as yet, proficient in them. The ritual is performed at mid-day after the preparation of the objects.

The first of these objects or items is an "altar" or "shrine" called **tatoemau'** (see also Marshall 1922:78–9). This is sometimes described as the "house of the Old Mother Rice" (**By Mo Pgha 'a' doe'**) but the term **tatoemau'** itself means, literally, "thing of the one bowl". It is a very simple bamboo structure consisting of a small platform raised on four posts with a ladder leading up to the platform from the ground. Like all Palokhi houses (and, indeed, Northern Thai rural houses), the ladder has an odd number of rungs, usually five or seven. The ladder is for the rice souls (**by koela**) to ascend to the platform to partake of the offerings that will be made to the rice. The house of the Old Mother rice is erected in the small plot in the swidden where the Old Mother Rice is planted.

The second item which is also made for the first stage of the rite is the ritual basket (**tasae'**) to replace the weather-worn one which was made earlier in the year for the planting ritual.

The third item consists of three articles which are collectively known as the **toemau'** ("one bowl") from which the "altar" or "shrine" derives its name. This consists of a small bamboo cup (**tapolo'**), a small stick "stirrer" placed inside the cup (**mau' bo**, "stick of the bowl") and a stylised plant made from bamboo (**nade' chu**, literally, "nostril hairs") which is also placed in the cup. The cup is filled with rice liquor if this is available; otherwise, some rice chaff (which is used to make the yeast necessary for the production of liquor) is used instead.

Figure 6.2 The Toemau'

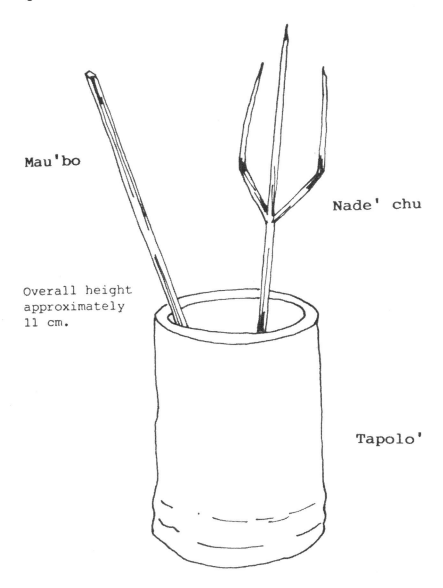

Mau'bo

Nade' chu

Overall height
approximately
11 cm.

Tapolo'

The Toemau' on the Platform of the Tatoemau or "House of the 'Old Mother Rice' ". The "house" is being prepared by Gwa. N the nade' chu ("nostril hairs") in the tapolo' or bamboo cup. mau'bo or "stick stirrer" has not yet been placed in the cup.

The ritual commences with an offering of a chicken (male or female) to the various elements which are believed to be a danger to the rice crop. The offering is made at the **tasae'**, the ritual basket into which these elements are collected and appeased. The prayer which accompanies the killing of the chicken begins with a line that, in fact, is addressed to rice.

By 'oe, ma na ba' takoe'e', takoetau	O rice, (I) do this so that you will receive that which is for you, that which protects you

This is followed by two lines which describe in dense metaphors all the ill-omens which portend disaster or calamity.

Li chi lau, cau'gwa hau poe "y'	The squirrel's urine falls, the crow cries in pain
Tho soepghau ni, taho kau'	The ill-omened bird ([?]ruddy ring dove) laughs, the barking deer calls out[15]

This is a list of what the Palokhi Karen believe are illomens that foretell disaster. They will not, for example, embark on a hunt if any of these signs are encountered. In this prayer, however, these portents serve to describe metaphorically the critical period in the growth of rice when the rice is thought to be vulnerable to the predations of pests, crop diseases and the elements.

The next part of the prayer elaborates on the preceding lines by describing what is being done to protect the rice, that is, the collection of the various dangers to the rice crop into the ritual basket.

Sae' xy' tatoe'ghe	The basket seeks that which is not good
Sae' xy' tatoe'gwa	The basket seeks that which is not pure
Sae' xy' tho soepghau ni, taho kau'	The basket seeks the ill-omened bird that laughs, the barking deer that calls out
Sae' xy' ta'a'ble	The basket seeks that which is slippery
Ta'a'ple', ta'a'chgha	That which is pointed, that which tramples
Sae' xy' pgha ku', pghakoe'njau 'a' ble	The basket seeks the people who cough, the human beings who are slippery

At this point, the throat of the chicken is slit and rubbed all over the ritual basket in order to smear it with the blood of the fowl. The prayer continues as this is done.

Li chi lau, the soepghau ni	The squirrel's urine falls, the ill-omened bird laughs

Cau'gwa hau poe' 'y', taho kau'	The crow cries in pain, the barking deer calls out
Sae' xy' tatoe'ghe	The basket seeks that which is not good
Sae' xy' tatoe'gwa	The basket seeks that which is not pure
Sae' xy' zy 'a' ble	The basket seeks the rats which are slippery
Sae' xy' tho 'a' ble	The basket seeks the birds which are slippery
Sae' xy' li'lu 'a' ble, noxae 'a' ble	The basket seeks the squirrels which are slippery, the flying squirrels which are slippery
Sae' xy' ta'a'lau, ta'a'la'	The basket seeks that which falls, that which collapses
Pgha ku' 'a' ble, pghakoe'njau 'a' ble	The people who cough, the human beings who are slippery
Sae' xy' tatoe' 'au'ba', tatoe' 'auhu'	The basket seeks the "not eating to fullness", the "not drinking to fullness"

At the end of the prayer, feathers are torn from the chicken and stuck on the blood smears on the ritual basket.

This prayer, like most Palokhi Karen prayers, consists of metaphors built around a simple theme which, in this case, is the containment of all that may endanger the rice crop. The most noteworthy feature of the prayer, however, is the recurrent references to "things that are slippery" (ta'a'ble). These references are based primarily on the idea that women who have just given birth, and new-born babies, are in a "slippery" condition. Slipperiness, however, is not merely descriptive of the physical condition of women and new-born babies; it also describes a **general** state that is believe to affect the whole community at childbirth. The Palokhi Karen have, for example, a prohibition on work outside the village on the day when a birth occurs. The reason for this prohibition, they say, is that if they do so, untoward consequences would result either for the mother and infant or for those who work outside the village. The belief and prohibition, quite evidently demonstrate that childbirth is a matter of concern to the community as a whole. In principle, it is similar to the belief that "crooked unions" would result in calamity and the destruction of rice crops for the whole community: the underlying logic of the two beliefs are similar in that the consequences of breaches of these prohibitions are **transitive**.

What is significant about the two beliefs and their associated prohibitions, it must be emphasised, is that both link cultural definitions of **reproductive processes** to the cultivation of crops, as well as the relations between individuals involved in such processes and the entire community. In the context of the rite of protection, the association between childbirth and the state of the rice crop at this stage of the swidden cycle possesses, as I shall show, a very specific significance.

However, it may be noted here that apart from the illomens which are mentioned, the image of the dangers that threaten the rice growing in swiddens is also evoked through the primary meanings attaching to the idea of a slippery state that comes about at childbirth. These meanings are further extended to fructivorous animals such as rats, squirrels, birds and so on, and also to people. There is no special significance to the term "coughing people" which is, here, an extension in the imagery of "slippery people" who are thought to be people who may steal the rice crop as well as those who through their "slippery" condition may bring about untoward consequences to the crop. The significance of the other referents in the prayer are less obscure and have to do with actual conditions which represent a destroyed crop, for example the trampling of the rice by feral pigs, deer, and so forth, and the crushing of the crop by the slipping of the charred remains of felled trees, and so on. The containment of "not eating to fullness, not drinking to fullness' is, of course, an alternative expression of the wish or desire that the year's harvest will be sufficient for the needs of the household.

The next stage of the ritual consists of two parts. The first part is the induction of a cool state in the swidden crops and members of the household. This is yet another expression of the belief — central to the Head Rite, marriage, "crooked unions" and the rite of planting — that a cool state is essential for the successful growth of rice and other swidden crops. The second part of the ritual follows from the first and consists of encouraging the growth of rice. In this stage of the ritual, a hen is offered to the Old Mother Rice. The choice of a hen clearly indicates the essential feminine nature of rice through a concordance of sex categories. It is a further example of how in certain ritual performances (of which the 'au' ma xae ritual is one), the Palokhi Karen maintain distinctions in gender through the sex of chickens that are used in these performances.

The first part of this stage of the ritual entails a prayer that is addressed to fire which is propitiated in order to achieve the cool state that is necessary. As only one chicken is offered (that is to say, the chicken for the Old Mother Rice), it may be asked why the Palokhi Karen do not also make an offering to fire. The reason is that they do not necessarily conceive of fire as an entity in the same category as the Old Mother Rice and other tutelary spirits. The reference to fire is, in point of fact, part of the ritual language which is for all practical purposes a **verbal** ritual, as a performative, designed to induce the cool state that is regarded as being so crucial for the growth of rice and swidden crops. The prayer goes as follows:

Me'u 'oe, coe moe 'au' na, coe soe 'au' na	O fire, I use and feed you, I send and feed you
Lae 'au' xae' cau'lau, khwa' cau'lau	Charring has eaten the knife cuts (that is, in the wood), the axe cuts (in the wood)
Ly 'au' ke na	Propitiating you (so that) you go back
Le 'au' khy na	The glowing eats you till you are cool
Ly khy na, ly ba' na	Propitiating you till you are cool, propitiating (and) affecting you
Khy dau' by, khy dau' hy	Cooling together the rice, cooling together the unhusked rice
Khy dau' tasu, khy dau' taphla'	Cooling together that which is planted, cooling together that which is hoed
Khy dau' mysa, khy dau' soekau	Cooling together the chillies, cooling together the brinjals
Khy khaeloe', khy khaeche	Cooling everything, cooling all
Khy dau' nauca, khy dau' khine	Cooling together myself, cooling together (?)thus
Khy dau' coe' phau'my, ma	Cooling together my woman, wife
Phomy, phokhwa	Daughter, son
Ma'pho, dae'pho	Son-in-law, daughter-in-law
Li	Grandchildren
Khy khaeloe', khy khaeche	Cooling everyone, cooling all
Si' toe' ko ba', si' toe' ghau ba'	So that none are affected by heat, so that none are affected by redness

The prayer continues in this vein in a highly repetitive manner. The single, dominant theme here is very clearly the creation of a cool state. It is extremely significant, however, that the induction of this state that is so necessary for the successful growth of crops also entails cooling all the members of the household who are carefully identified in the prayer. The identification of the household, or domestic group, with the crops that it cultivates which underlies the practice of the ritual ownership of swiddens is, thus, expressed here in a different form. At the same time, the identification of household members individually recalls the manner in which they are similarly referred to in **'au' ma xae** prayers where they are also associated with subsistence activities. The almost litanical form of these references in prayers from quite different ritual contexts is a clear confirmation of the strength and pervasiveness of the associations that they express and establish simultaneously.

At the end of the prayer, the next part of the ritual begins with a prayer addressed to rice. The opening lines of this prayer are:

| By 'oe, toemau' ghe na, toemau' gwa na | O rice, the toemau' beautifies you, the toemau' purifies you |
| Toemau' siso, toemau' la 'ae' 'au' ghe na | The sap of the toemau', the spreading leaves of the toemau' eat well for you |

These lines are difficult to translate but they are crucial to an understanding of the significance of the **toemau'** in the ritual. The use of **ghe** ("good", "beautiful") and **gwa** ("white", "pure") is, of course, a common feature of Palokhi ritual language. As we have seen from the Head Rite, they stand together for a state that is auspicious and harmonious. What is interesting in the first line, however, is its syntax in which the adjectives **ghe** and **gwa** are used as verbs in order to represent the transference of attributes from the **toemau'** onto rice. Adjectival verbs are not uncommon in Sgaw Karen and, for that matter, in other Karen dialects.[16] Here, however, they are used with particular effect. While the English terms "beautify" and "purify" may seem adequate enough, nevertheless, they do not quite convey the sense of the Karen. The construction of the Karen suggests rather more. The verbalisation of the adjectives **ghe** and **gwa** in this context carries with it a sense of "becoming" and "being for" or "being unto", so that the overall meaning of the line also contains the suggestion of a transference of the attributes denoted by the adjectives.

The symbolic function of the **toemau'**, suggested by these adjectival verbs, becomes more apparent in the next line. The reference to the "spreading leaves" of the **toemau'** has to do, in fact, with the exaggerated, stylised leaves of the bamboo plant (**na'de chu**) placed within the cup (**tapolo'**). The "sap" of the **toemau'**, on the other hand, refers to the rice liquor, or the substitute rice chaff, which is also placed within the cup. At the heart of this reference to the "sap" of the **toemau'** are images and metaphors which are derived from the process of making rice liquor. The yeast which is made from rice chaff and flour that is necessary for the production of rice liquor, if it is well made, and the successful fermentation of the liquor, for example, are both invariably described as having "risen well" (**thau ghe**). It is an expression which is also used to describe the successful growth of the rice crop. It may be noted also that in this second line the transference of the properties of the **toemau'** onto rice are expressed in an idiom of consumption, that is, eating. It is yet again a further indication of the importance of the idiom in representing structural relations in symbolic form which, as we have seen, occurs elsewhere in **'au' ma xae,** the Head Rite, and day-to-day patterns of commensalism.

The rest of the prayer enlarges on the theme established in these first two lines.

| Ma noe' chu than, ma noe' sa thau | Making your leaves (literally, "hairs") rise, making your panicles (literally, "fruit") rise |

Toemau' ghe na, toemau' gwa na	The toemau' beautifies you, the toemau' purifies you
Ha' ke, chae' pha', ha' ke 'au' loe' ghe	Return, (and be) stored, return and eat well of everything
Ma noe' su ghe, ma noe' sa ghe	Making your livers beautiful, making your panicles beautiful
Ma noe' chu thau, ma noe' sa thau	Making your leaves rise, making your panicles rise
Ma noe' chu cha', noe' sa cha'	Making your leaves full, making your panicles full
Toemau' siso, toemau' la 'ae' 'au' loe' ghe na	The sap of the toemau', the spreading leaves of the toemau' eats well of everything for you
Siso 'au' ghe, la 'ae' 'au' ghe	The sap eats well, the spreading leaves eat well

At the end of the prayer, the throat of the chicken is slit and its blood is smeared on the ladder, posts and platform of the "house of the Old Mother Rice", after which feathers are stuck onto the blood smears.

The two chickens are then cleaned, dressed and cooked in the field hut. Next, small pieces are taken from the extremities of the chickens, namely, the wing tips, the claws and tails which stand for the whole chickens, and these are wrapped up with some rice in banana leaves. These food offerings are placed on the platform of the shrine. A brief prayer, similar to the one above, is recited as this is done. Thereafter, the ritual officiants and other members of the household may proceed to eat.

The last stage of the ritual is relatively simple and involves the making and setting of three apotropaic devices within the plot where the Old Mother Rice is planted and another at the beginning of the path leading from the boundary of the swidden to the field hut.

The symbolism of these devices is, at a certain level, readily apparent. With one exception, they represent weapons of one kind or another. The three instruments set in the plot of the Old Mother Rice are the "elephant spears" (**bau koe'cau)**, the "throat squeezers" or "throat chokers" (**tathi'khau'**) and the "anus eater" (**ta'au'khi**). The "elephant spears" are three long, sharpened bamboo sticks placed in the ground equidistant from one another and bound roughly two-thirds of their lengths from the ends implanted in the ground. The "throat squeezers" are two bamboo poles which are split in two at their upper ends. They are stuck in the ground facing each other and the split ends are brought together around a short bamboo staff which is set into the soil mid-way between the bases of the "throat squeezers". The "anus eater" is a single bamboo pole split four ways almost to the base which is pushed into the ground. The four quarters of the upper portion are then bent over backwards and forced into the earth.

In Palokhi, there are two interpretations of the meaning of the "anus eater" which is the only device that does not resemble a weapon. The first view is that it represents a gaping mouth, much like the mouth of a trap, and if it encounters intruders (in a metaphorical sense), then the four arms of the "anus eater" spring back trapping the intruders. The other view is that the "anus eater" symbolises the fate that would befall intruders, that is, their anuses would be split four ways.

I suggest, however, that there is a deeper symbolism running through the assemblage of apotropaic devices than that which is ostensibly portrayed by the apparent shapes of these devices. While the "elephant spears" do, indeed, suggest the symbolic impalement of intruders, pests, and so on, the "throat squeezers" and "anus eater" symbolise perhaps rather more which, quite conceivably, is related to the idioms of consumption that are a consistent and recurrent feature of Palokhi rituals. Both devices have, as their foci, the extremities of the alimentary canal and their "manifest" symbolic functions are to effect a dysfunctioning of these extremities in a general sense. Accordingly, the protection offered by these apotropaic devices would therefore be no other than that which is founded upon a latent image of non-functioning or "closed" alimentary canals in predators. It is an image which would be wholly consistent with a perception of such predators as competitors in the consumption of rice. In the rite called "wrist-tying at the reaping of rice" (which I discuss later [pp. 408–13]), for example, the rice souls are called upon to return from "within the throats of rats".

The Symbolism of the Toemau' Reconsidered

The significance of the **toemau'** is worth a reconsideration at this stage. It is clear that the ritual and the use of the **toemau'** conform closely to the patterns in ritual described by Tambiah. There is undoubtedly an exploitation of the expressive properties of language, the sensory qualities of objects and the instrumental properties of action simultaneously, based on the principles of similarity and contiguity.

The purpose of the ritual is, at one level, obvious as the contents of the prayer indicate and it is none other than what the Palokhi Karen profess it to be: the nurturing and successful growth of the rice crop through the containment of various dangers and the creation of a cool state. What is not entirely obvious, however, is the **totality** of the symbolism of the **toemau'** in the context of the ritual and its structural position as a sequel to the rites of planting, within the larger context of swidden rites. There is only one indication of this and it concerns the "spreading leaves" and "sap" of the **toemau'**. These are clearly references to the stylised plant and liquor or chaff placed within the bamboo cup. Yet, it is the **toemau'** that is referred to rather than the stylised plant which is the key symbol that designates the physical state desired in the rice crop. This suggests that the symbolic plant is insufficient for the expressive aspects of the prayer. Or, to put it another way, the state of growth in the rice crop is not merely symbolised by the bamboo plant but by the **totality** of objects which make up the **toemau'** of which the plant is a constituent part.

If we consider the appearance of the **toemau'** carefully, it becomes apparent that apart from the stylised plant, the essential imagery of the cup and stirrer (the **tapolo'** and **mau' bo**) is identical to that of the water container and descending pole (**thi toe** and **kra' lau**) in the rite of planting the ritual basket of the yam. They are analogues of the same symbolic identity — produced by the image of a stick-in-a-container — the only difference being one of scale. The correspondence in imagery, its occurrence in the same general context of swidden rites, and its appearance in consecutively performed rituals argue against any arbitrary coincidence. I therefore suggest that the **primary** symbolism of the **toemau'** is none other than that in the case of the **thi toe** and **kra' lau,** that is, the conjunction of male and female in procreative mode.

Other than the difference in scale, which by no means reduces the significance of this primary symbolism, there is nonetheless one important difference — the inclusion of the stylised plant in the **toemau'**. If the symbolism is identical in both cases, then the inclusion of the stylised bamboo plant must represent an extension of the imagery or symbolism that lies at the core of both sets of ritual objects. Given the primary symbolism of both, the elaboration on the **toemau'** becomes wholly apparent and, indeed, it is almost literal. For it is none other than the emergence and growth of rice "arising" from the conjunction of male and female in procreative mode symbolised by the stick that lies within the container. The **toemau',** therefore, represents a logical development of the symbolism contained in the **thi toe** and **kra' lau** central to the rites of planting.

The extended meaning of the **toemau'** is borne out by a key feature of the prayer in the rite, namely, the references to "slipperiness" which are based on conditions associated with childbirth. They are not, then, merely metaphors for the dangers that threaten the rice crop; they are integral to the symbolic representation of the transition made by rice expressed by the transformation in meaning of the two sets of ritual objects, that is, from the **thi toe** and **kra' lau** to the **toemau'**. In other words, the allusions to "slipperiness" reveal, at the same time, that after the rice seed has been planted, the rice plants have been "born" and have entered a stage of growth in which their protection becomes essential to ensure that they are brought to a state of fruition which is the overt concern of the rite of protection. These references are, thus, integral to the totality of symbolic representations contained in the rite which, in short, are derived from a procreative model of society extended to the cultivation of rice in Palokhi.

The Rites of Harvesting

The rites of harvesting consist of a number of rites performed at different times as the season proceeds. It is not possible to deal with all the rites that are performed at this time and I shall, therefore, discuss only three. These are: "wrist-tying at the reaping of rice" (**ky cy' ku lau by**); the "eating of the head rice" (**'au' by kho**); and the final harvest celebration called the "descent of the land" (**kau lau we**) or the "rising of the New Year" (**thau ni sau**).

Wrist-Tying at the Reaping of Rice (Ki Cy' Ku' Lau By)

The wrist-tying ceremony is performed in the early morning of the first day of reaping, before the members of the household set out to work in their swidden. The ritual is very much a domestic one and its purpose is to call back the souls of all the members of the household back into their bodies and, as the term suggests, to bind the souls within the bodies of their respective owners.

The significance of the wrist-tying ceremony, which is performed again in the harvest season (on the first day of threshing and the second day of the New Year celebrations), cannot be fully appreciated without reference to the more important features of wrist-tying rituals in general. Ordinarily, wrist-tying rituals are only performed when a person is thought to be suffering from "soul loss" (**ba' kau' koela**).[17] In such circumstances, a ritual specialist (**soera**) is called in to perform the ritual which requires the preparation of food to entice the wandering soul (or souls) back into the body of the person concerned. Divination is employed to determine whether or not the soul or souls, have returned. If the souls are deemed to have returned, the wrists of the patient are bound, followed by those of other members of the household. Thereafter, all the members of the household proceed to eat. It is clear that these rituals have as their purpose the re-establishment of the "integrity" or "corporateness" of body and souls. Here, we may note that the ritual is held when a person undergoes what is regarded to be a critical period, and that an important aspect of the symbolism in the ritual is commensalism which establishes the interrelatedness or "corporateness", as it were, of all household members.

Both these features are integral to the rite of wrist-tying at the reaping of rice. There is, however, one important difference: the souls of rice are included in the ritual reflecting the close association between households and the rice that they cultivate, as well as a certain conception which likens rice to humans evident in the ritual ministrations that both receive. This may be seen in the prayer that is said in the ritual by the head of the household.

Koela 'oe,   O Souls

Ha' ke, 'au' me gwa, ke 'au thi chghi	Return, eat the white rice, return and drink the clear water
Lu pgha thi toe' ghe, pgha kau toe' ghe	To bath in the waters of (other) people is not good, the domain of (other) people is not good

These opening lines are significant for they show that in the ceremony, at this stage of the agricultural season, the restoration of the "integrity" or "corporateness" of souls, bodies and rice, has a **territorial** aspect. That is, it is conceived of in the context of the land, or domain, which the community inhabits, and which identifies the community. The prayer continues with invitations to the souls of the members of the household to partake of the food which has been prepared for the ritual:

Ke kwa, ke poe' chghi, poe' hy'	Return and look, return to our fallow swidden, our swidden
Ha' ke, 'au' me loe' 'a' gwa, 'au thi loe' chghi	Return, eat the all-white rice, drink the all-clear water
Tho nja loe' 'a' so, chau nja loe' 'a' so	The fat meat of the bird, the fat meat of the chicken
Ha' pgha thi toe' ghe, pgha kau toe' ghe	To go the waters of (other) people is not good, the domains of (other) people is not good
By loe' chi' pu, by loe' na pu	The rice in the wet-rice fields, the rice in the padi fields[18]
By 'a' lau chwi, by 'a' lau Zwa	The rice crouches down (literally, "goes down like a dog"), the rice bows down (literally, "goes down before "Zwa", the cosmogonic deity)[19]

At the end of this call to the souls of family members, the head of the household next calls upon the souls of rice to return to the swidden. In this call, the rice is described as "rice of the thirty-three mothers". Although the Palokhi Karen cultivate several varieties of rice in their swiddens, they certainly do not recognise thirty-three varieties in their ethno-botanical classificatory system. This particular reference is based on the belief that rice and humans are similar in the number of souls that they possess. As I noted in Chapter III (p. 105, n. 24), the number of souls attributed to humans does, in fact, vary from informant to informant. Thus, the actual number of souls credited to humans and rice is not nearly so important as the fact that **rice is likened to humans** in the ideology of religion and agriculture in Palokhi. It is this which gives the ritual of wrist-tying at the reaping of rice its particular significance.

(By) phi' 'i' soe'chi-soe' mo, by soe'chi-soe' mo	Glutinous (rice) of the thirty-three mothers, rice of the thirty-three mothers
Ha' ke phgho, ke ro, ke mycha 'i	Return dense and compact, return within the fence, return this morning
Ke di' 'a' pghe si, ke di' 'a' pghe phau	Returning full as a comb, returning and filling the granary

The last line above deserves comment because of the wealth of the metaphors employed and its polysemous nature. Si phau literally means "comb" and it is used here to convey the image not merely of the number of rice souls that are being called upon to return, but also of the plenitude of rice in the swidden. **Phau**, in this context, means "granary", but it is also the homophone of "flower" (the difference being a mid-tone and a low-falling tone). "Comb" and "flower" (**si phau**), however, many also mean "flowers in blossom" and, metaphorically, also "mistress" or "lover" in Sgaw Karen.[20] What we find here, therefore, is a super-imposition of various metaphors producing highly evocative images simultaneously. The overall impression conveyed in this line is a combination of a call to the thirty-three rice souls which return in a seried rank like the teeth of a comb, and a plea to a mistress or lover, as well as a declaration of the fullness of rice in the swidden that will abundantly stock the household granary.

Having called upon the souls of household members and rice, the head of the household goes on to say:

Ke di' 'a' pghe chghi, ke di' 'a' pghe hy'	Returning full in the fallow swidden, returning full in the swidden
Mycha 'i, coe ki ke na, kau' ke na	This morning, I tie (your wrists at) your return, I call (for) your return
Ke 'o' phgho, ke; ke ke 'o' ro, ke	Return and remain dense and compact, return; return and remain (in) the fence, return
Koela soe'chisoe' mo	Souls of the thirty-three mothers
Soe' gha, lwi gha	(Of) the three persons, the four persons

In the last two lines above, the head of the household refers simultaneously to the souls of rice and the four members of his family. Following from this, he next instructs the souls of the family members to collect the rice souls from wherever they have wandered or were taken by predators of the rice crop which, in the text that follows, are represented by rats.

Thy' phgho ke, thy' ro ke	Pull back dense and compact, pull back within the fence
By zy khau' pu	The rice (from) within the throats of rats[21]
Lae xy', ke 'au'	Go and seek, return and eat

| Ke, ke mycha 'i | Return, return this morning |
| Di' 'a' loe', di' 'a' che | (Remaining) all (of you) (remaining) everyone (of you) |

The prayer is highly repetitive. At the end of the prayer, the parents then take up the lengths of yarn which were earlier placed on the tray of food and proceed to bind the wrists of their children. No particular attention is given to birth order in the tying of wrists. When the wrists of all the children have been tied, the two parents then tie each others' wrists. With the wrist-tying completed, all the members of the household proceed to eat the meal from the tray after which they then go to their swidden to commence reaping.

The Eating of the Head Rice ('Au' By Kho)

In Palokhi, the rice that is first reaped is early ripening rice. The Old Mother Rice is not, usually, early ripening rice so that the reaping of swiddens does not always commence with the reaping of the entire crop of the Old Mother rice. Nevertheless, a sheaf of the Old Mother Rice is usually harvested and stored in the rafters of the field hut until the entire harvest is brought back to the village at the end of the harvest season, at which time the Old Mother Rice is brought back and stored above the rice in the granary. For many Palokhi households, the rice that is reaped in the early stages of the harvest season is brought back for immediate consumption because by this time their stocks of rice from the previous year have been exhausted. For other more fortunate households, the rice that has been reaped is left, bound in sheaves, on the stubble for to stooking prior to threshing at a later stage. For all households, however, the rice that has been reaped for immediate consumption is treated as the "head rice" (**by kho**) or "first rice".

The eating of the head rice takes place in the evening of a day that is deemed convenient for all members of the household, for it is important that all should be present for the rite. The ritual officiant is, significantly, the oldest married, or widowed, woman in the family. There are many levels at which the ritual may be interpreted. It is concerned, for example, with the process of converting rice into its edible form through the use of fire. This is apparent from the inclusion of the hearth and hearth-stones in the ritual which includes their propitiation. It is also concerned with the propitiation of rice itself for being eaten. At yet another level, it is also concerned with ensuring that rice is not lost in the process of preparing it for consumption. However, what is most important sociologically is the essentially female nature of the rite which marks it as a domestic rite through the idiom of processing and cooking rice, quite regardless of the mimimal sexual division of labour in Palokhi. It is the only agricultural rite of significance that demands a female officiant and it expresses the ideological categorisation of men and women and their complementarity, in agricultural production, through the mediation of a general opposition between the domestic and non-domestic domains.

On the evening of the ritual, a small portion of the "first rice" is set aside, unhusked, in a small bowl while the rest, sufficient for a meal for the household, is cooked in a pot. When the rice is cooked, the pot is placed near the hearth where the family normally takes its meals. Other accompaniments are also prepared and placed alongside the pot of rice. The ritual officiant then proceeds to make the preparations that are necessary for the ceremony. Three bananas are split lengthwise along their skins which are opened up to form a sort of container for the fruit inside. The bananas are then placed on the three hearth-stones in the fireplace as an offering to fire. There is no particular significance in the use of bananas because pieces of yam, tapioca or sweet potato may also be used. A fresh water crab is then cast onto the embers in the fire-place.

The ritual officiant then unravels a bunch of vines (called **ki'ko**), collected earlier in the day from the forest, and proceeds to garland the hearth posts with them.[22] As she does so, she picks up a few grains of the unhusked "first rice", a small handful of the cooked rice in the pot and plucks a leaf from the vines and chews on them. She also picks up small pieces of banana from the hearth-stones and breaks of a claw from the crab and chews on these as well. As she does this, she says the following prayer:

By loe' hy'	Rice of the swidden
'Au' nau, 'au' ti na	(I) eat you shared (with other things), (I) eat you mixed (with other things)
'Au' nau na dau' by be' hysa'	(I) eat you shared together with unhusked rice
'Au' nau na, 'au' ti na dau' soedau'	(I) eat you shared, (I) eat you mixed with prawns
Si toe' 'y, si toe' xau'	So that you do not rot, so that you do not (?)spoil
Si toe' phi', si toe' pau'	So that you do not take offence, so that you do not (?)
Si toe' wi, si toe' wau	So that you are not finished, so that you are not (?)exhausted[23]

The prayer continues in this vein at considerable length. As she chews and recites the prayer, the ritual officiant also spits out some of the contents of her mouth onto the hearth and around the fireplace.

There are some variations to the otherwise repetitive, indeed redundant, nature of the verses. For example, the rice is told that "people do so (that is, the ritual) for the future, people eat thus for the future" to bring about a "rising" of the "eating to fullness, the drinking to fullness". It is, significantly, also told that "You are the father, you are the mother". In the light of the distinction between procreativity and non-procreativity established by the systems of sex, gender and kin terms in Palokhi discussed in Chapter III, the conjunction of "father" and "mother" in this reference is clear: in the cognitive scheme that orders cultural categories, rice is treated as a **reproductive** entity alongside humans.

The ritual officiant continues to refill her mouth with more unhusked rice, cooked rice and so on, and next addresses the hearth directly.

Loechau soe' phloe'	(You) three hearth-stones
Me'u 'i, pgha moe 'au' 'au' na, pgha soe' 'au' na	This fire, people use and feed you, people send and feed you
Si toe' phi, si toe' pau'	So that you do not take offence, so that you do not (?)
Pgha 'au' ti na dau' li'lu, noxae	People eat you mixed with squirrels, flying squirrels

What is being expressed in the second and last line above are difficult to translate because of the polysemous nature of the term for "eat" in Palokhi, and as it is employed in these lines. The expression **pgha moe 'au' na,** for example, also means "people use you to eat" (that is, to prepare food). There is also the idea that fire — as it is used to prepare food or to burn off the fur of animals prior to cooking them — "eats" the food or animals. "Burning", to give another example, is spoken of in terms of "fire eating" (**me'u 'au'**) something. All of these ideas and associations present in these lines express the propitiation of fire and hearth, and the fact that they are regarded as co-eaters of human food. This is, thus, yet another example of the importance and power of idioms of eating, and their applications, in Palokhi.

Beyond the purpose of the ritual, in these two stages, obvious from the declarative sentences of intentionality in the prayer, it is possible to propose a further interpretation on the performance. They key feature is the mastication of food together with unhusked and husked rice. The food and rice, however, are not swallowed by the officiant. Instead, they are spat out around the hearth when it is propitiated, and again around the room later. A major theme in the prayer, however, is the shared eating of food with rice itself, fire, the hearth and "the doing of the steps, the doing of the **xae**" (see below), that is, the household and **'au' ma xae** respectively. Accordingly, I suggest that the mastication by the ritual officiant is in fact the symbolic acting out of the consumption of food by rice, fire, the hearth and the domestic group at one and the same time.

After propitiating rice, fire and the hearth, the officiant chews some more rice and food and circumambulates the room. As she does so, she repeats the prayer but this time, however, she spits out the contents of her mouth on the walls and corners of the room. There is a variation in the prayer which reveals still another aspect to the ritual.

Toe chau 'o', si pi' 'a' lau	One mortarful (of unhusked rice) present, so a pip descends[24]
Toe pi' 'o', pi' 'a' lau	One pip present, a pip descends

When she returns to the hearth, the officiant then proceeds to tie a **ki'ko** vine around the pot of rice, saying as she does so:

Ki nau noe' khau, ki tau noe' khau	Tying your neck shared, tying your neck (?)slowly
'Au' na dau' de' by, njari	Eating you with padi field frogs, njari fish ([?] mantis shrimp)
Dau' mauli', dau' taswau	With gibbons, with langurs
Dau' tamaxau', tamaxae — khaeloe'	With the household (literally, "the doing of the steps"), the doing of the xae (that is, performing the **'au' ma xae** ritual) — everything
Si toe' wi, si toe' wau	So that you are not finished, so that you are not (?)exhausted
Si toe' phi, si toe' pau'	So that you do not take offence, so that you do not (?)

At the end of this prayer, the ritual officiant or a married daughter takes a length of the **ki'ko** vine outside the house and binds the mortar in which rice is pounded to remove the husk. This is accompanied by a perfunctory prayer which acknowledges the use of the mortar and asks that one pip of husked rice be obtained from one pip of unhusked rice.

When this is done, rice from the pot containing the cooked "first rice" is spooned out onto two eating trays after which the women and girls of the family eat from one tray while the men and boys eat from the other.

That this is a pre-eminently domestic ritual is clear; but, where it differs from other domestic rituals marked by commensalism is the way in which it is almost entirely focused on the process of transforming unhusked rice into husked rice, cooking (indicated by the role of fire and the hearth), and the commensalism **with** food itself. Given the structural position of the rite in the cycle of agrarian rites and the cultivation of swiddens, that is, when the first of the harvest is brought back for consumption, the rite is undoubtedly concerned with marking the passage of swidden rice from its cultivated state to a state in which it may be domestically consumed.

Another important difference lies in the organisation of the familial commensalism that takes place at the end of the ritual, namely, the **segregation** of males and females during the eating of the "first rice" which is not present in other forms of commensalism, ritual or otherwise. The undoubtedly female nature of the ritual and its focus on the transformation of rice establishes all too clearly that the two are associated through a play on the process of preparing rice and cooking.

Cooking, as Davis observes (1984:176) in discussing the symbolic representations of the opposition between male and female among the Northern Thai, is perhaps the one proto-typical cultural activity almost universally associated with females. In Palokhi, however, there is only a minimal sexual division of labour and men actually do cook and, occasionally, pound rice. The rite of eating the first rice, therefore, does not assert or reflect the reality of social relations in this particular sense. What it expresses is the opposition and complementarity of the roles of female and male, as general cultural categories, through a **ritual** sexual division of labour resting on an implicit opposition between women and men, the domestic and non-domestic, and settlement and forest. It is a complementary opposition that is mediated by the symbolic transition of rice from its cultivated state to a domestically consumable one.

The Rites of the New Year (Lyta Thau Ni Sau)

The rites of the New Year, or the "rising of the New Year" (**thau ni sau**) as it is called in Palokhi, may be regarded in some senses as a harvest celebration but they are, in fact, rites which mark the passage from one agricultural cycle into the next and which are wholly oriented towards the new season. The New Year itself is also described by a complementary term: the "descent of the land" (**kau lau wae**). Both these expressions, as I showed in my discussion of the agricultural calendar in Palokhi, describe the succession of agricultural seasons and their constituent features according to natural or "organic" rythms.

The rites of the "rising of the New Year", or "descent of the land" consist of the following: "Soul calling at the descent of the land" (**phau' koela kau lau wae**); "libations at the descent of the land" (**khwae' ta kau lau wae**); and "wrist-tying at the descent of the land" (**ki cy' kau lau wae**). All these rites may equally be described in terms of the "rising of the New Year" instead of the "descent of the land".

An important condition on holding the rites of the New Year, however, is that all the households in the village must have performed their annual **'au' ma xae** first. Many of the agrarian rites that are conducted in Palokhi are, as we have seen, the responsibility of individual households. This is what we might expect given the nature of domestic social organisation and the sociology of agricultural production in Palokhi. **'Au' ma xae**, however, is a quintessentially domestic ritual intimately related to the ideology of kinship and the sociology of domestic group formation and fission. Nevertheless, the position of **'au' ma xae** in the annual cycle of ritual activities — that is, as a mandatory ritual precondition for the New Year rites — marks it, at least in this particular regard, as a proper calendrical ritual and, therefore, as an integral part of the cycle of agrarian rites in Palokhi. This is significant because it is one more example of how not only ritual performances but also their structural positions in the sequence of annual rites periodically affirm the identification of households with the process of agricultural production.

When all the households in Palokhi have conducted their **'au' ma xae** rituals, and have made the rice liquor and other preparations necessary for the New Year rites, the headman decides upon two consecutive days when they are to be held. The soul calling and libations are held on the evening of the first day while the wrist-tying is held on the following morning.

In the evening of the first day, the oldest married or widowed woman of each household performs the soul calling ritual. Although men may perform the soul calling, it is usually women who do so in Palokhi. Each woman carries a sling bag, into which a live chicken is placed, and goes to all the tracks which begin at the boundaries of the village with a "beating stick" (**nau phau' kra'**). The stick is an implement which is, characteristically, used in soul calling rituals. It is a slim bamboo stick, just under a metre in length. It is split four ways half way down its length and has three notches mid-way on the remaining half. Bits of food are placed in the notches to entice the souls of people to return. The stick is beaten on the ground such that it rattles because of the free split ends. It is this that gives the ritual its name of **phau' koela** (literally, "soul beating"). The prayer that is said in the ritual and the beating of the **nau phau' kra'** are accompanied by graphic gestures of collecting the souls and placing them into the bag. Unlike the soul calling prayers said during harvest rites in which the souls of rice are called back as well, the prayer is directed only to the souls of household members.

The prayer below, recited by the wife of the headman, is an example of the kinds of soul calling prayers which feature in the rites of the New Year. It begins onomatopoeically with a call which is invariably used in soul calling prayers in general. It is also the call to chickens when they are fed.

Prr, phomy koela, ke	Prr, souls of (my) daughter return
Phokhwa koela, ke	Souls of (my) son(-in-law) return
Coe li koela, ke	Souls of my grandchildren return
Coe li phau'my, coe li phau'khwa	(Of) my granddaughter, (of) my grandson
Ke 'o' loe' doe', 'o' loe' lau	Return and remain in the house, remain at the sleeping mat

'O' ply 'a' sau' toe'ghe	To stay with the spirits of the dead is not good
'O' chghe 'a' sau' toe'ghe	To stay with the ghosts of the dead is not good
Ke 'o' loe' zi, ke 'o' loe' xau	Return and remain in the village, return and remain at the house steps
Khoelau' koewi, koela	Touching one another, all souls[25]
Dau' mo, dau' pa	With mother, with father
Dau' py, dau' wae	With younger sister, with elder brother
Dau' pho, dau' li	With children, with grandchildren

The prayer continues in this fashion at considerable length. At the end of the prayer, the woman goes on to the next track and repeats the prayer until the ritual has been conducted at all the tracks beginning at the boundaries of the village. She then returns to the house where all the household members assemble and have their evening meal.

Although this ritual is designed to recall the souls of household members, similar to the wrist-tying rites at harvest time, there is one difference. In this case wrist-tying is not performed. It is a general recall of the souls in preparation for the wrist-tying ceremony which is performed on the next day after the family has eaten its first meal in the morning. It is worth noting also that the prayer is wholly unambiguous on the communality of household members which it expresses through the conjunctive **dau'** which relates all the members of the household together, and through the description of the proximity, indeed contiguity, of souls. To put it another way, the ritual brings together the individual members of the household in all their totality and, thus, "consolidates" them for the transition into the new agricultural season.

When all the households have had their meal, the festivities begin with various people beating gongs, clashing cymbals and singing in the open near the headman's house. This goes on until the headman calls in the Palokhi villagers for the "libations at the descent of the land" (**khwae'ta kau lau wae**) made to the Lord of the Water, Lord of the Land and other tutelary spirits. The size of Palokhi houses makes it impossible for any house to accomodate all the people in the village and this is equally true for the headman's house. For the "libations at the descent of the land", what usually happens is that all the male heads of households congregate in the headman's house while women and children stay outside. However, as with the Head Rite (the key features of which also distinguish this ritual), this is also a reflection of the fact that men dominate the ritual life of the community.

In the two New Year rites which I witnessed in 1981 (22–23 January) and 1982 (6–7 February), the serving of liquor during the "libations at the descent of the land" were done by Nae' Kha, the headman's son. The customary practice in Palokhi is that it is the male head of the household, his son-in-law or, occasionally, an unmarried son who serves the liquor on ritual and social occasions. The deviation from this practice in the headman's house, however, should be understood in the light of the prospective succession of Nae' Kha to the headmanship of Palokhi. Headmanship and the Head Rite, as we have seen, require the maintenance of a certain continuity of relationship with the Lord of the Water, Lord of the Land to enusre harmonious conditions for the on-going existence of the community. Nae' Kha's role in the "libations at the descent of the land" is, therefore, another aspect of the constitution of this continuity of ritual relationships integral to headmanship in Palokhi.

The organisation and structure of the "libations at the descent of the land" are identical to that of the Head Rite. Although the prayers are essentially similar in that they propitiate the Lord of the Water, Lord of the Land and request his protection, they differ somewhat in their temporal orientations. Whereas the prayers of the Head Rite are concerned with maintaining the status quo with the spirit of the domain in the agricultural year that is in progress, the prayer in the New Year rite is markedly proleptic; it is emphatic about the approaching year and, indeed, a general future.

The following is a prayer made by Tamu' the headman.

Sa, delau Thi Koe'ca, Kau Koe'ca	O descend Lord of the Water Lord of the Land
Palaukhi 'a' Koe'ca, Palauklo 'a' Koe'ca	Lord of the headwaters of Pang Luang, Lord of Pang Luang
Tado', tapgha 'a' Koe'ca	Lord of that which is great, Lord of that which is old
Koe'ca, loe' my, Koe'ca loe' hau	Lord in the mid-heavens, Lord of the earth
Mycha 'i, my ghe, la ghe	Today, the sun is beautiful, the moon is beautiful
Sa' lau ne loe' my ghe, la ghe, 'a' sau 'i	(We) desire the sun to be beautiful, the moon to be beautiful, anew here
Ma sunja, 'au' sunja	Working for the future, eating in the future
Ma klae, 'au' ba do'	Doing little, eating greatly
Ma sunja, 'au' sunja	Working for the future, eating in the future
Ma 'au' chi', ma 'au'	Cultivating (literally, "working to eat") padi-fields, cultivating wet-rice fields
Ma 'au' chghi, ma 'au' hy'	Cultivating fallow swiddens, cultivating swiddens
Ma sunja, 'au' sunja	Working for the future, eating in the future
Ma klae, 'au' ba' do'	Working little, eating greatly

Ma ci' (kae), ne ba' 'a'	Doing little, obtaining much
Sunja khaupa	(In) the future continuously
Kae' ba' ke by koe'ca hy koe'ca	(Let us) be again lords of rice, lords of unhusked rice
Kae' poe'na 'a' koe'ca	(Let us) be lords of buffaloes
Kae' tatau' 'a' koe'ca	(Let us) be lords of cattle
Kae' thau' 'a' koe'ca	(Let us) be lords of pigs
Kae' chau 'a' koe'ca	(Let us) be lords of chickens
Cy'noe chi ba thau Na	(Our) ten fingers are raised up in prayer to you
Ghe loe' Koe'ca 'i, Koe'ca kwa	It is beautiful here Lord, Lord look
Koe'ca kwa khaeloe' kwa khaeche	Lord watch over all, watch over everything
Kwa myna ty loe' myche	Watch over in the night till the dawn
Kwa mycha ty loe' hamy	watch over in the morning till the dusk
Ma he loe' 'a' 'au', ba, 'a' 'au ba	Bestow fullness in eating, fullness in drinking
Ma he loe' 'a' 'au' ba dau' zi, dau' xau	Bestow fullness in eating together (in all) the villages, together at all the house-steps
Kwa khaeloe'	Watch over all
Kwa khaeloe', kwa khaeche	Watch over all, watch over everything
Kwa phodi', kwa phosa	Watch over those still young, watch over the children
Kwa phau'my, kwa phau'khwa	Watch over the women, watch over the men

Later in the prayer, the tutelary spirit of the domain is specifically asked to protect the village and house-holders from all that may endanger them. The form in which this request is expressed makes it clear that the community and its well-being are conceived of in terms of a solidarity and corporateness which are defined by the physical boundaries of houses, the village, and the domain.

Kwa tacu', kwa tacha	Watch over the aches, watch over the pains
Kwa tatoe'ghe, kwa tatoe'gwa	Watch over that which is not good, watch over that which is not pure
Si' toe' thau loe' doe'	So that they do not ascend to the houses
Si' toe' thau loe' lau	So that they do not ascend to the sleeping mats
Toe' ghe	It is not good
Si' toe' hae thau zi	So that they do not ascend to the village
Toe' ghe	It is not good

Si' toe' hae thau xau	So that they do not ascend to the house-steps
Toe' ghe	It is not good
Plae ke	Divert them back
Plae ke su my do', kau lae	Divert them back to the great domain, the large country[26]
Su thi zi, su kau coe	To faraway waters, To distant domains
He loe' 'a' chghae doe', chghae lau	Bestow their dispersal from houses, their dispersal from sleeping mats
He loe' 'a' chghae zi, chghae xau	Bestow their dispersal from the village, their dispersal from house-steps
'O' loe', Koe'ca, 'i	Remain, Lord, here
Koe'ca kwa khaeloe', kwa khaechae	Lord watch over all, watch over everything

The prayer continues in this manner and then ends with the standard formula which closes all prayers to the Lord of the Water, Lord of the Land and other tutelary spirits.

Once the libations and prayers have been made in the headman's house, the headman and elders then proceed to the other houses to perform the ritual. This may be done on the same night or on the following day depending on how much time is left.

The "wrist-tying at the descent of the land" is performed on the following morning. In contrast to the libations in the headman's house of the previous night, it is a domestic rite performed, in conjunction with the eating of the early morning meal, by parents. It is similar to the wrist-tying rituals that I have already described and its purpose is also the same. After the ceremony, other people in the village are then invited to eat. As I noted in Chapter IV, this goes on throughout the day with the Palokhi Karen moving from house to house to eat and to drink the rice liquor which is also offered at the same time.

One notable feature of the festivities on the second day of the New Year rites is the custom of displaying new married women's skirts. This is done individually by house-holds, usually after the wrist-tying ceremony. The skirts are taken out and hung on bamboo poles which are the equivalent of clothes lines in Palokhi. Alternatively, they may be hung on the railings of verandahs. The overall effect is highly colourful, contributing to the festive air which characterises the rites of the New Year.

The Palokhi Karen explain the custom by saying that it makes the village look "beautiful" (ghe). This is undoubtedly true but, as we have seen, married women's skirts possess a very particular symbolic value in Palokhi. While their red colour signifies a state of "procreativity", a symbolic value which they share with men's shirts, their special application to fruit trees on the other hand singles them out as a more powerful symbol of this state. Given the dominant symbolism of married women's skirts, their use is entirely appropriate in the context of the New Year rites. Indeed, it is consistent with the general theme of the rites, that is, the consolidation of the community and renewal: the custom invokes the generative powers that are symbolised by married women's skirts for the new agricultural year.

In this chapter, I have described several rituals within the corpus of annual agricultural rites in Palokhi, in order to illustrate their principal features and the particular forms in which language and symbolic activity are employed, to demonstrate their major importance in the religious life of the community, and to show more generally their significance in terms of the cultural ideology of the Palokhi Karen. These rituals are organised around ideas, concepts and categories which are key elements in the way that the Palokhi Karen conceive of agricultural production, especially swidden cultivation, and of their viability as a community. In the religious life of the Palokhi Karen, it is evident that both agricultural production and the existence of the community are treated as interrelated, on-going processes. At the heart of this ideological relationship lies what may best be regarded as a procreative model of society extended to agriculture.

ENDNOTES

[1] In Palokhi, the cycle of wet-rice agricultural rituals is modelled on that of swiddens, but not in its entirety. It is based on a number of key rites such as the rites of planting, the rite of protection and some harvest rites which I discuss in this chapter. There are, in addition, some minor ritual practices which are borrowed from the Northern Thai but these do not provide the key symbolic motifs of the wet-rice ritual cycle. There are, however, two rites which are partly of Northern Thai provenance and they are important. These are, specifically, the rite of "propitiating the spirit of the dam" (known by the macaronic **ly faaj**) and the "wrist-tying of buffaloes" (**ki cy' poe'na**). Both are fitted in within the religious system of the Palokhi Karen in that the supreme spirit which is appeased, and appealed to, is the Lord of the Water, Lord of the Land. Indeed, the cycle of wet-rice agricultural rituals is in fact articulated within the cycle of swidden rites. For example, although the rites of planting and protection must be performed in swiddens and wet-rice fields by households which have both, it is not unusual to find such households performing only harvest rites in swiddens because they deem it sufficient for both fields.

[2] As I explain later, an important feature in ritual ownership is the health or "vitality" of the ritual owner. In Palokhi, most of the male heads of households have not reached an age, or are in a condition, where they might be regarded as having declined in health or "vitality". Hence the fact that the ritual officiant and ritual owner are one and the same person.

[3] Among the Sgaw Karen in Mae Sariang, however, this does not appear to be the case. Kunstadter reports that the ceremonial owner of the field is, often, a young child (male or female) who is selected by the family to be the owner of the field for a year. The rationale for this, according to Kunstadter, is that:

The Karen like to select a young field owner because of the probability that a young person has not been exposed to, nor had a chance to offend the spirits as much as an older person. If the field is bountiful, its young ritual owner will continue in this role as long as his (or her) luck holds, or until he has children of his own to take the responsibility; but if he is unlucky, he may never again assume ritual responsibility for fear that his unsuccessful relationship with the spirits will be repeated. (1978:86).

[4] In Palokhi, people were divided in opinion as to whether or not a former ritual owner could become one again. In practice, however, there was no instance of a person assuming the role again.

[5] Divination with chicken bones has been widely reported for the Karen. However, the methods and criteria for ascertaining favourable or unfavourable prognostications vary. An alternative method of divination with chicken bones, among the Karen, is excellently described by (Marshall [1922:280–4]).

[6] The term **my**, here, literally means "sun" and its use is based, of course, on the idea that clearing the forest canopy lets the sun in. However, perhaps because of this association, **my** may in fact be used as a metaphor for swiddens which is indeed the case in some other ritual texts. This sense of the term is also present in this line.

[7] This distinction is also to be found in one of the very few general food taboos that the Palokhi Karen have. Despite their very eclectic diet, they have a dietary prohibition on rats which live in or around the village (see also Hinton [1975:127]). As this prohibition cannot be related to any other aspect of Palokhi Karen culture, the explanation for it must lie in the anomalous habits of these rats which are neither domesticated nor wild but forage in both domains. The prohibition, therefore, would be of the same order as that on the pangolin amongst the Lele which Douglas discusses (1957) or on the cat amongst the Northern Thai (Davis [1984:171]). This separation of domains among the Karen has also been noted by Madha (1980: 59–60) and Mischung (1980:26–7).

[8] The Palokhi Karen do not have an elaborate cosmology. At any rate, they are unable to describe in any detail what might be regarded as a cosmological system. The only references to a cosmology occur in prayers such as this one, and in mortuary prayers in which the souls of deceased persons are instructed to go to the after-world (see also Mischung [1980:73–81]). The after-world is described symbolically in these prayers through the medium of a tree drawn out on the back of a winnowing tray with rice flour. A coin (a baht or sataang), which represents the souls of the dead person, is moved in various directions along the tree but the orientational references in the prayer are totally inverted. The base of the tree, for example, is spoken of as the top of the tree and vice versa. It is only from these references that we may infer something of the cosmology of the Palokhi Karen because the few myths that they possess offer no indication of a cosmology.

[9] An indication of the pejorative associations attaching to the words for "crooked" and "crossed" is, of course, to be found in the way that the Palokhi Karen describe prohibited unions. It may also be seen in the way stubborn, obdurate adults and children are described: they are said to have "crooked ears" (**na ke'**).

[10] **Ha'sa** is a Northern Thai term (**haksaa**) that has been used to form the dyadic complement of the Sgaw Karen **koetau**. The use of Northern Thai terms in Palokhi Karen ritual language is not uncommon as we have seen elsewhere. In this, Palokhi Karen ritual language displays a feature, amongst others, which is by no means uncommon. It is a characteristic of ritual languages distinguished by semantic parallelism, in multi-lingual or multi-dialectal contexts, as Fox (1971:234) has shown.

[11] **Pgho** refers esentially to what is probably best regarded as "ritual power". It may be applied to objects or to people and some animals such as elephants. Old or ancient objects, for example, may sometimes be said to have **pgho** especially if they possess ritual significance. Wild animals such as barking deer or wild boar which "cannot be killed" (**ma si toe' se**), that is, which constantly elude hunters, may also sometimes be said to have **pgho**. Similarly, elephants of advanced age with a reputation for intelligence may also be spoken of as having pgho. However, the word is more appropriately used with respect to people especially ritual specialists (**soera**). Ritual specialists who are repeatedly successful in healing rituals, for example, are said to be "men of **pgho**". Such men might well be described as possessing "charisma" in the Weberian sense of the term. In Palokhi, and indeed in the Mae Muang Luang-Huai Tung Choa area there was no person, animal or object that was recognised as such. A brief but interesting summary of the concept may be found in (Keyes [1977b:54]).

[12] Quite apart from being symbols of wealth, elephants **are** wealth for the Karen (see, for example, Hinton [1975:134–5] and Kunstadter [1978:103–5]). Few Palokhi Karen have ever seen bronze frog drums but they are regarded, as in many if not all other Karen communities, as being quintessentially Karen (see also Cooler [1979]). They are also, typically, objects which may be attributed with **pgho**. The identification with bronze drums is so strong that it forms the central motif of the coat-of-arms of the Karen National Union and Karen National Liberation Army, the separatist movement in Burma. In Palokhi, however, part of the value that is placed on such drums and rupees lies in the fact that they are seen to be old. This association is not overtly expressed but it may seen in the near-reverent way that the Palokhi Karen handle or admire such old objects. While it true to some extent that the value that is placed on these objects derives from their rarity, this does not explain the quasi-veneration accorded to them nor the belief that if they are sold or traded off, the result will be the destitution of the household. Some Palokhi households possess objects of no mean antiquity. The small assortment of objects include a bullet coin, a Bols genever clay bottle possibly dating back to late Ayuthian times, a

crude celadon covered jar of undoubtedly old provenance (Donald Gibson, pers. comm.) resembling primitive Northern Thai celadons, and a glass bead necklace similar to the Venetian glass beads extensively traded in parts of Southeast and East Asia via the Indian sub-continent.

[13] In this line, the use of the term "livers" should be understood in the context of the term **sa,** "fruit", "grains" or "panicles". **Sa** has the homophone **sa'** which means "heart". In ordinary speech, **sa'** coupled with transitive verbs denotes reflexive action or action that involves oneself. So, here the desire for fullness in rice itself is conveyed by the partially explicit and partially implicit organic analogy that is being drawn.

[14] **Taka'** means "riches" or "wealth" in Sgaw Karen. **Talae',** however, comes from the Northern Thai **laek** which means "to exchange".

[15] In describing a similar ritual in Burma, Marshall quotes part of a ritual text which goes as follows: "When the eagle flies, the crow is afraid. When the laughing bird laughs and the barking deer barks, let us not fear their bad omens" (1922:79). Despite the obvious differences, the similarities in this formula are striking. They do not merely suggest a common oral tradition among the Karen but a certain continuity through time and space as well. In Palokhi, the formula may sometimes be rendered as "the squirrel sits" (**li chinau**). Marshall identifies the "laughing bird" as a species of the genus **Lanius**.

[16] See Jones (1961:16) and Matisoff (1983:78).

[17] The expression literally means "having to call souls" or "being required to call souls". "Soul calling" is also performed in cases of what is probably best described as "spirit invasion" or **ba' soeta** which may be translated as "being required to do a sending". This represents a more complex situation as intruding spirits must first be "sent" before the souls of the afflicted person may be "called" to return. In either case, the most important feature is the restoration of souls to bodies. More generally, it reflects conceptions of "self" or "person" in which the joint integrity of souls and bodies is an important feature.

[18] **Na**, here, comes from the Northern Thai **naa** which means, of course, "padi-field" or "wet-rice field".

[19] This is one of the very few references in any context, in Palokhi, to the cosmogonic deity Zwa or Ywa which has been widely reported in the early literature on the Karen (see, for example, Cross [1853–54:300]; Mason [1861:97]; Marshall [1922:211–218]). While the Palokhi Karen appear to believe, very generally, in the existence of Zwa as a sort of high god there is no evidence in their day-to-day religious and ritual life to suggest that this belief occupies an important place in their religious system. Neither do they have myths about Zwa which the early Christian missionaries in Burma were so fond of recounting. For the Palokhi Karen, the most important figure in their religious system is the Lord of the Water, Lord of the Land. It is interesting to note that the Zwa tradition of the Karen does not feature prominently in contemporary studies of the Karen, suggesting that its importance to the Karen may have been overplayed by Christian missionaries. As Keyes also points out in his analysis of the Zwa tradition (1977b:52), missionary accounts have tended to colour all subsequent interpretations of the tradition. The difference between "Ywa" and "Zwa" is a simple linguistic transformation of the initial consonants which occurs fairly consistently among Sgaw Karen speakers as one moves east from Burma to Thailand.

[20] I must acknowledge here my indebtedness to Thra Pu Tamoo for explaining the intricacies of this portion of the prayer which would otherwise have remained obscure to me. Not all Palokhi ritual texts contain such a wealth of images. Unlike, say, the ritual texts of the Rotinese of Eastern Indonesia which are presented as public oratorical performances (Fox [1971, 1975, 1983]), Palokhi Karen ritual language is used in prayers which are for all practical purposes individualised performances. There is no audience as such even when there are a large number of villagers present. Under these conditions, and given the way that knowledge of ritual language is transmitted (as I have described before), there is very little cross-referral and discussion of the forms in ritual language. In these circumstances, it is not possible to talk of a proper canon in Palokhi ritual texts which, otherwise, would be established through public performances as is the case with the Rotinese (see, for example, Fox [1983]). Nevertheless, it is clear that there is a common stock of lexical items and semantic elements which make up dyadic sets that are structured in "formulaic phrases" as Fox calls it (1971:215). Contrary to the Rotinese, the very nature of the way in which ritual language is employed in Palokhi allows for individual improvisation and this particular line, I think, is an exceptionally good (if rare) example of such an improvisation.

[21] This brief reference bears a remarkable similarity with a Northern Thai prayer, also said during the harvest which Davis discusses (1984:255–6). In the part of the prayer which Davis examines, in the ritual that "recalls rice souls" (**suukhwaan khao**), the rice is asked to "flow" from the mouths of a host of animals, including the bamboo rat.

[22] I have not been able to identify the **ki'ko** plant. Marshall also reports its use, but in a different context. He says that the leaves are used to wrap the chicken bones used in swidden divination (1922:76). He does not, however, identify the vine.

[23] **Wi** means "to be finished", "to be completed", and so forth. **Wau,** however, has no intrinsic meaning so far as I have been able to ascertain. In transcribing and translating this text with the assistance of several men in Palokhi, I was unable to obtain any elucidation of the meaning of the word despite many queries. Some suggested that Soe Wae, the old lady who performed the ritual, had perhaps made up a word to complete the dyadic set. Soe Wae, however, claimed that **wau** meant the same thing as **wi**. In the absence of any other referent by which the term may be glossed, I have used here an English equivalent which may, perhaps, be regarded as permissible given the form of the oral tradition of the Palokhi Karen. Nevertheless, I must stress that the translation offered here is provisional for the reasons above.

[24] The **pip** referred to here is one of the standard measures of rice used in Palokhi which they have adopted from the Northern Thai. As I noted in Chapter V, it is equivalent to 22 litres.

[25] **Koewi**, according to the Palokhi Karen, is an alternative term for **koela** or "souls". It is not used in ordinary speech and is, therefore, specific to ritual language. I have used only the term "souls" in this translation for lack of an alternative term in English.

[26] The term **my** is derived from the Northern Thai **myang** which means "land", "country" or "domain", that is, a political unit, as well as "capital city".

Chapter VII

Conclusion: Cultural Reproduction and the Maintenance of Identity

In the late eighteenth century, Father Vincentius Sangermano made the following remarks about the Karen in Burma:

> It is worthy of observation that, although residing in the midst of the Burmese and Peguans, they not only retain their own language, but even their dress, houses, and everything else are distinguished from them; and what is more remarkable, they have a different religion. (Sangermano, quoted in Keyes [1979a:1]).

These observations are as true today of the Palokhi Karen in the Pa Pae hills as they were of the Karen amongst the Burmese and Mon of Burma in Sangermano's time. As I hope to have shown, following the argument set out in the introductory chapter to this study, much if not all of what is distinctively "Karen" about the Palokhi Karen—despite the fact that they are to be found in a predominantly Northern Thai socio-economic milieu and, indeed, are dependent to a greater or lesser extent on a regional economy to meet their subsistence needs—may be found in their "different" religion. I also hope to have shown that, "even in their dress, houses, and everything else" there are features, the significance of which can only be understood by reference to their indigenous, non-Buddhist, non-Christian religion.

By way of comparison and contrast, however, let me turn briefly to a consideration of two rather different examples of what "being Karen" might mean. In terms of my argument and analysis, both examples may be regarded as "ideal types" representing possibly extreme developments, conditioned by historical circumstances, in the directions which the **sociological relationship** between religion and identity (at its most general) may take in the context of intergroup relations involving the Karen. Nevertheless, they stand as very real experiences—at least for some Karen communities. The two examples which I refer to are the Telakhon, a Karen syncretic Buddhist millenarian movement, and the Karen separatist movement in Burma which is predominantly composed of Christian Karen in its leadership, body of armed men and, to some extent, civilian supporters. The relevance and interest of these two movements, for the present discussion, lie in what may be gleaned about the relationship between social organisation, religion, and some form of Karen identity, and in the possible elements of an answer to the question which I posed at the beginning—in what way or ways are Buddhist, Christian, and "animist" Karen "Karen"?

The Telakhon: Identifying Religious Change

The Telakhon movement has not been thoroughly documented, at least in its ethnographic details, but what is available in existing accounts is highly suggestive of the kinds of evidence which are relevant to the issues dealt with in this study in the case of the Palokhi Karen. There are only two accounts (Stern [1968] and Dodd [1962]) of the Telakhon which offer some details of this Karen Buddhist millenarian movement based on first-hand information.[1]

Stern's account of the Telakhon in one Karen community is principally concerned with an explication of the phenomenon of millenarianism based on Buddhist derived beliefs about a Future Buddha, **Arimetteya**, in terms of the significance of a certain Karen myth, as well as a sociological explanation of the phenomenon in terms of a version of Aberle's "relative deprivation" thesis.[2] The account of the Telakhon provided by Dodge is based on the same group of people. It is not altogether informative from an anthropological point of view but, as with Stern's description (which was based on a visit to the Telakhon a few years after Dodge's first visit), there are a few intriguing observations about social organisation and identification in the context of religious change.

In the earlier description of the Telakhon, Dodge (an American Baptist missionary based in Thailand) says that there were approximately 50 followers of Telasi, the self-proclaimed **Ariya** (that is, **Arimetteya**), at the village of Tee Maw near the Thai-Burmese border. Dodge also says, however, that there were reputedly 6,000 followers spread out in separate villages in Burma as well as Thailand. His overall impression of Tee Maw was that "it is essentially a Karen society, including Sgaw and Pwo" where the followers of Telasi "can wear Karen dress or else solid coloured shirts and longee" which most of the men wear, while "The women seem to wear typical Karen costumes all the time" (1962:i, 4).

The intriguing part of Dodge's observations, however, concerns what appears to be an element of hierarchical differentiation at Tee Maw. He reports that Telasi had two subordinates, the **"bukho"** or spiritual head, and the **"kokho"** or secular head, as well as a "scribe" who was also prominent at his meetings with the head of the Telakhon. Equally intriguing is Dodge's report that the head of the Telakhon made the suggestion that the mission of American Baptists establish a clinic and school in a valley about three days' walk from Sangklaburi. The leader of the Telakhon claimed that if the mission did so, "a thousand or more Karen would move there". Telasi, furthermore, offered to have the land cleared for them (1962:10). Judging from Dodge's account, it would seem that this valley lay well away from Tee Maw itself. What is intriguing about this brief account of the conversation with Telasi is that the leader of the Telakhon seems either to have had some power of disposition over land situated well away from his headquarters at Tee Maw, or that he at least believed he did.

The significance of these snippets of information provided by Dodge is that generally the society was "essentially Karen" and that where the social organisation of the Telakhon is concerned there was some form of hierarchy as well as some notion of territorial control attaching to leadership of the Telakhon. Though Dodge's descriptions are by no means conclusive, they contain elements which indicate some important differences in social organisation compared to that in Palokhi, nowithstanding the fact that Tee Maw is "essentially Karen" and the fact of Karen dress.

Stern's account of the Telakhon some years later is more detailed and it points to a far greater elaboration of life in the Telakhon. It is not possible to say whether the elaboration lies in the development of the Telakhon over a few years, or whether it lies in Stern's greater attention to detail; but the elaboration is significant.

The account of Telakhon organisation under the **Ariya,** provided by Stern, goes as follows:

> Beneath him there is now a complex administration comprising a religious head (**bu kho**) and a secular head (**kaw kho** — both terms are given in Sgaw), each assisted by a board, a central executive committee and subordinate counterparts under the inferior **yathe,** as well as a panel of elders, drawn from all the faithful, to serve as advisors to the central executive committee. Together, they manage the affairs of the sect, supervising the three major festivals of the year, maintaining communication with the membership and correspondence with outsiders, and overseeing corporate business concerns, which derive income principally through a house tax on members and from free-will gifts. Two secular departments, those of education and defense, seem as yet largely inoperative. The executive committee also sits as a court in maintaining observance of a code of controlling sexual conduct with traditional Karen stringency, but also forbidding gambling, the use of intoxicants and narcotics, and acts which might foment internal discord; and further enjoining the raising of such animals as might be sacrificed to the spirits. To the conduct so regulated is added the encouragement of wearing Karen garb. (1968:315–6).

Stern comments later that,

> The issues of change and conservation in customary behaviour are neatly exemplified in the Telakhon observance of the wearing of Karen garb, an act which may be taken as expressive at once of an ethnic continuity with the mythic past, when the conditions of the millenium were laid down, and of that reunited nation of the Karen to which they look forward. (1968:321).

The doctrinal considerations and macro-political aspects (that is, the relations between the Karen and the polities of Burma and Thailand in historical times) of the Telakhon have been much explored and discussed not only by Stern but others as well (Keyes [1977a]; Hinton [1979]; Lehman [1979]; Tambiah [1984:300–2]; but see also Wijeyewardene [in press]) and I shall not, therefore, consider them here. The micro-political features and the identification of religious change are, however, worth noting.

Despite what may be regarded as its "charismatic" basis, it is unequivocally clear that the social organisation of the Telakhon is not only "bureaucratic" in nature (also in Weber's sense), but it displays **political** features. The bureaucratic aspect of the Telakhon is evident from Stern's description as is the political which is contained in some notion of territorial control and defence. This is consistent with the politico-religious complex associated with beliefs about **cakkavatti** and **Arimetteya**. As Stern describes it, the **Arimetteya** is preceded by "the messianic figure of the **cakkavatti**, a universal monarch, who solely through the exercise of his justice and love for all living beings will conquer mankind and thus lay the foundation for the new order (**dhamma**) of the Future Buddha, **Arimetteya**" (1968:300). The two may sometimes be conflated as seems to be the case with the leader of the Telakhon.

It is, however, the creation of two offices or positions in the bureaucratic organisation of the Telakhon out of a Karen context that is striking, namely, the **bu kho** and the **kau kho** (Dodge's **"kokho"** and Stern's **"kaw kho"**) functioning under the **Ariya** Telasi who is not only a religious figure but presents some semblance of being a ruler of sorts. **Kho** of course means "head" in Sgaw Karen and **kau** "stream valley" or more broadly "domain", as I have noted before. The etymon of **bu** is either Mon (**pon**, as Stern suggests) or Thai (**bun**), both ultimately deriving from the Pali **punna**, "merit".[3] In Palokhi, as we have seen, the only "head" is the village headman, the **zi kho**, who functions essentially as an intermediary between the community and the Lord of the Water, Lord of the Land.

The administrative complex of the Telakhon (to which we might add its "corporate business concerns") and these two "heads" are so radically different from the system of head-manship and village organisation which, as I have shown, are intimately linked to religion in Palokhi, that we may well be justified in saying that they represent very different social systems.

Wijeyewardene has argued, in his paper on "The Theravada Compact and the Karen" where he examines not only the Telakhon but other movements in Northern and North-eastern Thailand and similar contemporary developments in Thailand, that

> … we need to look at the operation of Buddhism in society not so much as the operation of a single tendency or dichotomy, but as a number of

sometimes opposed principles. The millenarian tendency ... applied not only to individuals and communities who were "deprived", but was also a factor in the activities of monarchs themselves. Charismatic figures may sometimes not be so much millenarian, but represent the manifestation of a point of view put forward by [Trevor] Ling — a Buddhist view of society which was concerned with creating a society in which salvation was possible. In its modern manifestation, I suggested that we have a sociological view of the role of Buddhism; and traditionally, what appear to be millenarian movements were attempts to define the socio-religious nature of the society. (Wijeyewardene, **in press**).

The Telakhon is quite evidently one such attempt to define, or redefine, the socio-religious nature of society, Dodge's general impression notwithstanding.

Indeed, this redefinition was probably so successful at Tee Maw that it was necessary to "mark" it somehow as a "Karen" phenomenon. I would suggest that this is the import of the encouragement to wear Karen dress noted by Stern, and it is probably the use of Karen dress (and the use of Sgaw Karen) at Tee Maw which led Dodge into describing Tee Maw as an essentially "Karen" society. Even if Dodge was correct, when he first visited Tee Maw, it is clear from Stern's account that Karen dress was not merely a matter of what **could** be worn, but what **ought** to be worn. It is almost as if the Telakhon was in danger of becoming (or being seen as) something else that necessitated the encouragement of the wearing of Karen dress. Dodge is quite explicit that the language spoken in the Telakhon was Sgaw Karen (1962:7), so the language was probably not entirely sufficient in itself to distinguish the identity of the movement if, as I argue, an additional possibly more conspicuous "marker" was required. Although Stern is essentially correct in seeing the "issues of change and conservation" in the wearing of Karen dress, these issues are not perhaps as neatly exemplified as he suggests.

The encouragement of Karen dress in the Telakhon, I suggest, was an attempt to assert an identity, a means of identifying socio-religious change in the form of the Telakhon as a "Karen" development because the cultural substance, as it were, of the community at Tee Maw had **changed.** It is possible also that the conscious references to the Karen myth, and its apparently indigenous millenarian content, which Stern discusses, were of the same order.[4] This is not to say, however, that socio-religious change in the form of the Telakhon necessarily meant an absolute hiatus in cultural continuity at Tee Maw, but rather that the socio-religious change was sufficient and significant enough to require a **conscious** attempt to identify the change. In terms of the argument presented at the beginning of this study, I would suggest that the cultural ideology of the

Tee Maw Karen had undergone a transformation and that they cannot be regarded as being "Karen" in the same sense that the Palokhi Karen are "Karen".

Similar considerations are contained in the Karen separatist movement, but the separatist movement is also extremely interesting for what it shows of how transformations in cultural ideologies, of the kind that I am interested in here, may be disguised by the manipulation of traditional Karen symbols and adductions of a mythical past rationalised in the form of a theory of racial origins. In principle, the issues are not dissimilar to those in the Telakhon.

From "Tribe" to "State": An Official View of Karen Identity

The Karen separatist movement has been in existence in Burma since 1949, one year after Burma gained independence from the British. The movement has received some scholarly attention by historians and political scientists and has merited brief comments in the anthropological literature on the Karen.

Keyes' short account of Karen nationalism (1977b:56–8) provides the essential background to the emergence of the separatist movement in Burma which is now based in several strongholds on the Thai-Burmese border. As Keyes notes,

> The activities of the Christian missionaries among the Karen must be recognized as perhaps the most important factor in the development of a Karen national movement, a movement that has attracted many non-Christian Karens. (1977b:56).

The reason for this, as Keyes points out, was that Christian missionaries initiated the development of a Karen literate tradition through the introduction of schools, the construction of printing presses which served both religious and secular needs. Equally important was the fact that Karen Christian churches provided a supralocal network of connections and organisation.

Out of this background has emerged the Karen National Union (KNU), a political organisation, and its military arm, the Karen National Liberation Army (KNLA), as they are now known.[5] The aim of the KNU is the establishment of an independent Karen state which they call Kawthoolei or "The Land of Lilies". The Karen separatists, under the leadership of General Saw Bo Mya who is both President of the KNU and Commander-in-Chief of the KNLA, occupy a certain amount of territory in Burma and this is, for all practical purposes, their **de facto** state.

There is a semblance of a government complete with cabinet ministers holding various portfolios, but in the final analysis these are somewhat artificial creations which do not mean very much, at least in terms of ministerial powers as they are conventionally understood. The real administrative structures of Kawthoolei are army command structures modelled on the British Army, that is its organisation and order of battle. This consists of five brigades and an elite battalion. Each of these brigades and the battalion are responsible for an operational sector which together form the administrative and constituent territories of Kawthoolei. The principal tasks of these units are, of course, the defence of their sectors and the conduct of operations against Burmese government troops when they move into these sectors. The elite battalion has additional, rather more offensive tasks.

The commanders of these units are responsible for the collection of taxes or levies on goods in the black market trade between Thailand and Burma. The income from these levies is turned over to the government, as it is called, though it is nothing but the headquarters of the KNLA. The income thus received is used to finance the movement's never-ending military confrontation with the Burmese government. Income is also obtained from the sale of timber and some minerals in Thai markets. A certain amount of income in kind, namely rice, is also collected from Karen villages in Kawthoolei. Unit commanders are said to receive nominal salaries, but all amenities such as housing, road and water transport and so forth are provided. Part of the income from the levies are redistributed to unit commanders for the purpose of equipping and paying their regular troops and conscripts who are said to serve for two years. Generally, however, units are required to be self-sufficient in food, and some commanders in fact have their own sources of income deriving from the sale of livestock in Thailand or from their own farming businesses.

The important point to note about the separatist movement is that it represents an active or activist manifestation of Karen nationalism and, like Karen nationalism, grew out of a history and system of Christian missionary patronage in Burma. Its leadership is predominantly composed of Christian (Baptist and Seventh-Day Adventist) Karen, many of whom are Sgaw, though for all practical purposes little weight is attached to Sgaw-Pwo differences. The two major languages used by members of the KNU and KNLA are Sgaw Karen and English, although Burmese is also sometimes used, especially by Karen from Rangoon and Moulmein who have joined the movement.

The separatist movement is undoubtedly political in its motivation, but it is the cultural logic of the movement that is relevant here. This is best exemplified in official and quasi-official accounts of what is best regarded as the "mythical charter" (in Malinowski's sense) of the movement. Perhaps the most fascinating aspect of this "charter" is that much of it rests on the ethnological speculations and conjectures of the early missionaries and British colonial administrators in Burma, based on a number of Karen myths.

The first myth, which bears certain resemblances to the story of the Garden of Eden in the Old Testament, tells the story of the creation of the first ancestral couple by a cosmogonic deity, Y'wa. According to the myth, Y'wa forbade them to eat a certain fruit but a serpent, Mu kaw li, feminine in its conception, persuades them to do so and the couple then become subject to the processes of aging, disease, and death. The second myth relates that Y'wa gave his children, amongst whom numbered the Karen, books of knowledge. The Karen, however, lose the book through their negligence and it is destroyed. Y'wa nevertheless promises them that some day "foreign brothers" would bring a "golden book" for them. Both myths are discussed by Keyes who says:

> These two myths greatly impressed the American Baptist missionaries who began work among the Karens in the early part of the nineteenth century. The first story so paralleled the Biblical story of the Garden of Eden, including the fact that the name Y'wa was very similar to the Hebrew Yahweh, that the missionaries concluded that the Karens must be the descendants of one of the ten lost tribes of Israel. Moreover they quickly presented themselves as the foreign brothers bringing the Karens the golden book. The fact that missionaries were the first to record these myths has led to their interpretations colouring the understanding of them ever since. Contrary to such interpretations, Y'wa cannot in fact be seen (at least prior to Christian missionization) as a high god that approximates the biblical conception of God. For the Karen, Y'wa represents a natural state, including the distinctions between men, some of whom are literate and others of whom, like the Karens, are not.

> The cosmogonic deities, Y'wa and Mu kaw li, are but one type of supernatural power recognized by the Karen. In addition are the rather large number of animistic divinities, that is, minor gods and spirits, that belong to the Karen pantheon. Of these animistic beings, the most important are the "Lord of Land and Water," that is, a territorial god, and the ancestral spirit, called **bgha**. (1977b:52).

Keyes' discussion is generally persuasive, but at least one missionary, Francis Mason, attempted to fit if not the ten lost tribes theory then most certainly its assumption of migrations to a theory of the origins of the Karen based on another myth to explain the presence of the Karen in Burma. It is, it might be added, perhaps the only indigenous Karen myth with a millenarian colour and it is the one discussed by Stern.

There are a number of versions of the myth, described by early missionaries. The following account draws on a somewhat later version provided by the Reverend David Gilmore (1911). Very briefly, the myth recounts the travels of another mythical ancestor or patriarch who kills a wild boar. He uses one of the boar's tusks to make a comb and as he combs his hair with it, he becomes young again. His family does the same, becoming young again. His children bear a great many offspring, and they in their turn have many children. As they all use the comb, their numbers are not reduced by death and the land they occupy becomes overpopulated. The old-young patriarch therefore decides that he should set out in search of new land to settle. As he travels further afield, he loses his children or descendants after he crosses a "sandy river" or "river of sand". The descendants are left behind because of some misadventure. The myth ends with a declaration that when the descendants are freed from sin, the patriarch will return and lead his descendants across the river to the pleasant land which he has found beyond.

The point to note about this myth is the reference to the "river of sand" or "sandy river". As Gilmore says:

> Dr. Mason interpreted it to mean a "river of running sand", i.e., a river consisting of sand. He came to the conclusion that the desert of Gobi was meant by this, and interpreted the legend to mean that the Karens had crossed this desert during the migration into Burma. Subsequent writers have followed Dr. Mason here. (1911:81).

Although Gilmore and some other missionaries were unconvinced by Mason's ethnological conjectures, it is evident that some version of them has found its way into the political ideology of the Karen separatist movement.

In a publication available in Kawthoolei (Saw Moo Troo and Mika Rolley, n.d.), an article whose purpose is to establish that the Karen separatist movement has nothing in common with communism is prefaced by a definition of what it means to be a Karen, what a Karen heritage consists of, and a statement on the historical origins of the Karen.[6] The definition is expressed thus:

> According to the tribal traditions of the Karens their earliest known patriarch is Poo Htot-meh-pah, boar tusk's father. Hence in answer to the question "Who is a Karen?" one of the answers should be (1) one who can claim his ancestry to Poo Htot-meh-pah and (2) one who possesses, maintains and cultivates the legacies bequeathed to him by the said fore-bear and his predecessors. (Saw Moo Troo and Mika Rolley n.d.:1).

As for the Karen heritage, the author says, "As a nation, we have at least eight", and proceeds to present them "in order of merit and value". They are: The knowledge that there is a God, the Divine Being; High moral and ethical standards; Honesty; Simple, quiet and peaceful living; Hospitality; Language; National costumes; and Aptitude for music.

The origin of the Karen, which is clearly an implicit justification for a prior right to land, goes as follows:

> From central Mongolia our forefathers moved down south to Tibet and afterwards further down along both sides of the Irrawaady [sic], Sittang and Salween rivers settling down scatteringly everywhere between these rivers and thickly in the Irrawaddy Delta. After them came the Talaings

and the Burmese respectively in bigger waves. Then they lived together
or side by side with the subsequent settlers most of them became
Buddhists [sic]. (Saw Moo Troo and Mika Rolley n.d.:2).

Although the pamphlet is not, strictly speaking, an official publication issued
by the Kawthoolei government — it is described on the first page as "An
appraisal by an inside observer who is not a politician and who does not aspire
to be one" — it undoubtedly seeks to present views which are endorsed by the
separatist movement.

A similar type of pamphlet entitled **The Karen Revolution in Burma**
(Lonsdale n.d.) presents the same ethnological speculations in greater detail,
with what can only be described as a touching faith in the power of dates, in an
appendix entitled "The Origin of the Karens". The first three pages of this
appendix are reproduced in Appendix I.

The official view of the basis of a Karen identity is hardly different from those
expressed in these pamphlets. Indeed, the consistent reiteration or representation
of this view at both levels would suggest that Mason's speculations have taken
on the status of a "culturally" based political doctrine, for they provide the
ultimate validation for the existence of Kawthoolei. In an interview with General
Saw Bo Mya (a Sgaw Karen and Seventh-Day Adventist), Bo Mya asserted:

> The Karen migrated down to China from Mongolia and down to Burma.
> The Karen are peace-loving people and for that reason they suffer.
> Thieving and robbing is not in the Karen line. The Burmese migrated
> after the Karen. The Burmese are more aggressive than the Karen and
> exploit all peoples. The came and encroached on Karen land and the
> Karen say that there is so much land so the Karen moved away. Because
> we are peace-loving people we gave way .... Later on the Burmese not
> only took away what the Karen owned but persecuted them.

After a long diatribe about the iniquities of the Burmese, he went on to say:

> From the point of view of the world, people may think we are a very
> backward group [because] we have not won the war. But, to speak
> seriously, the Burmese have received help from all over. But we have
> stood up against the Burmese and the rest of the world. So we are not
> perhaps such poor fighters .... So this is no mean feat on our part because
> we are fighting against all odds, and to think of it, it is like the whole
> world oppressing us. Inspite of all this and the odds, we feel that God
> is with us.

In many respects, the Karen separatist movement is virtually millenarian.
Though it is not predicated on a predicted emergence or arrival of a religious
figure, it nonetheless seeks to establish a new order which, if not a **dhamma,**

is most certainly based on a Christian view of a Karen society in which they, like the Christian meek they see themselves as, will come into their own and inherit **their** earth.

The political ideology of the separatist movement, however, cannot be a very neat edifice. It consciously draws upon myths and other symbols which are **regarded** as being quintessentially Karen: bronze frog drums, for example, provide the motif for the KNU's and KNLA's coat of arms, while Karen clothes (the "national costumes") are specially worn during Liberation Day parades and celebrations. There is, in other words, a deliberate utilisation of what are held or thought to be intrinsically Karen. Furthermore, as one Karen Seventh-Day Adventist lay preacher closely associated with the separatist movement views it, although all in Kawthoolei are Karen, yet not all are the same because there are those who are not **Christian** who eventually must be shown the way from "animism" and "uplifted".

As with the Telakhon, Karen nationalism and the separatist movement which have rather different roots in Christian conversion represent the manifestation of historical processes and a transformation in cultural ideology. And, similar to the Telakhon, the Christian Karen associated with the separatist movement I suggest are really not "Karen" in the sense that the Palokhi Karen are "Karen".

Back to Culture

The Telakhon Karen and the Karen Christian nationalists are somewhat extreme cases of how religious change may be seen to be associated with manifestly different forms of "being Karen". They are recognisably different from each other, and from the Palokhi Karen. More difficult to identify would be the kinds of differences which may exist in Karen communities which undergo religious conversion (whether to Buddhism or Christianity) but with perhaps less pronounced organisational or political changes. Unfortunately, little has been written on such communities and they must remain as an area to be investigated. The Telakhon and the Karen nationalists nevertheless offer useful insights into the question of religious, cultural, and ethnic change if taken as examples of what is possible in the relationship between religion and identity.

There can be no doubt that however it is internally defined by the people themselves, both the Telakhon Karen and the Karen separatists regard themselves as being unequivocally Karen. In the same way, the Palokhi Karen consider themselves to be quite unambiguously Karen, though they refer to themselves in their dialect as **pghakoe'njau** or "human beings". As I have already argued, whatever the criteria or "commonsense constructs" they may use to define their "Karen-ness", the definition itself must be considered tautological. Accordingly, any actor definition of identity (whether we choose to call it cultural or ethnic) has limited, if any, value for a sociological analysis. Sociological definitions according to some "marker" or sets of "markers", on the other hand, are I suggest not without their problems. While diacritica, such as language, may enable us to establish whether or not a group of people or a community may be taken as being of one ethnic group rather than another (say, Karen and Northern Thai), they become inadequate for the identification of intragroup differences, especially when these intragroup differences are of an order resembling that between larger groups. These intragroup differences are clearly exemplified by the Telakhon Karen, the Karen nationalists, and the Palokhi Karen.

This is easily seen in, for example, the use of Karen as a language (or, for that matter, dress or any other "symbol") as a "marker" of identity. It is only a marker in a nominal sense regardless of whether or not it is taken as such by the Karen themselves. As I have tried to show, very particular kinds of cultural meanings are expressed through the use of Sgaw Karen in Palokhi in relation to their ritual and social life. It is extremely unlikely that these meanings are similar to those expressed in the use of Sgaw Karen among the Telakhon or the Karen nationalists. Indeed, I would argue that they are very different. The fact that Sgaw Karen is used by all three therefore says very little about what this might signify in terms of their identification as Karen. The central issue here, in other words, is a clearer sociological understanding of the role of language (rather than language **per se**) as it is employed by the Karen. The same may be said for Karen dress, as I have tried to show in the case of the Palokhi Karen.

One conclusion which I would therefore draw from this brief examination of the Telakhon and the Karen separatist movement, in relation to the argument in this study, is that in discussing what is similar and different among communities which claim a "Karen" identity, an analytical concept like "cultural ideology", as I defined it earlier, has a certain utility. It makes it possible to identify what inter- and intragroup similarities and differences are without recourse to actor definitions of identity which would thereby implicitly restate a tautology at an analytical level; it also enables us to do so without recourse to some notion of "markers" of identity, the analytical status and applicability of which can only be relative. The concept of "ethnicity" as applied to the Karen in the contexts of religious change, however, raises precisely this problem, for if it is taken too far, it leaves us with a much too relativistic notion of ethnic identity in which the only irreducible element is the cultural distinctiveness of this identity. I would suggest that while the term "ethnicity" has its uses, the logic of its application must require us to examine more closely what is entailed by the notion of cultural distinctiveness, and to do so brings us back to culture. For analytical purposes, however, "culture" itself may be too general and it is here that something like "cultural ideology" may serve better.

In the case of the Palokhi Karen, the notion of a cultural ideology I believe enables us to grasp a great deal of what makes them distinctive not only in their own eyes, but in relation to other Christian or Buddhist Karen and, more generally, the Northern Thai as well. This cultural ideology is, as I have argued, best described as the structured relations between a "procreative model" of society and social processes, an integral part of which is a system of social classification based on the difference between male and female, cultural definitions of the relations between the two and the relationship between men and land, and a "model" of agricultural processes. The cultural ideology of the Palokhi Karen is "reproduced" in and through their religious system, a system which is dominated by men who play a crucial role in ritual life. In Palokhi, remaining distinctively Karen is a matter of cultural reproduction and the maintenance of identity.

ENDNOTES

[1] There are other Karen millenarian movements (see, for example, Keyes [1979b:20]; Hinton [1979:84–5]), but Stern's account of the Telakhon in Kanchanaburi province provides the most comprehensive discussion of the subject.

[2] Stern's application of this thesis is essentially political in its import, resting on an assumption that the **Ariya** (or **telakhon**) movement was a reaction to oppression by the Burmese. It is an analysis which has been criticised by Hinton on theoretical grounds and untested psychological assumptions (1979:91). While Hinton is, in my view, correct in his criticism, it is difficult to see how his alternative explanation that the phenomenon of "Karen prophets ... groping towards pan-Karen solidarity" is similar to the efforts of the Karen separatist movement is any different on theoretical or empirical grounds from that of Stern's. Sociological explanations of the type proposed by Hinton have, in their turn, been criticised by Wijyewardene (**in press**) for their "ring of Wagnerian metaphysics"(!). Though his focus is the "Theravada Compact and the Karen" Wijeyewardene, however, is concerned rather more with Buddhist millenialism as a particular application of "sociological Buddhism", in Ling's sense (1975), by those in Theravada Buddhist societies and polities who may be motivated by, amongst other things including historical conditions, the desire for power. He is very likely right in his assessment. While these discussions are extremely useful according to the kinds of sociological understandings that we may arrive at about Buddhism and, to some extent, about its manifestations among marginal groups (such as the Karen) in the context of the Theravada Buddhist states of Burma and Thailand, we still know very little about the details of life in Karen millenarian cults such as the Telakhon.

[3] For a discussion of the **bu kho** in recent times in a Pwo Karen community outside of a millenarian context, see Andersen (1976:269–74).

[4] I discuss a version of this later in the case of the Karen separatist movement (p. 452–3). In the case of the separatist movement, it is clear that the myth has become the foundation for nationalist Karen claims for a separate state. While I would agree with Stern's analysis of the myth, I would nevertheless suggest that the myth, as it is adduced in the Telakhon, is an "article of faith" as it were, consciously wedded to the complex of millenarian ideas, rather than say a matter of belief to which little or no reflection is given.

[5] The following descriptions of the Karen separatist movement are based on a visit to Kawthoolei in early 1982. I discuss elsewhere, in an unpublished paper (1985) the history of the Karen separatist movement and its organisational antecedents. Currently, the only reasonably comprehensive account of the Karen separatist movement is to be found in German (Sitte [1979]).

[6] Despite the apparently non-Karen names of some of the authors of the publications which I discuss here, it is possible that they are in fact Karen. I have already discussed the naming system in Palokhi; it would seem that a similar system also operates in the case of Christian Karen. The system, however, draws upon Christian and other English names or words with occasionally somewhat strange, if not bizarre, results. In the KNLA, there are a Lieutenant-Colonel Saw Oliver, a Colonel Saw Gladstone, and a Colonel Marvel.

Appendix A. The 'Au' Ma Xae Ritual[1]

The Palokhi Karen believe in "souls" (**koela**), and most of them agree that each person possesses thirty-seven souls, although this number varies from one informant to another, and also from place to place (Kunstadter, pers. comm.; see also Mischung [1980:57]). These souls are located in various parts of the body. The most important soul is the **koela kho thi'**, the principal soul which resides in the head and the loss of which would result in death. The Palokhi Karen also believe in "spirits" (**tamyxa**) and these spirits are said to inhabit such features of the natural environment as the forest, streams, tracks, and exceptionally large trees that are withered and standing. These spirits may be malevolent or, at best, indifferent in their relations with people, but all are manipulable through ritual intercession.

In addition to these spirits is an "entity" called **xae** which is often described as **bgha'** and is sometimes also equated with **si kho myxa** (see also Marlowe [1979:179]; Mischung [1980:82–3]).[2] **Xae** has been variously glossed by other researchers who have worked among Sgaw Karen as "ancestral spirits of kin groups called **dopuweh**" (Iijima [1979:107]), "ancestral or house spirit" which is the "controlling authority, the guardian of jural rules, and the dispenser of punishment for their infringement" (Marlowe [1979:178]), "ancestor spirit" (Madha [1980:199]), and "ancestor" (Mischung [1980:82]). In Palokhi, **xae** is conceived of as a very amorphous "entity" if, indeed, it may be said to be an "entity" at all. Most Palokhi Karen assert that it is neither soul (**koela**) nor spirit (**tamyxa**), while some say that it may be one or the other, but they are, nevertheless, uncertain on the point. The various meanings attributed to **xae** referred to above, however, do not in my opinion adequately describe how **xae** is conceived of among the Palokhi Karen. What **xae** "means" to the Karen of Palokhi can only be understood through an examination of the details of the ritual associated with it.

The ritual of **'au' ma xae** (which, literally, means "to eat, doing the xae" and is often abbreviated to **'au' xae**, that is, "to eat **xae**") falls within the larger body of rituals that have as their purpose the restoration of health and well-being to individuals. A large part of these rituals involves the re-establishment of a concord between the domain of souls and spirits, on the one hand, and the domain of people and the physical environment, on the other. Any dissonance between these domains — whether through the witting, or unwitting, actions of people giving offence to the spirits or through the malevolent designs of the spirits themselves — results in illness. In these terms, illness is really symptomatic of three general conditions: "soul loss" (**ba' tamyxa**), "spirit invasion" (**ba' soeta**), or of something "amiss" with the **xae** (**ba' ma xae** or **ba' xae**).[3] When illness presents itself, divination is, then, necessary to determine which of these three conditions exists so that the appropriate ritual may be conducted to restore a person's well-being. As with most forms of divination, divination in Palokhi is based on binary principles and analogic reasoning to "sort out" or eliminate, the possible causes of illness. In the Palokhi Karen scheme of things **ba' xae** usually (though not always) stands last in the order of possibilities.

If divination indicates that the **'au' ma xae** ritual is necessary, then further divination is required to determine whether it should be conducted by the mother or father of the person who is ill. Both parents may, however, decide to conduct the ritual, without recourse to divination. In either case, the mother has to conduct the ritual first followed by the father on the next night. Whether or not divination is resorted to, the elements in the ritual are the same. The personnel involved in the ritual, however, varies depending on generational depth, the composition of the family and, in the case of the patient, where he or she is located in terms of generational levels. In very general terms, this describes the basic considerations which inform the organisation of the **'au' ma xae** ritual. In practice, however, there are several permutations and complexities arising from these considerations and these are best explicated by referring to specific cases.

The first case which I consider here concerns a married couple, with children, and whose parents are all alive. This case would, therefore, involve either a nuclear family (that is, where the couple has moved out of the woman's natal home because a younger sister has married) or a stem family, consisting of parents and a married daughter with her husband and children, as a result of the custom of uxorilocal residence at marriage. Assuming that a child of the couple is in need of the **'au' ma xae** ritual, and divination reveals that the ritual must be conducted by both parents, further divination is then necessary to determine whether the ritual must be conducted using chickens for the ritual meal (a "small" **'au' ma xae**) or chickens and pigs (a "big" **'au' ma xae**). Pigs and chickens are specially reared for the express purpose of **'au' ma xae** rituals, and these animals may not be put to any other use. **'Au' ma xae** pigs are called **thau' kho thi'**, and the chickens **chau kho thi'**. These pigs and chickens are acquired by a couple after they are married for use in **'au' ma xae**. In Palokhi, the man usually buys a sow and hen and then "gives" them to his wife to rear for **'au' ma xae** purposes.

In Palokhi, there are slightly different interpretations as to what the "giving" of these animals means. Some say that these animals, therefore, "belong" to the woman, but others say that she rears them for the couple. To see the status of the **kho thi'** animals in terms of "ownership" however, would be to miss an essential aspect of the way in which the Palokhi Karen maintain a conceptual separation between the domains of male and female activity. There is only a minimal sexual division of labour in Palokhi, but one area where male and female activities are marked is the domestic domain, in which the rearing of pigs and chickens and, to some extent, the preparation of rice are seen to be essentially female activities. A sow and hen are acquired initially for **'au' ma xae** purposes because hereditary continuity of these animals is regarded, at least in theory, as being essential in conducting the ritual.[4] The actual use of these animals in **'au' ma xae**, however, depends on who holds the ritual and related considerations. If the wife holds the ritual, and both her parents are alive, then she uses a cock and hen corresponding to the sex of both her parents. If only one parent is alive, then she uses a fowl of the sex corresponding to that of the living parent. In the case of **'au' ma xae** that require pigs as well, then only one pig is used — a sow corresponding to the sex of the woman herself.

There are eminently pragmatic reasons why strict symmetry in the sexual symbolism in the case of pigs, paralleling that for chickens, is not observed. The Palokhi Karen say that pigs are more expensive than chickens, they take longer to rear, and besides much of the pork would be wasted after the ritual because it would not keep as well. If the husband holds the ritual, the same strictures apply with regard to the use of chickens in respect of his parents. Similarly, in a "big" **'au' ma xae** he would be obliged to use a boar. Nevertheless, even with all these stipulations, the animals cannot be used indiscriminately: due regard must be given to generational order and birth order in the lines of **chau kho thi'** and **thau' kho thi'**.

Furthermore, the pigs must be all-black and the chickens any colour but white. Given that the ritual may be held by the father and/or mother (husband and/or wife), the fact that there are two versions of **'au' ma xae**, "big" and "small", means that **'au' ma xae** may be carried out within a single night or may stretch over four days. A full-blown "big" **'au' ma xae**, for instance, would require the use of **chau kho thi'** on the first and second nights, followed by the use of **thau' kho thi'** on the third and fourth nights.

Assuming that both parents are to hold the ritual, and that further divination indicates that a small **'au' ma xae** should be performed, then the parents and their children must refrain from working on the days of the ritual. They must also wear "traditional" clothes. Towards the evening of the first night, the appropriate chickens are selected and killed. This may be done by either the father or mother.

It is worth noting here that the Palokhi Karen say that the blood of **'au' ma xae** animals should not be spilled. The chickens are therefore killed in one of two ways. They either have their necks wrung or are beaten over the head with the flat of a bush knife until they are unconscious before they are cast onto the hearth where they are burnt to remove the feathers. Pigs, being larger animals, are despatched in a different manner. They are clubbed on the snout or head after which they are throttled to death by placing a piece of wood across their throats with someone standing on the two ends of the wood so as to apply the necessary pressure. This stricture on the shedding of blood of **kho thi'** animals stands in striking contrast to the method of killing animals as offerings to the Lord of the Water, Lord of the Land and other spirits associated with rice cultivation and the expiatory rite for "crooked unions". In these cases, blood must be let as part of the offertory process. The Palokhi Karen also say that care must be taken to ensure that the organs and entrails of the **kho thi'** animals should not be damaged when the body cavity is slit open to remove them for cleaning. The chickens are cooked whole in a pot of water along with the the livers and hearts which are bound up with the intestines. The pigs are, of course, dismembered prior to cooking. Unlike the vegetable stews eaten on ordinary occasions, or the chicken and pork stews, which are cooked to feed helpers in cooperative agricultural tasks, the chicken or pork eaten during **'au' ma xae** rituals is usually cooked without adding the myriad spices and herbs, as well as salt, so common to Karen cuisine.[5]

When the chickens have been dressed and cooked, they are placed in a bowl together with the organs and intestines, and the bowl is set in the centre of a large circular eating tray. Rice is then spooned out around the bowl in the tray and the parents and their children will then sit around the tray or squat about the tray. As this first **'au' ma xae** is held by the mother of the child, the mother's parents are required to attend the ritual regardless of whether or not they are living in the same house. The parents of the woman sit a little away from the tray, and the ritual meal commences with the child's **father** picking a small piece of chicken from a thigh of each fowl and a handful of rice, which he then eats. The child's mother then does the same, followed by the children according to birth order.

When all the members of the nuclear family have eaten in this fashion, including the child who is ill, each of them takes a sip of water in the same order. The mother then calls to her parents, who have been sitting to one side throughout, to "come and eat, come and drink". Her parents approach the tray, and her father takes a piece of flesh from the cock which he wraps, with some rice, in banana leaf. Her mother does the same, but takes the flesh from the hen. The pieces must all come from the same thigh from which the child's father has initially picked. As they do this, they pray for the well-being of their daughter, son-in-law, and grandchildren specifying particularly the symptoms of the grandchild who is **ba' xae**. These prayers are addressed to the souls of their respective parents whether living or dead. When they finish the prayers, they shove the wrappings of rice and chicken through the slatted bamboo floor of the house.

The following is an example of an **'au' ma xae** prayer. It comes from an **'au' ma xae** rite performed by Rae', the ritual specialist in Palokhi, for one of his grandchildren. Rae''s wife had died several years before, while his son-in-law, Thi Pghe, had died in 1978. This particular **'au' ma xae**, thus, involves a three generation stem family in principle (see below) but the prayer may be regarded as being representative of all **'au' ma xae** prayers since there is little variation in these prayers. As with most prayers and ritual texts in Palokhi, this prayer is long and repetitive; I therefore present below only a portion of the prayer sufficient to show its principal features.

Coe mo koela, coe pa koela	Soul of (my) mother, soul of (my) father
Zaude toe, zaude cha	(My) loins hurt, (my) loins are painful
Ba' poe'y' cy' toe kha 'i	This hand is afflicted with aches
Moe 'a' blo' ke, moe 'a' bla ke	Cause well-being to return, cause healing to return
Tamy ma cu' 'ae', toe' ghe; taxa ma cha lae', toe' ghe	Spirits consume (us) with aches, (which is) not good; spirits consume (us) with pain, (which is) not good
Kri' noe sa', krau' noe sa'	Gird yourselves closely, bind yourselves closely
Tamy ma cu' 'ae', toe' ghe; taxa ma cha 'ae', toe' ghe	Spirits consume (us) with aches, (which is) not good; spirits consume (us) with pain, (which is) not good
Noe' kae' si 'kho, noe' kae' myxa	You are the si'khomyxa
Noe' poedi', noe' poedau' ta, se	You are able to remove, you are able to remove (all) together (these) things (that is, the afflictions)
Coe phomy koe'mata, koe''au'ta	My daughter goes working, goes for food
Koe'laeta, koe'keta	Setting forth, returning
Coe' phomy koe'laeta, koe'keta	My daughter sets forth, returns
Koe' hy' 'au' by be', hysa'	Swiddening to eat grains of rice, unhusked rice
'A' phokhwa toe gha ne	Her son over there
Coe li 'a' do' toe gha ne	My big grandson over there
'Oe' koe'mata, koe''au'ta	He goes working, goes for food
Koe'laeta, koe'keta	Setting forth, returning
Kwa chghi, kwa hy'	Watching over the fallow swidden, watching over the swidden
Lae loe' chghi, lae loe' hy'	Going to the fallow swidden, going to the swidden
Tamy ma cu' 'ae', toe' ghe; taxa ma cha 'ae' toe' ghe	Spirits consume (us) with aches, (which is) not good; spirits consume (us) with pain, (which is) not good

Kri' noe' sa', krau' noe' sa'	Gird yourselves closely, bind yourselves closely
Noe' kae' si'khomyxa	You are the si'khomyxa
Noe' poedi', poedau' ta, se	You are able to remove, you are able to remove (all) together (these) things (that is, the afflictions)
'O' loe' za 'a' ni toechi, 'a' la toekoeza	Remain with me for ten years, for one hundred months

The prayer continues in this vein with Rae' referring to the various conditions "afflicting" his two other grandchildren, and ends with the line "Remain with me for ten years, for one hundred months".

Although the rite was specifically held because his youngest grandchild was sick, it is worth noting that the conditions of **all** the members participating in the rite are mentioned. It is also significant that the relationships between members are described in terms of generational dyads, as indicated by the possessive pronouns, and that they are referred to according to generational and then birth order. Rae' begins by referring to himself, and then his daughter by the expression **"my** daughter", followed by his grandson whom he refers to as **"her** son" (the possessive **'a'** being attributive of **coe' phomy**), and then only as **his** grandson. This is a good indication of how the Palokhi Karen conceive of generational relationships, that is, in terms of successive steps of affiliation. Note also that the participants are not referred to by any collective term; they are referred to **individually**, which is indicative of the degree of importance accorded to individual social identities notwithstanding the fact that the ritual expresses their commonality through commensalism. The specific references to subsistence activities is, again, of considerable significance; they point to a perception that the health, well-being, membership and subsistence activities of domestic groups are inter-related. The ritual is a "totalising" one: it contains a great many conceptual associations which cover various facets of the lives of individuals and domestic groups.

Once these prayers are completed, everyone proceeds to eat his fill without regard for the order of precedence that dictated the ritualised eating of the chickens or, as the Palokhi Karen express it, the "eating of the **kho thi'**". During the eating of the **kho thi'**, however, all the participants must be extremely careful not to disrupt the proceedings by any sort of disorderly behaviour which might result in dropping the eating utensils or upsetting the cooking and water vessels. If any of these should happen, the very strict adherents of **'au' ma xae** say that the ritual must be conducted again because it has become ineffective. Similarly, if a child should complain that it has not had enough to eat, then the ritual should be performed again. Most Palokhi Karen, however, eschew observing these conditions on **'au' ma xae** on the grounds that if they were to do so, the ritual would be too burdensome as they would end up consuming their **kho thi'** animals faster than they reproduce.

On the next day, the child's father must conduct the ritual. Given the custom of uxorilocal residence at marriage, the father's parents must be called to attend the ritual from wherever they happen to live. The ritual is conducted in the same way as on the first night, with the father's parents addressing their prayers to the souls of their respective parents. If for some reason the father's parents are unable to attend the ritual, then the father, as he eats the **kho thi'**, will address a similar prayer to his parents' souls, while at the same time taking pieces of the appropriate fowl and some rice, and wrapping them separately in banana leaves. These bundles are kept aside for his parents in the eaves of the house, and after the ritual has been completed, they are taken to his parents at a later date. The rice and chicken which are kept aside are simply called "dried rice" (**me xe**). When the dried rice is sent to the parents, they eat it and say prayers for the well-being of their son and his family, just as they would had they been able to attend the ritual.

The foregoing description of **'au' ma xae** with chickens applies equally well to **'au' ma xae** with pigs. There is, however, one difference: **'au' ma xae** with pigs usually includes divination which is called "divining at the gall-bladder of the pig" (**ka thau' 'a' soedi**). If the gall-bladder is small, this means that the ritual will not be successful, although the ritual is nonetheless performed. If it is full, but is held by the mesentery across the junction of the two major lobes of the liver, then this is also taken as a sign that the ritual will be unsuccessful. If, however, the gall-bladder is full and is aligned with the junction of the two lobes, then it augurs well. If divination augurs ill, the Palokhi Karen say that the ritual should be conducted again, but they tend to ignore this for the same reasons that they tend not to observe the conditions on the ritual mentioned before.

'Au' ma xae (whether "big" or "small") where the parents of both of husband and wife are all alive represents an ideal type situation which is rare in Palokhi. More common are situations in which at least one of the parents is dead. In such circumstances, the ritual is carried out in much the same way and the structure of the ritual remains the same: the surviving parent of either spouse attends the ritual and says the same prayer while making the offerings of rice and chicken, or pork, to the souls of his, or her, parents.

If, however, both the parents of the husband and/or wife are dead, then the **'au' ma xae** ritual is conducted in a slightly different manner, although the **kho thi'** is eaten in the same way described above. If the child's mother's parents are deceased, then there will be only one chicken, a hen (corresponding to the sex of the mother), used on the first night of the ritual. At the end of the eating of **kho thi'**, the mother will then take a piece of the chicken and some rice, and wrap them in banana leaf saying a prayer to the souls of her deceased parents for the well-being of the family. The offering is then shoved through the floor of the house, after which the family proceeds to eat its fill. Similarly, if the father's parents are dead, then a cock is killed for the second night of the ritual, and the father will say a prayer and make the offering to the souls of his parents after the eating of the **kho thi'**.

The next case I consider is when both parents of the spouses are dead and when one of the spouses is also deceased. Under these circumstances, only the surviving parent performs the **'au' ma xae** ritual. The order of commensalism remains the same, and at the end of the eating of the **kho thi'**, the father or the mother as the case may be, says the prayer and makes the offering to his or her parents' souls.

If, however, both the husband and wife are dead, then the orphaned children can no longer have **'au' ma xae** performed for them. In Palokhi Karen reckoning, it is not possible for orphans to be **ba' xae**. If grandparents of the orphans are alive, they cannot perform the ritual for the orphans, nor can married siblings of the orphaned children. The Palokhi Karen offer no explanation for this beyond saying that it is parents who must perform **'au' ma xae** for their children.

Thus far I have considered cases in which the personnel involved in the ritual span two or three generations, and the person who is **ba' xae** is in the lower (or lowest) of generation. In the various permutations of these cases, the ritual is always held by the parents of the person who is **ba' xae**. Another significant feature of the ritual is that these parents call upon their parents to attend the ritual. The latter then call upon the souls of their deceased parents to heal and restore the well-being of the descendants in need of the ritual. If the grandparents of the person who is **ba' xae** are dead, then their souls are called upon by his or her parents to heal and restore the well-being of the family. In other words, the ritual entails a "connecting up" of generations in such a way that the parents in the last surviving generation (whichever the level) call upon the souls of their deceased parents. At each level, however, there is in the structure of the ritual an evident recognition of the bilaterality of parenthood. Or, in more general terms, the ritual complex, as a whole, appears to place an emphasis on generational continuity through filial relationships, traced bilaterally.

The features of the ritual described above are also present when the person who is **ba' xae** is a parent. There is, however, an important difference in the organisation of the ritual in terms of who is required to attend and, here, a certain asymmetry emerges in the form of a matrilateral bias in the organisation of the ritual. For example, if the person or any of his or her siblings is **ba' xae** then either of the parents or both (depending on the outcome of divination) will have to perform the ritual. Whatever it is, the ritual is conducted in the manner described earlier, that is, the **kho thi'** is eaten first, followed by a prayer and offerings to the souls of the person's grandparents. The order of eating, however, is a little different because the participants span three generations. The person's father eats first, followed by the mother after which the person and his or her siblings eat according to birth order. If the siblings are married and have children, the children of sisters attend the ritual but the children of brothers do not. The spouses of siblings do not attend the ritual either. Accordingly, if the person who is **ba' xae** is a woman with children, then her children are required to attend the ritual but not her husband. On the other hand, if the person who is **ba' xae** is a married man with children, his wife and children do not attend the ritual. Participation in this kind of **'au' ma xae** is, thus, based on links traced through the female line. The children of female participants eat immediately after their mothers. For instance, if the person who is **ba' xae** has an elder and younger sister both of whom have children, then the order of eating the **kho thi'**, as far as they are concerned would be: eZ, eZ's children (according to birth order), ego, ego's children (also according to birth order, assuming of course that ego is a woman), yZ, and so on. Should a sister be dead, her children would nonetheless be required to participate in the ritual. It is only in **'au' ma xae** of this sort (where the participants span three generations) that orphans participate, that is, by virtue of links through the female line.

The corollary to this kind of **'au' ma xae** is, of course, to be found in **'au' ma xae** conducted for a person's father or his siblings, by that person's paternal grandparents. He or she would, necessarily, be excluded from these **'au' ma xae** by the principle that dictates attendance at the ritual in this larger, all-encompassing form, namely, the tracing of links of affiliation through the female line.

This principle in the organisation of the form of **'au' ma xae** described above operates only in the context of the ritual. It does not constitute the basis for organising kin groups for any other purpose whatsoever in Palokhi. The parallels between this basis for organising **'au' ma xae** in its more embracing form and the way in which the lines of pigs and chickens are maintained for the purposes of **'au' ma xae** are, however, striking.

As I noted before, sows and hens are acquired, initially, by married couples for use in their rituals. Specifically, sows and hens are acquired because the females of the species bear offspring which the males do not. Furthermore, as some informants explained the matter, the only means of ascertaining continuity of lines was through the females of the species — because any number of males could copulate with them and, consequently, any attempt to trace continuity of these lines of **kho thi'** animals through boars and cocks would be futile. In other words, the obvious facts of "maternity" and parturition make the female of the species a "natural" criterion by which the continuity of lines may be unambiguously traced because the reproductive process is physiologically "marked" in females, whereas is it not in the case of males.

Although the Palokhi Karen do not express it in any overt or even implicit manner, I suggest that the parallel ways in which lines are traced in **'au' ma xae** animals, and people in the organisation of **'au' ma xae** rituals (of the kind described above), are not coincidental. They are based on analogous principles — sexual reproduction through females, and the lack of ambiguity in tracing lines of "descent" (or affiliation) on the basis of the facts of "maternity" and parturition. Yet, although the principles are analogous, there is a major difference between the two in the ritual complex: **'au' ma xae** rituals also involve — at each generational level of the participants — a recognition of the bilaterality of parenthood, that is, of maternity **and** paternity. **'Au' ma xae**, as a ritual complex, therefore contains a parallelism based on the analogous principles of tracing "descent" on the basis of "maternity" and parturition, as well as an opposition based on "non-paternity" in animal reproduction and "paternity" in human reproduction.

Despite the importance of this ritual complex in the lives of the Palokhi Karen, they are nonetheless unable to provide reasons to explain the practice of **'au' ma xae**. Nor are they able to recount a myth (in the Malinowskian sense of a "charter") to account for the performance of the ritual, and which might provide a further basis for understanding the ritual. Mischung, however, has reported such a myth from Chom Thong. The myth is suggestive indeed and lends support to the interpretation of **'au' ma xae** that I have advanced above. Part of the myth documented by Mischung, relevant to my argument, reads as follows:

> In the olden times, there was once a great war in which nearly all Karen men died. There were only as many men left as it would take to fill a pail with coconuts, but there were as any women as it would take to fill a bucket with sesame seeds. After that war, more than ten women had to share one man. There were also lots of children, they were like animals. Many of them were ill, and there was nothing the Karen could do about it. Then Ywa (the creator-god) came down to the Karen and said: "Perform the **au qai** rite!", and he also told them how to do it. "If you or your wives and children are ill, perform the **au qai!**"

> The Karen asked: "How shall we do this **au qai**?" Ywa explained everything. In this ritual, they were to call the souls of their parents who had died in the war, and these would come to help. This was because all of the old people had died during this war. Before that time, there might have been a lot of other rites, but after the war there were only young people left, and when they grew old they did not have any knowledge and were like animals. (Mischung [1980:86])

As Mischung remarks, in his commentary following the myth (1980:87), the central piece of information being communicated in the myth is that without the rite, the Karen would be like animals instead of human beings. This is, indeed, the theme of the myth. But, it is significant that the theme should be expressed in terms of such an evident concern with the distinction between animality and humanity based on the **sexual and reproductive behaviour** of animals and humans, and on the issue of **non-monogamous** unions of which the Karen disapprove. The myth, thus, expresses precisely those concerns which, as I suggested, are embedded in the **'au' ma xae** rituals of Palokhi.

These concerns are also to be seen in the notion of **xae.** I refrained, earlier, from trying to define **xae** because, as it should be obvious by now, it is not any easy thing to do — in the absence of unequivocal indigenous explanations — without taking into consideration the various permutations and complexities of the **'au' ma xae** ritual. An examination of these permutations and complexities of the ritual does, however, bring us closer to an understanding of what **xae** "means". Rather than calling the **xae** "ancestral spirit", and so forth, I think it would be more accurate to regard it — despite the risk of some reification of the Karen concept — as a kind of shared "consubstantial essence" (or, perhaps, even a shared "state") which comes into existence with the formation of a marital union and the birth of children.

To begin with, the linguistic evidence argues against interpretations such as "ancestor spirit", because **xae** (although possessing the synonym **bgha'**) is not "soul" (**koela**) or "spirit" (**tamyxa**). Furthermore, **xae** is not invoked in the prayers said during the ritual. It is the souls of deceased parents in the immediate ascending generation that are invoked. **Xae,** therefore, stands on its own apart from these entities and, consequently, the indications as to what it "means" must be sought elsewhere in the ethnographic data.

The most pertinent of these data are to be found in certain aspects of the ritual. First, **'au' ma xae** can only be perfomed by parents for their children, and not even grandparents or married siblings of the children may do so. Second, unmarried children cannot themselves perform the ritual and it is only when they marry and have children of their own that they may, then, perform the ritual even when their parents are alive. Third, and perhaps most conclusively, orphans cannot have **'au' ma xae** performed for them. They only participate in **'au' ma xae** under two conditions: when the ritual is performed by their maternal grandparents for siblings of their mother, and when they themselves marry and have children of their own. Finally, when persons are **ba' xae**, the ritual is not conducted solely for them; the ritual also involves primary kin in the case of nuclear families holding the ritual, and lineal and collateral kin organised on the basis of links through the female line in the case of larger kin groups when the ritual is, nevertheless, performed by the parents of those who are **ba' xae**. The commonality, or better still, the communality of those involved in **'au' ma xae** is indicated by two important considerations: first, the transitive consequences of infringements of marriage rules (resulting in "crooked unions" in which kin of parties to such unions fall ill; second, by the enumeration in **'au' ma xae** prayers, by name, of those (other than the person who is **ba' xae**) involved in the ritual and their respective "symptoms" of "dis-ease".

The weight of the evidence is, I think, sufficient to warrant the wider interpretation of **xae** that I have proposed. Nevertheless, we are left with one aspect of the ritual unresolved, namely, the status of **xae** in kin groups larger than the nuclear family. I think it is safe to say that **xae** is the same, and that its genesis and transmission lie in nuclear family formation, even when **'au' ma xae** may include larger kin groups. The groups themselves are organised on "natural" principles, that is, the tracing of group affiliation on the basis of the facts of "maternity" and parturition. However, what makes **'au' ma xae** a preeminently "cultural" thing is, as I argued earlier, the recognition of paternity in the bilateral structure of the ritual. It is, in other words, important to recognise that there are two rather different principles at work in the **'au' ma xae** ritual.

If the ideology of kinship and **'au' ma xae** could be said to be "sociological", it would be so in a way which stresses the marital relationship and the procreation of children, rather than the larger kin groups which participate in the ritual. The sociological aspects of the kinship system, that is, marriage and residential patterns, household formation and fission, and the structure of **'au' ma xae** make this clear. The ideology of kinship and **'au' ma xae** also stresses the continuity of domestic groups associated through shared **xae** in a three generation cycle, which ends with the death of parents, whereupon the families of married siblings become fully separate units conducting their own **'au' ma xae** when the cycle repeats itself.

ENDNOTES

[1] 'Au' ma xae or 'au' xae (as it is often abbreviated) has been rendered as **aukhre** (Kunstadter [1979]), **awkre** (Marlowe [1979]), **oxe** (Iijima [1970, 1979]) **Aw(G)he** (Madha [1980]) and **au qai** (Mischung [1980]). Mischung's spelling follows the Calmon system for writing Sgaw Karen in the Latin alphabet and it is in fact used by several hundred Karen (Mischung [1980:v]). This appendix is based on a published paper (Rajah [1984]). I have, however, omitted parts of this paper, and also included additional ethnographic details here in order to address more directly the concerns dealt with in Chapter III.

[2] These alternative terms are intriguing and require some explanation. The Palokhi Karen are unable to explain the differences, but the explanation is I believe simple if we disabuse ourselves of the notion that they necessarily refer to the same thing. If we consider the contexts in which these terms are used, **xae** and **sikhomyxa** quite clearly have specific referents. **Xae** is used only in general reference to the ritual and I present an interpretation of its meaning in the text of this discussion. **Sikhomyxa**, on the other hand, is only used in prayers and it quite clearly refers to the souls of deceased parents. **Bgha'** is more difficult to determine. It appears to be a generic term being, as I was told in Northern Thai, both **phii** ("spirit") and **khwaan** ("soul") or something similar. My interpretation is that if **bgha'** may be spoken of as if it means "souls" and "spirit", it is probably neither though it may be similar to the two. Given the "identifiability" of **xae** and **sikhomyxa**, I suggest that **bgha'** probably means the "souls/spirits of deceased grandparents" in a general sense.

[3] Here, I use the term "illness" in the sense that Lewis (1976) has defined it. "Soul loss" and "spirit invasion" are merely convenient glosses for the Karen terms which describe these ideas in a rather elliptical fashion and which, therefore, do not bear direct translation.

[4] This is yet again another expression of the importance of continuity of ritual relationships in Palokhi Karen religious conceptions. See also Kunstadter (1978:102) and the note on p. 467.

[5] The concern with continuity in 'au' ma xae appears here in a different form. All 'au' ma xae must be performed in an "identical" manner. Thus in the very first 'au' ma xae that the couple conduct, they can if they wish use spices and salt in cooking the chicken or pork. This means, however, that all subsequent chickens and pigs must be cooked in exactly the same way. This is clearly impracticable because the availability of herbs and spices is contingent upon the succession of cultigens in swiddens. Similarly, salt, although now easily available in Northern Thai village shops, was in former times a scarce commodity and the domestic supply of which could never be certain. It is also interesting to note that some Palokhi Karen will, at the very first 'au' ma xae, deliberately nick one or two of the organs of the chicken or pig with a knife and make a tear in the intestines, so that should they accidentally damage the innards of the chickens or pigs in future 'au' ma xae, they need not fear that the ritual has been imperfectly conducted.

Appendix B. Labour Expended on Agricultural Activities and Co—Operative Labour Exchanges in Palokhi (21 January 1981 – 31 December 1981)

Of the 19 households in Palokhi, five (H1a, H2, H3, H4, and H8) had swiddens and wet-rice fields, five (H5, H11b, H12, H13a, H13b) cultivated only swiddens, while seven (H1b, H6, H7, H9, H11a, H14, and H16) cultivated only wet-rice fields. Two households (H10 and H15) did not own any fields. It should be noted, however, that some households shared in the cultivation of fields and thus had access to both swiddens and wet-rice fields as in the case of H1a and H1b and H11a and H11b, and H13a and H13b.

The data in the first table (Table B.1) are meant to illustrate general patterns in the relationships between the amounts of labour expended by households (from domestic supplies of labour) on work in their own fields, labour that is received, and labour that is contributed, in co-operative exchanges. Although the records for some households are not available, in the cultivation of wet-rice fields, the available data are sufficient to show in broad, general terms the relative distribution of labour in agricultural activities and co-operative labour exchange done by households.

The second and third tables (Tables B.2 and B.3) are matrix tables which show, in more detail, the actual amounts of labour received and given in co-operative labour exchanges among households. For purposes of comparison and illustration, the labour expended by households which shared in the cultivation of a swidden (H1a and H1b, H11a and H11b, H13a, H13b and H13c) are indicated **as if** they were provided as co-operative work. This is to show the relative amounts of labour supplied by households in jointly working a field. As discussed in the case studies presented in Chapter IV, they reflect the different commitments of these households in the cultivation of fields where the fields are regarded as being owned by a particular household which, thus, has a greater responsibility for its cultivation.

It should also be noted that the data contained in these three tables are based on the 1981 agricultural season in Palokhi. They do not, therefore, relate to the data on agricultural production presented in Chapter V which are based on the 1980 agricultural season. The data in the tables were obtained on the basis of interviews of all households in Palokhi (except where indicated as unavailable [NA]) conducted regularly at intervals ranging from three days to a week, from 21 January 1981 to 31 December 1981.

Table B.1. Labour Expended by Households in Palokhi in Swidden and Wet—rice Cultivation (21 January 1981 – 31 December 1981) in Man-days

Household	Household size	Household dependency ratio	Swidden Cultivation			Wet-rice Cultivation		
			Total Labour expended by household in own swidden	Total Labour received in co-operative exchange	Total Labour given in co-operative exchange	Total Labour expended by household in own field	Total Labour received in co-operative exchange	Total Labour given in co-operative exchange
H1a	6	66.6	-	-	-	72.5	44.5	48.5
H1b	6	66.6	>163.5	>117.0	>90.5	60.5	51.0	36.0
H2	12	41.6	259.0	78.0	106.0	224.5	32.5	54.0
H3	11	18.2	120.5	31.0	96.0	234.5	43.5	37.0
H4	6	66.6	53.5	108.5	71.5	NA	35.5	25.0
H5	5	60.0	69.0	85.0	53.0	-	-	27.0
H6	7	71.4	-	-	3.0	89.0	12.0	15.0
H7	5	60.0	-	-	4.5	40.0	16.0	4.0
H8	9	44.4	52.5	76.5	56.0	NA	26.0	35.5
H9	8	62.5	-	-	9.0	NA	21.0	1.0
H10	5	60.0	-	-	3.0	-	-	1.0
H11a	2	50.0	-	-	-	-	-	-
H11b	8	50.0	>52.0	>43.0	>51.0	>NA	>22.0	>16.5
H12	3	33.3	37.5	90.5	61.0	-	-	25.5
H13a	7	71.4	>	>	>	-	-	8.0
H13b	4	50.0	>87.0	>59.5	>56.5	-	-	1.0
H13c	4	50.0	>	>	>	-	-	-
H14	3	33.3	-	-	13.0	NA	4.0	4.0
H15	2	50.0	-	-	-	-	-	-
H16	5	20.0	-	-	15.0	NA	36.5	5.5

Table B.2. Matrix of Labour Exchanged by Households in Palokhi in Swidden Cultivation (21 January 1981 – 31 December 1981) in Man-days

Households receiving labour	H1a	H1b	H2	H3	H4	H5	H6	H7	H8	H9	H10	H11a	H11b	H12	H13a	H13b	H13c	H14	H15	H16	Total labour received by household
Households supplying labour																					
H1a	×	8.0	16.0	10.0	14.0	8.0	–	2.0	11.0	–	2.0	1.0	8.0	18.0	5.0	–	–	5.0	–	5.0	113.0
H1b	3.5	×	–	–	–	–	–	0.5	–	–	–	–	–	–	–	–	–	–	–	–	4.0
H2	6.0	5.0	×	15.0	12.5	8.5	–	1.0	10.0	–	–	1.0	5.0	7.0	4.0	1.0	–	1.0	–	1.0	78.0
H3	2.0	–	8.0	×	5.0	2.0	–	–	5.0	1.0	–	–	1.0	5.0	–	2.0	–	–	–	–	31.0
H4	14.0	6.0	25.0	11.0	×	13.5	–	1.0	11.0	3.0	–	1.0	9.0	9.0	4.0	4.0	–	1.0	–	1.0	108.5
H5	8.0	1.0	14.0	9.0	14.0	×	–	1.0	12.0	–	–	9.0	9.0	10.0	4.0	1.0	–	–	–	2.0	85.0
H6	–	–	–	–	–	–	×	–	–	–	–	–	–	–	–	–	–	–	–	–	–
H7	–	–	–	–	–	–	–	×	–	–	–	–	–	–	–	–	–	–	–	–	–
H8	7.0	3.0	17.0	9.5	10.0	7.0	3.0	–	×	2.0	1.0	–	5.0	6.0	3.0	1.0	–	1.0	–	1.0	76.5
H9	–	–	–	–	–	–	–	–	–	×	–	–	–	–	–	–	–	–	–	–	–
H10	–	–	–	–	–	–	–	–	–	–	×	–	–	–	–	–	–	–	–	–	–
H11a	2.0	2.0	–	6.0	–	–	–	–	1.0	–	–	×	–	–	–	–	–	–	–	–	12.0
H11b	1.0	5.0	–	8.0	8.0	4.0	–	–	2.0	1.0	–	×	×	3.0	5.0	3.0	–	1.0	–	1.0	31.0
H12	11.0	–	13.0	16.5	9.0	10.0	–	–	1.0	1.0	–	×	9.0	×	1.0	5.0	–	3.0	–	4.0	90.5
H13a	5.0	–	5.0	5.0	1.0	–	–	–	1.0	1.0	–	×	1.0	1.0	×	14.5	–	3.0	–	–	36.5
H13b	1.0	–	–	6.0	2.0	–	–	–	2.0	–	–	–	1.0	2.0	9.0	×	–	1.0	–	–	23.0
H13c	–	–	–	–	–	–	–	–	–	–	–	–	–	–	×	×	×	–	–	–	–
H14	–	–	–	–	–	–	–	–	–	–	–	–	–	–	–	–	–	×	×	–	–
H15	–	–	–	–	–	–	–	–	–	–	–	–	–	–	–	–	–	×	×	–	–
H16	–	–	–	–	–	–	–	–	–	–	–	–	–	–	–	–	–	–	–	×	–
Total labour given by household	60.5	30.0	106.0	96.0	71.5	53.0	3.0	4.5	56.0	9.0	3.0	3.0	48.0	61.0	30.0	26.5	–	13.0	–	15.0	689.0

273

Table B.3. Matrix of Labour Exchanged by Households in Palokhi in Wet-rice Cultivation (21 January 1981 – 31 December 1981) in Man-days

Households receiving labour	Households supplying labour																				Total labour received by household
	H1a	H1b	H2	H3	H4	H5	H6	H7	H8	H9	H10	H11a	H11b	H12	H13a	H13b	H13c	H14	H15	H16	
H1a	x	13.5	7.0	5.0	6.0	3.0	-	-	2.0	-	-	-	1.0	5.0	2.0	-	-	-	-	-	44.5
H1b	16.0	x	3.0	1.0	4.0	1.0	4.0	4.0	5.0	-	-	-	2.0	4.5	1.0	-	-	2.0	-	3.5	51.0
H2	5.0	1.5	x	11.0	2.0	2.0	1.0	-	1.0	-	-	-	3.0	4.0	2.0	-	-	-	-	-	32.5
H3	5.0	2.5	14.0	x	3.0	5.0	-	-	3.0	-	-	-	2.0	4.0	2.0	-	-	1.0	-	2.0	43.5
H4	8.0	1.0	9.0	2.0	x	7.5	1.0	-	4.0	-	-	-	1.0	1.0	1.0	-	-	-	-	-	35.5
H5	-	-	-	-	-	x	-	-	-	-	-	-	-	-	-	-	-	-	-	-	-
H6	-	1.0	2.0	-	-	-	x	-	7.0	-	-	2.0	-	-	-	-	-	-	-	-	12.0
H7	-	3.0	4.0	1.0	1.0	1.0	1.0	x	5.0	-	-	-	-	-	-	-	-	-	-	-	16.0
H8	3.0	3.0	3.0	4.0	2.0	2.0	8.0	-	x	-	-	-	1.0	-	-	-	-	-	-	-	26.0
H9	3.0	-	3.0	3.0	3.0	2.0	-	-	2.0	x	-	-	2.0	2.0	-	1.0	-	-	-	-	21.0
H10	-	-	-	-	-	-	-	-	-	-	x	-	-	-	-	-	-	-	-	-	-
H11a	5.0	3.0	-	2.0	1.0	-	-	-	-	-	-	x	-	1.0	-	-	-	-	-	-	12.0
H11b	1.0	1.0	4.0	3.0	-	1.0	-	-	-	-	-	-	x	-	-	-	-	-	-	-	10.0
H12	-	-	-	-	-	-	-	-	-	-	-	-	-	x	-	-	-	-	-	-	-
H13a	-	-	-	-	-	-	-	-	-	-	-	-	-	-	x	-	-	-	-	-	-
H13b	-	-	-	-	-	-	-	-	-	-	-	-	-	-	-	x	-	-	-	-	-
H13c	-	-	-	-	-	-	-	-	-	-	-	-	-	-	-	-	x	-	-	-	-
H14	-	-	2.0	-	1.0	-	-	-	1.0	-	-	-	-	-	-	-	-	x	-	-	4.0
H15	-	-	-	-	-	-	-	-	-	-	-	-	-	-	-	-	-	-	x	-	-
H16	2.5	6.5	3.0	5.0	2.0	3.5	-	-	5.5	1.0	1.0	-	2.5	3.0	-	-	-	1.0	-	x	36.5
Total labour given by household	48.5	36.0	54.0	37.0	25.0	27.0	15.0	4.0	35.5	1.0	1.0	2.0	14.5	25.5	8.0	1.0	-	4.0	-	5.5	344.5

Appendix C. A Note on Work and Wage Work in Palokhi

By the very nature of their subsistence system where the fields and forests, on which the Palokhi Karen depend so much for food, are situated outside the village but within the stream valley or domain, whilst the **loci** of the cash economy are formed primarily by Northern Thai settlements such as Ban Mae Lao and Ban Pa Pae, it is not surprising therefore that "work" and "wage work" should be seen in terms of distinctions in spatial relationships with the village as a focal referent. These distinctions are reflected in the verbal categories for "work" and "wage work" and their usages.

In Palokhi, there is a generic term for "work" as an activity, **mata**, which is formed from the verb **ma** ("to do", "to make") and **ta** ("thing" or "things"). **Tama**, on the other hand, means "work" in the sense of something that is done but it is rarely used except when something specific is being referred to, whereas **mata** is always heard, especially in conjunction with the word **lae**, "to go". **Mata** covers a whole range of activities — from the various agricultural tasks in swiddens and wet-rice fields to the making of tools, baskets, guns and the building of houses. It is also a common reply (**lae mata**, "going to work") to the question "where are you going?" (**na lae su lau**) which functions as a standard greeting, after which a more specific response may follow such as "going to weed" (**lae khlau nau**), "going to pick tea" (**lae dae' naumy**), and so on.

There are two terms which are the complementary opposites of **mata**. These are **'o' doe'** and **lae ha'**, and they refer to what people in Palokhi regard as essentially non-work activities. **'O' doe'** means "to be at home" (literally, "to be in the house" or "to remain in the house") but, in fact, even when they are "in the house", the Palokhi Karen are busy performing a myriad number of tasks, for example, collecting firewood, drawing water, mending garden fences, feeding their chickens and pigs, and so forth. **Lae ha'**, which always connotes leisure and enjoyment, however, means "to go visiting" (literally, "to go walking") which may be anywhere outside one's home or Palokhi. By the very nature of their subsistence system where the fields and forests, on which the Palokhi Karen depend so much for food, are situated away from the village, it is not surprising that **mata** is always coupled with **lae**, but it is nonetheless significant that activities outside the village (with the exception of **lae ha'**) should be regarded as work whereas activities within the village are not.

Against all these categories for work and non-work activities, stands the term for "wage work" or "wage labour" (which is also coupled with the word "to go"), **ha' ca**, a loan word now fully assimilated into the lexicon of the Palokhi Karen from the Northern Thai **hap caang**, "to hire a worker" or "to engage for wage work".[1] The use of this term as a loan word is by no means peculiar to

Palokhi or the Karen communities in the Mae Muang Luang-Huai Thung Choa area. Hamilton (1976:131) has also noted its use in the Pwo Karen community of Ban Hong in Hod, and this suggests that there is no indigenous term for this sort of work, or that if there is it does not enjoy any currency. In Palokhi, **ha' ca** or **lae ha' ca** is always used even when the Karen refer to wage work among themselves. **Ha' ca** may, however, be glossed in Karen by a short-hand general term which provides an interesting insight into how wage work is conceived of in Karen thought.[2] The term is **ma laeta** (or **lae ma laeta**) which, roughly translated, means "to work-exchange things" (where **lae,** "exchange" [possibly from the Northern Thai **laek** with the same meaning], is tonally different from **lae,** "to go"). Wage labour, therefore, is seen in terms of an exchange of something for one's labour (rather than, say, the sale of one's labour which would be impossible to express in Palokhi Karen). The significance of this gloss for **ha' ca** is, perhaps, better appreciated if we contrast it with the Karen term for co-operative labour exchange in agricultural activities which is **ma dau' lau (poe') sa'.** The literal translation of this expression is "to work with (our) hearts falling together", but a more idiomatic translation would be "to work mutually". Indeed, this is the essential sense of the term as indicated by **lau sa',** a phrase that invariably denotes mutual, reciprocal action or common activity. The important point here is that the provision of labour on a reciprocal basis (that is, what we might call "labour exchange") is not seen to be "exchanged"; only objects or goods are "exchanged". **Ha' ca,** on the other hand, is seen as kind of exchange transaction.[3] **Ma laeta** itself may be elaborated upon in order to make a distinction between the kinds of payments made for wage work, that is, money or cash payments, and rice wages. The former is called **ma ne ce',** "to work and obtain money", while the latter is called **ma lae 'au' by,** "to work-exchange eating unhusked rice". While the first expression is straightforward enough, the second is unusual that **'au' by** is not the conventional way of describing the eating of rice which is **'au' me,** meaning "to eat cooked rice". Nor does it reflect the nature of rice wages which are invariably made in the form of husked or milled rice which the Palokhi Karen call **hy sa'** (or **by hy sa'**). What underlies this formulation for work paid in rice wages is a very fundamental idea about the relationship between work and rice: rice that is obtained by work is rice from one's field and it is based, of course, on the agricultural experience of the Karen.

These terms and expressions are important in showing how the Palokhi Karen view wage work according to culturally held notions about the nature of work. The ideas encapsulated in these descriptions are implicit in their use of the term **ha' ca.** The retention and use of the Northern Thai term, however, is itself significant. We have already seen that a distinction is made between work and non-work, where work is viewed in terms of activities performed outside the village. This is also true of wage work which is undertaken not merely outside the village but of the environment which the Palokhi Karen utilise for subsistence purposes — usually in Northern Thai villages and sometimes in Lisu villages and units of the Royal Forestry Department in the watershed. While wage work is performed "outside", it is also work which is different from ma ta and the difference is indicated by the use of the term **ha' ca.** But, I suggest that **ha' ca** as a borrowed Northern Thai linguistic category also marks this sort of work in another significant sense: it is work that falls within a different domain — not necessarily Northern Thai, although it is very often the case, but one that is essentially non-Karen. This is associated with a certain attitude, in Palokhi, that agricultural work is intrinsically satisfying — or, at least, meaningful in the sense that its product is directly consumable for sustenance — while wage work to support oneself entirely is not.

Despite the arduous nature of agricultural work, the Palokhi Karen regard wage work for a living as being harder and more demanding than agricultural work. This is not peculiar only to Palokhi. Marshall, a keen observer of the Karen, put this rather more strongly in describing the employment of Karen in the forestry industry in Burma some sixty years ago; he notes that "the Karen has a distaste for steady work under supervision, especially if the immediate overseer is a Burman" (1922:87). This is really more a reflection of attitudes towards a way of life rather than the nature of wage work itself. They do not, of course, describe it in quite this way; what they say is that wage work is "not enjoyable" (**toe' my').** A good instance of this feeling towards wage work and agricultural work may be seen in the return to farming by the households which worked for several years in units of the Royal Forestry Department in the Mae Muang Luang-Huai Thung Choa area. It is also to be seen in the sentiments that the Palokhi Karen evince with regard to households that are virtually wholly dependent on wage work for a living and households that fail to make the most of agricultural production; these households are considered unfortunate or, to put it another way, as somehow "second-class" members of the community.

I think it would not be far wrong to say that the ultimate aspiration of the Palokhi Karen in general is to cultivate fields and to be entirely self-sufficient in agricultural production. But, this would not be just a desire generated by the inadequacies of their agricultural system; it represents a sort of ideal which has intrinsic value as a way of life and it is reflected in their verbal categories for agricultural work and wage work.

ENDNOTES

[1] McFarland (1944:704) gives, as the meaning of **rap caang** (the Central Thai equivalent of **hap caang**), "to engage as an hireling".

[2] The Karen expressions for **ma laeta** and its elaborations that I discuss here are less commonly used compared to the Northern Thai term. They might, perhaps, be better described as explanations in Karen for the Northern Thai term. However they are regarded, it is clear that they indicate a particular view of wage work in terms of the semantics of words available in Karen. It is this that I wish to stress: the

Palokhi Karen can only express the meaning of the Northern Thai term in ways that are significant to them but that this is done by employing words which have particular meanings in a Karen context of experience. The Karen must, of course, be able to explain somehow the Northern Thai term but when they do, it is not done arbitrarily. Nevertheless, it would seem that the Karen expressions do not satisfy or else we might expect them to be used instead of the Northern Thai term. I suggest, later, a reason why this might be so.

[3] I am not implying by this that the Karen in Palokhi therefore regard their labour, or the work that they do, as some sort of object or that they are necessarily "alienated" (in the Marxist sense of the term) from the work that they do and the products of their labour in wage work situations.

Appendix D. Swidden Cultivation in Palokhi[1]

The swidden cycle in Palokhi usually commences in late January, or early February, with the selection of various possible sites for swiddening. There is, of course, no clear-cut line of demarcation between agricultural cycles in terms of agricultural activities because even as they are bringing in their harvests from their swiddens and wet-rice fields, the Palokhi Karen are already considering where they will swidden next. In most cases, they do in fact have a general idea of where they intend to swidden next because they have considered the possibilities in the course of the previous year. The Palokhi Karen do not have a carefully worked out rotational fallow system for swiddens such as the Lua', for instance, have and their swiddening practices in this respect show rather more similarities with those of the Karen which have also been described by Kunstadter (1978: 81–2). Nor do the Palokhi Karen cultivate swiddens in contiguous blocks of land as do the Pwo Karen studied by Hinton (1975:106ff.).

The selection of swidden sites is very much a matter of individual household choice which is not unduly constrained by the need to make accommodations with other households, or with neighbouring communities. The reason for this is that they are virtually the sole occupants of the middle part of the Huai Thung Choa valley and, therefore, do not face competition for the forest resources of the valley with their Northern Thai neighbours who live downstream and who are engaged primarily in wet-rice agriculture. Neither do they face any competition from their closest Karen neighbours from the village of Pong Thong who are small in number and whose swiddening needs are sufficiently met by the forests of the smaller Pong Thong stream valley.

The evaluation of forest areas is guided by several factors, the most important of which is the state of vegetative regrowth of the forest. The Palokhi Karen have two terms which distinguish between two types of forest cover although this distinction is, in fact, not very clear. The first term, **pgha,** refers to the forest in general but it may also refer to old, or very old, secondary forest. The second term, **chghi,** refers to swiddens which have been left fallow for a period ranging from as short as one year to 20 or 30 years, or even more. The distinction, therefore, is ambiguous since long established **chghi** could be described as **pgha.** In my observation the term **chghi** is more consistently applied to secondary forest of which the Palokhi Karen have positive knowledge of previous cultivation obtained either at first hand or through an observation of the nature of the state of secondary regrowth, while the term **pgha** is used to refer to areas where the evidence of previous cultivation is all but absent, that is, forest which has reached, what Spencer calls (1977:39), a "fairly stable equilibrium of ecological succession".

The ambiguity in the application of these terms, nevertheless, requires some explanation and I think it is probably to be found in ecological changes in Northern Thailand and an older usage of the term made no longer relevant as a result of these changes.[2] It is likely that these two terms originally referred to primary forest and secondary, or previously cultivated, forest and that the distinction has been lost with the elimination of primary forests in the region. The difference between these two terms, as they are used in Palokhi, is thus nominal and does not feature in the way that the Palokhi Karen decide upon swidden sites. Indeed, when they talk of clearing the forest for a swidden, they almost always talk in terms of clearing **chghi.**

In actual practice, however, **chghi** which are used for swiddening are forests that have regenerated for over thirty years at least because households in Palokhi have yet to return to swiddens that they previously cultivated in the history of their settlement in the Huai Thung Choa valley. This is very unusual indeed for any Karen community so far described in contemporary accounts, and the reason has to do with the still very favourable ecological conditions in the valley. The Palokhi Karen also take into account other considerations in deciding where to cut their swiddens but these considerations are not given equal weight by all households. Some households say, for instance, that good swiddening areas are those which have dark or black soil (as opposed to red soil) and that the soil should not taste sour or salty. Another criterion which some households say they use is the presence of litter or humus on the ground. Still others claim that the presence of a certain small-stemmed, thick-walled species of bamboo called **wa su,** or "black bamboo" **(Bambusa tulda),** is a good indicator of suitable locations for swiddening. Considerations of slope are not very important, but areas with very steep slopes are avoided because their higher degree of erodibility results in loss of seed and crops along with the soil during the rainy season. Other physiographic characteristics such as a general even-ness of terrain and the absence of large rocks as well as the presence of a small gully or drainage line are regarded as desirable because work is made easier in such terrain, while the presence of a drainage line ensures access to water that is required for drinking and cooking in the course of working in the swidden throughout the year.

On the basis of these various considerations, a few sites are chosen by each swiddening household. The reason why more than one site is usually selected is because the final choice of a site is determined by divination which is an essential part of the process of site selection (see Chapter VI). This, then, saves the household the inconvenience of seeking out alternative sites again if divination indicates that a site is unsuitable for swiddening.

Clearing of Swiddens (Phae' Lau Hy')

Once swidden locations have been finally decided upon, the process of clearing may begin. This is done in the cool dry, and then hot dry months of February and March, sometimes extending into early April. The clearing of swiddens involves two main tasks — slashing away the bush, undergrowth and small trees, and felling large trees. Slashing is done by both men and women, while the chopping down of trees is a task that is performed only by men. The work is done by households on a co-operative labour exchange basis. As with other agricultural tasks of this nature, the work teams are formed on an **ad hoc** basis with households soliciting assistance a few days in advance. Work teams, in Palokhi, therefore are not fixed in composition or numbers throughout the year or, for that matter, throughout any particular phase in the agricultural cycle. The teams are usually largest in the early stages of any particular phase which requires co-operation, after which their numbers dwindle as the work gets done and household members turn to other tasks.

Slashing is done with bush knives (**xae'**) which are either made by the blacksmith in the village, or purchased at the large Northern Thai settlement of Ban Pa Pae. The entire site is slashed first, after which the trees are felled with axes (**kha'**) which are bought in local stores. In Palokhi, as with other Karen swiddening communities elsewhere, swiddens are cleared below ridge tops which means that there is always a tree line above swiddens (see, for example, Grandstaff [1980:6], Uhlig [1978:39], but cf. Kunstadter [1978:83]). The Palokhi Karen say that by not clearing the vegetation in these places, the regeneration of the swidden when it is left fallow is facilitated by seed falling downslope from the vegetation on the ridge tops. Trees are chopped down at about waist height, or slightly above. If the trees are exceptionally large, however, simple scaffoldings are erected to enable the axemen to chop the tree higher up its length where the girth of the tree is smaller. The scaffolding consists of two sturdy saplings bound together to form a cross which is then leant against the tree allowing the axemen to stand on the lower arms of the crossed saplings from where they can then chop down the tree. As with many other swiddeners, the Palokhi Karen make attempts to bring down several trees at a time by partially cutting them and then bringing them down by felling a tree against the line of partially cut trees. In Palokhi, almost all trees are chopped down in swiddens, regardless of their size and species. This practice differs from that reported for other Karen communities and the reason for it is that the Palokhi Karen do not feel a need to preserve some trees in swiddens, as there are still areas with plentiful forests available to them and hence the lack of incentive to assist in the process of forest regeneration.[3]

When swiddens have been cleared, they are left to dry for a few weeks before they are burnt. In Palokhi, the swiddens which were cleared in 1980 were left to dry for about four weeks in the hot dry season before they were burnt.

Burning Swiddens (Chu Hy')

After the swiddens have dried in the hot season, they are burned before the onset of the rains. Prior to burning, however, fire-breaks are constructed in the swiddens in order to reduce the risk of setting the adjacent forests aflame. This consists of throwing the dried slashed vegetation at the perimeter of swiddens inside and, sometimes, by clearing a little of the undergrowth that abuts onto the cleared swiddens. Not much time is spent on this task, and it is undertaken by household members with, occasionally, some assistance from another household. The firing of swiddens is also carried out by small teams of two or three men on a labour exchange basis. This is done by men who start fires at different points at the perimeter of swiddens. These points are usually chosen downslope at the base of swiddens, near the little streams where swiddens are often cleared, as a line of retreat once the swiddens are ablaze. Slash is piled up to provide a good source of fuel for the starting fires which are lighted with torches of fresh pinewood, the resin in the wood being inflammable. The swiddens are burnt in the late morning and within a few hours the dried slash and trees are reduced to ashes. Although they are careful enough to make fire-breaks, the Palokhi Karen do not organise fire-fighting teams as a precaution against fires which may go out of control and burn the adjacent forests (see also Kunstadter 1978: 83).

After the swiddens have been burnt, they are left to cool and they are then inspected a few days later to see if the burning has been satisfactory. In 1980 and 1981 all swiddening households were successful with the first fires in their swiddens and, therefore, did not need to reburn them. The re-burning of swiddens entails the gathering of ill-burnt or unburnt slash into piles and a second firing. The purpose of this is, of course, to ensure a more even spread of ash which acts as a source of nutrients for the crops and, secondly, to remove more of the fallen timber from the area to be cultivated.

Planting (Tho Hy')

About a week to a fortnight after the swiddens have been burned, the first swidden crop is planted. This is maize (**Zea mays**) which is a minor crop that the Palokhi Karen cultivate as a supplement to rice and it is usually eaten when stocks of rice are low. This seems to be a widespread practice among Karen cultivators (see Hinton [1975:189]; Kunstadter [1978:85]) but in Palokhi the role of maize as a supplementary crop is minor compared with that for the Pwo Karen described by Hinton. This is because the availability of wage labour opportunities in Northern Thai villages has led the Palokhi Karen to supplement their harvests of rice with rice purchased from the Northern Thai which, to them, is more preferable to eating a "starvation crop". The maize is planted entirely on a household basis, that is, households providing the labour required for the task entirely from their own pool of labour. The work is carried out with the use of a digging stick, which is a short length of bamboo or wood tipped with an iron blade resembling a small hand-spade with a straight edge. The maize seeds are dropped into the holes made by the tool at various places in the swidden.

After the maize has been planted, rice is planted next. The planting of rice is the most labour intensive task in the cultivation of swiddens as the work needs to be done as quickly as possible, before the arrival of the rains, over a large area. Co-operation in this is, therefore, absolutely essential in Palokhi and it is during the planting phase of swiddening that the work groups are largest in the agricultural cycle with the possible exception of harvesting. Planting is done by dibbling, using long thin bamboo poles of about two to two and a half metres in length which are tipped with an iron blade similar to the blade of the digging stick. Indeed, often they are one and the same. Sometimes, if there are not enough of these blades, a short section of bamboo may be cut to tip the dibbles. Dibbling is invariably done by men while sowing is done by women, boys and girls. Most of the rice planted in Palokhi swiddens is ordinary, that is, non-glutinous rice, while small areas are given to glutinous rice. The Palokhi Karen recognise up to eight varieties or strains of ordinary rice and all are preferred to glutinous rice. The latter is usually used to make rice cakes on certain ritual occasions, for rice liquor and the remainder is eaten when stocks of ordinary rice have run out. The rice seed of these two kinds of rice are kept separate and are planted separately.[4] The seed is brought to the swiddens in baskets or sacks and they are distributed to the sowers who fill their sling bags with the seed and follow the line of dibblers, filling the dibble holes with seed. The holes are not covered after seeding.

The work parties usually commence work in the early morning and continue planting until noon when they rest for about an hour or two. At this time, the first major agricultural ritual is performed by the headman (if present) and by other older men in the party, after which food is served to helpers by the household whose swidden is being planted. This is also the first time that food is offered to members of work gangs; in clearing and burning, helpers bring their own food to eat at mid-day.[5] Planting continues in the afternoon until the swidden is fully planted or, if that is not possible, until the end of the working day which is normally at about 5 pm.

On the first day of rice planting, household members will also plant their other crops as well, but this task is less urgent than the planting of rice itself as they can return to complete the planting of these crops in following days. A list of the crops grown in Palokhi swiddens is given in Appendix D. All crops are planted in one of two ways: either mixed with the rice seed, or planted separately by broadcasting seed between dibble holes, and around the field hut. Tubers, which are also planted on this first day of planting and on subsequent days, must be placed into the ground; this is often done by digging up the soil with a bush knife, after which the soil is tamped back with the foot. At the end of the day, a brief ritual (called "planting the ritual basket of the yam", **chae' lau nwae tasae'**) is conducted (see Chapter VI). Thereafter, catch crops continue to be planted in swiddens for several days on a household basis. If there still remains rice seed to be planted, this is done with small work teams made up of two or three co-operating households. During the two or three weeks that follow, a variety of other tasks are also carried out in swiddens, namely, fencing and the construction of various traps and alarms worked by wind or water.

Weeding (Khlau Nau)

Soon after planting, the rainy season begins — usually in the middle of April — and the Palokhi swiddens quickly become full with the shoots of growing crops, and weeds. This marks the time when the laborious task of weeding must begin. It is also the time when the Palokhi Karen must prepare their wet-rice terraces for planting. The beginning of the wet season thus introduces a period when labour has to be allocated among a number of tasks. For some households, the stocks of rice from their previous year's harvest may, in fact, be depleted or exhausted so that they also have to look for wage work in order to obtain rice. In these circumstances, they are faced with even more difficult problems in allocating their domestic supply of labour among competing demands on their time.

In the early stages of the wet season, in swidden cultivation, weeding is however a pressing necessity because the growth of weeds takes place faster than that of the rice crop and threatens to choke out and overshadow the growing rice shoots. Weed growth, moreover, occurs continuously throughout the rainy season and so there is a great need to keep it in check. Weeding is, as Kunstadter observes, "the most time consuming, most labour consuming, most uncomfortable, and most disliked portion of swidden agriculture" (1978: 90). Because of the many competing demands for their labour, the Palokhi Karen are unable to organise the weeding of swiddens on a regular, concerted, co-operative labour exchange basis. All Palokhi households are busy attending to their various subsistence tasks during the wet-season and this makes the co-ordination of weeding among households difficult. Instead, weeding is usually done on a household basis and it is spread out over the rainy season. It is most intensive in the early to middle stages of the wet season when the weeds are rapidly growing. Once the weeds are removed (or as much of them as may be managed by each household), this offers a respite during which time the rice and other crops have a chance to grow and, to some extent, contain the growth of weeds by shading them out. The sporadic weeding that takes place in the later stages of the wet season then suffices to keep weed growth in check which allows the rice crop to mature.

Reaping (Ku' Lau By)

In late September or October the rains usually end and the rice crop in Palokhi swiddens begins to mature. Because there are several varieties of rice, the crop ripens at different stages. The early ripening varieties of rice, for instance, are ready for harvesting in late September or early October; the later ripening varieties are only ready for harvest in November. Harvesting of the rice crop, therefore, is spread out over several weeks in Palokhi. The harvesting of rice entails three different tasks — reaping, threshing and transporting the crop for storing in household granaries in the village. Like planting, harvesting is marked by co-operative labour exchange because all three tasks require a considerable amount of labour inputs within relatively short spaces of time (though to a lesser degree than that in planting) which individual households, with their limited internal supplies of labour, cannot provide.

As with planting, the first day of reaping is marked by the attendance of a large number of workers drawn from other households to assist in the work in the swidden of one household. The first day of reaping is one which is ritually significant for the household and it begins with a ritual wrist-tying ceremony in the house before the household members set out to their swidden accompanied by the helpers from other households. Reaping is done with sickles, and these are either made in Palokhi or purchased in Ban Mae Lao or Ban Pa Pae. The rice is reaped close to the ground, a handful at a time (that is, as they have grown from the dibble holes) and each bunch is tied up or bound with some straw into a sheaf which is then placed on the stubble. The rationale for this practice is that it prevents the accumulation of moisture on the sheaves or rice which would otherwise cause it to deteriorate, as the rice is often left in the fields for a few days before being collected and made into stooks. There is also a good reason for reaping the rice close to the ground: when the rice is stooked, the sheaves are placed on the ground in a circle with the uppermost part of the stalks (that is, which bear the grains) lying towards the centre of the circle, and the stook is built up in this manner by laying down more and more stalks of rice onto the first lot on the ground. The lower half of the rice stalks are, thus, on the outside and they form a thatch-like structure over one another and over the rice grains. Keeping the stalks long at reaping is, therefore, essential for well-constructed stooks in order to prevent moisture from reaching the rice grains. The purpose of binding the stalks of rice into sheaves is to make the task of collecting the harvest easier.

It is worth noting here that as with planting, a mid-day meal is prepared for the helpers who come to assist a household in the reaping of its swidden.

However, unlike planting, no rituals are performed to propitiate the "Lord of the Water, Lord of the Land". The only ritual that is performed is a household ritual which is addressed to the souls of members of the household and to the rice soul (see Chapter VI).

After the swidden of a particular household has been reaped on the first day, the work teams dissolve and are reconstituted to work in the swiddens of other households — regardless of whether the first swidden was completely reaped or not. The work teams move on in this way until debts in labour services are more or less discharged. Smaller groups then get together to carry out the remaining work of reaping the rice left in swiddens. This method of co-operative labour exchange fits in well with the fact that the rice crop ripens at different stages. These smaller teams also perform other tasks besides reaping the rice that remains on the stalk in Palokhi swiddens, namely, carrying the sheaves of rice for stooking, clearing an area of ground on which to build the rice stooks, and constructing the stooks.

It should be noted that by this time, towards the end of reaping swidden rice, the competing demands for labour that each household faces intensifies. In this period, the rice in wet-rice fields are ready to be harvested as well and, thus, the households which are engaged in agricultural production have to allocate their labour among several different tasks and to meeting their various obligations arising from receiving the labour services of others. The smaller teams which are found working at this stage of the agricultural cycle are thus the outcome of decisions made which attempt to balance the commitments of households to ensuring that their own harvests are managed and brought in, the need to obtain assistance to do this, and the countervailing obligation to repay the labour debts thus incurred which reduces the labour time put into attending to their own needs.

Threshing (Phau' Lau By)

The first day of threshing is again a ritually significant day for the household and another wrist-tying ceremony is conducted in the house before the household members go to their swidden. Threshing is also marked by an injunction that all those who thresh on the first day must continue with the work on subsequent days until all the rice is threshed. The effect of this injunction is that only household members end up threshing their harvest. Although I discuss the significance of this injunction and other rituals associated with the harvest season in Chapter VI, it may be noted here that this season has the largest number of rituals of all the phases in the agricultural cycle of Palokhi. The overall importance of the rituals at harvest time, however, lies in the way the association between households and their rice crops are symbolically expressed.

Threshing is done on a clearing along the slope of the swidden near the stacks of rice, carved out of the hill-side with a hoe. The threshing ground is made firm by placing retaining logs along the contour of the slope and packing the earth tight against the logs until a flat surface is obtained. On this clearing, a large threshing mat (**khlaumy**) is placed with its ends made to curve upwards by means of supporting posts, or merely by resting them on the side of the hill and the top-most retaining log. Sheaves of rice are taken from the stooks and thrown, beaten and shaken on the mat. Then a man or woman steps onto the mat and kneads the rice stalks with the feet while fanning the rice with a large winnowing fan in broad, sweeping arcs. The fanning creates a draught of air which blows away the chaff and broken stalks while the heavier grains of rice remain in the mat. When all the grains have been separated from the stalks in this way, the stalks are removed by hand and the mat is rolled up to bring the rice together after which it is scooped up by hand or by means of a bamboo cup (or any small container that is available) and poured into a 22 litre kerosene tin in order to measure the amount of rice. Each time the tin is filled, a tally is kept by making a bend in a long, flat sliver of bamboo, and the rice is then poured into sacks or baskets to be stored either in temporary granaries in the swidden but or taken back to the household granary in the village. When all the rice has been harvested, the amount of rice obtained can then be determined in **pip**, the Northern Thai term for the volume of the kerosene tin which the Palokhi Karen have adopted, by counting the number of bends in the bamboo splint.

Threashing may also be done in a different way, although it is not common in Palokhi swiddens. This is actually a practice adopted from the Northern Thai and which is more commonly used in threshing the wet-rice harvest. It entails building a small threshing rack consisting of two long saplings which rest on the forked ends of wooden supports implanted into the ground at the threshing area. The rice stalks are then beaten on the rack thus dislodging the grains which fall onto the threshing mat which is placed under the rack.

Transporting and Storing the Harvest (Gwi By, Pha' By)

This last stage in the agricultural cycle in swiddens is carried out entirely by household members. It may be done during the threshing phase in stages, as the rice is threshed or it may be done right at the end of the season in a few days continuously. Whether it is done one way or the other depends on whether or not the household has built a temporary granary in the swidden hut. Most households in Palokhi prefer to transport their rice harvests back to the village as soon as they are threshed because they are afraid that the rice may be stolen or eaten by field rats, birds and so on, if left in the swiddens. This last stage of the agricultural season in swiddens is marked by a ritual which is performed when the last batch of rice is borne back to the village and, as with all the rituals performed at this time, it is wholly a household affair.

ENDNOTES

[1] The agricultural practices of the Karen, described by various researchers, show broad similarities although variations do exist. These variations are, however, relatively minor. Kunstadter's account (1978) of Karen swidden and wet-rice agricultural practices is the most detailed and comprehensive available and much of what he has to say about the Laykawkey Karen, in Mae Sariang, is equally applicable to the Palokhi Karen. In this appendix on swidden agriculture in Palokhi, I therefore present a brief account of the various swiddening activities in Palokhi sufficient to show what takes place in the agricultural cycle and to indicate points of similarity and difference, where relevant, between what takes place in Palokhi and that in other Karen communities as found in existing descriptions on Karen agricultural practices.

[2] The Karen are widely reported to be secondary forest swiddeners and they have probably been so for a very long time (but see Grandstaff [1976:152]). Whatever the reasons for the shift from primary to secondary forest swiddening (which Grandstaff examines in considerable detail), the cultivation of secondary forests has meant that the Karen now occupy those parts of the highlands of Northern Thailand characterised by the presence of Dry Dipterocarp and Mixed Deciduous Forests. Karen terminology, however, does not make distinctions of this sort. The distinction — which may be inferred from the way that **pgha** and **chghi** are used — is one between forest that has been previously cultivated and forest that has not. Given the major ecological changes that have taken place in Northern Thailand, I think it is not unreasonable to make the further inference that this distinction is indeed an old one which had real meaning before such changes took place. The oral tradition of the Karen (which appears to possess a fair degree of continuity over time and space) suggests that **chghi** is more important in their perception of their environment than **pgha** as far as swiddening is concerned. In many of the prayers said in rites that are performed in association with swidden cultivation, **chghi** is invariably paired with **hy'** ("cultivated field" or swidden).

[3] In the village of Dong Luang (Mae Sariang), the Pwo Karen leave some trees standing in swiddens to assist in the regeneration of forest in fallow swiddens, as well as to retard soil losses because the roots of the trees hold the soil together (Hinton 1975: 84). The trees are, however, pollarded to prevent them from shading the rice crop. In Mae Tho, the Sgaw Karen do not fell trees which have a diameter of more than 15 centimetres at waist height but they are pollarded as in Dong Luang (Nakano 1978: 419). Though the Palokhi Karen are aware of the importance of having a tree line above their swiddens to seed fallow swiddens (and, thus, facilitate the process of regeneration), the fact that they do not leave standing trees in their swiddens is, nevertheless, a good indication that they feel no need to make additional efforts to propagate natural processes because of the ample forests around them.

[4] Other Karen cultivators are also reported to grow several varieties or strains of rice (Kunstadter [1978:87]; Hinton [1975:93]). Unlike the Karen studied by Kunstadter, the Palokhi Karen do not make special efforts to cultivate certain strains of rice, particularly early ripening ones to reduce the waiting period for harvests, during which time their stocks of rice have been consumed. In this regard, they are therefore more similar to the Pwo Karen studied by Hinton. As far as their own rice crop is concerned, the Palokhi Karen prefer ordinary rice to glutinous rice although when they purchase rice from the Northern Thai, it is glutinous rice that they obtain because it is cheaper and it is usually the only rice available as the Northern Thai only grow and consume this sort of rice. Iwata and Matsuoka (1967:309) say that most hill communities in Northern Thailand (with the exception of the Hmong and Yao) cultivate principally glutinous rice, while Watabe (1976:87) says that in one Lua' village he found both varieties of rice grown, presumably in equal amounts (but cf. Kunstadter [1978:87]). Most Karen, however, cultivate ordinary rice as the principal grain and glutinous rice in small quantities. On the basis of archaeological evidence, Watabe postulates that there is a high probability that hill or upland rice in early times was glutinous and that if deliberate selection of glutinous rice is not assumed, then this rice was progressively replaced by ordinary rice. The reason being that the genes responsible for the characteristics of ordinary rice are dominant and that hybridisation frequently recurs which would lead eventually to the predominance of this rice if selection was not practised by cultivators. If this is the case, then it is not impossible on the other hand that the Karen — given their preference for ordinary rice — have in fact enhanced the process by favouring ordinary rice in swidden cultivation.

[5] The manner in which food is shared in conjunction with the performance of agricultural rituals is significant because it appears to symbolically express certain sociological arrangements in Palokhi in relation to agricultural production. I have discussed the symbolic and ideological aspects of two modes of commensalism, that is routine domestic commensalism and feasting in the rites of the New Year, in Chapter IV; but in Chapter VI, I discuss other aspects of ritual commensalism in the particular context of agricultural rites in Palokhi.

Appendix E. Crops Grown in Palokhi Swiddens[1]

Common Name	Karen Name	Botanical Name	Harvested/Collected
1. Ordinary rice	by	**Oryza sativa** sp./var.	September - November
2. Glutinous rice	by pi' 'i'	**Oryza sativa** sp./var.	September - November
3. Maize	by khae sa	Zea mays	July - August
4. Taro	nwae	Colocasia esculenta	August -
5. Yam	nwae se	**Dioscorea** sp.	August -
6. Yam	nwae choe	**Dioscorea** sp.	August -
7. Winged yam	nwae doe	Dioscorea alata	August -
8. Tapioca	ke' bo	Manihot esculenta	July - February
9. Sweet potato	nwae caupa	Ipomoea batatas	September - February
10. Mustard greens	sa 'badau'	Brassica juncea	June - July
11. Cockroach berry	soekhau	Solanum aculeatissimum	August - November
12. Eggplant	soekhau kha	Solanum indicum	October -
13. Eggplant	ma' khwae sa	Solanum torvum	September -
14. Tomato	soekhau chi	Lycopersicon esculentum	June - January
15. Bitter cucumber	si phy de	Momordica aharantia	September -
16. Cucumber	si kha sa	**Momordica** sp.	October -
17. Snake gourd	da xy sa	Trichosanthes anguina	June - October
18. Angled loofah	doe re sa	Luffa acutangula	July - October
19. Smooth loofah(?)	to' kwae sa	**Luffa** sp.(?)	June - October
20. White gourd	lu sa	Benincasa cerifera	August - January
21. Pumpkin	lu khae bau	Cucurbita pepo	August - October
22. Pumpkin	lu khae sa	Cucurbita moschata	September - October
23. Melon	di my	Cucumis melo	September - November
24. Melon	di khwa	**Cucumis** sp.	September - November
25. Melon	di ploe'	**Cucumis** sp.	September - November
26. Cow pea(?)	poe thau sa	**Vigna sinensis** (?)	September - November
27. Red bean	soe be'	Vigna umbellata	October - November
28. Chilly	mysa phado'	**Capsicum anuum** var. grossum	July -
29. Chilly	mysa pho	**Capsicum anuum** var. acuminatum	July -
30. Chilly	mysa be'	Capsicum frutescens	July -
31. Basil	hau' koe' wau	**Ocimum** sp.	August -
32. Mint	hau' pghi	**Mentha** sp.	July -
33. Sesame	nisau	Sesamum indicum	October -
34. Lemon grass	hau' koe' wau toepho	Cymbopogon citratus	July -
35. Turmeric	soeghau	Curcuma domestica	June -
36. Sugar cane	koethi	**Saccharum** sp.	September -
37. Tobacco	njasu'	Nicotiana tabacum	September - October
38. Job's tears	boe'	Coix lachryma jobi	September - December

ENDNOTES

[1] This list of crops grown in Palokhi swiddens is the result of a collaborative effort with Wieland Kunzel of the University of Freiburg conducted in August - September 1980. Specimens of cultigens were first collected and identified according to their Karen names in Palokhi. They were then taken to the Department of Botany, Chiang Mai University, where Wieland Kunzel was able to establish their common and botanical names with the assistance of Acharn Wilaiwan Anusarnthorn. The periods when these cultigens are harvested or collected are based on information provided by the Palokhi Karen. It may be

noted that the number of cultigens grown in palokhi swiddens is considerably less than those grown in Karen swiddens identified by Kunstadter (1978). I am very much indebted to Wieland Kunzel for initiating the work on cultigens in Palokhi and for generously making available his various notes on them, and to Acharn Wilaiwan for her help in identifying the specimens of cultigens from Palokhi.

Appendix F. Wet-Rice Cultivation in Palokhi

Planting of Dry-bed Nurseries (Tho Ta Ka)

The first task in the actual cultivation of wet-rice in Palokhi is the planting of rice seed in nurseries. This is done in dry-bed nurseries and it is a practice which is by no means unusual in Northern Thailand as it is also done by some Northern Thai (Davis [1984:151]), Lua' and Karen (Kunstadter [1978:93]; see also Moerman [1968:53] and Iwata and Matsuoka [1967:310]). The planting of rice seed in this manner is called by the Palokhi Karen, **tho ta ka**, a combination of the Karen for swidden planting, **tho hy'**, and the Northern Thai term for rice nursery, **taa kaa**. The Palokhi term is apt indeed, for the technique of planting wet-rice seed is similar to that of planting rice in swiddens. The nursery is a small plot of land close to the wet-rice field which is cleared of vegetation and burnt, after which the seed is planted by dibbling. The work is done by individual households, often with a husband and wife working together. Unlike swiddening, however, there are no rituals associated with the planting of wet-rice seed in dry-bed nurseries.

Building Dams (Ma Faaj)

The next stage in the wet-rice season is the building of dams, called **ma faaj** which is again a compound term of Karen and Northern Thai (**faaj**, "dam" or "weir"). Before the dams are erected in the Huai Thung Choa, irrigation canals have to be checked and cleared of leaves and sediment, their walls rebuilt if they have been eroded, and their entrances to wet-rice terraces cleared if they are blocked, and so on. The dams are erected every year because they are not permanent structures. They consist of logs, branches and pieces of wood which are thrust into the stream bed, or placed firmly among rocks, at appropriate places and built up in this fashion in order to raise the level of the stream until it reaches the level of the land where the irrigation canals begin. In some cases, trees may be felled across the stream so that they act as a kind of retaining wall against which branches and pieces of wood are placed in order to erect the dam.

There are five dams across the Huai Thung Choa serving the total of twelve plots of wet-rice terraces. Each dam is shared by a number of households (ranging from two to four per dam) and the work of making the dams is also shared by these households. The ritual that is performed at the dam after its construction is usually led by the oldest cultivator, that is, the household that first made use of a dam. The ritual is not necessarily held immediately after the dam has been built however; it is usually held after the rice seedlings have been transferred from their nurseries into the terraces, in the middle of the wet season. The ritual is conducted as much to propitiate the spirit of the stream as to ensure the successful growth of the wet-rice crop.

Once the dams are built, the water is allowed to flow into the wet-rice terraces via irrigation canals which are cut along contour lines leading to the fields that are fed by the stream. The irrigation canals enter the fields at their upper-most terraces and, from here, the water is directed to lower terraces by means of sluices which are embedded in the dikes or bunds which separate the terrace plots in the field. The sluices are made from a short section of bamboo which is open at one end and closed at the other by the node in the bamboo but which has a small opening cut just before and above the node. The sluices are set in the bunds in such a way that the open ends life in the higher terrace, while the other end leads out to the lower terrace with the opening facing upwards. The sluices thus act as valves which impede the water flowing through them so that the seedlings, when they are planted, around the sluices are not damaged or uprooted by the gush of water entering the lower terraces.

The inundation of terraces at this stage of the season is essential before work can commence in them. The reason for this is that in the dry season the earth in the terraces has dried up and become hard and compact. It is also held together by the roots of the stubble from the previous harvest which are left in the fields although buffaloes are let in to graze when the fields lie fallow. The condition of the earth in terraces before and at the onset of the rainy season thus makes ploughing an impossible task, hence the necessity to inundate the terraces first in order to make the earth soft enough to plough (see also Kunstadter [1978:93]) or to hoe.

Hoeing (Pla' Chi') and Ploughing (Tha Chi', Thaaj Chi')

When the wet-rice fields have been soaked and softened, the task of ploughing begins. In some cases, where the terraces are too small for buffaloes to move in, hoeing is done to break up the earth instead of ploughing. It is interesting to note that while the hoeing of wet-rice fields is described by a full Karen term in palokhi, ploughing is not, containing as it does the Northern Thai term for "plough", **thaaj**. This is because the Karen have their own word for "hoe" and "wet-rice field" (see also Jones [1961: 157]), but not for plough. The ploughshares, which the Palokhi Karen use, are all purchased from Northern Thai shops, but the frames are made in Palokhi. A further interesting feature about the influence of Northern Thai on ploughing in Palokhi is the use of Northern Thai commands in driving buffaloes, **khwaa** ("right") and **tauj** ("turn around"). Although some buffaloes in Palokhi actually belong to Northern Thai and therefore "they understand only Northern Thai", nonetheless, the Palokhi Karen will often use these commands when they handle their own buffaloes.

Ploughing is hard work indeed, but it can only be done by two men at a time — one to lead the buffalo, and another to work the plough. All wet-rice cultivating households have buffaloes but almost all of them make mutual arrangements of one sort or another in ploughing. The most common of these are work exchange arrangements between households which have only one adult male capable of undertaking the hard work of ploughing which women cannot, and which old men are unable to because of their infirmity. Those households which have more working age males are, of course, able to carry out the ploughing of their fields entirely with their own internal supplies of labour. It is also worth noting that in Palokhi, the buffaloes which do not belong to the villagers have been left with them by Northern Thai, or Karen, on agistment. This is a great advantage to the households which rear them because they may use the animals without charge, and at the same time acquire buffaloes eventually according to the terms of agistment agreements which usually specify equal shares in the calves bred by the buffaloes on agistment (see Appendix G).

The process of ploughing itself has the effect of breaking up the earth and mixing the stubble and buffalo dung left by grazing buffaloes into the soil. It thus assists, though only partially, in recycling nutrients back into the soil. This process would be more efficient if the stubble were burnt prior to flooding and ploughing (Hanks [1972:37]) but, in Palokhi, this is hardly ever done and, when it is, only parts of fields are treated in this way.

Harrowing (Phoe Chi', Phya Chi')

Ploughing is only the first step in preparing the wet-rice terraces for the planting of seedlings. It is followed by harrowing which further breaks up the earth — which has been turned into lumps of mud by ploughing — into smaller pieces or lumps. As with ploughing, the term for this process is derived from the Northern Thai term for the implement that is used in it — **phya**, "harrow" or "rake". The harrows are made in Palokhi and are modelled on those of the Northern Thai just as the ploughs are. Similar to ploughing, the task of harrowing requires two men and a buffalo, and the work arrangements are the same as well. The work is no less strenuous than ploughing because the harrows have to be kept steady and manipulated through the resistant lumps of mud, and thrown at regular intervals to shed the mud that accumulates before and in-between the tines of the harrow.

Where the terraces are too small for harrowing to be done with buffaloes, further hoeing may be necessary to continue the process of breaking up the soil and mud. This, however, is usually done as part of the initial hoeing of these micro-terraces.

Smoothening (Kwa 'bleta, Toe' Chi', Toek Naa)

The process of harrowing, if it is thoroughly done, and the on-going inundation of the wet-rice fields turns the mud in terraces into a thick consistency, but the surface of which is usually uneven because the mud accumulates at various places during harrowing. It is necessary to smoothen the surface, that is, to distribute the mud evenly in each plot, because the mud eventually settles down to form the bed into which the rice seedlings are planted and take root. If the surface were left uneven, an uneven bed would result beneath the water level in terraces making the thorough planting of seedlings impossible. Smoothening is done with a plank that is harnessed to the buffalo which is made to drag the plank, or board, around the terrace thus distributing the mud around the terrace. The process is simply called by a karen term, **kwa'bleta**, which means "to sweep smooth", or by the Northern Thai term **toek naa** ("to smoothen the wet-rice field"), or again a combination of karen and Northern Thai as in **toe' chi'**. This is also a task that requires the efforts of two men, but it is not unusual for one man to do it because the board does not require much handling as ploughs and harrows do.

Once smoothening is completed, the wet-rice fields are not worked for some time to allow the mud to settle at the bottom of the terraces. This generally coincides with the initial growth period of the rice shoots in nurseries.

Planting (Su By)

By late June or early July, the seedlings in the dry-bed nurseries are ready for transplanting into the wet-rice terraces. The seedlings, which the Palokhi Karen call by their own term, **by pho** ("little rice [plant]") or **ta ka**, the same Northern Thai term for nursery, have to be removed first from the nurseries and this is usually done by households on an individual basis in preparation for transplanting when other households come to assist in the task on a co-operative labour exchange basis. Removing the seedlings is called **thae' ta ka**, "clearing the **ta ka**", and it entails careful uprooting of the seedlings from the nursery bed so as not to damage the roots. The seedlings are tied in bundles with bamboo withes, each about the size of a handful, and the bundles are then stacked by the field hut ready for the work team to plant which is usually done on the following day. The planting of seedlings is called **su by**, an entirely Karen term. The organisation of labour for planting the seedlings is similar to that in the planting of swiddens, that is, all households contribute their labour, which is then reciprocated when it is their turn to transplant their seedlings. As with swiddening, planting in wet-rice fields is extremely labour intensive for the same reasons, namely, the necessity to get as much done over a large area in a short period of time, hence the large work teams. After the first day of planting, the work teams move on to other fields, until all the fields have been planted. It is not uncommon, of course, for households to find that not all of their terraces have been planted on the first day, and so smaller teams are formed to carry out the work of planting that remains.

The task of planting itself requires first the trimming of the seedlings to about 30 to 35 cm in length. The reason for this practice is that with the reduced height of the seedlings, they are less likely to topple over while they are still taking root in the terrace beds. The seedlings are trimmed in bundles with a bush knife and they are cast into the terraces where they float around. The work teams enter the terraces and pick them up and plant them directly using their fingers to protect the roots as they are inserted into the terrace beds. The seedlings are planted about 20 cm apart in an irregular fashion unlike some Northern Thai cultivators who attempt to plant seedlings in straight rows.

The planting of wet-rice is, in so far as its ritual aspects are concerned, modelled on what takes place in swiddens but only to a limited extent. There is, for instance, a small crop of "Old Mother Rice" that is planted which is the focus of planting rites. It is significant that the "Old Mother Rice" in Palokhi fields are protected, at the time of planting, by "hawks' eyes" (**taa liaw**, a Northern Thai term) which is a typically Northern Thai agricultural practice (see Davis [1984:160, 292]). The "planting of the ritual basket of the yam" which characterises swidden planting is not, significantly, carried out in wet-rice fields. The prayers that are said when wet-rice is planted, however, are the same as those said in swidden planting and are addressed to the "Lord of the Water, Lord of the Land". The work teams on the first day of planting are also offered food at mid-day, as in swidden planting.

After the swiddens have been planted, the wet-rice fields are fenced to keep out cattle and buffaloes. This work is done solely on a household basis.

Weeding (Pla' Kha Na)

During the growing season of wet-rice, that is, roughly from July through September, the only agricultural task that needs to be performed in wet-rice terraces is weeding. Although the Palokhi Karen have their own term for "weed", as we have seen, the weeds that grow on the bunds and dikes of wet-rice terraces are referred to by their Northern Thai name, **khaa naa**. The process of weeding is called "hoeing weeds" (**pla' kha na**) and it describes how the weeds are removed. As in swiddening, this is done sporadically because it conflicts with tasks that need to be performed in swiddens, namely, weeding and the collection of cultigens. During this time, the stocks of rice in Palokhi begin to run out, if they have not been exhausted already, and the Karen therefore have to seek employment in Northern Thai villages so that they can buy rice with the wages that they earn. It is also a period when tea buyers and **miang** merchants come around Ban Mae Lao to buy tea leaves, and the Palokhi Karen also take this opportunity to earn money by picking tea in their own tea gardens, or those of the Northern Thai, in order to obtain money as well.

The weeding season in the wet-rice cycle is also the time when a rite to protect the rice in the wet-rice fields has to be performed. This practice is clearly derived from the cycle of agricultural rites associated with swidden cultivation. The name of this rite, in wet-rice fields, is called **bghau chi'** after the **bghau hy'** ritual in swiddens which I discuss in Chapter VI.

Harvesting (Ku' Lau By)

By late September and early October, the rice in Palokhi terraces are about ready for harvesting. Before it can be harvested, however, the terraces must be drained of water and this is done by breaching the dams in the Huai Thung Choa. At this time of the year, the wet season is also approaching its close, and within a week to a fortnight of breaching the dams, the wet-rice terraces are completely dry. The harvesting of wet-rice is similar to that of swidden rice and, as I have already described the three phases involved (that is, reaping, threshing and the transport and storing of the harvest) in Appendix D, I shall not therefore deal with this aspect of the wet-rice cycle in Palokhi.

However, it may be noted that this particular stage in the wet-rice cycle is not surrounded by the rituals associated with its corresponding stage in the swidden cycle unless the cultivation of wet-rice is the sole form of agriculture undertaken by a household. That is to say, where households cultivate both swiddens and wet-rice fields, the rituals in swiddens are deemed to suffice for wet-rice fields as well. Quite apart from the calendrical system, this is a clear indication of the ideological weight attached to swiddening in Palokhi despite the very important part played by wet-rice agriculture in the subsistence economy of the Palokhi Karen.

Appendix G. The Agistment of Buffaloes and Cattle in Palokhi

The rearing and agistment of buffaloes and cattle is a common, and probably long established practice, in Northern Thailand. In one of the few sociological studies of livestock rearing and related issues, in the highlands of Northern Thailand, Falvey (1977) observes that while cattle rearing in the highlands has been in existence for as long as highland areas have been populated, the rearing of buffaloes is most likely a more recent phenomenon brought about by two main factors, namely, an increasing shortage of grazing areas in the lowlands and increasing wet-rice cultivation by highland communities in highland areas. Falvey's observations especially with regard to the karen are particularly interesting as they are very much applicable to the Palokhi Karen as well. In his survey of various highland communities, he notes that the mean buffalo population was highest for the Akha, followed by the Karen, and then only by the Northern Thai, Lisu and Hmong, reflecting a correlation with the cultivation of wet-rice in these communities. Equally interesting is his observation that the mean number of households tending cattle and buffaloes (self-owned and on agistment) was highest among the Karen (1977:27). Falvey also adds that while the Karen own buffaloes because they are needed in the cultivation of wet-rice, the tending of large livestock, particularly cattle, is practised by rich families "as a means of accumulating wealth as an insurance against crop failure" (1977:40). All these remarks are, by and large, true for the Palokhi Karen.

The following table shows the number of households which own and tend on agistment buffaloes and cattle in Palokhi. The general patterns in the ownership and agistment of buffaloes and cattle in Palokhi are very similar to that described by Falvey. The reasons are also very much the same.

All the households which own buffaloes also cultivate wet-rice fields, and the ownership of buffaloes is clearly associated with the use of buffaloes in the cultivation of wet-rice. Cattle, on the other hand, are not employed as beasts of burden or pack animals in Palokhi, but they are nevertheless reared on agistment owned, although only by a few households. Whether the livestock is owned or tended on agistment, the purpose of these households (apart from having buffaloes to work in their wet-rice fields), is to eventually own a small herd of buffaloes or cattle, or both. In its most general sense, this may be regarded as a form of accumulation of wealth, but more specifically, as Falvey points out, livestock thus reared and owned act as a "cash reserve". In this sense, buffaloes and cattle represent wealth quite different from wealth in the form of elephants and bronze drums (see Chapter VI, p. 432, n. 12) which are "prestige" possessions. Buffaloes and cattle are more easily liquidated assets and are a hedge against crop failure or large shortfalls in agricultural production when large amounts of rice need to be acquired to meet domestic consumption requirements.

Table G.1. Buffaloes and Cattle Owned and Agisted in Palokhi

Household	Buffaloes		Cattle	
	Owned	Agisted (from)	Owned	Agisted (from)
H1a	6	—	—	—
H2	1	5 (Karen—Huai Sai Luang)		2 (Northern Thai— Huai Mao)
H3	4	—	—	—
H4	2	—	1	—
H6	1	—	—	—
H7	1	—	—	—
H8	1	2 (Karen—Huai Dua)	—	2 (Northern Thai— Mae Lao)
				2 (Northern Thai— Thung Choa)
H9	2	—	—	—
H11a	3	—	—	—
H13a	—	—	3	2 (Karen—Mae Tho)
H14	1	—	—	—
H16	2	—	—	—
Total	22	7	4	8
Mean	2	3.5	2	2

The buffaloes and cattle that are owned by the Palokhi Karen have been acquired in several ways—inheritance, direct purchase or agistment. The agistment arrangements are, in their broad outlines, similar to that reported by Falvey (1977:91–2) whether the parties are Karen and Karen, or Karen and Northern Thai, that is, the tender of the livestock receives every second calf as a fee. Agistment is known by its Northern Thai term **liang phaa** or the Karen expression **by' lae ne 'o'** which roughly means "to rear and obtain in exchange", in Palokhi.

Most agistment agreements in Palokhi are of the sort in which the tender receives the second calf in payment for tending the stock which are usually female buffaloes or cows. In some cases, however, half shares in each calf may be agreed upon and if, or when, the calf is sold (also upon agreement), the proceeds are shared by the stock owner and the tender. If bulls are agisted, however, the agreement between owner and tender usually specifies half-shares in the appreciated value of the stock during the time in which it is tended, if it is sold. Agistment agreements, however, place all burden of risk on the tender in that if stock on agistment dies through neglect or is stolen, the tender must then make full restitution according to the market value of the stock at delivery and half its appreciated value at the time of its death or loss. Notwithstanding the element of risk in agistment, it is nonetheless a very worthwhile arrangement, particularly from the perspective of the Palokhi Karen, because the tending of stock requires very little labour and no on-going expenses in the form of feed. The buffaloes and cattle in Palokhi are usually herded by boys between the ages of seven and eleven, and regularly by a Khamu' man who settled in Palokhi as a dependent of H2. The buffaloes and cattle are led out in the mornings and allowed to graze in the forest and they are herded back to the village in the evenings. In 1981, only one household (H8) realised money from agisted stock. A calf from one of the two cows agisted by a Northern Thai woman in Ban Thung Choa was sold to a Northern Thai for Bht 1,200 and this was shared equally by H3 and the Northern Thai woman. Some households, however, sold their own stock to other Karen in the village or to Northern Thai elsewhere. H1a for instance, sold one buffalo to a Karen working in the Flower Plantation of the Royal Forestry Department's Watershed Unit 1 valued at Bht 1,700 (which was paid for in cash and rice in instalments) and a buffalo calf to H6 for Bht 1,000. H11a and H16, on the other hand, sold a buffalo each to Northern Thai for Bht 2,700 and Bht 2,500 respectively. The market price of large livestock varies according to the age of the animals and also according to whether purchasers come to Palokhi looking for a sale, or whether the Palokhi Karen go out seeking purchasers. In the former case, clearly older animals command better prices, while in the latter case, better prices are generally obtained if buyers come to Palokhi looking for animals to buy.

The following is a list of the approximate prices of buffaloes and cattle according to age, in Palokhi. Bulls, particularly in the case of buffaloes, tend to be priced higher (by about Bht 500) than females of equivalent age because of their generally longer effective working life as females cannot be worked when they are in calf.

Table G.2. Approximate Prices of Buffaloes and Cattle by Age, in Palokhi (1980–81)

Age in Years	Price of Buffaloes (in Bht)	Price of Cattle (in Bht)
1	1,100	1,000
2	2,500	2,000
3	4,200	2,500
4	5,500	NA
5	8,000	NA

Appendix H. Examples of Household Budgets in Palokhi

The tables in this appendix, based on seven household budgets in 1981, illustrate the extent to which the Palokhi Karen are linked to an external, cash based economy primarily through their need for rice in order to make up shortfalls in agricultural production. The households include those with rice surpluses (H2) and those which were unable to cultivate rice for one reason or another (for example, H5 and H13b) as well as those which cultivated rice but did not produce enough for their domestic requirements (H1a, H1b, H3, and H6). These households are, therefore, generally representative of most if not all households in Palokhi.

Perhaps the most striking feature of these examples of household budgets is that all the households are involved in the cash economy of the Pa Pae hills to one extent or another. This is shown very clearly in all the tables but Table H.1 in. particular demonstrates the importance of the **miang** and tea industries.

The data were obtained on the basis of interviews, conducted regularly at intervals ranging from three days to a week, from 21 January 1981 to 31 December 1981.

Table H.1. Examples of Household Budgets: Income Earned from Miang and Tea Related Activities (21 January 1981 – 31 December 1981)

Household	Wage Labour In Palokhi			Wage Labour Outside Palokhi			Leaf-picking in Gardens (Man days)	Quantity of Leaf sold (Kg)	Income from Sale of Leaf		Total Number of Days Worked (Man days)	Total Income Earned	
	Days Worked (Man days)	Income Earned		Days Worked (Man days)	Income Earned				Cash (Baht)	Rice (Baht)*		Cash (Baht)	Rice (Baht)*
		Cash (Baht)	Rice (Baht)*		Cash (Baht)	Rice (Baht)*							
H1a	—	—	—	11.0	218.0	108.0 [24.0]	31.75	313.6	1,164.2	—	42.75	1,382.2	108.0 [24.0]
H1b	—	—	—	14.0	203.0	45.0 [10.0]	43.5	236.9	947.0	—	57.5	949.3	45.0 [10.0]
H2	—	—	—	20.0	351.0	—	15.5	102.5	465.0	—	35.5	816.0	—
H3	13.0	118.0	96.75 [21.5]	62.5	1,773.0	157.5 [35.0]	1.5	16.0	24.0	—	77.0	1,797.0	242.5 [56.5]
H5	11.0	39.0	146.25 [32.5]	79.25	1,276.0	391.5 [87.0]	9.0	101.4	219.5	—	99.25	1,495.5	537.75 [119.5]
H6	—	—	—	2.0	16.0	—	112.75	2,107.5	4,433.5	2,704.5 [601.0]	114.75	4,449.5	2,704.5 [601.0]
H13b	4.5	88.5	45.0 [10.0]	28.25	710.0	121.5 [27.0]	5.0	102.0	153.0	—	37.75	951.5	166.5 [37.0]

* Rice incomes are given in Baht; the figures in brackets show the actual amounts of rice in litres.

Table H.2. Examples of Household Budgets: Income Earned in Palokhi from Wage Work, Sales, and Services (21 January 1981 – 31 December 1981)

| | Wage Labour | | | | Sales | | | | | | | |
| | Days Worked (Man days) | Wages | | Opium Cash (Baht)** | Food (Vegetables, Fish, Confections, Sundry goods, etc.) | | Others (Tobacco, Liquor, Smithing Work, etc.) | | Poultry and Livestock | | Ritual Services |
Household		Cash (Baht)	Rice (Baht)*		Cash (Baht)	Rice (Baht)*	Cash (Baht)	Rice (Baht)*	Cash (Baht)	Rice (Baht)*	Cash (Baht)
H1a	–	–	–	–	–	–	12.0	–	615.0	–	–
H1b	–	–	–	–	–	–	42.0	–	–	–	–
H2	–	–	–	–	113.0	–	120.0	–	9.0	–	–
H3	2.5	78.0	–	–	100.0	–	112.0	–	13.0	–	–
H5	1.0	–	99.0 [22.0]	75.0 [3.0]	7.0	99.0 [22.0]	37.0	–	–	–	70.5
H6	0.5	–	4.5 [1.0]	10.0 [0.25]	45.0	–	67.0	–	–	–	–
H13a	6.0	53.0	171.0 [38.0]	–	–	–	–	112.5 [25.0]	–	–	–

* Rice incomes are given in Baht; the figures in brackets show the actual amounts of rice in litres.

** Incomes received in the form of opium are given in terms of their cash value, that is in Baht. The actual amounts of opium received are given in brackets in tua, a Northern Thai unit of measurement approximately equivalent to 4.8 grammes.

Table H.3. Examples of Household Budgets: Income Earned Outside Palokhi from Wage Work, Sales, and Services (21 January 1981 – 31 December 1981)

| Household | Wage Labour | | | Sales | | | | | | | |
| | Days Worked (Man days) | Wages | | Opium Cash (Baht)** | Others (Tobacco, Liquor, Smithing Work, etc.) | | Poultry and Livestock | | Ritual Services | Forest Products | |
		Cash (Baht)	Rice (Baht)*		Cash (Baht)	Rice (Baht)*	Cash (Baht)	Rice (Baht)*	Cash (Baht)	Cash (Baht)	Rice (Baht)*
H1a	—	—	—	—	—	135.0 [30.0]	1,210.0	369.0 [82.0]	—	—	—
H1b	—	—	—	—	—	—	110.0	387.0 [86.0]	—	—	—
H2	11.5	323.0	—	—	667.0	—	2,300.0	—	—	125.0	—
H3	27.5	584.0	38.7 [8.5]	—	740.0	—	800.0	—	—	900.0	—
H5	11.0	219.0	81.0 [18.0]	75.0 [2.0]	75.0	9.0 [2.0]	—	—	340.75	40.0	—
H6	1.5	40.0	49.5 [11.0]	200.0 [4.0]	3,171.0	99.0 [22.0]	350.0	72.0 [16.0]	—	280.5	—
H13a	13.5	345.0	72.0 [16.0]	—	287.0	13.5 [3.0]	—	—	—	234.5	—

* Rice incomes are given in Baht; the figures in brackets show the actual amounts of rice in litres.
** Incomes received in the form of opium are given in terms of their cash value, that is in Baht. The actual amounts of opium received are given in brackets in tua, a Northern Thai unit of measurement approximately equivalent to 4.8 grammes.

Table H.4. Examples of Household Budgets: Expenditures in Palokhi on Wages, Goods, and Services (21 January 1981 – 31 December 1981)

Household	Wage Labour				Purchases						
	Days Worked (Man days)	Wages Paid		Opium Cash (Baht)***	Food (Vegetables, Fish, Confections, Sundry goods, etc.)		Others (Tobacco, Liquor, Smithing Work, etc.)		Poultry and Livestock		Ritual Services Cash (Baht)
		Cash (Baht)	Rice (Baht)*		Cash (Baht)	Rice (Baht)****	Cash (Baht)	Rice (Baht)*	Cash (Baht)	Rice (Baht)*	
H1a	5.0	—	NA [44.0]	—	42.0	—	122.0	—	100.0	—	23.0
H1b	10.0	—	NA [35.0]	—	47.5	—	86.0	—	26.0	—	77.75
H2	7.5	56.0	NA [14.0]	10.0 [0.25]	85.0	—	86.0	—	120.0	—	—
H3	3.5	15.0	NA [4.0]	—	131.0	—	158.0	—	150.0	—	—
H5	1.0	—	NA [11.0]	—	7.0	—	133.0	99.0 [22.0]	10.0	—	—
H6	—	—	—	5.0	14.0	—	131.0	—	600.0	—	—
H13b***	—	—	—	—	79.0	—	—	—	—	—	—

* In 1981, wage work was mainly done by a young girl (an only daughter) to earn some money and rice to support her sick mother. Her work consisted primarily of milling rice for some of the wealthier households in Palokhi (for example, H1a, H1b, H2, and H3) as well as child-minding. The work that she did was hardly essential to these households as they could quite easily do it themselves. Her employment, therefore, was motivated by a charitable concern for her and her mother's welfare. When her mother died in April, she was fostered out to a Northern Thai family in Ban Mae Lao, as I have noted before (Chapter III, n. 23, p. 197). She was paid rice wages in the form of milled non-glutinous rice grown by these households. As the Palokhi Karen do not generally sell the rice which they cultivate, it is difficult to impute a cash value to the rice and for this reason I have not indicated the cash values of these wages in the table. Where I have indicated the cash value of rice wages, the rice which was used for payment was glutinous rice purchased in Northern Thai settlements.

** In this table, the expenditures on opium are given in Baht while the quantities of opium are given in tua in brackets. The purchases shown in the table are small and were bought essentially for medicinal purposes. They do not represent purchases by addicts (whose households are not reflected in the table) which were substantial but proved difficult to determine or estimate.

*** "Rice" is sometimes used to "purchase" other items in Palokhi. Such transactions are therefore exchange transactions in reality. In the table, the rice used in this way is indicated in litres and, where the rice is glutinous rice originally purchased in Northern Thai settlements, their cash values are also indicated in brackets.

**** The data for H13b in this table are not as reliable as those for other households and this explains to some extent why its expenditures appear somewhat small in comparison. It should be noted, however, that H13b shared a number of economic functions with H13a (as discussed in Chapter IV, pp. 206–11) and several items (for example, tobacco) were obtained from the parental household without having to buy them from other households. As I have also pointed out, H13a and H13b were relatively poor and this also explains the lower levels of expenditures of the household in this table.

Table H.5. Examples of Household Budgets: Expenditures Outside Palokhi on Rice and Other Goods and Services (21 January 1981 – 31 December 1981)

Household	Rice Baht*	Opium Cash (Baht)**	Food (Vegetables, Fish, Confections, Sundry goods, etc.)		Others (Tobacco, Liquor, Smithing Work, etc.)		Ritual and Medical Services Cash (Baht)	Rent Cash (Baht)	Transport Cash (Baht)	Taxes Cash (Baht)
			Cash (Baht)	Rice (Baht)***	Cash (Baht)	Rice (Baht)***				
H1a	1,150.5 [247.0]	-	330.5	-	656.5	-	85.0	-	35.0	10.0
H1b	1,248.5 [290.0]	-	596.0	NA [4.0]	448.0	-	113.75	-	68.0	-
H2	-	-	1,084.0	-	2,324.5	-	14.25	-	71.0	10.0
H3	420.0 [89.0]	5.0 [0.125]	821.5	-	2,433.5	-	-	-	180.0	10.0
H5	403.5 [82.5]	5.0 [0.125]	551.0	-	604.5	-	20.0	-	227.0	25.0
H6	1,527.5 [313.0]	160.0 [4.0]	598.0	-	1,260.5	-	70.0	1,500.0	87.0	10.0
H13b	666.0 [167.0]	-	54.5	-	31.5	-	-	-	10.0	-

* The amounts of rice purchased are given in litres; the figures in brackets show the cash values (in Bht) of the corresponding amounts of rice.

** The opium purchased is given in terms of their cash values, that is Bht; the corresponding amounts purchased are given in tua (in brackets), a Northern Thai unit of measurement approximately equivalent to 4.8 grammes.

*** The rice shown in this column is rice used as a medium of exchange. I have not indicated the cash value of the rice as it was rice grown in Palokhi by H1b and therefore difficult to impute a value to it.

Appendix I. The Origin of the Karen: An "Official" History

The origin of the Karens

According to tradition the home-country of the Karens was the land called by them—.' Htee-Hseh-Meh-Ywa' 'Water pushes sand flows'. It means that it was a land that Sand Moves or Flows as a river-' The River of Sand'. Perhaps it might be the Gobi desert, which is directly towards the north. That region is in Mongolia. Thus is seems that the Karens came from Mongolia, and they were a tribe of the Mongolian race. It was as suchthat the Karens were described by a great many historians as an off-shoot of the main race the Mongolian race.

The First migration of the Karens into Burma.

All western historians and the missionaries, working among the Karens had mentioned that the home of the Karens was in what (to the Karens) was known as Kaw-Si' or the 'Country-Si' probably Sinkiang, a region in western China. That was before they came into Burma. The Chinese and the Shans have stated that the river Yangtse (which means the Yang river) came from the country of the Yang (the Yang or the Karen). This plainly shows that the Karens or the Yangs or the Carians had lived some where in the west of China, in the region where the Yangtse takes its source.

The Karens entered Burma along three routes-

(1) The Mekong valley route.

(2) The Irrawaddy valley route.

(3) The Salween valley route.

(1) The Mekong river rises in Tibet and flows through China down south through Laos. Cambodia and enters the Gulf of Thailand. Some history books mentioned that the Karens established cities and government in Chiang Mai, but they were overthrown by the Thais, and Karens moved into the mountains, to Mae Sariang and across the other side of the Salween.

(2) The second migratory group followed along the valleys of the Shwe-li and the Irrawaddy. The Pwo Karens built the town of Prome (Pwo-Wai' -meaning the' Pwo-town). Some went down south to the Irrawddy Delta-to such places as Ma-u-bin, Bassein, Myaung-Mya, etc.

(3) The third group entered what now is known as the Shan States, moving down to southern Shan State. They are here known as the Pa-o Karens, some stayed on in Karenni State (the Red Karens). Some of this group went westward

to Toungoo, Shwe-Gyin, Thaton, Moulmein, Tavoy and Mergui saw these Karens settling on these places.

Karen tradition has it that the first migration of the Karens was in the year B. C. 1125 and the second one was in B.C739. They were the first migratory group to arrive in this region now called Burma. In those days according to Karen tradition the sea shore was at Prome (then called Pwo-way). The Karen calender year is (739/ the year of our Lord A.D. 1939)-1939 was the year the Government of Burma recognised and confirmed it. Thus the Karen year this time will be (739 / 1977) 2716 year-the 739 was the year 739 B.C. when the Karens came into Burma in their second migration into Burma. Professor Luce of the Rangoon University and Professor Peam of the Eastern Historical Research Society endorsed the statement of the Karen calender year.

The Karens came in earlier than the Shans, and due to the dominance of the Shans, the Karens moved down south towards the delta regions of the great river valleys along which they came. The Karens moved down south at the time over two hundred years before the Mon and the Burmese came over from India.

When the Karens first settled down they called this land 'Kaw Lah' -the Green Country' and they were then a free people but gradually the Mons (a new group evolved from the mixed marraige of the Indians and the people of the land in Tavoy and Moulmein regions) and the Burmans (the people emerging from the inter-marriage of the Indian 'Bramin' and the people in the country) pushed into the Karen settlements. These Karens being peaceful and self-effacing had again to move away into the mountain fastness or away from established settlements which became the possessions of these later settlers who had all the traits or (mostly all) of the Indian culture, statescraft and other attributes of the so-called civilization.

The present day Karens are found in-

(1) The Delta of the Irrawaddy-

Bassein, Myaung-mya, Ma-u-bin, Pya-pon, Henzada, Tharawaddy and some in the Prome district.

(2) The Eastern Hills-

Toungoo, Papun, Thaton, Moulmein, Pa-an, Tavoy, Mergui and Pegu districts and also in Karenni, southern Shan States and in Pyin-ma-na hills.

(3) The western regions-

The Pwo and Sgaw Karens here live amongst the Burmese and thus having come in contact in most of their dealings with the Burmese, these Karens can speak the Burmese language well, but in the eastern hills they live apart and have very little contact with the Burmese, resulting in having very little command of the Burmese language. The Karens both living in the deltas and the eastern hills are behind the Burmese in their standard of living.

The Karen Tribes

A nation has its own characteristics, there being four-

(1) It's tradition,

(2) t's language, character and culture,

(3) The Land in which it settlesdown

(4) It's individualistic policies of economy, the Karens have all these characteristics, and though a nation, there are many tribes.

On May 6, 1936, the governor of Burma issued a statement, announcing that there are eleven Karen tribes-

(1) Sgaw (2) Pwo (3) Pa-O (4) Paku (5) Mon-Ney-Bwa (6) Bwe (7) White Karen (8) Padaung (9) Eastern Bwe (Ka - renni or Kayah (10) Con-Ker (11) Geh-Bah.

Chronology

1. Migration of the Karen from Mongolia B.C. 2617
2. Arrival of the Karens in East Turkistan B.C. 2013
3. Migration of the Karens from East Turkistan B.C. 1866
4. Arrival of the Karens in Tibet B.C. 1864
5. Migration of the Karens from Tibet B.C. 1388

    (The Karens settled down in Tibet for 476 years)
6. Arrival of the Karens in Yunnan in China B.C. 1385
7. Migration of the first group from Yunnan to S.E. Asia B.C. 1128
8. Arrival of the first group Karens who entered S.E. Asia B.C. 1125
9. Migration of the second group of the Karens from Yunnan to S.E. Asia B.C. 741
10. The last arrival of the second group to enter S.E. Asia B.C. 759

Bibliography

1. The Karen History by Saw Aung Hla.
2. The Karens of the Golden Chersonese by Lt. Col. A. R. Memahon
3. The Loyal Karens of Burma by D.M. Smeaton, M. A.
4. The travel of Marco Polo. The Venetian Vol I and II, edition 1903 by Sir. H. Yule
5. The travel of Marco Polo, The Venetian by John Measefield.
6. History of China, 1929, by W.E. Soothill
7. An outline History of China, 1296, by Gwen and Hall

8. A sketch of China History. Ancient and Modern etc. Vol I and II 1834 by Rev. Charles Gutstaff

The Karens under the Feudal Masters

The Karens are agriculturists and like peace and quietness. They dislike rowdiness and so the majority would rather stay away from big cities with their activities and noises. For over two hundred years they enjoyed a free life under the leadership of their own patriach of the village, here in this land they has seen built up from mere islands in the sea, into an alluvial-filled land of mountains, and rivers. But when the Mons and the Burmese came in, there started frictions and disagreements in temperament of different cultures. Thus the Karens moved away leaving their settled lands to these new comers. This went on time after time and the Karens avoided strifes by moving away.

During the time of the Mon and the Burmese monarchial rule, the Karens were ill-used to work in the building of pagodas, and digging channels for irrigational water courses. They had been told when young about how their forefathers were carriers earth and stones in baskets which the Burmese kings had them special-made. The woven strings attached to the baskets had harness of wood or bamboo, which harness could be hooked on to the shoulders to relieve the strain on the head. The special harnesses were sickles, and the baskets must be loaded till the straps became so taut they twanged like the strings of a Violin. Any one incapable of fulfilling the alloted was beaten to death. In certain cases the women met un-sightly deaths and the children were put into wooden and pounded to death or else, were thrown up with a sword or a spear pointed to receive them as they dropped back to earth. These are not fancies but facts handed down through the various generations. The Karens could not expect any mercy or understanding from those in powers (The book 'The Karens and their travails' by Thra T. Thanbya, had been banned from publication but might still be in an American Missionary Library).

The Karens had been made to feel so un-worthy being ill-treated, oppressed and massacred all through these centuries, that have developed an inferiority complex. The more enlightened ones have reservation about trusting of the Burmese who-ever are in power. Perhaps the genes of the Karen babies in their mothers wombs had undergone so drastic a change that a Karen born of woman, naturally had an ingrained sense to be wary of a Burma. In spite of such terrible physical frustrations, the Karens are still holding on to some national characteristics a sense of honesty, a desire to entertain visitors, a willingness to take part in the communical activities. In this modern world of permissiveness, the Karen family is a closely-Knitted unit. They still remain loyal to their people and their country.

The Karens under the British Colonial Rule

After the Anglo-Burmese war of 1825, the British took the Arakan and Tenessarim states. In 1852 lower Burma fell into the hands of the British. In the third Anglo-Burmese war of 1886, the whole of Burma came under the control of the British. Christian missionaries followed the British rulers. Christianity preaches love, deliverance from bondage (of sin) and blessings to the poor and the oppressed. These attributes of Christianty closely correspond to the Karen traditional ideals. Naturally the Karens were easily converted to Christianity.

Under the British rule, the Karens were allowed to learn their language and the government recognised the students of the tenth standard sitting for a Karen

These pages above are facsimiles of the first three pages of Appendix I to **The Karen Revolution in Burma** (Lonsdale, n.d.).

Bibliography

Acciaioli, G. 1981. Knowing What You're Doing: A Review of Pierre Bourdieu's **Outline of a Theory of Practice. Canberra Anthropology.** 4(1):23–51.

Althusser, L. 1969. **For Marx** (transl. B.R. Brewster). Harmondsworth: Penguin Books.

Andersen, K.E. 1976. Elements of Pwo Karen Buddhism. In **Lampang Reports,** ed. S. Egerod and P. Sorensen. Copenhagen: Scandinavian Institute of Asian Studies.

Austin, J. 1962. **How to do Things with Words.** London: Oxford University Press.

Barth, F. 1969. Introduction. In **Ethnic Groups and Boundaries,** ed. F. Barth. Boston: Little, Brown and Co.

Barthes, R. 1972. Myth Today. In **Mythologiques,** R. Barthes. St. Albans: Paladin.

Benedict, P.K. 1972. **Sino-Tibetan — A Conspectus.** Cambridge: Cambridge University Press.

Benjamin, G. 1980. Semang, Senoi, Malay: Culture-history, Kinship, and Consciousness in the Malay Peninsula. Unpublished Manuscript.

_____. 1985a. Between Isthmus and Islands: Notes on Malayan Palaeo-sociology. Paper presented at the 12th Congress of the Indo-Pacific Association, Penablanca, Philippines, 26 January - 2 February, 1985.

_____. 1985b. In the Long Term: Three Themes in Malayan Cultural Ecology. In **Cultural Values and Tropical Ecology in Southeast Asia,** ed. K.L. Hutterer, A.T. Rambo, and G. Lovelace. Ann Arbor: University of Michigan.

Bock, C. 1884. **Temples and Elephants: Narrative of a Journey through Upper Siam and Laos.** London: Sampson, Low, Marsden, Searle and Rivington.

Bourdieu, P. 1977. **Outline of a Theory of Practice** (transl. R. Nice). Cambridge: Cambridge University Press.

Burling, R. 1970. **Man's Many Voices: Language in Its Cultural Context.** New York: Holt, Rinehart and Winston, Inc.

Chapman, E.C. 1967. **An Appraisal of Recent Agricultural Changes in the Northern Valleys of Thailand.** Bangkok: Department of Land Development.

_____. 1983. The Huai Thung Choa Project: Its Role, Environmental Setting, and Objectives. In Natural Resource Development and Environmental Stability in the Highlands of Northern Thailand: Proceedings of a Workshop organised by Chiang Mai University and the United Nations University, ed. E.C. Chapman and Sanga Sabhasri. **Mountain Research and Development.** 3(4):318–25.

Cohen, P.T. 1984. Opium and the Karen: A Study of Indebtedness in Northern Thailand. **Journal of Southeast Asian Studies.** 15(1):150–165.

_____ and G. Wijeyewardene. 1984a. Introduction. In Spirit Cults and the Position of Women in Northern Thailand, ed. P. Cohen and G. Wijeyewardene. **Mankind.** (Special Issue no. 3). 14(4):249–71.

_____ and G. Wijeyewardene, eds. 1984. Spirit Cults and the Position of Women in Northern Thailand. **Mankind.** (Special Issue no. 3). 14(4).

Cooler, R.M. 1979. **The Karen Bronze Drums of Burma: The Magic Pond.** Ph.D. Thesis. Cornell University.

Cooper, R.G. 1984. **Resource Scarcity and the Hmong Response.** Singapore: Singapore University Press.

Cross, E.B. 1853–54. On the Karens. **Journal of the American Oriental Society.** 4:291–316.

Davis, R.B. 1984. **Muang Metaphysics: A Study of Northern Thai Myth and Ritual.** Bangkok: Pandora.

Dodge, P. 1963. Two Weeks on an Elephant: Diary of the First Visit to the Telakhon of Thailand, November – December, 1962. Mimeo.

Donner, W. 1978. **The Five Faces of Thailand.** Institute of Asian Affairs (Hamburg). London: C. Hurst and Co.

Douglas, M. 1957. Animals in Lele Religious Thought. **Africa.** 27:46–58.

Durrenberger, P. 1974. The Regional Context of the Economy of a Lisu Village in Northern Thailand. **Southeast Asia.** 3(1):569–75.

Endicott, K. 1970. **An Analysis of Malay Magic.** London: Oxford University Press.

Falvey, L. 1977. **Ruminants in the Highlands of Northern Thailand.** Chiang Mai: Tippanetr Press.

Firth, R. 1963. Bilateral Descent Groups: An Operational Viewpoint. **Occasional Papers of the Royal Anthropological Institute.** 16:22–37.

_____. 1973. Food Symbolism in a Pre-Industrial Society. In **Symbols: Public and Private,** R. Firth London: George Allen and Unwin.

Fox, J.J. 1971. Semantic Parallelism in Rotinese Ritual Language. **Bijdragen Tot de Taal-, Landen Volkenkunde.** 127(2):215–55.

_____. 1974. "Our Ancestors Spoke in Pairs": Rotinese Views of Language, Dialect, and Code. In **Explorations in the Ethnography of Speaking,** ed. R. Bauman and J. Sherzer. Cambridge: Cambridge University Press.

_____. 1975. On Binary Categories and Primary Symbols. In **The Interpretation of Symbolism,** ed. R. Willis. London: Malaby Press

_____. 1979. The Ceremonial System of Savu. In **The Imagination of Reality,** ed. A.L. Becker and Aram Yengoyan. Norwood, New Jersey: Ablex Publishing Corporation.

_____. 1983. The Rotinese Chotbah as a Linguistic Performance. In **Accent on Variety,** ed. A. Halim, L. Carrington and S.A. Wurm. Canberra: Pacific Linguistics.

Frake, C. 1969. Notes on Queries in Ethnography. In **Cognitive Anthropology,** ed. S. Tyler. New York: Holt, Rinehart and Winston.

Frazer, J.G. 1919. **Folklore in the Old Testament,** vol. 2. London.

Freeman, J.D. 1958. The Family System of the Iban in Borneo. In **The Developmental Cycle in Domestic Groups,** ed. J. Goody. Cambridge: Cambridge University Press.

_____. 1960. The Iban of Western Borneo. In **Social Structure in Southeast Asia,** ed. G.P. Murdock. Viking Fund Publications in Anthropology, no. 29. Chicago: Quadrangle Books.

_____. 1961. On the Concept of the Kindred. **Journal of the Royal Anthropological Institute.** 91:192–220.

Geertz, C. 1966. Religion as a Cultural System. In **Anthropological Approaches to the Study of Religion,** ed. M.Banton. ASA Monographs 3. London: Tavistock Publications.

_____. 1973. Ideology as a Cultural System. In **The Interpretation of Cultures,** C. Geertz. London: Hutchinson and Co.

Geertz, H. and Geertz, C. 1964. Teknonymy in Bali: Parenthood, Age-Grading, and Genealogical Amnesia. **Journal of the Royal Anthropological Institute.** 94(2):94–108.

Gilmore, A. 1911. Karen Folklore, I. **Journal of the Burma Research Society.** 1:75–82.

Goody, J. 1982. **Cooking, Cuisine and Class.** Cambridge: Cambridge University Press.

Grandstaff, T.B. 1976. **Swidden Society in North Thailand: A Diachronic Perspective Emphasizing Resource Relationships.** Ph.D. Thesis. University of Hawaii.

Grathoff, R. 1970. **The Structure of Social Inconsistencies: A Contribution to a Unified Theory of Play, Game and Social Action.** The Hague: Martinus Nijhoff.

Haas, M. 1964. **Thai-English Student's Dictionary.** Stanford: Stanford University Press.

Hackett, W.D. 1953. **The Pa-O People of Shan State, Union of Burma.** Ph.D. Thesis. Cornell University.

Hallett, H.S. 1890. **A Thousand Miles on an Elephant in the Shan States.** Edinburgh and London: William Blackwood and Sons.

Hamilton, J.W. 1976. **Pwo Karen: At the Edge of Mountain and Plain.** The American Ethnological Society, Monograph 60. St. Paul: West Publishing Co.

Handelman, D. 1979. Is Naven Ludic? Paradox and the Communication of Identity. In The Power of Ritual: Transition, Transformation and Transcendence in Ritual Practice, ed. B. Kapferer. **Social Analysis.** (Special Inaugural Issue). 1(1):177–91.

Hanks, L.M. 1966. The Corporation and the Entourage: A Comparison of Thai and American Social Organisation. **Catalyst.** 2:55–63.

_____. 1972. **Rice and Man.** Chicago: Aldine.

Heald, P.S. 1900. **The Social Progress of the Karens Under Christianity.** B. Div. Thesis. University of Chicago.

Hinton, P. 1973. Population Dynamics and Dispersal Trends Among the Karen of Northern Thailand. In **Studies of Contemporary Thailand,** ed. R. Ho and E.C. Chapman. Department of Human Geography, Publication HG/8. Canberra: Australian National University.

_____. 1975. **Karen Subsistence: The Limits of a Swidden Economy in North Thailand.** Ph.D. Thesis. Sydney University.

_____. 1983. Do the Karen really exist?. In **Highlanders of Thailand,** ed. J. McKinnon and Wanat Bhruksasri. Kuala Lumpur: Oxford University Press.

Hurni, H. 1979. First Results of a Study on Soil Erosion in the Mae Muang Luang Ecosystem (Northern Thailand). Paper presented to the Workshop on the United Nations University-Chiang Mai University Joint research project on Agro-forestry and Highland-Lowland Interactive Systems, November 1979.

_____. 1982. Soil Erosion in Huai Thung Choa-Northern Thailand: Concerns and Constraints. **Mountain Research and Development.** 2(2):11–56.

_____ and Sompote Nuntapong. 1983. Agro-forestry Improvements for Shifting Cultivation Systems Soil Conservation Research in Northern Thailand. In Natural Resource Development and Environmental Stability in the Highlands of Northern Thailand: Proceedings of a Workshop organised by Chiang Mai University and the United Nations University, ed. E.C.. Chapmand and Sanga Sabhasri. **Mountain Research and Development.** 3(4): 338–45.

Iijima, S. 1970. Socio-cultural Change Among the Shifting Cultivators through the Introduction of Wet Rice Culture — A Case Study of the Karens in Northern Thailand. **Memoirs of the College of Agriculture.** Kyoto University, Agricultural Economics Series 3. 97:1–41.

_____. 1979. Ethnic Identity and Sociocultural Change Among the Sgaw Karen in Northern Thailand. In **Ethnic Adaptation and Identity: The Karen on the Thai Frontier with Burma.**, ed. C.F. Keyes. Philadelphia: Institute for the Study of Human Issues.

Iwata, K. and M. Matsuoka. 1967. Agricultural Practices Among Thai Yai, Thai Lu and Certain Hill Tribes in Northern Thailand. **Nature and Life in Southeast Asia** 5:295–312.

Jakobson, R. 1956. Two Aspects of Language and Two Types of Aphasic Disturbance. In **Fundamentals of Language,** R. Jakobson and M. Halle. The Hague: Mouton.

_____. 1970. Language in Relation to Other Communication Systems. **Linguaggi nella Societa nella Tecnica.** Milan: Edizion di Communita.

Jones, R.B. 1961. **Karen Linguistic Studies.** Berkeley and Los Angeles: University of California Press.

Judd, L.C. 1977. **Chao Rai Thai: Dry Rice Farmers in Northern Thailand.** Bangkok: Suriyaban Publishers.

Kahn, J.S. and J.R. Llobera, eds. 1981. **The Anthropology of Pre-capitalist Societies.** London: The Macmillan Press.

Kapferer, B. 1979a. Introduction: Ritual Process and the Transformation of Context. In The Power of Ritual: Transition, Transformation and Transcendecne in Ritual Practice, ed. B. Kapferer. **Social Analysis** (Special Inaugural Issue). 1(1):3–19.

Keen, F.G.B. 1978. The Fermented Tea (**Miang**) Economy of Northern Thailand. In **Farmers in the Forest,** ed. P. Kunstadter, E.C. Chapman, and Sanga Sabhasri. Honolulu: University Press of Hawaii.

Keyes, C.F. 1977a. Millenialism, Theravada Buddhism and Thai Society. **Journal of Asian Studies.** 36(2):283–302.

_____. 1977b. **The Golden Peninsula.** New York: MacMillan Publishing Co.

_____. 1979a. Introduction. In **Ethnic Adaptation and Identity: The Karen on the Thai Frontier with Burma.** Philadelphia: Institute for the Study of Human Issues.

_____. 1979b. The Karen in Thai History and the History of the Karen in Thailand. In **Ethnic Adaptation and Identity: The Karen on the Thai Frontier with Burma.** Philadelphia: Institute for the Study of Human Issues.

_____, ed. 1979. **Ethnic Adaptation and Identity: The Karen on the Thai Frontier with Burma.** Philadelphia: Institute for the Study of Human Issues.

_____. 1981. The Dialectics of Ethnic Change. In **Ethnic Change,** ed. C.F. Keyes. Seattle: University of Washington Press.

Kraisri Nimmanahaeminda. 1965. Put Vegetables into Baskets, People into Towns. In **Ethnographic Notes on Northern Thailand,** ed. L.M. Hanks, J. Hanks, and L. Sharp. Data Paper no. 58, Southeast Asia Program, Department of Asian Studies. Cornell University.

Kunstadter, P. 1967. The Lua' and Sgaw Karen of Maehong-sorn Province, Northwestern Thailand. In **Southeast Asian Tribes, Minorities and Nations,** ed. P. Kunstadter, vol. 2. Princeton: Princeton University Press.

_____. 1969. Hill and Valley Populations in Northwestern Thailand. In **Tribesmen and Peasants in North Thailand,** ed. P. Hinton. Chiang Mai: Tribal Research Centre.

_____. 1972. Demography, Ecology, Social Structure and Settlement Patterns. In **Structure of Human Populations,** ed. A.J. Boyce and G.A. Harrison. Oxford: Clarendon Press.

_____. 1978. Subsistence and Agricultural Economies of Lua' and Karen Hill Farmers, Mae Sariang District, Northwestern Thailand. In **Farmers in the Forest,** ed. P. Kunstadter, E.C. Chapman, and Sanga Sabhasri. Honolulu: University Press of Hawaii.

_____. 1979. Ethnic Group, Category, and Identity: Karen in Northern Thailand. In **Ethnic Adaptation and Identity: The Karen on the Thai Frontier with Burma,** ed. C.F. Keyes. Philadelphia: Institute for the Study of Human Issues.

_____. 1983. Highland Populations in Northern Thailand. In **Highlanders of Thailand,** ed. J. McKinnon and Wanat Bhruksasri. Kuala Lumpur: Oxford University Press.

_____. 1983. Karen Agro-forestry: Processes, Functions, and Implications for Socio-economic, Demographic, and Environmental Change in Northern Thailand. In Natural Resource Development and Environmental Stability in the Highlands of Northern Thailand: Proceedings of a Workshop organised by Chiang Mai University and the United Nations University, ed. E.C. Chapman and Sanga Sabhasri. **Mountain Research and Development.** 3(4):326–37.

Kunzel, W. 1983. Ethnic and Spatial Differences in Wage-Labour Employment and in the Introduction of Coffee at Huai Tung Choa, Thailand, 1979–80. In Natural Resource Development and Environmental Stability in the Highlands of Northern Thailand: Proceedings of a Workshop organised by Chiang Mai University and the United Nations University, ed. E.C. Chapman and Sanga Sabhasri. **Mountain Research and Development.** 3(4):357–62.

Kunzel, W. n.d. Karen Agriculture in Northern Thailand: Trends and Prospects. Unpublished Manuscript.

La Fontaine, J.S. 1978. Introduction. In **Sex and Age as Principles of Social Differentiation,** ed. J.S. La Fontaine. ASA Monograph 17. London: Academic Press.

Leach, E.R. 1964. **Political Systems of Highland Burma.** London: The Athlone Press. (First published 1954).

LeBar, F.M., G.C. Hickey, and J.K. Musgrave, eds. 1964. **Ethnic Groups of Mainland Southeast Asia.** New Haven: Human Relations Area File Press.

Lehman, F.K. 1967. Kayah Society as a Function of the Shan-Burman-Karen Context. In **Contemporary Change in Traditional Societies,** ed. J. Steward. Urbana: University of Illinois Press.

_____. 1979. Who are the Karen, and If So, Why? Karen Ethnohistory and a Formal Theory of Ethnicity. In **Ethnic Adaptation and Identity: The Karen on the Thai Frontier with Burma,** ed. C.F. Keyes. Philadelphia: Institute for the Study of Human Issues.

Levi-Strauss, C. 1966. **The Savage Mind** (English transl.). London: Weidenfeld and Nicholson.

_____. 1969. **The Elementary Structures of Kinship** (transl. J.H. Bell, J.R. von Sturmer and R. Needham). Boston: Beacon Press.

Lewis, G. 1976. A View of Sickness in New Guinea. In **Social Anthropology and Medicine,** ed. J.B. Loudon. ASA Monograph 13. London: Academic Press.

Lewis, J.L. 1924. **The Burmanization of the Karen People: A Study in Racial Adaptability.** M.A. Thesis. University of Chicago.

Lewis, P. and E. Lewis, 1984. **Peoples of the Golden Triangle.** London: Thames and Hudson.

Ling, T. 1975. **The Buddha: Buddhist Civilization in India and Ceylon.** Harmondsworth: Penguin Books.

Lonsdale, M. n.d. **The Karen Revolution in Burma.** n.p. Loudon, J.B. 1976. **Social Anthropology and Medicine.** ASA Monograph 13. London: Academic Press.

McCarthy, J. 1900. **Surveying and Exploring Siam.** London: John Murray.

McFarland, G.B. 1944. **Thai-English Dictionary.** Stanford: Stanford University Press.

Madha, Michael Abd-Rehman. 1980. **Economic Development and Social Change: The Structure of Two Sgaw Karen Communities in North-West Thailand.** Ph.D. Thesis. Cambridge University.

Marlowe, D.H. 1969. Upland-Lowland Relationships: The Case of the S'kaw Karen of Central Upland Western Chiang Mai. In **Tribesmen and Peasants in North Thailand,** ed. P. Hinton. Chiang Mai: Tribal Research Centre.

_____. 1979. In the Mosaic: The Cognitive and Structural Aspects of Karen-Other Relationships. In **Ethnic Adaptation and Identity: The Karen on the Thai Frontier with Burma,** ed. C.F. Keyes. Philadelphia: Institute for the Study of Human Issues.

Marshall, H.I. 1922. **The Karen People of Burma: A Study in Anthropology and Ethnology.** Columbus: Ohio State University.

Mason, F. 1865. Religion and Mythology of the Karens. **Journal of the Royal Asiatic Society.** (Bengal Branch). 34(2):173–88, 195–250.

_____. 1866. Physical Characters of the Karens. **Journal of the Royal Asiatic Society.** (Bengal Branch). 35(2):1–30.

_____. 1968. On Dwellings, Works of Art, etc., of the Karens. **Journal of the Royal Asiatic Society.** (Bengal Branch). 37(2):125–69.

Matisoff, J.A. 1983. Linguistic Diversity and Language Contact. In **Highlanders of Thailand,** ed. J. McKinnon and Wanat Bhruksasri. Kuala Lumpur: Oxford University Press.

Milner, G.B. 1969. De l'Armature des Locutions Proverbiales: Essai de Taxonomie Semantique. **L'Homme.** 9(3):49–70.

Mischung, R. 1980. **Religion in a Cgau (Sgaw) Karen Village of Western Upland Chiang Mai Province, Northwest Thailand.** Final Report presented to the National Research Council of Thailand. Mimeo.

Mitchell, J.C. 1974. Perceptions of Ethnicity and Ethnic Behaviour: An Empirical Exploration. In **Urban Ethnicity,** ed. A. Cohen. ASA Monographs 12. London: Tavistock Publications.

Moerman, M. 1968. **Agricultural Change and Peasant Choice in a Thai Village.** Berkeley and Los Angeles: University of California Press.

Morgan, L.H. 1871. **Systems of Consanguinity and Affinity of the Human Family.** Smithsonian Contributions to Knowledge 17. Washington: Smithsonian Institution.

Nakano, K. 1978. An Ecological Study of Swidden Agriculture at a Village in Northern Thailand. **Tonan Ajia Kenkyu.** 16(3):411–46.

———. 1980. An Ecological View of a Subsistence Economy Based Mainly on the Production of Rice in Swiddens and in Irrigated Fields in a Hilly Region of Northern Thailand. **Tonan Ajia Kenkyu.** 18(1):40–66.

Oliver, T. 1978. Bullets, Saddles and Horse's Hoofs. **Arts of Asia.** 8(3):94–101.

Ortner, S. 1973. On Key Symbols. **American Anthropologist.** 15(5):1338–46.

Prayad Pandee and E.C. Chapman. 1983. Recent Changes in Land Use and Land Cover at Huai Tung Choa. In Natural Resource Development and Environmental Stability in the Highlands of Northern Thailand: Proceedings of a Workshop organised by Chiang Mai University and the United Nations University, ed. E.C. Chapman and Sanga Sabhasri. **Mountain Research and Development.** 3(4):346–52.

Pendleton, R.L. 1963. **Thailand: Aspects of Landscape and Life.** New York: Duell, Sloane and Pearce.

Penny, D.H. 1969. Growth of "Economic Mindedness" Among Small Farmers in North Sumatra, Indonesia. In **Subsistence Agriculture and Economic Development,** ed. C.R. Wharton. Chicago: Aldine Publishing Co.

Potter, J.M. 1976. **Thai Peasant Social Structure.** Chicago: University of Chicago Press.

Rajah, A. 1975. **Bomoh Practices and Bomoh Belief Systems.** Field Report. Department of Sociology, University of Singapore.

———. 1983. Implications of Traditional Karen Land-use Systems for the Introduction of New Cropping Systems: Some Observations from Ban Hua Lao, Huai Thung Choa, Northern Thailand. In Natural Resource Development and Environmental Stability in the Highlands of Northern Thailand: Proceedings of a Workshop Organized by Chiang Mai University and the United Nations University, ed. E.C. Chapman and Sanga Sabhasri. **Mountain Research and Development.** 3(4):352–6.

_____. 1984. **'Au' Ma Xae:** Domestic Ritual and the Ideology of Kinship Among the Sgaw of Palokhi, Northern Thailand. In Matrilineal Cults and the Position of Women in Northern Thailand, ed. P. Cohen and G. Wijeyewardene. **Mankind.** (Special Issue no. 3). 14(4):348–56.

_____. 1985. From "Tribe" to "State": The Evolution of the Karen Separatist Movement in Burma. Unpublished manuscript.

Renard, R.D. 1980. Kariang: **History of Karen T'ai Relations from the Beginnings to 1923.** Ph.D. Thesis. University of Hawaii.

Saw Moo Troo. n.d. Karens and Communism. In **Karens and Communism, and Karens fight for Peace,** Saw Moo Troo and Mika Rolley. n.p.

Scott, G. 1922. Among the Hill Tribes of Burma — An Ethnological Thicket. **The National Geographic Magazine.** 41(3):293–321.

Sitte, F. 1979. **Rebellenstaat im Burma-Dschungel.** Graz: Verlag Styria.

Smeaton, D. 1887. **The Loyal Karens of Burma.** London: Kegan Paul, Trench and Co.

Somphob Larchrojna. 1975. **Karen Medicine.** M.A. Thesis. Sydney University.

Sophon Ratanakhon. 1978. Legal Aspects of Land Occupation and Development. In **Farmers in the Forest,** ed. P. Kunstadter, E.C. Chapman, and Sanga Sabhasri. Honolulu: University Press of Hawaii.

Sorokin, P. 1957. **Social and Cultural Dynamics.** Boston: Porter Sargent.

Spencer, J.E. 1966. **Shifting Cultivation in Southeastern Asia.** Berkeley and Los Angeles: University of California Press.

Stern, T. 1965. Research upon Karen in Village and Town, Upper Khwae Noi, Western Thailand. Mimeo.

_____. 1968. **Ariya** and the Golden Book: A Millenarian Buddhist Sect among the Karen. **Journal of Asian Studies.** 27(2):297–328.

Tambiah, S.J. 1968. The Magical Power of Words. **Man** (NS). 3(2):175–208.

_____. 1973. Classification of Animals in Thailand. In **Rules and Meanings,** ed. M. Douglas. Harmondsworth: Penguin Books. (Excerpt from S.J. Tambiah. 1969. Animals are Good to Think and Good to Prohibit. **Ethnology.** 8[4]:424–59).

_____. 1979. A Performative Approach to Ritual. **Proceedings of the British Academy.** 65:114–69. London: Oxford University Press.

_____. 1984. **The Buddhist Saints of the Forest and the Cult of Amulets.** Cambridge: Cambridge University Press.

Thannarong Viboonsunti, Benchaphun Shinawatra, and Prasert Wongbhan. n.d. Socio-economic Study of the Tribal Villages in Huey Thung Choa. Mimeo.

Tribal Research Centre. 1978. **Distribution of Major Highland Ethnic Group Village Settlements.** Map. Chiang Mai: Tribal Research Centre.

Truxton, A.S. 1958. **The Integration of the Karen Peoples of Burma and Thailand into their Respective National Cultures: A Study in the Dynamics of Culture Contact.** M.A. Thesis. Cornell University.

Uhlig, H. 1980. Problems of Land Use and Recent Settlement in Thailand's Highland-Lowland Transition Zone. In **Conservation and Development in Northern Thailand,** ed. J. Ives, Sanga Sabhasri, and Pisit Voraurai. Tokyo: United Nations University.

Van Roy, E. 1971. **Economic Systems of Northern Thailand: Structure and Change.** Cornell: Cornell University Press.

Watabe, T. 1976. The Glutinous Rice Zone in Thailand — Patterns of Change in Cultivated Rice. In **Southeast Asia: Nature, Society and Development,** ed. Shinichi Ichimura. Monographs of the Centre for Southeast Asian Studies, Kyoto University. Honolulu: University Press of Hawaii.

Wijeyewardene, G. 1966. **A Preliminary Report on Kinship and Land Tenure in a North Thai Village.** Report presented to the National Research Council of Thailand. Mimeo.

_____. 1968. Address, Abuse and Animal Categories in Northern Thailand. **Man** (NS). 3(1):76–93.

_____. 1971. A Note on **Patrons** and **Pau Liang. Journal of the Siam Society.** 59(2):229–33.

_____. 1974. Kinship: An Essay in its Logic and Antecedents. Unpublished manuscript.

_____. **In press.** The Theravada Compact and the Karen. **Sojourn.** 2(1).

White, B.N.F. 1980. Rural Household Studies in Anthro-pological Perspective. In **Rural Household Studies in Asia,** ed. H.P. Binswanger et al. Singapore: Singapore University Press.

Willis, R. 1975. **The Interpretation of Symbolism.** London: Malaby Press.

Yao Souchou. 1983. **Class, Culture and Structural Domination in a Colonial Situation: Changing Community Leadership on Cheung Chau Island, Hong Kong.** Ph.D. Thesis. University of Adelaide.

Made in the USA
Middletown, DE
21 March 2023

27262272R10190